EL MACAYO

A Prehistoric Settlement in the Upper Santa Cruz River Valley

Edited by William L. Deaver and Carla R. Van West

With contributions by
Anthony Della Croce
William L. Deaver
Robert A. Heckman
Juerena R. Hoffman
Richard G. Holloway
Barbara A. Murphy
Marcy H. Rockman
Steven D. Shelley
Sharon F. Urban
Carla R. Van West

Report prepared for
Public Works Department
Santa Cruz County
2150 N. Congress Drive
Nogales, Arizona 85621

Technical Series 74
Statistical Research, Inc.
Tucson, Arizona
2001

Statistical Research Technical Series

Series editor: Jeffrey H. Altschul
Volume editor: Barbara K. Montgomery
Production manager: Lynne Yamaguchi
Graphics manager: Cynthia Elsner Hayward
Production assistants: Karen Barber, Dan Shapiro

Cover design: Cynthia Elsner Hayward
Cover art adapted from parrot/macaw pin created by McBride Lomayestewa, Second Mesa Hopi Tribe

Published by Statistical Research, Inc.
P.O. Box 31865
Tucson, Arizona 85751-1865

ISBN 1-879442-74-4

First printing: June 2001
2 4 5 3 1

Typeset and printed in the United States of America.
Printed on acid-free paper.

CONTENTS

LIST OF TABLES

ABSTRACT

Agency: The Bureau of Land Management served indirectly as lead agency. Santa Cruz County, Arizona (Department of Public Works), was the direct sponsor of the work. Work was conducted under Arizona State Museum (ASM) Permit 1996-70ps; ASM Repository Service Agreement, March 11, 1996; and Agreement on Burial Discoveries: Case No. 95-24.

Project Title: Archaeological Data Recovery and Analysis at El Macayo (AZ EE:9:107 [ASM])

Project Description: Mitigation of adverse effects to a National Register–eligible prehistoric village site on a portion of the 94-acre new county complex parcel proposed as a baseball field and exercise path

Location: El Macayo is a large village site located in part on the Santa Cruz County Complex property in Nogales, Arizona. The site is positioned at 1,146 m (3,760 feet) above mean sea level on the west bank of Nogales Wash and the north bank of Mariposa Wash.

Summary: Archaeological data recovery was undertaken by Statistical Research, Inc., at the site of El Macayo (AZ EE:9:107 [ASM]), a prehistoric village located on land occupied by the Santa Cruz County Complex in Nogales, Arizona. Fieldwork was conducted by a crew of four archaeologists and a physical anthropologist under the direction of William L. Deaver between April 16 and May 23, 1996. By the end of 28 days of fieldwork, 177 features had been exposed, identified, and mapped. Of these 177 features, 11 pit structures, 11 burials, 19 pits, and 1 miscellaneous feature were partially or fully excavated. Analysis and interpretation of architectural, ceramic, lithic, shell, floral, faunal, and burial data suggest that the village was occupied over a period of six centuries between A.D. 550 and 1150. The multicultural occupants of the site were foragers and farmers who had access to material goods produced in the Gila-Salt and Tucson Basins and in the Trincheras region of Sonora. After A.D. 950, they were producers of a local pottery tradition with links to the traditions of the Santa Cruz series documented for the Tucson Basin area. Yet, they likely were neither Hohokam nor Trincheras and perhaps are best described as a local culture. Agriculture may have been less important here than elsewhere in the southern Southwest, and the preference for inhumation burial suggests a significant departure from contemporaneous burial customs to the north.

ACKNOWLEDGMENTS

Data recovery, analysis, and interpretation of cultural remains at El Macayo were rewarding experiences for us who were involved. Because of contract requirements, we concentrated our efforts on a rather small, but well-used, portion of the landscape. Yet, we came to understand far more about the prehistory of the borderlands than the limited size of that archaeological place would suggest. That experience was enriched by the kindness and assistance of a number of individuals.

The Santa Cruz County Public Works Department staff were wonderfully helpful. Director Ken Zehentner and Assistant Director Victor Gabilondo could not have been more supportive. They cleared the excavation area of shrubs and vegetation to assist us in laying out our grid, they provided us with a backhoe and backhoe operator, and they kindly stored our tools and equipment when we were conducting fieldwork. They also came down frequently to check on our progress, and shared knowledge of the area with us. Later, when we needed archival data from their files, they cheerfully fulfilled our requests for assistance. Without their assistance, the project would have suffered.

Bureau of Land Management (BLM) Archaeologist Max Witkind vicariously participated in our project. Given that the Santa Cruz County parcel had been under BLM jurisdiction until 1987, there was some question as to the role that the BLM might play in legal matters and review responsibilities. Max determined that the BLM would review documents but that we would deal directly with the Arizona State Museum (ASM) on permits and human remains issues.

Repatriation Coordinators Lynn Teague and Gwinn Vivian of ASM secured a burial memorandum of agreement for us prior to fieldwork (Agreement on Burial Discoveries: Case No. 95-24). We all anticipated that human remains and funerary objects would be found in our data recovery efforts, as they had been in the two previous subsurface investigations at the site (Gardiner and Huckell 1987; Slawson 1991). That we did so was wise: multiple human graves were exposed on the first day of fieldwork. Eventually, the inhumation burials of 13 humans, one dog, and one macaw were discovered. However, only those graves that were disturbed were excavated and removed (nine humans and the two animals). All other locations were mapped but left undisturbed.

The partial remains of nine human individuals and their associated offerings were repatriated to the Tohono O'odham Nation. Arrangements were handled through the Tohono O'odham Cultural Committee in the person of Mr. Joe T. Joaquin. After excavation, the human remains were carried to our Tucson office and were examined by a physical anthropologist (see Chapter 9). In the autumn of 1996, Edward Encinas and Bennett Encinas of the San Xavier District of the Tohono O'odham Nation retrieved the remains and copies of our documentation from our Tucson facilities.

Fieldwork was undertaken by SRI crew members Jay Sandor, John Logan, Lorey Cachora, and Lisa Shelley under the supervision of Field Director William Deaver and Principal Investigator Carla Van West (ASM Permit 1996-70ps; ASM Repository Service Agreement, March 11, 1996). Physical anthropologist Juerena Hoffman conducted the in-field recovery and documentation of human remains. Historical archaeologist Matthew Sterner documented and investigated historical-period features along the margins of the project area. Volunteers Cherie Freeman, Maria Levy, and Peg Nugent assisted the crew on different occasions. Photographic documentation of our excavations was enhanced by the skills of Kurt Brei, who used a low-elevation blimp to take aerial views of excavation units.

Laboratory personnel Darell Clark, Gina Logan, and Kristy Ratliff, under the supervision of Laboratory Director Su Benaron, processed artifacts and environmental data, prepared collections for analysis, and entered field data into databases. Ceramic artifacts were identified and analyzed by Robby Heckman. Lithic artifacts were described by Tony Della Croce. Shell artifacts were documented by Sharon Urban. Nonhuman animal bone was inventoried by Marcy Rockman. The macaw burial was documented by Steve Shelley. Botanical samples (macrobotanical and pollen) were described by Richard Holloway. All chronometric samples were taken by Bill Deaver; he also was responsible for their interpretation. Juerena Hoffman completed the physical inspection and documentation of the human remains begun in the field.

Administrative support was provided by Carey Dean and Project Manager Debbie Altschul. SRI President Jeffrey Altschul guided the data recovery and compliance process from beginning to end.

The final report was produced by Karen Barber and Lynne Yamaguchi, with illustration support from Cynthia Elsner Hayward, Judy Roman, Chuck Riggs, Susan Martin, and Lisa Folb. The report greatly benefited from the editorial skills of Barbara Montgomery and Dan Shapiro.

Bill Deaver deserves the greatest amount of recognition for the successful completion of this project. His attention to detail, his curiosity about the past, and his dedication to the task at hand are exemplary. He recognized the significance of data recovered by this project, and he used it to narrate a much richer and more complex story of what happened in the middle Santa Cruz River valley than anyone before. Bill is commended for his consistent effort and is much appreciated for his contributions to southern Arizona prehistory.

—Carla R. Van West
May 10, 2001

ONE

Introduction

Carla R. Van West & William L. Deaver

I n the late spring of 1996, personnel from Statistical Research, Inc. (SRI), carried out archaeological excavations on a prehistoric site in Nogales, Arizona, for Santa Cruz County (Figure 1). This report presents the results of data recovery efforts at AZ EE:9:107 (ASM), also referred to as El Macayo Village in honor of a rare military macaw (*Ara militaris*) burial recovered from this site. (Hereinafter, the "ASM" suffix will be dropped; all site numbers should be assumed to be Arizona State Museum [ASM] designations unless otherwise noted.)

This chapter briefly describes El Macayo and summarizes previous archaeological work conducted at the site. The remainder of the chapter is devoted to placing our work at El Macayo in its spatial, temporal, and research contexts. This is accomplished by a short description of the site as we understand it today, a review of the physical environment and potential economic resources available to the settlement's inhabitants, a sketch of the culture history of the Nogales area, and a synopsis of our research design for this project.

Project Background

In 1987, the Santa Cruz County Board of Supervisors initiated a process that would transfer 94.8 acres of patented land from the U.S. Department of the Interior, Bureau of Land Management (BLM), to Santa Cruz County for its use as a "New County Complex" (W. Max Witkind, personal communication 1999) (Figure 2). As part of their obligations under this Recreation and Public Purposes Act agreement (44 Stat. 74, as amended by 43 USC 846 et seq.; PL 99-632), Santa Cruz County was required to comply with federal directives concerning the identification, evaluation, and consideration of prehistoric and historical-period cultural resources on this land (Sections 106 and 110 of the

National Historic Preservation Act of 1966, as amended; the Archaeological Resources Protection Act of 1979; and the Native American Graves Protection and Repatriation Act of 1990), as well as Arizona state law regarding human remains and objects of cultural heritage (ARS 41-844). Consequently, Santa Cruz County has funded (1) the cultural resources inventory of the 94-acre parcel (Neily and Euler 1987), (2) a testing program to evaluate the significance and integrity of the three sites identified within this parcel, including AZ EE:9:107 (Gardiner and Huckell 1987), (3) a second testing program to better define the extent of subsurface remains at AZ EE:9:107 (Slawson 1991), and (4) a data recovery program to mitigate anticipated adverse impacts to a portion of the site proposed for a recreation facility (this report).

A request for proposals to conduct archaeological data recovery, analysis, and write-up was issued in October 1994. SRI was awarded this contract in July 1995. Fieldwork was conducted April 13–May 23, 1996. Processing and analysis were undertaken in 1996, and write-up was completed in 1997. A draft report was submitted in the spring of 1998 and reviewed by the State Historic Preservation Office (SHPO) in the fall of 1998. The draft report was reviewed and approved by the BLM in the winter of 1999. This document represents the final report of this data recovery effort.

Previous Archaeological Work at El Macayo

El Macayo was recorded first in 1983 as an extensive sherd-and-lithic scatter with more than 2,000 surface artifacts and given the designation AZ EE:9:1 (BLM) by Don Simonis (1983) during a field inventory of BLM land. The

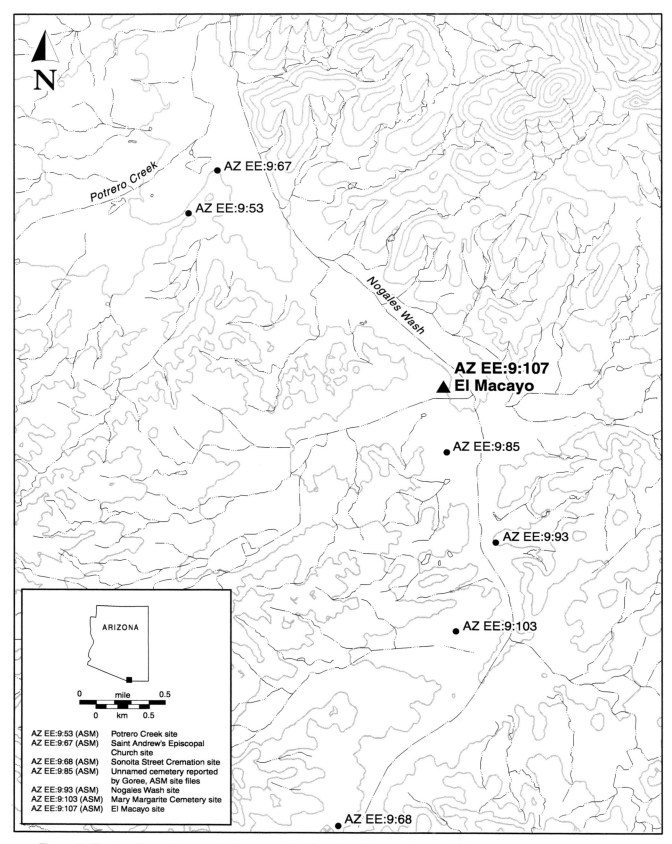

Figure 1. The location of the project area on the Nogales, Arizona-Sonora, 7.5-minute USGS quadrangle map.

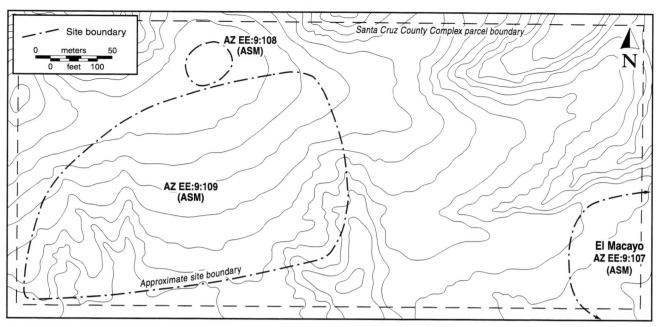

Figure 2. The location of AZ EE:9:107 (ASM) relative to the Santa Cruz County Complex parcel (after Gardiner and Huckell 1987:Figure 1).

site was shown to ASM archaeologist Sharon Urban in February 1985 by county employee and amateur archaeologist Ray Brown during an informal reconnaissance of Nogales area sites. At that time, it was assigned an ASM site number, AZ EE:9:102, and was given the name "the Oliver site," in honor of an acquaintance of Brown. Later, in April 1987, ASM Cultural Resource Management Division archaeologists Robert Neily and Thomas Euler conducted an official survey of the 94-acre property when management of the land was transferred to Santa Cruz County by the BLM (Neily and Euler 1987). Neily and Euler recorded this site and assigned it another ASM site number, AZ EE:9:107. Consequently, the site has two ASM site designations. In this report, we use the later designation, AZ EE:9:107, or its new name, El Macayo, to refer to this site.

ASM archaeologists mapped and conducted limited test excavations at three sites (AZ EE:9:107–109) on the 94-acre property during an eight-day period in August 1987 (Gardiner and Huckell 1987). At AZ EE:9:107, El Macayo, they excavated 182 linear meters of fill in five backhoe trenches (Trenches 1–5) and identified 31 prehistoric features in the walls of these trenches. These features included 7 pit houses, 7 bell-shaped pits, 13 pits of miscellaneous function, 2 possible human cremations, and 2 human inhumations (Figure 3). The types and diversity of artifacts and architectural forms indicated that El Macayo was a substantial Hohokam village with high integrity and potential for yielding significant information on prehistoric lifeways. Analysis of the ceramics suggested that the site was occupied during the A.D. 700–1200 period. Despite historical-pe-

riod land use on and in the vicinity of the prehistoric village, much remained of the former residential location. Consequently, recommendations for three alternative treatment plans were made: avoidance, burial, or data recovery (Gardiner and Huckell 1987:28–30).

Santa Cruz County subsequently determined that two options, avoidance and burial, were not feasible and that more testing was necessary to determine the geographic extent of the subsurface remains. Therefore, a second program of limited excavation was undertaken by Cultural and Environmental Systems, Inc. (CES), archaeologists to delimit the northern, western, and southern boundaries of the site (Slawson 1991). Fieldwork was conducted during a four-day period in September 1991, and an additional 185 linear meters of fill were excavated in seven trenches (Trenches 6–12). These subsurface exposures revealed the presence of seven additional features: three pit houses, three pits, and one human inhumation burial (see Figure 3). Results of the 1991 CES testing program conformed with those obtained by ASM in 1987. On the basis of the ceramics recovered, CES suggested that the occupation span was somewhat shorter than previously thought, likely between A.D. 750 and 1150. The additional trenches indicated that the presence of the subsurface materials corresponded closely with surface artifact distributions. Thus, CES suggested that the northern boundary of the village was somewhere between Trenches 8 and 9, the western boundary was the slope of the hill to the west, and the southern boundary (as well as the eastern boundary) was located beyond the property line of the county complex (Slawson 1991:14–15).

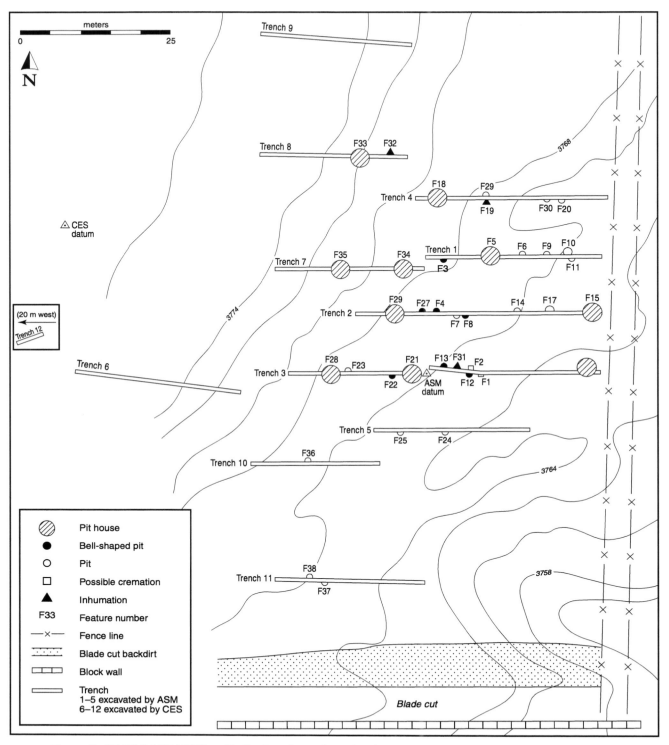

Figure 3. AZ EE:9:107 (ASM), with the locations of previously excavated trenches and identified features (after Gardiner and Huckell 1987 and Slawson 1991).

To proceed with proposed developments on the county parcel, the Santa Cruz County Board of Supervisors authorized that a contract be let for additional data recovery at El Macayo as recommended by CES (Slawson 1991:16).

El Macayo Site

El Macayo is a prehistoric habitation site in Nogales, Arizona (see Figure 3). Only the far western margin of this once extensive village is contained within the Santa Cruz County Complex parcel; most of the site is on private land now occupied by the Bird Hill Trailer Park (see Figure 2). The site lies at 1,146 m (3,760 feet) above mean sea level (AMSL), about 300 m (984 feet) west of Nogales Wash, 150 m (492 feet) south of a small unnamed wash draining into Nogales Wash, and immediately north of Mariposa Canyon. As a result of the work reported here, we believe that the village may have been occupied as early as A.D. 650 and as late as the early 1200s but certainly was inhabited from A.D. 850 to 1150, an occupational span equivalent to the late Colonial and Sedentary periods of the Hohokam cultural sequence. Dates are inferred largely from the co-occurrence and proportions of decorated ceramic types with known production periods, such as the Trincheras series type Trincheras Purple-on-red (and its companion types); the Santa Cruz series types Rillito Red-on-brown, Rincon Red-on-brown, and Tanque Verde Red-on-brown; and the Gila series types Gila Butte Red-on-buff, Santa Cruz Red-on-buff, and Sacaton Red-on-buff.

El Macayo is inferred to have been a village (alternatively, a large hamlet) occupied year-round at the confluence of Nogales Wash and Mariposa Canyon. Over the centuries, it appears to have been inhabited by a population practicing agriculture, wild-plant collection, and hunting. These inferences are supported by data on the range and abundance of artifact types and subsurface features and solid evidence of the storage and use of plant and animal remains. That the location provided a relatively stable opportunity for habitation over a number of generations is inferred from several lines of evidence. Numerous closely positioned and often superimposed pit houses, hearths, roasting pits, food storage facilities, and human and animal burials attest to the continuous use and reuse of this advantageous landform. Further, unambiguous evidence of the on-site use and processing of domesticated crops such as corn, as well as evidence of the many mundane tasks of daily life (e.g., eating, sleeping, food preparation, and tool making), add support to the conclusion that El Macayo was a year-round residence. The proximity of the site to Nogales and Mariposa Washes, with their seasonal flow of water and arable soils, as well as the settlement's proximity to arable nonriverine soils, suggests that the residents of El Macayo were well positioned to exploit opportunities for floodwater and high-water-table farming in the bottomlands and runoff farming on the sloping terraces above the streams.

Despite the limited amount of excavation and analysis conducted at the site, El Macayo has proven to be a rich source of information on the pre-Classic Formative period traditions of the upper Santa Cruz River valley. Data resulting from work at this site can be compared profitably to data obtained from more-intensively studied sites in the area with contemporaneous occupations. Among these, of course, are Paloparado (Brown and Grebinger 1969; Di Peso 1956), three of the four Baca Float sites (Doyel 1977a, 1977b), Potrero Creek (Grebinger 1971a, 1971b), and the Nogales Wash site (Jácome 1986).

Physical Setting and Environmental Characteristics

A consideration of El Macayo's location with respect to its physical setting provides insight into why early occupants of the region may have selected this location as a suitable habitation and why it continued to serve as a settlement for several centuries. Here, we review the salient geological, physiographic, climatic, hydrological, edaphic, and biotic characteristics of the region surrounding El Macayo, and we suggest the combination of environmental factors that likely contributed to its establishment and continued use.

Geology and Topography

Nogales, Arizona, is located within the Sonoran Desert section of the basin-and-range physiographic province of North America. Here, as elsewhere, alluvium-filled valleys are bordered by roughly parallel, northwest-southeast-trending mountain ranges of various dimensions, elevations, and geological structure. Upland areas above 1,600 m (5,250 feet) AMSL, which support a different suite of biotic and mineral resources than the lowlands, are within 32–40 km (20–25 miles)—roughly a long day's walk. Most of these uplands are volcanic mountains ranging in elevation from 1,524 to 2,881 m (5,000 to 9,453 feet) AMSL: the Tumacacori, Atascosa, and Pajarito Mountains to the west; the Sierra de Pinitos to the south; the Patagonias to the east; and the lofty Santa Ritas farther to the north. A small but prominent igneous intrusion only 13.7 km (8.5 miles) northeast of AZ EE:9:107 is Mount Benedict (1,381 m, or 4,565 feet AMSL), about midway between Nogales Creek and the Santa Cruz River. Another prominent volcanic hill less than 6.4 km (4 miles) from El Macayo and 2.4 km (1.5 miles) south of the international border is Cerro Oco-toso (elevation 1,400 m, or 5,512 feet AMSL). This hill constrains the growth of Nogales, Sonora, on its eastern margin.

The presence, form, and composition of these mountains and hills significantly influence rainfall patterns, surface runoff, soil composition, and biotic communities. They also provide sources of raw material for flaked and ground stone tools. For example, various types of igneous rock, including rhyolite, andesite, dacite, and related volcanic tuffs, form parts of the Atascosa, Tumacacori, San Cayetano, Patagonia, and Santa Rita Mountains. Consolidated conglomerates and tuff make up portions of the Atascosa Mountains and the adjacent, high-elevation alluvial fans. Siliceous stone, such as chert and chalcedony; various types of sedimentary rock, such as sandstone and limestone; and metamorphic rock, such as quartzite and slate, are found in portions of the Santa Ritas, including the drainages.

The twin border settlements of Nogales, Arizona, and Nogales, Sonora, are located within a pass (Nogales Canyon) that separates numerous volcanic hills, Pleistocene terraces, and irregular uplands characteristic of this portion of the Basin and Range Province. It is through this pass that Nogales Wash flows. El Macayo Village is located at the base of a low ridge that is the remnant of a Pleistocene age river terrace, now a few hundred meters west of Nogales Wash and immediately north of Mariposa Canyon. The village was built on and within Quaternary age sediments that were deposited primarily as alluvium and secondarily as colluvium and aeolian sediments.

Climate

The climate of the Nogales area is semiarid and typical of the southern Southwest. Precipitation is delivered primarily in two or three seasons (summer, winter, autumn), but most of the annual total falls in the summer. Temperatures are hot in the summer and cool in winter; snowfall is rare.

Precipitation and temperature data for Nogales have been recorded by one or more stations (Old Nogales, Nogales, and Nogales 6N) since as early as 1892 (Western Regional Climate Center [WRCC] 2000). These WRCC data (Figure 4) reveal that Nogales, Arizona, on average, receives 42.4 cm (16.68 inches) of annual precipitation. About 60 percent of the total falls as short, but intense, rainstorms in July, August, and September that affect limited areas and can cause rapid runoff, flash floods, and localized erosion. The summer moisture generally comes from the south; sources include the Gulf of Mexico, the Gulf of California, and the tropical eastern Pacific (Adams and Comrie 1997; Douglas et al. 1993); consequently, precipi-

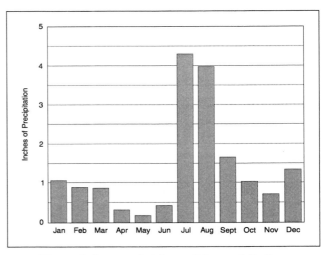

Figure 4. Average total monthly precipitation for Nogales, Arizona, 1892–1999 (data from the Western Regional Climate Center).

tation is generally greater on the southern slopes of the mountains. In contrast, only about 25 percent of the annual total is delivered in the form of widespread winter storms of low and steady intensity that occur more irregularly from December through March. Winter moisture derives from the Pacific Ocean by way of southern California and comes into the Nogales area from the west. A third, small, irregular, but often significant peak (about 10 percent) occurs in the autumn months of October and November. When these unusual storms occur—the result of waning tropical disturbances off Baja California—they often are heavy and last several days, resulting in local flooding. The spring months of April through June are typically dry and contribute only 5 percent of the total annual precipitation. Fall and winter precipitation is the most variable contributor to annual moisture, whereas summer rain is the most predictable temporal component. Consequently, pre-Hispanic agriculture in southern Arizona evolved largely in response to the availability of predictable summer moisture and not the less-regular fall and winter moisture.

The WRCC data (Figure 5) also indicate that Nogales regularly experiences low temperatures between 25° and 30°F during the winter months and high temperatures around 95°F during the summer months. Nightly and daily extremes as low as 6°F and as high as 110°F, however, have been recorded (Sellers and Hill 1974:346). The frost-free period (i.e., number of consecutive days with minimum temperatures greater than 32.5°F) generally begins in early April and continues through mid-November, resulting in a potential growing season of more than 220 days. Thus, pre-Hispanic agricultural systems had a relatively wide window of time in which planting, cultivation, and harvest could take place, even if the summer rains came late.

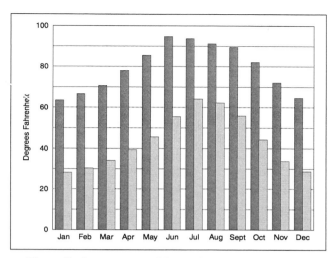

Figure 5. Average monthly maximum and minimum temperatures for Nogales, Arizona, 1892–1999 (data from the Western Regional Climate Center).

Soil Resources

The General Soil Map for Santa Cruz County indicates that much of the eastern Nogales area is classified as typical of the Lampshire-Chiricahua-Graham Soil Association. These soils tend to be shallow and cobbly and of the texture of loam, clay loam, or sandy loam. They are present on the lower mountains and foothills west of the Santa Cruz River and on parts of the Patagonia Mountains (Richardson et al. 1979). Bedrock underlying the Lampshire-Chiricahua-Graham Soil Association is predominantly rhyolite, andesite, granite, tuff, or tuff conglomerate.

Three mapped soil units underlie or are adjacent to El Macayo Village. The soils into which the archaeological features of the village were excavated are classified as Caralampi gravelly, sandy loams with 10–20 percent slopes. Immediately east and south of the village are the floodplains and low terraces of Nogales Wash and Mariposa Canyon, which contain sizable areas of Pima and Grabe soils (east and south, respectively). Of the more than five dozen soil units mapped in Santa Cruz County, only five units—the Grabe soils, Grabe-Comoro Complex soils, Comoro soils, Pima soils, and Guest soils—are considered agricultural soils when floodwater or irrigation is applied (Richardson et al. 1979:Sheet 114). A comparison of plotted site locations (site files, ASM) and the distribution of soil types for Santa Cruz County (Richardson et al. 1979) reveals that, by far, most pre-Hispanic habitation sites in the Nogales area—large and small (from Tubac to the international border)—are located on terraces above or on the margins of the floodplains of the Santa Cruz River and its major tributaries. Sizable patches of one of these five soil types are present on or border these terraces. That El Macayo Village was

established on a landform adjacent to two patches of Pima and Grabe soils, then, is consistent with the pattern of site establishment for the region.

The Caralampi gravelly, sandy loam underlying El Macayo is a deep, well-drained, slightly acid soil that formed in old alluvium weathered from granite, andesite, rhyolite, dacite, and tuffs. Here, as elsewhere in south-central Santa Cruz County, these soils are Ustollic Haplargids (a type of Aridisol) found on long, narrow ridge remnants of dissected old alluvial fans formed during the Pleistocene or before. Given their moderate slopes, erosion potential, low available water capacity, and slow permeability, they are generally not suitable for nonirrigated farming (Richardson et al. 1979:13, 88).

The Pima soil found in Nogales Wash is a deep, well-drained soil formed in recent alluvium (Anthropic Torrifluvent, an Entisol) that has weathered from mixed igneous, sedimentary, and metamorphic rock (Richardson et al. 1979:36–37). As a series, Pima soils are fine, silty sediments with a high available water capacity; they are among the best agricultural soils in Santa Cruz County.

The Grabe soil found at the mouth of Mariposa Canyon is a deep, well-drained soil formed in recent alluvium (a Typic Torrifluvent, a type of Entisol) from mixed igneous and sedimentary rock. Grabe soils develop in narrow areas on floodplains adjacent to major streams. With their high available water capacity, moderate permeability, and nearly ideal loamy texture, Grabe soils are considered the best agricultural soil in the upper Santa Cruz River valley and produce the highest per-unit yield in every category of irrigated crop (Richardson et al. 1979:51). Agricultural yields on Grabe soils are followed closely by yields on Grabe-Comoro soils, Comoro soils, Pima soils, and Guest soils.

Water Resources

Nogales, Arizona, is located in the upper watershed of the Santa Cruz River. The Santa Cruz River is an intermittently flowing desert stream some 362 km (225 miles) long that collects surface runoff from a 22,200-km^2 area in southern Arizona and northern Mexico (Webb and Betancourt 1992:4). Its source lies in Arizona's San Raphael Valley, where it drains the southern slopes of the Canelo Hills, a portion of the western slopes of the Huachuca Mountains, and the eastern slopes of the Patagonia Mountains. From there, it flows southward into Sonora, Mexico, then loops back into the United States at a point about 10 km (6 miles) east of Nogales and continues northward to its junction with the Gila River west of Phoenix.

Some researchers (e.g., Doyel 1977a; Grebinger 1971a) consider the upper Santa Cruz River to be that portion of the river from its headwaters to the point where it returns to Arizona. We suggest that geological and hydrological characteristics of the river, rather than political boundaries, are more appropriate criteria for distinguishing the upper from the middle reach of the river valley. Thus, we consider the upper Santa Cruz River drainage to be that portion of the river that extends from its headwaters in the San Rafael Valley to its junction with Sonoita Creek. This upper reach has a narrow stream channel and a constricted floodplain, which is bounded on both sides by mountains less than 1,829 m (6,000 feet) in elevation that are drained by relatively short ephemeral streams. In contrast, the middle Santa Cruz River is defined as that portion of the river that stretches from Sonoita Creek to the Rillito Gaging Station northwest of Tucson, where the surface flow largely disappears until it reaches the Gila River west of Phoenix. This reach is bounded by lower, volcanic mountain ranges on the west (e.g., the Tumacacori, Sierrita, and Tucson Mountains) and higher, more complex ranges on the east (i.e., Santa Ritas, the Rincons, and the Santa Catalinas) that have longer, more substantial tributaries draining their northern, western, and southern slopes.

According to geologists Schwalen and Shaw (1957:3), the Santa Cruz River and its major tributaries flowed in relatively shallow swales and regularly overflowed their banks across their floodplains prior to 1890. After that time, these drainages entrenched into their valley floors to depths between 1.5 and 7.6 m (5 and 25 feet) in the upper Santa Cruz River valley, likely as a result of long-term trends in alluvial-water-table cycles, exacerbated by erosion caused by historical-period overgrazing, drought, and instabilities from the 1887 San Bernardino Valley earthquake (Bryan 1925; Cooke and Reeves 1976; DuBois and Smith 1980; Hastings and Turner 1965). Thus, it is likely that hydrological conditions conducive to natural floodwater-type agriculture, as well as simple irrigation farming, were present along Nogales Wash and within Mariposa Canyon at various times in their history.

El Macayo Village is located immediately north of the junction of Mariposa Canyon and Nogales Wash, both small, upper-watershed tributaries of the Santa Cruz River. The existing portion of the village is also 100 m (330 feet) south of a small unnamed arroyo that drains the western portion of the hill on which the Santa Cruz County Complex is built and that flows into Nogales Wash. The sources of water for Mariposa Canyon are the eastern slopes of the Pajarito Mountains in both southern Arizona and northern Mexico, whereas the sources of Nogales Wash are the slopes of the low volcanic hills on either side of Nogales Canyon. No water flows into Nogales Wash from Mariposa Canyon at present, but seasonal water probably did reach Nogales Wash before 1890. Nogales Wash flows northward for 4.3 km (2.7 miles) before it joins Potrero Creek. From that point, Potrero Creek flows northward for 5.5 km

(3.4 miles) before it joins the Santa Cruz River near the Nogales International Waste Water Treatment Plant, south of Rio Rico. A few springs are depicted on Nogales area maps, and it is likely that groundwater, as well as seasonal flows in now-intermittent drainages, provided the domestic, agricultural, and construction-related water required for village life.

Biotic Communities

Nogales, Arizona, is located within the Chihuahuan semidesert grassland of the southern Southwest and northeastern Mexico (Brown 1994). This biome is at a higher elevation than the Sonoran desert scrub environment to the north and at a lower elevation than the Madrean evergreen woodland in the nearby mountain ranges. Thus, environmental resources potentially accessible to the occupants of El Macayo included not only the plant, animal, soil, and stone resources of the surrounding semidesert grassland and its riparian corridors, but also the upland resources of the Madrean evergreen woodland and conifer forests near the margins of the upper Santa Cruz River valley. The occupants of El Macayo would also have had, within a 64-km (40-mile) radius, access to the biotic resources of the Plains grassland east of the Patagonia Mountains near the modern-day community of Sonoita, Arizona, as well as a small area of subtropical Sinaloan thorn scrub north of the Mexican town of Imuris, Sonora.

The dominant forms of vegetation in semidesert grassland are, of course, grasses, but trees and shrubs also are important floral components. The quantity and predictability of average annual precipitation during the primary growing season (April through September) largely determines the productivity of the grasslands. In prehistoric times, most of the grasses were bunchgrasses, but because of overgrazing and suppression of fire, sod grasses have outcompeted many native varieties. Today, the dominant grasses of the semidesert grassland are the summer-active perennial black grama (*Bouteloua eriopoda*) and the water-loving tobosa (*Hilaria mutica*). Common shrubs and trees include mesquite (*Prosopis velutina*), catclaw (*Acacia greggii*), one-seed juniper (*Juniperus monosperma*), Mormon or Mexican tea (*Ephedra trifurca* or *E. antisyphilitica*), desert hackberry (*Celtis pallida*), and ocotillo (*Fouquieria splendens*). Drainages commonly support cottonwood (*Populus* sp.), desert willow *(Chilopsis linearis)*, western soapberry *(Sapindus saponaria)*, Mexican blue oak *(Quercus oblongifolia)*, and Emory oak *(Quercus emoryi)*. Leaf succulents and cacti are important components of the semidesert grassland. Succulent species typically include the sotols (*Dasylirion*), beargrasses (*Nolina*), agaves (*Agave*), and yuccas (*Yucca*). Cactus species include the barrel cactus (*Ferocactus wislizenii*), cane cholla (*Opuntia imbricata* and *O.*

spinosior), desert Christmas cactus (*O. leptocaulis*), prickly pear (*Opuntia* sp.), and a variety of hedgehog and pincushion cacti (*Echinocereus* and *Mammillaria*). Forbs and "weeds" of potential economic importance to foragers are seasonally abundant. For example, spring species include filaree (*Erodium*), buckwheat (*Eriogonum*), and mallow (*Sphaeralcea*), whereas summer species include spiderling (*Boerhaavia)*, white-mat (*Tidestromia*), amaranth (*Amaranthus*), and devil's claw (*Martynia*).

Economically important and well-represented mammals of the semidesert grassland include black-tailed jackrabbit (*Lepus californicus*), spotted ground squirrel (*Spermophilus spilosoma*), cotton rats (*Sigmodon* sp.), wood rats (*Neotoma* sp.), white-tailed deer (*Odocoileus virginianus*), and the ubiquitous coyote (*Canis latrans*). Formerly, pronghorn (*Antilocapra americana*) frequented the semidesert grassland, but with the reduction of grass and the invasion of scrubby trees and shrubs (e.g., mesquite, juniper, cacti, burroweed, and snakeweed), mule deer (*Odocoileus hemionus*) and javelina (*Dicotyles tajacu*) have extended their range and density in this zone. In addition, numerous birds, reptiles, and amphibians are well represented in the grassland, woodland, and riparian habitats of south-central Arizona. The uplands are dominated by oaks and chapparal at elevations between 1,372 and 1,981 m (4,500 and 6,500 feet) AMSL and yellow pines above 1,981 m (6,500 feet) AMSL. It is in these higher-elevation settings that the white-tailed deer finds its primary habitat, and a variety of conifer and oak trees and volcanic stone resources are located.

Summary

A review of environmental characteristics and the natural resources of the Nogales area suggests that an abundant variety of plant, animal, soil, water, and mineral resources were available to the pre-Hispanic inhabitants of the upper Santa Cruz River region during the Formative period. The occupants of El Macayo potentially had access to a variety of wild and encouraged economically important plant resources, desirable animal species, serviceable construction timber and fuel wood, high-quality arable land, and sources of agricultural and domestic water in proximity to their settlement. The most limiting resource to sustained habitation probably was the supply of water, particularly in spring and early summer. By establishing a settlement adjacent to some of the best agricultural soils in the region, at the junction of two drainages with water sources in two different uplands, the inhabitants of El Macayo increased their chances of receiving floodwater for their crops during the summer growing season. Further, these drainages likely supported a riparian habitat that offered many useful plants and animals.

Prehistoric Archaeological Context

The Precolumbian history of settlement and cultural dynamics in the upper Santa Cruz River valley is fragmentary and known only in outline; relatively little archaeological research has been conducted, and much remains to be learned. Human history in the upper Santa Cruz River valley likely began in the Paleoindian period, although no sites clearly dating to this early time period have been identified. This landscape certainly was used in the late Archaic and early Formative periods, but few sites visible today on the modern ground surface contain sufficiently unambiguous time-diagnostic artifacts to produce a well-developed picture of the nature and extent of early agricultural lifeways. To date, the best-documented period is that from about A.D. 750 to about 1300, when groups of people practicing a generalized subsistence economy based on farming, gathering, and hunting settled portions of the river valley and stayed long enough to leave behind many traces of their occupation. Local groups who interacted in various ways with Phoenix Basin and Tucson Basin groups to the north (glossed here as "Hohokam") and Magdalena Valley and Altar Valley groups to the south (glossed here as "Trincheras") have been documented. Sometime after A.D. 1450, ancestral Pima populations, such as the Tohono O'odham and Sobaipuri, lived along portions of the middle and upper Santa Cruz River before the coming of the Europeans in the sixteenth century—a time we refer to as the protohistoric period. Historical records available after Father Kino's 1691 arrival in what is now southern Arizona add considerable detail to the narrative outline, but even these are inadequate to fully document patterns of settlement, land use, and the interaction of cultures in the upper Santa Cruz River valley for the late seventeenth through late nineteenth centuries. Not until the coming of the railroad, the cessation of Apache raiding, and the beginning of sustained settlement in the Nogales area (ca. 1880) do we have a reasonable amount of information on the peoples and practices of southern Arizona.

History of Archaeological Research

The first archaeological explorations in the region encompassing southern Arizona and northern Mexico date to the late 1800s and early 1900s (Huntington 1912, 1914; Lumholtz 1912; McGee 1895). From these reconnaissances came the earliest clues that Precolumbian populations resembling the ancient populations of central Arizona had also lived in the Pimeria Alta. In addition, early investigators documented a variety of archaeological site types, including the enigmatic *cerros de trincheras*, which were thought to have had defensive, religious, or even agricultural or domestic functions.

Not until the 1920s and 1930s was problem-oriented research into the nature of early settlement specifically in the upper Santa Cruz River basin conducted (Gladwin and Gladwin 1929a, 1929b; Sauer and Brand 1931). The surveys of this period were somewhat more rigorous and had as their goal the recording of basic site types and pottery inventories. Such studies were used to define the influence of the "Red-on-buff Culture" of southern Arizona (i.e., the Hohokam; Gladwin and Gladwin 1929a) and suggest that the early populations of the upper Santa Cruz River valley not only interacted with the red-on-buff- and red-on-brown-pottery-making populations farther to the north, but also with red-on-purple-pottery-making people to the south. Trincheras sites in Sonora were recorded in more detail, and data were amassed on settlement distributions (Sauer and Brand 1931).

The 1920s and 1930s also mark the first efforts in "salvage archaeology" for the Nogales area. In 1928, and again in 1934, Byron Cummings of ASM responded to requests to examine and retrieve cremated remains and other artifacts unearthed during construction in downtown Nogales (B. Cummings, letters, 1928 and 1934, additional site information file, ASM, Tucson). In 1928, he was shown a set of cremations from Sonoita Street, a location assigned the ASM site number of AZ EE:9:68 by Laurens Hammack in 1968, when he, too, was asked to salvage additional cremations from the same location. The second set of cremations was unearthed in 1934 near the federal building.

In 1941 and in 1952–1953, two important surveys were undertaken along the Santa Cruz that have served as important baselines for the upper and middle Santa Cruz River valley (Danson 1946; Frick 1954). Both were conducted as master's theses within the University of Arizona, Department of Anthropology, and both were aimed at establishing local chronological sequences and identifying cultural influences and interactions. Danson surveyed the upper Santa Cruz River from its headwaters in the San Rafael Valley downstream to the town of Tubac and recorded 126 sites. With these data, he established a basic chronological sequence for the upper Santa Cruz River basin—a temporal framework used by most researchers in the Nogales area until quite recently.

Although his survey was largely confined to the edge of the floodplain and the terraces and bluffs adjacent to the channel, Danson classified his 126 sites into seven prehistoric categories and three historical categories. He also proposed a developmental chronology for the upper Santa Cruz basin, based primarily on potsherds recovered from the site and secondarily on architectural size and complexity. While acknowledging that settlement in the Archaic

period was likely, Danson's documented occupation sequence spanned from the Colonial through the Classic period of the Hohokam sequence, which he assigned to A.D. 500–1400. Further, his survey supported the historical records that suggested that Piman speakers, probably including Sobaipuri, Tohono O'odham, and Pima, were present by at least the 1600s. He found ample evidence of Spanish presence in the upper Santa Cruz River valley, which included ranches, towns, and missions, such as Calabasas, Guevavi, and Tumacacori. He also noted significant quantities of Trincheras culture pottery, pottery from the Dragoon Tradition to the east, and pottery he considered a "local type" influenced by both the Hohokam and Trincheras Traditions.

Frick (1954) examined lands on both sides of the middle Santa Cruz River and only a few upland localities between Sahuarita and Tubac; 216 sites were recorded. Three clusters of sites were located: one at the north end near Continental, one near the Canoa Ranch, and one near Tubac. Sites were assigned to one of four descriptive site types—all presumed to date to the prehistoric Formative era. No sites were assigned to the Paleoindian, Archaic, Pioneer, protohistoric, or early historical period. Frick used the Hohokam classificatory scheme to assign occupation dates to sites and assigned them to either the Colonial (Rillito), Sedentary (Rincon), or Classic (Tanque Verde and Tucson) period. Frick observed that pre–Tucson phase material culture in his survey area strongly resembled pre–Tucson phase materials in the Tucson Basin proper. However, his late Classic period sites had neither the Pantano Red-on-brown nor the Gila Polychrome pottery typically found in Tucson; rather, his sites exhibited a combination of Tanque Verde Red-on-brown and Sells Red. He speculated that populations in his portion of the Santa Cruz River valley had more in common with populations in the Papaguería, the Empire Valley, and the San Pedro River valley than with populations in the northern Tucson Basin in the late Classic period.

The first major excavation in southern Arizona was conducted in 1953 and 1954 by Charles Di Peso (1956) of the Amerind Foundation at Paloparado Ruin (AZ EE:8:2)—a site that continues to serve as the baseline against which nearly all Formative period sites in the upper and upper-middle Santa Cruz River valley are measured. The site is an extensive multicomponent, prehistoric and early-historical-period settlement located on a terrace above the confluence of Peck Canyon and the Santa Cruz River. It contains pre-Classic, Classic, and protohistoric or early-historical-period components (Wilcox 1987). It was first reported by Sauer and Brand (1931) and was assigned a site number by Danson in 1941. In the 1960s, an additional locus of the site was investigated by Brown and Grebinger (1969) when the construction of Interstate Highway 19 between Tucson and Nogales was routed through the site. Although subsequent researchers (e.g., Wilcox 1987) have refuted a number of Di

Peso's conclusions concerning the various dates of occupation and his claim that the settlement was the historical location of San Cayetano de Tumacacori, this site still remains the most completely excavated and reported settlement in southern Arizona south of Tumacacori.

The pace of archaeological research quickened in the 1960s, primarily as a result of the construction of Interstate 19 between Tucson and Nogales. Additional sites were recorded (R. G. Vivian, site cards, ASM), and several sites were excavated, including the Archaic period Carmen site (Brown 1967) and the Formative period Potrero Creek site (Grebinger 1971a, 1971b). Excavations at the eighteenth-century Guevavi Mission by the Arizona Archaeological and Historical Society between 1964 and 1966 resulted in only a small report (Robinson 1976) but rekindled interest in the historical-period archaeology of the region (e.g., Fontana [1971] on Calabasas Mission and Fort Mason).

The 1970s witnessed the birth of the conservation movement in American archaeology, and new forms of survey, programs of data recovery, and agendas for resource protection and interpretation came into being. Surveys in the Rio Rico area (Cunningham 1972); emergency salvage of two sites with cremations in the city of Nogales, AZ EE:9:85 (Goree 1972) and AZ EE:9:67, the St. Andrew's Episcopal Church site (Reinhard 1978); excavations at AZ DD:8:122, 127, 128, and 129 prior to construction along Interstate 19 Doyel 1977a); and excavations at Tubac Presidio (Shenk and Teague 1975) and Tumacacori Mission (Barton et al. 1981; Fratt 1981a, 1981b; Shenk 1976) exemplify the work of this period.

Since 1980, more than 50 projects have been undertaken in the Nogales area between the international border and Tubac, most of them contracted to satisfy legal requirements of the National Historic Preservation Act of 1966 (P.L. 89-665, as amended). Table 1 is a compilation of the known projects in an area covered by seven 7.5-minute U.S. Geological Survey (USGS) topographic maps encompassing the upper Santa Cruz River and its tributaries at the point where it enters the United States downstream to Tubac. Most of these have been small-scale, noncollection surveys, but a few represent emergency salvage projects; programs of data recovery undertaken by state, federal, or municipal agencies; and privately funded programs of reconnaissance and research. Not including acreage examined by early surveyors such as Sauer and Brand (1931) or Danson (1946), approximately 7,200 acres have been examined, resulting in the documentation of more than 150 sites in the seven-map area (Table 2). Despite the small percentage of survey coverage (3 percent) relative to the size of the area (some 285,000 acres), it is likely that the range of site types encountered is reasonably representative of this portion of southern Arizona.

Sites recorded in the upper Santa Cruz basin include the following types. Artifact scatters with and without features have been interpreted to represent habitation sites, temporary encampments, resource procurement and -processing locales, agricultural fields, quarries, cemeteries, and historical-period trash dumps. In addition, sites with substantial aboveground architecture have been interpreted to represent *cerros de trincheras*, mesa- or mountaintop rock enclosure lookouts or shrines, rock corrals, and historical-period houses, missions, and forts. Finally, pictographs within rockshelters and on patinated boulders, as well as a variety of linear features, such as historical-period roads, railroad grades, canals, and erosion control features, have been recorded.

Cultural-Historical Narrative for the Precolumbian Era

The following section summarizes the culture history of the Nogales area as it has been pieced together by those researchers who have surveyed, excavated, and analyzed data since the late 1800s. This summary is incomplete for periods for which time-diagnostic artifacts are few (e.g., the Archaic, Early Formative, and protohistoric periods) and where cultural deposits lie buried under several meters of sediment (e.g., Paleoindian).

Paleoindian and Archaic Periods (ca. 10,000 B.C.–A.D. 1)

Little is known of the early hunting-and-gathering peoples of the Nogales area, the Paleoindians and the Archaic peoples (Mabry 1998b). No Paleoindian or Early and Middle Archaic sites have as yet been identified in the upper Santa Cruz River valley, although a few isolated Paleoindian projectile points (Mabry 1998b:Figures 3.3, 4.2) and a meager number of Late Archaic sites have been recognized to date (Mabry 1998b:Figure 6.1, Table 7.3). What is known about these early occupations in the southern Southwest originates from better-known localities in the San Pedro River valley (Altschul et al. 1997; Hemmings 1970; Huckell 1990; Sayles and Antevs 1941; Whalen 1971), the northern portion of the middle Santa Cruz River valley (Ayres 1970; Brown 1967; Huckell 1988), and the Tucson Basin region (Agenbroad 1967; Doelle 1985; Ezzo and Deaver 1998; Huckell 1982, 1984a, 1984b, 1990, 1995; Mabry and Holmlund 1998; Matson 1991; Roth 1989, 1995; Whittlesey and Ciolek-Torrello 1996).

The discovery of a mammoth innominate found in a gravel bar deposit 10 feet below the modern ground surface along a tributary to the Santa Cruz River, a few miles east of Nogales (B. Huckell, notes on the Griffen Mammoth Locality, 1978, additional site file information labeled "AZ EE:9," ASM), highlights the serendipitous nature of

Table 1. Recorded Surveys and Data Recovery Projects between Tubac and the International Border

Project Name	Year	ASM Proj. No.[a]	Affiliation	Reference	Area (acres)	New Sites (n)	Site Nos.	Collected?
Incidental Reconnaissance Survey	1895	na	BAE	McGee 1895:372–373	not provided			info. not provided
Reconnaissance in Pimeria Alta	1909–1910	na	private	Lumholtz 1912; see McGuire and Schiffer 1982:106–110	not provided			info. not provided
Reconnaissance in Pimeria Alta	1910–1912	na	CI	Huntington 1912; see McGuire and Schiffer 1982:106–110	not provided			info. not provided
Gila Pueblo "Sherd Surveys"	1928–1929	na	Gila Pueblo	Gladwin and Gladwin 1929b	not provided			info. not provided
Examination of cremations on Sonoita Street	1928	na	ASM	B. Cummings, files, ASM	not provided			info. not provided
Reconnaissance of southern SW and northern Mexico	1930	na	UCB	Sauer and Brand 1931	not provided			info. not provided
Examination of cremations near federal building	1934	na	ASM	B. Cummings, files, ASM	not provided			info. not provided
Excavations at Tumacacori	1934	na	NPS	Beaubien 1937	not provided			info. not provided
Tubac to head of Santa Cruz River	1941	1	UA	Danson 1946	35	126	AZ EE:10:1–36; EE:9:3–49; DD:12:1–5; DD:8:2, 12–49	yes
Sahuarita to Tubac, Middle Santa Cruz River	1952	1	UA	Frick 1954	80	216	AZ DD:8:50–114; DD:4:1–73; EE:1:1–77; EE:5:4	yes
Excavations at Paloparado site	1953–1954	na	AF	Di Peso 1956; Wilcox 1987	not provided	1	AZ DD:8:2	info. not provided
Excavations at Tumacacori	1955	na	NPS	Vivian 1955	not provided			info. not provided
Excavations at Guevavi Mission	1964–1966	na	AAHS	Robinson 1976; also Kessell 1970	not provided	1	AZ EE:9:1	yes
ADOT, I-19, Nogales to Tucson Survey	1964	8	ASM	Vivian, site cards, 1964–1966	not provided	17	AZ EE:9:51–52; BB:13:41–45, 48–51; EE:1:86; DD:8:124–125; EE:9:53–54, 68	yes
Excavations at Tumacacori	1964	na	NPS	Caywood 1965	not provided			info. not provided

Project Name	Year	ASM Proj. No.[a]	Affiliation	Reference	Area (acres)	New Sites (n)	Site Nos.	Collected?
Data recovery at the Carmen site	1966	na	ASM	Brown 1967	not provided	1	AZ DD:8:125	yes
Data recovery at Potrero Creek site	1966	na	ASM	Grebinger 1971a, 1971b	not provided	1	AZ EE:9:53	yes
Data recovery at Sonoita and International Streets	1969	na	ASM	Reinhard 1978	not provided	1	AZ EE:9:68	yes
Rio Rico Survey	1972	1	private	Cunningham 1972	1200	24	AZ DD:12:25–32; EE:9:69–84	yes
Emergency salvage recording at a cremation area	1972	na	ASM	Goree, site card and files, ASM	not provided	1	AZ EE:9:85	yes
Excavations at Tubac Presidio	1974–1975	na	ASM	Shenk and Teague 1975	not provided			yes
Excavations at Tumacacori	1979	na	ASM	Fratt 1981a, 1981b	not provided			yes
Data recovery on the Baca Float Land Grant #3 for ADOT	1977	na	ASM	Doyel 1977a	not provided	4	AZ DD:8:122, 127, 128, 129 (England Ranch)	yes
ADOT Intersection Improvements	1980	222	ASM	no documentation	not provided	—		no
Data recovery at St. Andrew's Episcopal Church	1982	na	ASM	Reinhard and Fink 1982	not provided	1	AZ EE:9:67	yes
Data recovery at Nogales Wash site	1982	na	PAHS	Jacome 1986	not provided	1	AZ EE:9:93	yes
Nogales International Wastewater Treatment Plant	1986	181	GPI	no documentation	7.6	—		no
Nogales Wash–Potrero Creek	1987	na	SRI	Shelley and Altschul 1987	not provided	1	AZ EE:9:104	no
Tubac Villa, Roy Ross Realty	1987	119	ASM	Bayman 1987	80	1	AZ DD:8:137	no
Santa Cruz Transmission Line: Amado to Tubac	1989	127	DM	O'Brien et al.1989	158	1	AZ DD:8:139	no
Ray Sanchez 20-acre subdivision in Nogales	1989	158	CES	Maldonado 1987	20	—		no
Twin Buttes Pipeline Access Road (EPNG Co.)	1991	123	ACS	Neily 1991	87	0, 14 isolates		
Amado–Tumacacori survey for U.S. West Communications	1991	254	SWCA	G. Seymour 1991	not provided	6	AZ DD:8:140–144, plus prev. recorded DD:4:203, DD:8:129	no

continued on next page

Project Name	Year	ASM Proj. No.[a]	Affiliation	Reference	Area (acres)	New Sites (n)	Site Nos.	Collected?
Proposed Guevavi Ranch Preserve survey for Santa Cruz County	1991	291	SWCA	D. Seymour 1991a	210	7, 2 isolates	AZ EE:9:133–139	info. not provided
Guevavi survey sponsored by City of Nogales	1991	293	SWCA	D. Seymour 1991b	280	21, 3 isolates	AZ EE:9:112–132	no
Excavations at Guevavi and Calabasas	1991	na	NPS	Burton 1992a, 1992b	44			info. not provided
Survey of Nogales section of U.S.-Mexico border for USACE (JTF6)	1991	308	GM	Martynec et al. 1994	161	10	AZ EE:9:140–149	no
U.S. West Communications—Hwy. 82 cable replacement	1992	16	IAR	Scott 1995	not provided	—		no
Nogales Fire Department Survey	1992	79	SWCA	Phillips 1995	2.4	1, 5 isolates	AZ EE:9:150	no
Mariposa Road (State Route [SR] 189) Upgrading Project (ADOT)	1992	133	DM	Bruder 1992	34	1	not provided	no
SR 189 ROW Survey for U.S. West	1992	165	TROW	Roth 1992	0.39	0, 3 isolates		no
Bonita Villa Partners	1993	73	SRI	Lindsay 1993	6.2	0, 1 isolate		no
Tubac-Tumacacori Fire Department	1993	83	SWCA	Roberts 1993	1.2	1	AZ DD:8:145	no
Nogales Housing Authority Survey	1993	289	CES	Sullivan 1993	7.06	—		no
Sonoita Creek State Park Boundary Fencing Survey	1994	29	ASP	Montero 1993	45.5	2	AZ EE:9:156, 157	no
ADOT Frank Reed Road	1994	76	ARS	Eighmey 1994	5.8	—		no
Old Tucson Road Survey for ADOT	1994	179	ARS	Stone 1994	20.9	2, 2 isolates	AZ EE:9:154, 155	no
Nogales Mariposa Canyon Line Replacement for El Paso Natural Gas	1994	253	ACS	Adams 1994	2	0, 1 isolate		no
Data recovery on the Buena Vista Ranch	1994	na	SRI	Neily 1994	not provided	1	AZ EE:9:151	yes
Asarco survey for Asarco, Inc.	1995	24	DA	Swartz 1995	58	2, 7 isolates	AZ EE:9:160, 161	no
Mariposa Canyon survey for Granite Construction Co.	1995	49	TROW	Carpenter and Tompkins 1995	68	1	AZ EE:9:159	no
Tucson-Nogales Fiber Optic Cable ROW for GST Lightwave, Inc.	1995	72	ACS	Adams and Hoffman 1995	454	12	AZ DD:8:147, BB:13:480, DD:8:2-12, 28, 61, 141–143; EE:1:32, EE:9:154–155, BB:13:1–12	no
South River Road survey for the WLB Group	1995	152	DA	Thiel 1995	not provided	5	AZ EE:9:162–164, 117, 112	no

Project Name	Year	ASM Proj. No.[a]	Affiliation	Reference	Area (acres)	New Sites (n)	Site Nos.	Collected?
Hacienda de las Flores survey for Cimarron Associates, LLC	1995	174	AA	Slawson 1995	not provided	0, 4 isolates		no
Pena Blanca survey for Pena Blanca Properties	1995	180	SWCA	Teris and Doak 1995	65	—		no
Mariposa Road/I-19 for ADOT	1995	212	ARS	Stone 1995	1.53	—		no
I-19/Chavez Siding for ADOT	1995	403	ARS	Barz 1995	21.8	1, 8 isolates	AZ DD:8:148	no
Nogales Housing Authority Survey for NHA	1995	431	CES	Huett 1995	6.15	0, 3 isolates		no
Circle Z Trails survey	1996	180	AA	Sullivan 1996	39.5	4, 4 isolates	AZ EE:5:32, 33, 39; EE:9:169	no
ADOT Business 19/Nogales for ADOT	1996	389	ARS	Lite 1996a	63	1, 5 isolates	AZ EE:9:176	no
SR 189/Nogales for ADOT	1996	393	ARS	Lite 1996b	29.4	1	AZ EE:9:172	no
I-10 between Nogales and Amado for ADOT	1996	408	ARS	Lite et al. 1996	219??	14, 65 isolates	AZ EE:9:173–175; DD:12:36, 37; DD:8:162–170	info. not provided
SR 82, Nogales to Sonoita, SR 90	1996	459	ARS	Hathaway 1996	484.9	10, 12 isolates	AZ EE:5:35–38; EE:6:64, 65; EE:9:166–168,178	no
Business 19/SR 189/Nogales for ADOT	1997	146	ARS	Lite and Palus 1997	10.6	1	AZ EE:9:177	no
SR 289 Nogales Maintenance for ADOT	1997	303	ARS	Palus 1997	215.85	3, 7 isolates	AZ DD:12:38, 40, 41	no
Nogales survey for Associated Consulting Engineers, Inc.	1997	423	SWCA	Lascaux 1998	10	1, 8 isolates	AZ EE:9:179	no
Rio Rico survey for SCS Engineers	1998	99	SWCA	Carpenter and Tompkins 1998	40	1, 2 isolates	AZ DD:8:171	no
Tubac survey for Santa Cruz County Public Works Department	1998	253	SWCA	Olson 1998	12.6	—		no
Guevavi Ranch Pipeline survey	1999	6	DA	Swartz 1999a	3.3	1	AZ EE:9:180	no
I-19 Ruby Road to Rio Rico survey	1999	104	DA	Swartz 1999b	not provided	0, 8 isolates		no
Country Club Road survey	1999	na	SRI	Gregory et al. 1999	not provided		AZ EE:9:67	no

Key: AAHS = Arizona Archaeological and Historical Society; ADOT = Arizona Department of Transportation; ARS = Archaeological Research Services; ASM = Arizona State Museum; BAE = Bureau of American Ethnology; CI = Carnegie Institution; DM = Dames and Moore; GPI = Gutierrez-Palmenberg, Inc.; PAHS = Pimeria Alta Historical Society; SRI = Statistical Research, Inc.; SWCA = SWCA Environmental Consultants; TROW = Tierra Right-of-Way; UA = University of Arizona; UCB = University of California at Berkeley
[a] Applies only to survey projects submitted to ASM; not applicable to excavation projects.

Table 2. Recorded Sites between Tubac and the International Border

ASM Site No.[a] & Name (If Given)	Recorder or Reference	Inferred Classification	Descriptive Type	Size
EE:8:2 (Paloparado)	Di Peso 1956	habitation	artifact scatter and structural remains	not provided
EE:8:12 (Paloparado, lower terrace)	Brown and Grebinger 1969	habitation	artifact scatter and structural remains	not provided
DD:8:22	Danson 1946	habitation	sherd area and walled enclosure	75 × 50 m
DD:8:25	Danson 1946	habitation	sherd scatter	250 × 150 m
DD:8:27	Danson 1946	habitation	recent Mexican, mission?	75 × 40 m
DD:8:28	Danson 1946	not provided	sherd-and-lithic scatter	100 × 75 m
DD:8:30	Danson 1946	not provided	sherd scatter	20 × 10 m
DD:8:33	Johnson, site card, 1983	1751 fort	El Presidio Real de San Ignacio de Tubac	not provided
DD:8:42	Danson, Caywood, Getty, site card, 1941	habitation	mound and sherd scatter, largest in valley	500 × 300 m
DD:8:44	Danson, Getty, Caywood, site card, 1941	habitation	rock-walled structure with enclosure wall	25 × 15 m
DD:8:47	Danson 1946	not provided	sherd scatter	75 × 100 m
DD:8:48	Danson 1946	not provided	sherd scatter	25 × 25 m
DD:8:49	Danson 1946	campsite	sherd scatter	5 × 5 m
DD:8:72	Frick 1954	habitation	sherd scatter and historic ruin	50 × 50 m
DD:8:75	Frick 1954	habitation	mesa-top rock enclosure	100 × 250 m
DD:8:87	Frick 1954	not provided	sherd scatter	25 × 75 m
DD:8:88	Frick 1954	campsite	sherd-and-lithic scatter	25 × 25 m
DD:8:90	Frick 1954	not provided	artifact scatter	50 × 50 m
DD:8:92	Frick 1954	campsite/quarry	flaked and ground stone scatter	50 × 50 m
DD:8:94	Frick 1954	habitation	sherd scatter	0.7 miles × 100 m
DD:8:95	Frick 1954	campsite	sherd scatter	10 × 10 m
DD:8:115	Frick 1954	not provided	four circular rock walls on mountain peak	not provided
DD:8:120	E. B. Sayles, site card	habitation, Classic period	habitation	15 acres
DD:8:123	Johnson, site card, 1959	habitation	walled hillside	not provided
DD:8:128	Doyel 1977a; Lite et al. 1996	habitation	not provided	not provided
DD:8:129	Doyel 1977a; Lite et al. 1996	habitation, Sobaipuri	not provided	not provided
DD:8:130	Lite et al. 1996	habitation	not provided	not provided
DD:8:135	Sharon Urban, site cards, 1982, 1983	not provided	rock corral, dry-laid masonry, historical	21 × 21 m
DD:8:136	Sharon Urban, site cards, 1982, 1998	Archaic campsite	lithic scatter	100 × 30 m
DD:8:137/33	Bayman 1987	not provided	not provided	not provided
DD:8:139	O'Brien et al. 1989	not provided	lithic scatter	350 × 175 m
DD:8:140	G. Seymour 1991	habitation, Rillito phase?	artifact scatter	140 × 100 m
DD:8:141	G. Seymour 1991	not provided	artifact scatter	20 × 20 m
DD:8 142	G. Seymour 1991	habitation, Rincon phase	artifact scatter	100 × 30 m
DD:8:143	G. Seymour 1991	habitation, Rincon phase	artifact scatter	100 × 30 m
DD:8:144	G. Seymour 1991	campsite	lithic scatter	20 × 15 m
DD:8:145	Dart 1994; Roberts 1993	habitation	artifact scatter	100 × 70 m
DD:8:147	Adams and Hoffman 1995	not provided	lithic scatter—rhyolite	85 × 58 m
DD:8:164	Lite et al. 1996	habitation	artifact scatter	183 × 52 m
DD:8:165	Lite et al. 1996	burial	historical cemetery, early 1900s	27 × 21 m

ASM Site No.ᵃ & Name (If Given)	Recorder or Reference	Inferred Classification	Descriptive Type	Size
DD:8:166	Lite et al. 1996	habitation	prehistoric artifact scatter, historical grave	215 × 150 m
DD:8:167	Lite et al. 1996	habitation	sherd-and-lithic scatter	150 × 52 m
DD:8:168	Lite et al. 1996	processing/procurement	lithic scatter	150 × 183 m
DD:8:169	Lite et al. 1996	processing/procurement	lithic scatter	107 × 183 m
DD:8:170	Lite et al. 1996	processing/procurement	lithic scatter	215 × 150 m
DD:8:171	Carpenter and Tompkins 1998	processing/procurement	lithic scatter	40 × 25 m
DD:12:1	Danson 1946	campsite	sherd scatter	40 × 50 m
DD:12:2	Danson 1946	not provided	sherd scatter	100 × 100 m
DD:12:3	Danson 1946	not provided	sherd scatter	35 × 20 m
DD:12:4	Danson 1946	not provided	sherd-and-lithic scatter	100 × 50 m, 25 × 25 m
DD:12:5	Danson 1946	habitation	artifact scatter	150 × 150 m
DD:12:25	Cunningham and Goree, site card, 1972	habitation	artifact scatter with architecture	180 × 240 m
DD:12:26	Cunningham and Goree, site card, 1972	habitation	artifact scatter with architecture	220 × 50 m
DD:12:27	Cunningham and Goree, site card, 1972	habitation	artifact scatter with architecture	400 × 450 m
DD:12:28	Cunningham and Goree, site card, 1972	habitation	artifact scatter with architecture	200 × 1200 m
DD:12:29	Cunningham and Goree, site card, 1972	habitation	artifact scatter with architecture	400 × 200 m
DD:12:30	Cunningham and Goree, site card, 1972	habitation	lithic scatter, structural foundations	200 × 250 m
DD:12:31	Cunningham and Goree, site card, 1972	habitation	lithic scatter, structural foundations	250 × 600 m
DD:12:32	Cunningham and Goree, site card, 1972	habitation	artifact scatter with architecture	275 × 600 m
DD:12:37	Lite et al. 1996	habitation	artifact scatter	365 × 150 m
DD:12:38	Palus 1997	road	linear historic road—Old Ruby Road	10 miles
DD:12:39	Palus 1997	habitation	artifact scatter, agricultural features	220 × 115 m
DD:12:40	Palus 1997	habitation	artifact scatter, one rock feature	185 × 100 m
DD:12:41	Palus 1997	erosion control	historic rock alignments	377 × 67 m
EE:9:1 (Guevavi Mission)	Robinson 1976	mission	NRHP-listed site, listed 1971	1 acre
EE:9:2 (Calabasas Mission)	Fontana 1971	mission, habitation	NRHP-listed site, listed 1971	not provided
EE:9:3	Danson 1946	habitation	artifact scatter and mound	150 × 100 m
EE:9:27	Danson 1946	habitation?	artifact scatter	150 × 75 m
EE:9:28 (Indian Hill)	Urban, site cards, 1982, 1984	not provided	masonry, petroglyph, artifact scatter	300 × 200 m
EE:9:29	Danson 1946	not provided	sherd-and-lithic scatter	25 × 15 m
EE:9:30	Danson 1946	habitation?	sherd scatter, ground stone	150 × 150 m
EE:9:31	Danson 1946	habitation?	sherd scatter, ground stone	100 × 100 m
EE:9:32	Danson 1946	habitation	artifact scatter	150 × 150 m
EE:9:33	Danson 1946	habitation	artifact scatter	75 × 50 m
EE:9:34	Danson 1946	habitation	artifact scatter, one trash mound	0.5 × 0.5 mile
EE:9:35	Danson 1946	habitation	sherd-and-lithic scatter	0.5 × 0.25 mile

continued on next page

ASM Site No.[a] & Name (If Given)	Recorder or Reference	Inferred Classification	Descriptive Type	Size
EE:9:42	Danson 1946	not provided	sherd-and-lithic scatter	25 × 40 m
EE:9:43	Danson 1946	not provided	sherd-and-lithic scatter	25 × 25 m
EE:9:53 (Potrero Creek)	Grebinger 1971a, 1971b; Lite et al. 1996	habitation, Rillito-Rincon phases, primarily	artifact scatter	200 × 200 feet
EE:9:54	Vivian and Wrasse, site card, 1966; Lite et al. 1996; Stone 1995	habitation	artifact scatter	100 × 100 feet
EE:9:64	Fontana, Greenleaf, Ayres, site card, 1967	not provided	artifact scatter	not provided
EE:9:65 (Fort Mason)	Fontana, Greenleaf, Ayres, site card, 1967	fort	artifact scatter, foundations?	not provided
EE:9:66	Fontana, Greenleaf, Ayres, site card, 1967	not provided	artifact scatter, historical period	not provided
EE:9:67 (St. Andrew's Church site)	Reinhard 1978; Reinhard and Fink 1982; Gregory et al. 1999	habitation, Rincon phase-Classic period?	artifact scatter, pit houses, cremations	60 × 60 m
EE:9:68 (Sonoita Street cremations)	Hammack, site card, 1969	burial	cremations	not provided
EE:9:85	Goree, site card, 1972	burial, habitation?	cremations in two rows, possible pit house	not provided
EE:9:87 (San Cayetano de Calabasas)	Melot, site card, 1976; Urban, site card, 1983	mission, habitation	adobe church/visita; settlement	10 acres
EE:9:88 (Pete Kitchen Ranch)	Melot, site card, 1976; Wilson 1974	habitation	historical ranch building	not provided
EE:9:89 (Old Nogales City Hall/Fire Station)	Rothweiler and Gregory 1980	historic public building	NRHP-listed site, listed 1980	not provided
EE:9:92 (Old Santa Cruz County Courthouse)	Wilson 1977	historic public building	NRHP-listed site, listed 1977	not provided
EE:9:93 (Nogales Wash site)	Urban, site card, 1982; Jacome 1986	habitation	artifact scatter, pit houses, cremations	200 × 200 m
EE:9:94 (Cielo Negro)	Morales, site card, 1982; Urban, site card, 1983	rock art	rockshelter, pictographs	18 × 8 m
EE:9:96 (Ray Brown Village)	Urban, site cards, 1982, 1984	habitation	artifact scatter	200 × 200 m
EE:9:97 (Ray Brown Village #2)	Urban, site cards, 1982, 1984	habitation	artifact scatter	not provided
EE:9:99 (Samantha Star/ Kino Springs site)	Urban, site card, 1982; Dart 1994; Roberts 1993	habitation	artifact scatter	not provided
EE:9:101 (Victoria site)	Urban, site cards, 1982, 1984	processing/procurement	lithic scatter, bedrock mortars	300 × 50 m
EE:9:102 (El Macayo)	see EE:9:107, number replaced			
EE:9:103 (Mary Margarite site)	Urban, site card, 1985	habitation and burial	prehistoric artifact scatter, historical cemetery	200 × 400 m
EE:9:104	Shelley and Altschul 1987	artifact scatter	prehistoric artifact scatter, historical artifact scatter	175 × 200 m
EE:9:105	Shelley and Altschul 1987	artifact scatter, historic structure	prehistoric artifact scatter, historical structure	18 × 20 m
EE:9:107 (El Macayo)	Neily and Euler 1987; Gardiner and Huckell 1987; this report	habitation	artifact scatter	125 × 70 m
EE:9:108 (1916–1917 Natl. Guard Camp)	Neily and Euler 1987; Gardiner and Huckell 1987	processing/procurement	lithic scatter, one rock pile	48 m diam.
EE:9:109 (1916–1917 Natl. Guard Camp)	Neily and Euler 1987; Gardiner and Huckell 1987	campsite	1916 National Guard encampment	350 × 700 m
EE:9:110 (Thelma Street Dump)	Urban, site card, 1990	historic dump	historical dump, 1900–1940s	90 × 60 m
EE:9:112	Seymour 1991b; Thiel 1995	habitation	prehistoric scatter, historical habitation and trash	180 × 240 m
EE:9:113	Seymour 1991b	habitation	artifact scatter	50 × 10 m

ASM Site No.[a] & Name (If Given)	Recorder or Reference	Inferred Classification	Descriptive Type	Size
EE:9:114	Seymour 1991b	not provided	artifact scatter	70 × 90 m
EE:9:115	Seymour 1991b	not provided	artifact scatter	15 × 20 m
EE:9:116	Seymour 1991b	habitation	prehistoric artifact scatter, historical structure, two canals	30 × 60 m
EE:9:117	Thiel 1995; Swartz 1999	habitation and burial	prehistoric midden and pit house, historical trash+	80 × 61 m
EE:9:118	Seymour 1991b	processing/procurement	two possible canal segments and buried deposits	60 m
EE:9:119	Seymour 1991b	habitation	prehistoric and Upper Piman artifact scatter	275 × 240 m
EE:9:120	Seymour 1991b	historic canals	canals—one historical, one prehistoric or early historical	1.5 miles long
EE:9:121	Seymour 1991b	processing/procurement, late nineteenth century	artifact scatter, historical canal	65 × 30 m
EE:9:122	Seymour 1991b	not provided	prehistoric artifact scatter, historical trash	50 × 27 m
EE:9:123	Seymour 1991b	not provided	prehistoric or protohistoric artifact scatter	50 × 30 m
EE:9:124	Seymour 1991b	not provided	boulder cluster	15 × 20 m
EE:9:125	Seymour 1991b	historic canal	canal	0.5 mile
EE:9:126	Seymour 1991b	historic canal, kiln, and upper Piman?	multicomponent scatter, kiln, canal	95 × 110 m
EE:9:127	Seymour 1991b	habitation	prehistoric artifact scatter, historical feature, trash	58 × 27 m
EE:9:128	Seymour 1991b	not provided	lithic scatter, two rock alignments	60 × 25 m
EE:9:129	Seymour 1991b	habitation, Trincheras?	artifact scatter	90 × 60 m
EE:9:130	Seymour 1991b	habitation	artifact scatter with subsurface features	45 × 125 m
EE:9:131	Seymour 1991b	habitation	artifact scatter with subsurface features	40 × 35 m
EE:9:132	Seymour 1991b	habitation, Upper Piman (Sobaipuri)	artifact scatter with subsurface features	75 × 70 m
EE:9:133	Seymour 1991a	habitation	artifact scatter	100 × 400 m
EE:9:134	Seymour 1991a	habitation	historical foundation, trash	40 m diam.
EE:9:135	Seymour 1991a	not provided	artifact scatter	60 × 30 m
EE:9:136	Seymour 1991a	habitation	historical foundation and artifact scatter	40 m diam.
EE:9:137	Seymour 1991a	habitation, Trincheras?	prehistoric village, twentieth-century habitation	400 m diam.
EE:9:138	Seymour 1991a	habitation, upper Piman camp?	prehistoric and protohistoric artifact scatter	500 m diam.
EE:9:139	Seymour 1991a	habitation	artifact scatter	not provided
EE:9:140	Martynec et al. 1994	processing/procurement	lithic scatter	20 × 20 m
EE:9:141	Martynec et al. 1994	processing/procurement	lithic scatter	120 × 100 m
EE:9:142	Martynec et al. 1994	processing/procurement	lithic scatter	40 × 50 m
EE:9:143	Martynec et al. 1994	processing/procurement	lithic scatter	40 × 80 m
EE:9:144	Martynec et al. 1994	processing/procurement	lithic scatter	50 × 80 m
EE:9:145	Martynec et al. 1994	processing/procurement	flaked and ground stone scatter	110 × 220 m
EE:9:150	Carpenter and Tompkins 1995	unknown		
EE:9:153	Seymour 1992	habitation, Sobaipuri-Piman, historical	artifact scatter and structural remains	40 × 30 m
EE:9:154	Adams and Hoffman 1995; Stone 1994	road	historical road and features	not provided

continued on next page

ASM Site No.[a] & Name (If Given)	Recorder or Reference	Inferred Classification	Descriptive Type	Size
EE:9:155	Adams and Hoffman 1995; Stone 1994	habitation	prehistoric artifact scatter	35 × 40 feet
EE:9:156	Montero 1993	rock art	rockshelter, pictographs	32 m
EE:9:157	Montero 1993	processing/procurement	lithic scatter	300 × 90 m
EE:9:158	Urban, site cards, 1985, 1994	habitation	historical structure	4 × 5 m
EE:9:159	Carpenter and Tompkins 1995	processing/procurement	lithic quarry	120 × 90 m
EE:9:160	Swartz 1995	not provided	sherd-and-lithic scatter	50 × 25 m
EE:9:162	Thiel 1995	prehistoric habitation, historic burial	prehistoric artifact scatter; historical cemetery	40 × 35 m
EE:9:163	Thiel 1995	prehistoric processing/procurement, historic habitation	prehistoric flaked and ground stone; historical structure/trash	168 × 53 m
EE:9:164	Thiel 1995	not provided	sherd-and-lithic scatter	198 × 50 m
EE:9:165	Sullivan 1996	not provided	lithic scatter	180 × 35 m
EE:9:172	Lite et al. 1996	railroad	railroad route for NM and AZ RR 1882	200 × 10 feet
EE:9:173	Lite et al. 1996	limited-activity site	sherd-and-lithic scatter	130 × 90 m
EE:9:174	Lite et al. 1996	not provided	artifact scatter	145 × 105 m
EE:9:175	Lite et al. 1996	not provided	sherd-and-lithic scatter	200 × 105 m
EE:9:176	Lite 1996a; Lite et al. 1996	road	historical road segment	6 miles × 40 feet
EE:9:177	Lite and Palus 1997	habitation	vernacular style house, 1940s–1960s	50 × 30 feet
EE:9:179	Lascaux 1998	not provided	lithic scatter, rock pile, terraces	150 × 120 m
EE:9:180	Swartz 1999a	not provided	sherd scatter	30 × 5 m

Key: NRHP = National Register of Historic Places
[a] All ASM site numbers have the prefix "AZ."

identifying potential Paleoindian remains in the upper Santa Cruz River valley. Similarly, sites inferred to date to the Archaic have only rarely been identified or tested (e.g., AZ DD:8:125, the Carmen site, and AZ DD:8:136), and in lowland contexts, they, too, are likely to be buried under many meters of sediment.

Early Formative Period
(400 B.C.–A.D. 700)

Almost nothing is known of the early agriculturalists of the Nogales area who preceded the Hohokam, Trincheras, and local traditions of the southern Southwest between the first few centuries B.C. and about A.D. 700. Today we refer to this time period as either the Early Formative, Early Agricultural, or Early Ceramic horizon. The Early Formative represents the time when ceramic containers were added to the inventory of material goods of Late Archaic foragers and part-time farmers and when agricultural production and sedentary ways of life became increasingly important. Although the Early Formative adaptation has been recognized in and described for the Tucson Basin and localities north (e.g., Ciolek-Torrello 1995; Deaver and Ciolek-Torrello 1995; Halbirt and Henderson 1993; Huckell et al. 1987;

Mabry 1998a; Mabry and Clark 1994; Mabry et al. 1997; Whittlesey 1995), it has not yet been documented in the Nogales area (Mabry 1998a:Figure 6.2)—although it certainly exists.

It is likely that some of the many artifact scatters in the upper Santa Cruz River valley that are manifested as distributions of surface artifacts with plain ware pottery and no painted pottery represent settlements associated with the earliest ceramic-bearing traditions of the Early Formative period—the Plain Ware horizon (ca. A.D. 1–425) (Deaver and Ciolek-Torrello 1995). Similarly, it is probable that artifact scatters with red-slipped pottery in addition to early plain ware are characteristic of the subsequent development, the Red Ware horizon (ca. A.D. 425–650; Deaver and Ciolek-Torrello 1995). Finally, it is reasonable to assume that sites possessing decorated pottery with simple, red-painted designs are representative of the final, but short-lived, ceramic tradition of the Early Formative period—the Early Broadline horizon (ca. A.D. 650–700) (Deaver and Ciolek-Torrello 1995). Whittlesey (1996:55) suggested that evidence exists for the emergence of regional subtraditions during the Early Formative period. With time, excavation, and comparative studies of ceramics, the Nogales area may prove to have a distinctive Early Formative period ceramic tradition, such as the Tucson and Phoenix Basins have been shown to possess. The oldest pottery found at excavated sites such as Paloparado, Potrero Creek, Nogales Wash, and El Macayo likely dates to the end of the Early Formative period.

Middle Formative Period
(A.D. 700–1150)

The Middle Formative period represents the time when the settlements of early farming peoples of the upper Santa Cruz River basin, including folks believed to be affiliated with the Hohokam and Trincheras cultures, become archaeologically visible. The Hohokam, as a distinct cultural entity, appeared first in the Phoenix Basin (alternatively referred to as the Gila-Salt Basin) at about A.D. 700 during the Snaketown phase of the Pioneer period, seemingly in conjunction with the introduction of large-scale, canal irrigation agriculture (Figure 6). The Tucson Basin exhibits a cultural sequence related to the Phoenix Basin sequence, although little is known of Pioneer period developments in the Tucson Basin prior to A.D. 500. To the south in the upper-middle and upper Santa Cruz basin, the nature and extent of the Pioneer period occupation are poorly known and are inferred from a small number of early ceramics identified at excavated sites such as Paloparado (Di Peso 1956), Potrero Creek (Grebinger 1971a, 1971b), and El Macayo (this report).

Several models have been developed to account for the Hohokam occupation in the Tucson Basin and middle Santa Cruz River valley, although none to date have included the upper Santa Cruz in their purview. Grebinger (1971a) and Haury (1976), for example, suggested that the Hohokam of the Gila-Salt Basin moved southward into the riverine areas along the Santa Cruz and displaced the indigenous populations who had lived in these areas, driving these less forceful peoples onto smaller drainages and more marginal desert lands. According to these models, the colonizing Hohokam occupied large centralized settlements, used irrigation technology, and maintained a distinctive and formal social organization and religious pattern. In contrast, Doyel (1977b, 1984) viewed the Hohokam of the Tucson Basin and areas south as a people who possessed a highly diversified agricultural and foraging economy that required a less formal organizational pattern and who lived in dispersed noncentralized settlements. Alternatively, Doelle (1988) suggested that the initial Hohokam settlements were located in the optimal floodwater- and irrigation-agriculture areas of the Tucson Basin, but by A.D. 800/850 or so (i.e., the Rillito phase), these prime areas were fully occupied, and subsequent settlements were located in more marginal settings.

Whatever the origins of Middle Formative period populations, by A.D. 700 archaeological manifestations in the Tucson Basin are generally characterized as Hohokam, although they were sufficiently different from those in the Phoenix Basin to warrant a separate cultural sequence (Wallace et al. 1995). By the eighth century A.D., occupation in the Tucson Basin was characterized by the presence of large settlements with public architecture (i.e., ball courts) that appear to have functioned as the primary centers of dispersed communities made up of clusters of small sites associated with a few larger sites (Doelle 1985; Doelle and Wallace 1986). This pattern of settlement persisted for more than two centuries and is referred to as the Hohokam Colonial period (A.D. 750–950).

Sustained occupation dating from the Colonial period also appears to have extended into the middle and upper Santa Cruz River basin, as indicated by large-area surveys in the middle basin (Frick 1954; Huber 1996) and the upper basin (Danson 1946; D. Seymour 1991a, 1991b), as well as excavations at several settlements in the middle and upper Santa Cruz River valley. These include Colonial period components at three of the four Baca Float sites (AZ DD:8:122, 127, and 128) (Doyel 1977a), Paloparado (AZ DD:8:2 and 12) (Brown and Grebinger 1969; Di Peso 1956; Wilcox 1987), Potrero Creek (AZ DD:9:53) (Grebinger 1971a, 1971b), AZ DD:7:22 near Arivaca (Whittlesey and Ciolek-Torrello 1992), Nogales Wash (AZ EE:9:93) (Jácome 1986), and El Macayo (AZ EE:9:107) (Gardiner and Huckell 1987; Slawson 1991; this report). Of these, only the extensive and long-lived Paloparado seems to have functioned as a primary village, similar to primary villages in the Tucson Basin. Another candidate is AZ EE:9:3, at the confluence of Sonoita Creek and the Santa Cruz River, which, according to Neily (1994:89), contains a ball court.

Sites in the middle and upper Santa Cruz River valley reflect interaction with the Tucson Basin and Phoenix Basin Hohokam. Exchange and emulation of Hohokam ceramics, architectural styles, and mortuary practices are examples of this influence, although contemporary burial customs were quite variable. In the Nogales area, Middle Formative period mortuary customs included both inhumation and cremation interments. Ceramics of the middle and upper Santa Cruz River valley also suggest that interaction was maintained with the Trincheras culture of the Rio Concepción basin to the south (Bowen 1972, 1976; Braniff Cornejo 1992; Johnson 1960; McGuire and Villalpando 1993).

During the Hohokam Sedentary period (A.D. 950–1150), occupation at a number of larger sites in the upper-middle and upper Santa Cruz River area, including Paloparado, Potrero Creek, Nogales Wash, and El Macayo, appears to have intensified (Danson 1946). To the north, this period is marked by a substantial increase in the number of settlements and the use of previously unoccupied areas. Doelle et al. (1987), in a survey of the southern Tucson Basin, noted that there were shifts in the locations of primary village ball court sites along the Santa Cruz at this time.

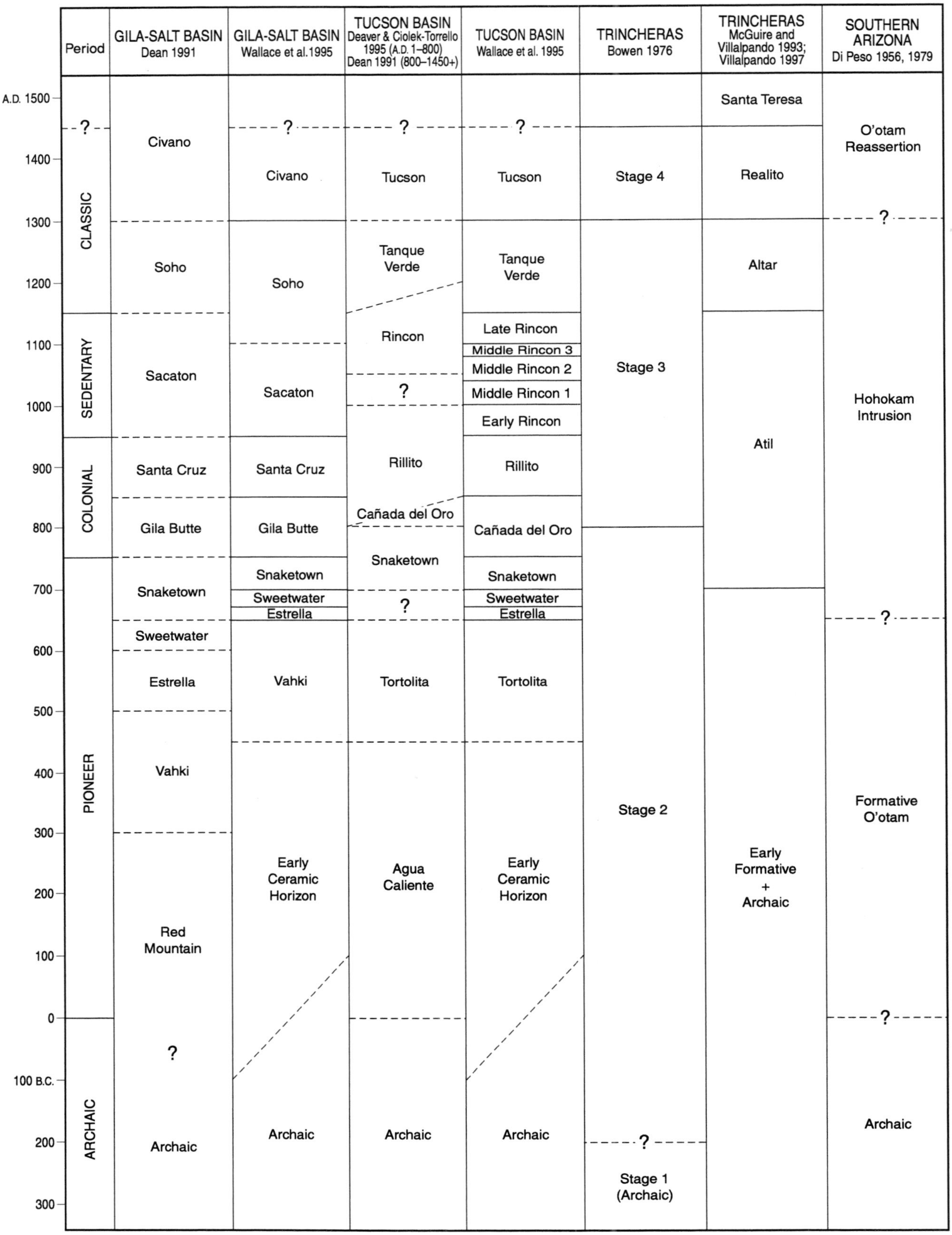

Period	GILA-SALT BASIN Dean 1991	GILA-SALT BASIN Wallace et al.1995	TUCSON BASIN Deaver & Ciolek-Torrello 1995 (A.D. 1–800) Dean 1991 (800–1450+)	TUCSON BASIN Wallace et al. 1995	TRINCHERAS Bowen 1976	TRINCHERAS McGuire and Villalpando 1993; Villalpando 1997	SOUTHERN ARIZONA Di Peso 1956, 1979
						Santa Teresa	
CLASSIC	Civano	Civano	Tucson	Tucson	Stage 4	Realito	O'otam Reassertion
	Soho	Soho	Tanque Verde	Tanque Verde		Altar	
SEDENTARY	Sacaton	Sacaton	Rincon	Late Rincon / Middle Rincon 3 / Middle Rincon 2 / Middle Rincon 1 / Early Rincon	Stage 3	Atil	Hohokam Intrusion
COLONIAL	Santa Cruz	Santa Cruz	Rillito	Rillito			
	Gila Butte	Gila Butte	Cañada del Oro	Cañada del Oro			
	Snaketown	Snaketown / Sweetwater / Estrella	Snaketown	Snaketown / Sweetwater / Estrella			
PIONEER	Sweetwater / Estrella	Vahki	Tortolita	Tortolita			
	Vahki				Stage 2	Early Formative + Archaic	Formative O'otam
	Red Mountain	Early Ceramic Horizon	Agua Caliente	Early Ceramic Horizon			
ARCHAIC	Archaic	Archaic	Archaic	Archaic	Stage 1 (Archaic)		Archaic

Figure 6. Comparative cultural chronology for southern Arizona.

Because of limited survey and excavation in the upper Santa Cruz region, however, it is not known whether a similar occupational expansion occurred there as well.

Sites in the upper Santa Cruz River valley inferred to represent Colonial period habitation, other than those referenced above, include AZ DD:8:140 (G. Seymour 1991), early occupations at the Mary Margarite site (AZ EE:9:103) (Urban, site files, ASM), and a cremation area on the south side of Mariposa Canyon near Nogales Wash (AZ EE:9:85) (Goree, site files, ASM). Sites in the upper Santa Cruz River valley inferred to represent Sedentary period occupation include AZ DD:8:142 and 143 (G. Seymour 1991), the Saint Andrew's Episcopal Church site (AZ EE:9:67) (Gregory et al. 1999; Reinhard and Fink 1982), and the Sonoita Street cremation area (AZ EE:9:68) (Reinhard 1978).

Late Formative Period
(A.D. 1150–1450)

At about A.D. 1150 or 1200—the end of the Hohokam Sedentary period and the beginning of the Hohokam Classic period—the material culture, spatial distribution, and size of settlements over a broad area of the American Southwest changed dramatically. In the Tucson Basin, the Classic period (A.D. 1150–1450) was characterized by the occupation of fewer but larger nucleated settlements; production and exchange of different ceramic styles; use of innovative architectural forms consisting of aboveground, multiroom adobe structures enclosed within adobe walls to form domestic compounds; development of new forms of public architecture (e.g., platform mounds surmounted by special structures); and a shift from cremation burial to inhumation burial that is taken to be an important change in religious ideology and practice.

Populations also seem to have increased and aggregated into fewer but larger settlements in the middle and upper Santa Cruz River valley during Classic period times. These changes, for example, were observed at the Paloparado Ruin, a settlement occupied at least into the early Classic period (A.D. 1150–1300) (Di Peso 1956; Wilcox 1987). According to Wilcox (1987), Paloparado was characterized by a complex settlement structure and public architecture (i.e., a banquette or walkway and a large plaza) that is hypothesized to have served integrative functions for a dispersed community. In addition, Wilcox (1987) has interpreted the presence of a discrete burial area at Paloparado, associated with a walled compound containing unique mortuary remains, as suggesting the practice of status ranking within late Classic Hohokam society. Ceramics recovered from Paloparado indicate large-scale interaction with populations in the Tucson Basin, the Gila-Salt Basin, the Papaguería, and the Trincheras culture area.

During the late Classic period (A.D. 1300–1450), *cerros de trincheras,* or hilltop settlements with walled hillside terraces, were constructed in northern Sonora and southern Arizona (Downum 1993; Downum et al. 1994; Stacy 1974). Although defensive functions have been suggested for some *trincheras* sites, many appear to be essentially habitation and agricultural sites (Downum et al. 1994). At least four of these sites have been located near Nogales (Downum et al. 1994:273; site files, ASM), but none has been investigated systematically.

Other than long-lived sites, such as Paloparado and El Macayo, sites in the upper Santa Cruz River valley inferred to represent Classic period habitations include AZ DD:8:42, which Danson (1946) judged the largest habitation site in the upper Santa Cruz River valley; AZ DD:8:90 and 94 (Frick 1954); and AZ DD:8:120 (Sayles, site files, ASM).

The Late Formative is the final prehistoric period in southern Arizona. What follows is a long and poorly understood period beginning after the abandonment of fifteenth-century prehistoric sites and lasting until the time of sustained contact between Native American and European populations in the American Southwest (Whittlesey 1996:72–80). This period is known as the protohistoric and is variously dated from A.D. 1450 to 1540, when Coronado made his journey into what is now Arizona and New Mexico; from A.D. 1450 to 1691, when Kino first visited San Cayetano del Tumacacori; or from A.D. 1450 to 1776, when the Spanish presidio of Tubac was moved to Tucson (Whittlesey 1996:72). Sites attributed to protohistoric Sobaipuri or Upper Pima occupation in the upper Santa Cruz River basin include AZ DD:8:129 (England Ranch Ruin) (Doyel 1977a); AZ EE:9:119, 123, 126, 129, 132, 133, 138, and 153 (D. Seymour 1991a, 1991b, 1992; G. Seymour 1991); and possibly AZ DD:8:49 (Danson 1946).

For the purposes of this document, we conclude this brief culture history with the close of the Precolumbian period, as it frames the occupation of El Macayo in the Santa Cruz County Complex property. For descriptions of the archaeological manifestations of the protohistoric and early historical periods in southern Arizona, the reader is referred to Whittlesey et al. (1994) and Whittlesey (1996).

Finally, it should be mentioned that an extremely valuable source of historical-period information for Nogales, Arizona, has been made available as a result of archaeological work on the Santa Cruz County Complex parcel. Gardiner (1987) and Gardiner and Huckell (1987) have compiled research undertaken to document historical-period site AZ EE:9:109. This is the location of the National Guard encampment that existed in Nogales, Arizona, from 1916 to 1918 in response to attacks along the United States–Mexico border by Pancho Villa and his supporters. Data available in these reports provide insight into the political events of a little-known but important chapter in our country's and state's recent history.

Summary

Despite more than 100 years of archaeological research in the upper Santa Cruz River basin, relatively little of the history of settlement and cultural dynamics in the region is known. Only the Middle Formative period has been documented in any detail, and that remains sketchy because of isolated survey projects and infrequent programs of excavation and analysis. A general review of site location and site description data on file at ASM, however, revealed several archaeological patterns worth noting. First, there is a surprising number of habitation sites among the list of recorded sites for the region, and many of these are very long-lived—if it is valid to use time-diagnostic ceramic types as a reasonable proxy for length of occupation. Apparently, a tradition of "deep sedentism" (Lekson 1990) is a defining characteristic of settlement behavior in this portion of southern Arizona. Second, the largest and longest-occupied habitations are without exception located adjacent to sizable patches of high-quality arable soil and surface water within the bottomlands of the Santa Cruz and its primary tributaries. Third, the diversity of ceramic types present on sites assigned to the Colonial, Sedentary, and early Classic periods suggests that local populations had frequent and sustained interaction with extralocal populations north, south, and east of the upper Santa Cruz River valley. Finally, it seems fair to say that the upper and middle Santa Cruz were heavily populated areas in prehistoric times. That they did not support larger populations is probably a function of the inhabitants' inability to create large-scale irrigation systems, a situation undoubtedly related to topographic and hydrological factors.

Research Design

The overarching goals of the 1996 data recovery program for El Macayo were to understand how successive generations of inhabitants made their living, how they related to one another and to other pre-Classic period populations around them, and how they responded to the environmental and cultural changes that took place during the A.D. 650–1150 period.

To approach these goals, four broad themes or historic contexts were identified as important and addressable research domains for data recovery investigations at El Macayo (Van West 1994). These included (1) chronology, (2) site structure, (3) subsistence, and (4) cultural affiliation and interaction. The following section summarizes the research design conceived prior to the 1996 fieldwork. It constituted an approach to research that seemed most appropriate given the results of the previous programs of testing, and it provided a structure for our data recovery methods and modes of analysis.

Chronology

Interpretation of the archaeological record results, in large measure, from the careful documentation of the spatial and temporal attributes of archaeological materials and the thoughtful search for patterning across these two dimensions. Moreover, the establishment of cultural sequences or the refinement of existing dating schemes is basic to virtually all research questions concerning cultural process and culture change. Whereas many investigators working in the upper Santa Cruz River valley have borrowed a temporal scheme developed primarily to describe Hohokam traditions in south-central Arizona, most would acknowledge that it is not truly applicable to the occupations of the Nogales area. Thus, the need to build and refine local chronologies is a persistent challenge.

Toward this end, the spatial relationships of artifacts and features encountered during fieldwork were documented, datable contexts were sampled, and all time-diagnostic materials were collected. A specific goal of the chronological studies at El Macayo was to date as many structures and features as possible. This was seen as an endeavor basic to the study of site structure and the organization of activity space within the settlement. Consequently, stratigraphic relationships were recorded in detail, organic material suitable for radiocarbon assay was recovered, and thermally altered features were sampled using archaeomagnetic methods. Postfieldwork analysis focused on the assignment of calendar dates to chronometrically sampled features, the establishment of construction sequences for particular loci within the site, and the combination of these results with those inferred from time-diagnostic artifacts to build a general site occupation sequence.

Site Structure

Analyses of site structure and intrasite settlement patterns are important avenues of research into social organization, population size, settlement growth, intensity of use, and duration of occupation. Successful studies of site structure are dependent on the exposure of significant areas of occupational space and well-preserved architectural remains. Where these topics have been studied at sites excavated in south-central Arizona (Di Peso 1956; Doyel 1977a; Grebinger 1971a, 1971b), researchers have been able to learn a great deal about the size and organization of the founding population, where different activities took place, and the direction and nature of growth in the village. We hoped we might be able to expose a sufficient number of structures and related features based on the combined work of ASM, CES, and SRI to gain some insight into the principles and practices governing the development of the settlement over time.

The combined map of subsurface features (see Figure 3) suggested that the densest concentration of architectural remains on the county-owned portion of the site was located between Trench 8 on the north and Trench 3 on the south. Further, the possibility of at least one cemetery east of Datum B (Trench 3) existed. Despite the fact that only a small portion of a much larger site remained, it was thought that it was still possible to reconstruct aspects of prehistoric social organization by examining the spatial arrangement of houses, adjoining courtyards or plazas, courtyard groups, cemeteries, and a variety of extramural features and activity areas. Should a sufficient number of features be dated, then some information on settlement growth might be gained.

We hoped that additional trenching and rapid mechanical stripping would allow us to expose buried features, note doorways and orientations where they were preserved, and measure the distances between clusters of houses, extramural features, and activity areas. Although the bases of two previously discovered storage pits were located more than 1.5 m (4.9 feet) below the current ground surface, we noted that the floors of most of the prehistoric structures were located within 45 cm (18 inches) of the surface (Gardiner and Huckell 1987; Slawson 1991). We hoped that if we unearthed enough structures, we might be able to suggest the size of household and courtyard groups and estimate the number of contemporary houses at any one point in time.

Subsistence

Economic adaptations in the Nogales area are not well documented. Although researchers assume that the Formative period occupants of the upper Santa Cruz River region were at least part-time farmers, it is not known to what degree prehistoric groups depended on agriculture for their annual caloric requirements. Neither is it known to what extent habitation sites in the region represent year-round occupations or part-time residences used to exploit seasonally available resources. Consequently, we envisioned the recovery of food remains in the form of macrobotanical and pollen samples, as well as animal bone, in conjunction with functional analysis of architectural spaces and nonarchitectural features used for food preparation and storage, to be an important area of inquiry.

The 1987 test excavations at El Macayo produced evidence of the cultivation of corn (charred cupules, glume, and chaff); the collecting of mesquite or palo verde beans,

grasses, spiderling, and possibly prickly pear fruit; and the gathering of oak and either willow or cottonwood for fuel wood (Gardiner and Huckell 1987:24–25). Given the large number of extramural pits and storage cists observed in the profiles of pit houses, we expected to recover numerous sediment samples for macrobotanical and pollen analysis, as well as faunal remains. These materials would provide important information on the variety of food items in the diets of late Colonial and Sedentary populations of the Nogales area and potentially offer clues as to their season or seasons of procurement and use.

Cultural Affiliation and Interaction

The upper Santa Cruz River region is located in a geographic area between the prehistoric Hohokam of the middle Santa Cruz, Tucson Basin, and Papaguería areas to the north and the prehistoric Trincheras culture of Sonora to the south. Archaeological materials and cultural patterns associated with Hohokam and Trincheras traditions are found in varying proportions in sites recorded in the Nogales area. For example, researchers who excavated and analyzed materials from the Nogales Wash site (Jácome 1986), the Potrero Creek site (Grebinger 1971a), and Paloparado Ruin (Di Peso 1956) suggested that the inhabitants of these sites were either participants in or in close contact with Tucson Basin Hohokam culture. In contrast, researchers who investigated sites such as AZ DD:7:22 at Arivaca (Whittlesey and Ciolek-Torrello 1992) and Buena Vista (Neily 1994) suggested that the inhabitants of these settlements appeared to have been more closely related to the Trincheras culture populations.

These inferences are based on the presence of materials (e.g., ceramic vessels or stone palettes) and traits (e.g., burial practices or house forms) presumed to represent contact and interaction with individuals and ideas from other populations. It is not known, however, whether the pre-Hispanic settlements of the Nogales area were populated by more than one cultural group, whether entire settlements were participants of one cultural tradition or another, or even if the settlements were inhabited by local groups unlike either dominant tradition. Given El Macayo's intermediate location, a significant effort was made to elucidate patterns that could shed light on the cultural affiliations and potential intergroup interactions among the inhabitants of El Macayo and their neighbors.

Prior to fieldwork, archaeological materials and patterns found frequently in archaeological contexts and believed to be linked with the creation of distinctive cultural identities and cultural practices were identified. Principal among these were the presence and preponderance of distinctively local ceramics or ceramic traits, unique stylistic or technological traits in other classes of material, unusual architectural conventions and site plans, mortuary customs, rock art, and locally specific economic patterns. Of these traits, we expected that ceramic and architectural data would be the most readily available sources of information on cultural identity at El Macayo. We understood that comparisons, even of these categories, would likely be unbalanced, given that so few Trincheras sites have been studied systematically or excavated, and that much greater research effort has been devoted to material remains associated with the Hohokam. Similarly, little comparative architectural and spatial-organizational data are available for the northern Sonoran traditions when compared to those of southern Arizona. Nevertheless, we hoped that ceramic clays and tempers could be studied in some detail, and that it would be possible to determine local versus nonlocal production of given ceramic types as an early step in the identification of distinctive cultural traditions.

Data Recovery Approach

To achieve our research objectives in a cost-effective manner, we proposed (1) to coordinate controlled hand excavation with judicious mechanic stripping and trenching and (2) to focus our efforts on a judicious sample of architectural and occupational spaces, as per recommendations made by Slawson (1991:16). Initially, we proposed to excavate completely three of the 10 known pit houses, sample the remainder for chronometric dates and subsistence remains, and record and sample all other pits and subsurface features for botanical and faunal remains. We further proposed to fully document and sample new features identified by any new excavation and fully map the remaining structures and associated features to reveal site structure and spatial organization. By the end of our six weeks of fieldwork, we had achieved these goals and more.

The project was divided into five phases. During Phase 1, the data recovery plan was developed and submitted to the Arizona SHPO and the BLM (pursuant to a memorandum of agreement executed for this project) for review and acceptance.

Phase 2 constituted all prefield arrangements and the actual fieldwork. SRI first requested and obtained an excavation permit from ASM (ASM Permit 1996-70ps, March 22, 1996). Second, we requested and obtained a repository agreement from ASM to curate the archaeological materials and subsequent data produced by our data recovery efforts (Notice of Intent to Provide Repository Services, March 11, 1996). Third, SRI initiated a request to secure a burial memorandum of agreement (BMOA) (as specified in Section 106 of the National Historic Preservation Act of 1966, as amended) on the supposition that additional human

remains and associated grave goods would be encountered during the project (Agreement on Burial Discoveries: Case No. 95-24). All permissions, agreements, and acceptances were obtained by the spring of 1996, and fieldwork was scheduled. Field investigations were carried out between April 13 and May 23, 1996. After the completion of the fieldwork, an interim letter report was prepared and sent to the Santa Cruz County Department of Public Works acknowledging that the data recovery had been completed.

Phase 3 involved the analyses of materials recovered during fieldwork. As per our BMOA, human remains and associated funerary items were inspected and documented first to ensure timely repatriation. These remains and their documentation were transferred to representatives of the Tohono O'odham Nation on October 24, 1996.

During Phase 4, a draft report synthesizing the results of fieldwork and analyses was prepared and submitted to Santa Cruz County, the BLM, the state archaeologist, and SHPO for review. This draft was reviewed and accepted by Santa Cruz County and agencies and returned for final production. The present document represents the final version of this report.

Finally in Phase 5, the collections will be prepared for submission to ASM for curation as per our repository agreement with that institution.

Organization of This Report

The remainder of this report presents the results of our data recovery efforts. Chapter 2 describes the results of fieldwork, including descriptions of site stratigraphy, excavation methods, architecture, and burials. Chapters 3–5 provide the results of material culture analyses; Chapter 3 describes the ceramics, Chapter 4 describes flaked and ground stone, and Chapter 5 describes shell artifacts recovered from our efforts at El Macayo. Chapters 6 and 7 present the results of the faunal analyses; Chapter 6 describes the nonhuman bone remains, and Chapter 7 describes the macaw recovered in a formal burial. Chapter 8 presents the results of pollen and flotation analysis and discusses the economic plant remains recovered from excavation. Chapter 9 presents the results of the osteological study of the human skeletal remains recovered by our fieldwork. Chapter 10 summarizes the results of our data recovery efforts and addresses the research questions. Chapter 11 contains recommendations for the continued protection of the site and its information potential, and concludes our report. Eight appendixes are also included in this report. Three are provided in full (Appendixes A, G, and H); five (Appendixes B–F) are presented in abbreviated form. The complete versions are on file at ASM, where the collections have been curated.

T W O

Excavation Results

William L. Deaver

One hundred seventy-seven prehistoric features were defined during the 1996 data recovery program at El Macayo (Figure 7). Added to the 38 features identified in previous excavations, a total of 215 prehistoric features have been identified on the portion of the site owned by Santa Cruz County (Table 3). These features include the remains of 24 pit structures, 13 human burials, 3 animal burials, 4 possible burials, and 172 pits and other features. Excavations to date indicate that this site was intensively occupied over a long period. The intensity of occupation is readily evident in the frequency of superimposed features. Because of this practice, the number of identified features is a minimum estimate of the total number of prehistoric cultural features present. The length of the occupation is indicated by the wide temporal range of painted pottery types identified (see Chapter 3). Based on known changes in painted design styles over time for the prehistoric ceramic traditions of southern Arizona, the decorated ceramics found at El Macayo indicate an occupation spanning five centuries from ca. A.D. 650 to 1150.

This chapter describes our findings during the 1996 excavations at El Macayo. Artifacts were recovered from 12 arbitrary excavation units and 38 features (Table 4). Recovery contexts included the site surface, 1 trench, 5 stripping units, 6 test pits, 9 pit houses, 10 burials, and 19 pits. Analyses of the artifacts and material items recovered from the excavations are described in succeeding chapters.

Site Stratigraphy

Four soil units used to identify, interpret, and define prehistoric cultural features were identified at El Macayo. Unit I is a shallow (10–15-cm-thick) layer of loose brown to dark brown, silty and sandy sediments containing prehistoric, historical-period, and modern artifacts at the surface of the site. Generally, this unit is the root zone of the grasses and forbs growing at the site and is the active soil layer. The contact between Unit I and the underlying Unit II is gradational over several centimeters.

Unit II is the main culture-bearing deposit (30–70 cm thick). Our Unit II label is equivalent to Stratum 60 identified by Gardiner and Huckell (1987). The sediment matrix is soft and has been churned by rodent activity. The matrix of this unit is generally a brown to dark brown, very fine to fine, silty sand with inclusions of gravels, small stones, and larger rocks (Gardiner and Huckell 1987:5). These sediments probably represent colluvial sediments eroding from the hill above and west of the site, and aeolian deposits derived from the floor of Nogales Wash to the east that were mixed with the occupational debris. Many of the larger rocks were probably the remains of prehistoric features or trash disposal. In general, Unit II is unstratified; extensive rodent disturbance appears to have contributed to the homogenization of the deposit. Occasional lenses of light to dark gray ash representing a variety of prehistoric human activities are still visible, however. Many of the features that we identified were visible only at the base of Unit II, where they had been excavated into the underlying, preoccupation soil, Unit III. As noted first by Gardiner and Huckell (1987), the fill of the features is undifferentiated from the general Unit II deposit. It is quite likely that many of the features we identified originated within the Unit II deposit, but there was no enduring evidence.

Units III and IV are preoccupation soil formations that underlie Unit II. Unit III is a weakly developed calcic horizon situated directly beneath Unit II across the site. Many of the cultural features are excavated into the top of this unit. The calcic horizon formed in a silty sand very similar to the matrix of Unit II. Consequently, Unit III is soft and crumbly. Unit IV is a reddish brown, argillic alluvium containing pebbles and boulders that form the ridge on which El Macayo is situated. This unit is exposed at the modern ground surface at the northern and western boundaries of the

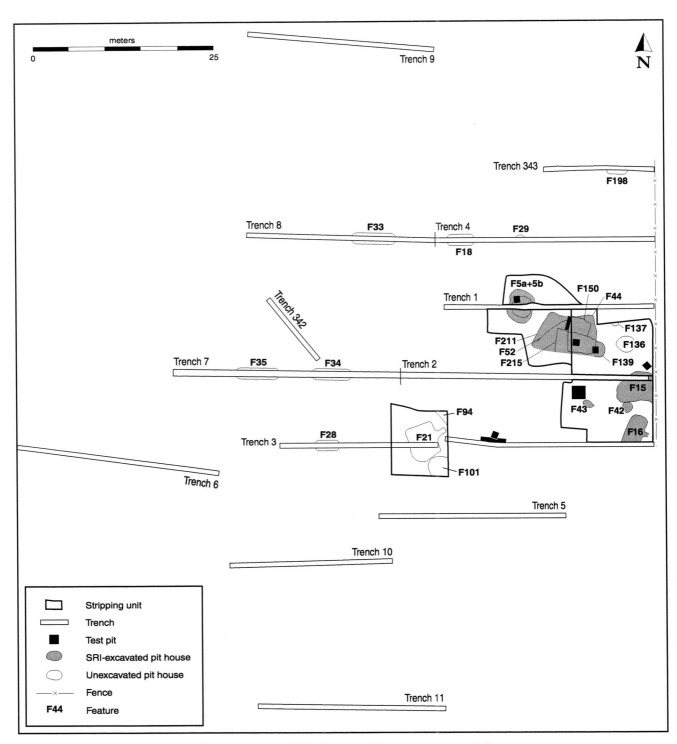

Figure 7. Overview of ASM, CES, and SRI excavations at El Macayo.
(CES Trench 12 is outside of the site area, and therefore not shown.)

Table 3. Inventory of Prehistoric Archaeological Features Identified at El Macayo

Feature Number	Feature Type	Northing	Easting	Discovery Phase	Feature Number	Feature Type	Northing	Easting	Discovery Phase
1	human cremation	100.00	109.00	ASM 1987	41	rock cluster	111.64	128.71	SRI 1996
2	human cremation	101.00	107.25	ASM 1987	42	pit house	105.80	125.91	SRI 1996
3	pit	120.00	103.00	ASM 1987	43	pit house	106.42	120.48	SRI 1996
4	pit	111.00	102.00	ASM 1987	44	pit house	116.00	119.50	SRI 1996
5	pit house	120.20	111.00	ASM 1987	45	pit	117.75	112.81	SRI 1996
6	pit	120.00	116.50	ASM 1987	46	pit	117.69	109.68	SRI 1996
7	pit	110.50	105.00	ASM 1987	47	pit	116.84	109.79	SRI 1996
8	pit	110.50	106.50	ASM 1987	48	pit	117.34	110.34	SRI 1996
9	pit	120.50	120.50	ASM 1987	49	pit	113.93	112.05	SRI 1996
10	pit	120.50	123.75	ASM 1987	50	pit	116.32	111.78	SRI 1996
11	pit	120.50	124.75	ASM 1987	51	pit	114.99	113.71	SRI 1996
12	pit	100.00	107.00	ASM 1987	52	pit house	115.20	115.60	SRI 1996
13	pit	101.00	103.00	ASM 1987	53	pit	113.34	116.45	SRI 1996
14	pit	110.50	115.50	ASM 1987	54	pit	115.28	112.58	SRI 1996
15	pit house	109.00	127.00	ASM 1987	55	pit	113.50	114.69	SRI 1996
16	pit house	102.50	127.00	ASM 1987	56	pit	115.50	114.87	SRI 1996
17	pit	110.50	120.75	ASM 1987	57	pit	116.76	107.61	SRI 1996
18	pit house	131.00	102.50	ASM 1987	58	pit	118.12	107.42	SRI 1996
19	human inhumation	131.00	111.00	ASM 1987	59	pit	118.85	106.32	SRI 1996
20	pit	131.00	123.00	ASM 1987	60	pit	119.69	106.46	SRI 1996
21	pit house	100.00	97.00	ASM 1987	61	pit	119.04	107.46	SRI 1996
22	pit	100.00	94.00	ASM 1987	62	pit	112.67	112.43	SRI 1996
23	pit	100.00	86.50	ASM 1987	63	pit	116.81	110.81	SRI 1996
24	pit	90.00	103.00	ASM 1987	64	pit	118.93	112.78	SRI 1996
25	pit	90.00	95.00	ASM 1987	65	pit	119.14	113.27	SRI 1996
26	pit	131.00	111.00	ASM 1987	66	pit	116.53	122.23	SRI 1996
27	pit	110.50	99.50	ASM 1987	67	pit	115.58	121.27	SRI 1996
28	pit house	100.00	83.75	ASM 1987	68	pit	96.26	93.89	SRI 1996
29	pit house	110.50	94.75	ASM 1987	69	pit	96.40	95.13	SRI 1996
30	pit	131.00	121.00	ASM 1987	70	pit	99.36	94.01	SRI 1996
31	human inhumation	101.00	107.00	ASM 1987	71	pit	101.23	93.55	SRI 1996
32	human and dog inhumation	138.50	95.00	CES 1991	72	void	—	—	—
33	pit house	138.50	89.50	CES 1991	73	pit	114.10	116.82	SRI 1996
34	pit house	118.50	96.00	CES 1991	74	pit	117.68	116.88	SRI 1996
35	pit house	118.50	85.50	CES 1991	75	pit	119.26	118.42	SRI 1996
36	pit	84.00	80.00	CES 1991	76	pit	117.27	121.23	SRI 1996
37	pit	73.00	82.00	CES 1991	77	pit	117.66	121.54	SRI 1996
38	pit	73.00	79.50	CES 1991	78	pit	118.08	120.91	SRI 1996
39	human inhumation	112.25	125.75	SRI 1996	79	pit	117.76	111.45	SRI 1996
40	human inhumation	113.02	128.39	SRI 1996	80	pit	114.82	112.47	SRI 1996
					81	pit	103.99	92.76	SRI 1996
					82	pit	114.80	112.47	SRI 1996
					83	pit	105.40	94.60	SRI 1996
					84	pit	103.79	95.18	SRI 1996
					85	pit	105.28	97.00	SRI 1996

continued on next page

Feature Number	Feature Type	Northing	Easting	Discovery Phase	Feature Number	Feature Type	Northing	Easting	Discovery Phase
86	pit	104.60	97.61	SRI 1996	133	pit	115.90	129.05	SRI 1996
87	pit	104.30	97.48	SRI 1996	134	pit	113.06	127.51	SRI 1996
88	pit	104.57	98.20	SRI 1996	135	pit	114.06	127.13	SRI 1996
89	pit	104.84	98.76	SRI 1996	136	pit house	114.71	125.38	SRI 1996
90	pit	104.86	99.43	SRI 1996	137	pit house	117.50	124.13	SRI 1996
91	pit	104.31	99.45	SRI 1996	138	pit	113.11	126.08	SRI 1996
92	pit	103.50	98.89	SRI 1996	139	pit house	114.00	121.50	SRI 1996
93	pit	104.58	99.95	SRI 1996	140	pit	111.80	122.00	SRI 1996
94	pit house	104.55	99.48	SRI 1996	141	pit	111.25	121.99	SRI 1996
95	pit	101.28	98.01	SRI 1996	142	burial?	111.21	124.74	SRI 1996
96	pit	101.41	99.71	SRI 1996	143	pit	111.09	123.30	SRI 1996
97	pit	101.37	100.22	SRI 1996	144	pit & macaw inhumation	112.39	123.18	SRI 1996
98	pit	100.36	99.53	SRI 1996	145	burial?	113.10	124.61	SRI 1996
99	pit	100.48	100.19	SRI 1996	146	burial?	113.46	123.04	SRI 1996
100	pit	98.98	100.15	SRI 1996	147	human inhumation	115.06	123.03	SRI 1996
101	pit house	97.86	98.24	SRI 1996	148	burial?	113.52	124.53	SRI 1996
102	pit	97.29	100.24	SRI 1996	149	pit	116.59	124.33	SRI 1996
103	pit	97.09	99.09	SRI 1996	150	pit house	117.00	119.00	SRI 1996
104	pit	96.77	99.60	SRI 1996	151	human inhumation	102.26	95.41	SRI 1996
105	pit	123.05	110.35	SRI 1996	152	pit	103.36	94.75	SRI 1996
106	pit	95.88	99.22	SRI 1996	153	pit	109.02	122.07	SRI 1996
107	pit	96.06	98.70	SRI 1996	154	pit	109.13	121.23	SRI 1996
108	pit	96.22	98.16	SRI 1996	155	pit	107.93	121.70	SRI 1996
109	pit	96.87	98.14	SRI 1996	156	human inhumation	102.00	95.31	SRI 1996
110	pit	96.02	97.23	SRI 1996	157	pit	107.57	121.39	SRI 1996
111	pit	117.20	124.00	SRI 1996	158	pit	107.30	120.91	SRI 1996
112	pit	122.80	109.60	SRI 1996	159	pit	106.63	121.23	SRI 1996
113	pit	115.80	113.34	SRI 1996	160	pit	105.38	121.57	SRI 1996
114	pit	118.75	113.32	SRI 1996	161	pit	105.31	119.91	SRI 1996
115	pit	117.36	122.92	SRI 1996	162	pit	105.96	119.86	SRI 1996
116	pit	122.58	114.15	SRI 1996	163	pit	106.32	119.11	SRI 1996
117	pit	124.20	114.41	SRI 1996	164	pit	107.12	119.36	SRI 1996
118	pit	124.48	112.29	SRI 1996	165	pit	107.91	118.96	SRI 1996
119	pit	123.69	110.78	SRI 1996	166	pit	107.79	118.35	SRI 1996
120	pit	124.27	110.65	SRI 1996	167	pit	108.52	118.11	SRI 1996
121	pit	124.45	109.30	SRI 1996	168	pit	108.07	116.91	SRI 1996
122	void	—	—	—	169	pit	106.02	118.09	SRI 1996
123	void	—	—	—	170	pit	104.66	117.10	SRI 1996
124	void	—	—	—	171	pit	103.85	118.43	SRI 1996
125	pit	121.10	113.23	SRI 1996	172	pit	103.36	117.36	SRI 1996
126	pit	115.45	123.23	SRI 1996	173	pit	104.73	117.85	SRI 1996
127	pit	116.03	123.91	SRI 1996	174	pit	104.70	118.43	SRI 1996
128	pit	115.87	126.83	SRI 1996	175	pit	104.59	119.07	SRI 1996
129	pit	117.33	128.66	SRI 1996	176	pit	102.80	119.92	SRI 1996
130	pit	116.68	127.90	SRI 1996					
131	pit	116.45	128.84	SRI 1996					
132	human inhumation	114.68	128.91	SRI 1996					

Feature Number	Feature Type	Northing	Easting	Discovery Phase
177	pit	105.97	118.85	SRI 1996
178	pit	113.25	119.00	SRI 1996
179	pit	115.20	117.20	SRI 1996
180	pit	103.05	95.74	SRI 1996
181	pit	102.43	94.46	SRI 1996
182	pit	101.01	95.19	SRI 1996
183	pit	105.10	125.50	SRI 1996
184	pit	106.60	126.00	SRI 1996
185	pit	105.40	127.30	SRI 1996
186	dog inhumation	106.20	127.60	SRI 1996
187	pit	104.66	123.60	SRI 1996
188	pit	111.20	126.36	SRI 1996
189	pit	119.60	116.35	SRI 1996
190	pit	119.56	114.60	SRI 1996
191	pit	140.50	114.08	SRI 1996
192	pit	140.50	115.00	SRI 1996
193	pit	140.62	116.79	SRI 1996
194	pit	140.57	118.34	SRI 1996
195	pit	140.46	129.24	SRI 1996
196	pit	139.84	128.82	SRI 1996
197	pit	140.00	126.60	SRI 1996
198	pit house	140.05	125.11	SRI 1996
199	pit	140.00	118.22	SRI 1996
200	pit	140.00	116.44	SRI 1996
201	pit	140.46	129.86	SRI 1996
202	pit	101.81	95.39	SRI 1996
203	pit	114.00	121.90	SRI 1996
204	pit	112.90	120.60	SRI 1996
205	pit	112.60	120.10	SRI 1996
206	pit	113.52	118.06	SRI 1996
207	pit	113.40	117.40	SRI 1996
208	pit	118.60	117.85	SRI 1996
209	pit	114.65	120.64	SRI 1996
210	pit	117.00	118.00	SRI 1996
211	pit house	117.00	115.50	SRI 1996
212	pit house	116.00	118.00	SRI 1996
213	human inhumation	101.25	106.44	SRI 1996
214	human inhumation	117.00	126.00	SRI 1996
215	pit house	115.50	117.00	SRI 1996
216	pit	115.20	115.60	SRI 1996
217	pit	107.70	127.25	SRI 1996
218	pit	108.00	126.60	SRI 1996
219	pit/posthole	108.88	127.40	SRI 1996

prehistoric settlement of El Macayo and beyond. The thickness and depth of these units are unknown because they extend beyond the depths of our backhoe trenches and excavations.

Excavation Units

Excavation units took the form of test pits (TPs), trenches, stripping units (SUs), structures, burials, pits, and indeterminate features. Each is described below.

Trenches

Two backhoe trenches were excavated by SRI to help define the northern and western boundaries of the settlement. Trench 342 was excavated near the western boundary of the site to explore the contact of the culture-bearing fill (Unit II) with the cobbly terrace deposits (Unit IV). The trench was excavated at an angle roughly perpendicular to the soil contact. The trench was 10.7 m long and was excavated to a depth of 0.2 m. This exploration revealed a thin mantle of culture-bearing sediments overlying a cobbly substratum. No features were discovered in this trench.

Trench 343 was placed 10 m north of and parallel to ASM Trench 4 (see Figure 7). It began at the fence separating the county parcel and the trailer park, and extended 20 m to the west where further excavations were restricted by a cluster of trees. The trench was excavated to a maximum depth of 60 cm. It revealed a 20–40-cm-thick layer of culture-bearing deposits (Unit II) overlying the weakly developed calcic horizon (Unit III). This deposit tapered to the west. Eleven archaeological features were identified in the trench walls, including nine probable pits and two possible structures.

Test Pits

Test pits were excavated manually. Three types of test pits were used to explore subsurface deposits. The first type included units excavated to obtain a vertically controlled sample of Unit I and II deposits above and within the pit houses selected for excavation prior to mechanical removal of overlying deposits. These test pits were square in plan, either 1 m or 2 m on a side, and were excavated in arbitrary levels. The first level was approximately 10 cm deep and corresponded to the thickness of Unit I. Subsequent levels were 20 cm in depth.

Table 4. Summary of Artifacts Recovered from El Macayo

Provenience	Ceramics		Lithics		Faunal			Total
	Sherds	Vessels	Flaked Stone	Ground Stone	Unworked	Worked	Shell	
General site								
Surface	1	—	—	1	—	—	—	2
Trench								
TR 343	40	—	—	—	—	—	—	40
Stripping units								
SU 56	167	—	6	2	1	—	—	176
SU 57	187	—	20	5	4	—	1	217
SU 80	43	—	—	3	2	—	—	48
SU 118	16	—	—	3	1	—	—	20
SU 122	82	—	1	5	2	—	1	91
Test pits								
TP 58	187	—	31	1	5	—	—	224
TP 60	438	—	104	—	1	1	1	545
TP 71	1,010	—	244	6	14	2	5	1,281
TP 103	398	—	83	2	5	—	3	491
TP 108	144	—	38	1	—	—	—	183
TP 291	324	—	69	—	7	—	—	400
Pit houses								
Feature 5								
Fill/roof fall	604	—	162	1	24	—	2	793
Posthole fill	139	—	145	—	8	—	1	293
Subfloor pit fill	72	—	7	—	1	—	—	80
Feature 15								
Floor	21	—	3	—	—	—	—	24
Posthole fill	16	—	7	—	—	—	—	23
Subfloor fill	104	—	19	—	2	—	1	126
Feature 16								
Fill	246	—	38	2	5	—	—	291
Floor	—	1	—	—	—	—	—	1
Posthole fill	15	—	5	—	2	—	—	22
Feature 42								
Fill	5	—	—	—	—	—	—	5
Floor groove	20	—	2	—	—	—	—	22
Feature 43								
Fill	4	—	—	—	—	—	—	4
Feature 44								
Roof fall	559	—	110	4	26	—	2	701
Floor	12	1	5	52	—	—	—	70
Hearth fill	3	—	—	—	—	—	—	3
Ash pit fill	1	—	3	—	—	—	—	4
Feature 139								
Fill	201	—	3	—	9	1	—	214
Floor	—	—	—	1	—	—	—	1
Feature 150								
Fill	71	—	37	—	—	—	—	108

Provenience	Ceramics		Lithics		Faunal			Total
	Sherds	Vessels	Flaked Stone	Ground Stone	Unworked	Worked	Shell	
Feature 212								
Posthole fill	260	—	130	2	15	—	—	407
Pits								
Feature 45	1	—	—	—	—	—	—	1
Feature 50	71	—	15	—	1	—	—	87
Feature 51	181	—	43	1	1	—	1	227
Feature 53	51	—	22	—	17	—	—	90
Feature 55	11	—	5	—	1	—	—	17
Feature 69	24	—	—	—	—	—	—	24
Feature 73	4	—	3	—	—	—	—	7
Feature 74	2	—	1	—	—	—	—	3
Feature 78	14	—	4	—	—	—	—	18
Feature 80	4	—	5	—	—	—	—	9
Feature 105	9	—	8	—	2	—	—	19
Feature 112	208	—	54	1	9	—	1	273
Feature 144	193	1	48	2	1	1		246
Feature 178	60	—	9	1	—	—	2	72
Feature 179	51	—	22	—	2	—	1	76
Feature 203	15	—	—	—	1	—	—	16
Feature 208	18	—	10	1	1	—	—	30
Feature 210	54	—	25	—	6	—	—	85
Feature 216	19	—	6	—	—	—	—	25
Human burials								
Feature 31								
Trench backdirt	112	—	24	2	—	—	—	138
Feature 39								
Burial fill	35	—	—	—	—	—	—	35
Feature 40								
Burial fill	14	—	4	—	12	—	—	30
Feature 147								
Burial fill	3	—	—	—	—	—	—	3
Feature 151								
Burial fill	14	—	7	—	3	—	2	26
Disturbance	11	—	3	—	23	—	—	37
Funerary offering	—	3	—	508	—	—	529	1,040
Feature 156								
Burial fill	1	—	—	—	—	—	—	1
Funerary offering	—	—	—	1	—	—	2	3
Feature 213								
Burial fill	47	—	24	—	3	—	—	74
Feature 214								
Funerary offering	—	1	—	—	—	—	—	1
Nonhuman burials								
Feature 144.01	—	—	—	—	274	—	—	274
Feature 186	—	—	1	—	192	—	—	193
Total	6,617	7	1,615	608	683	5	555	10,090

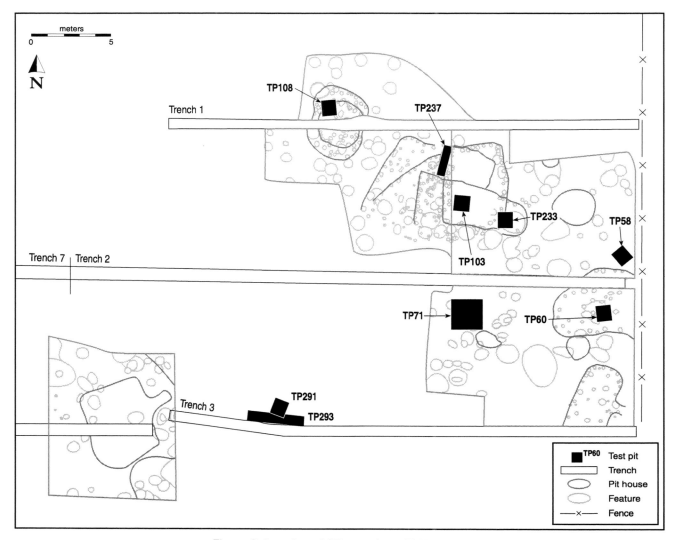

Figure 8. Location of SRI test pits at El Macayo.

The second type of test pit was an irregularly shaped unit placed in a pit house. These were excavated to obtain a screened sample of the remaining fill and may represent one-quarter, one-half, or some other fraction of the structure. The sizes and shapes of these pits were largely determined by the outline of the structure. Because the deposits removed from these test pits were clearly part of the pit house fill, the artifacts recovered from these test pits are summarized below in the discussion of the excavated pit houses.

The third type of test pit was a rectangular unit (TP 293) used to carefully remove the overburden above an inhumation (Feature 213). Because the overburden was composed of former sheet trash unrelated to the burial below, and because a controlled sample of this overburden had already been collected (see TP 291), the removed sediments were not screened.

Only the first type of test pit is discussed in this section. The locations of these exploratory excavation units are shown in Figure 8. A summary of the artifacts recovered from these units can be found in Table 4; a summary of the painted ceramic types by level is presented in Table 5. The other two types of test pits are described in the feature descriptions.

Test Pit 58

This test pit was a 1-by-1-m unit placed on the north side of ASM Trench 2 above pit house Feature 15. Three levels were excavated to a total depth of approximately 53 cm. The uppermost level was a dark brown, silty colluvium containing fine gravels with grass and wood debris. Level 2 contained modern glass, wire, and other metal fragments. A cluster of pebbles, designated Feature 41, was

Table 5. Summary of Identified Painted Pottery Types from Test Pits at El Macayo

Pottery Type	Test Pit 58			Test Pit 60				Test Pit 71				Test Pit 103				Test Pit 108		Test Pit 291		Total
	L1	L2	L3	L1	L2	L3	L4	L1	L2	L3	L4	L1	L2	L3	L4	L2	L3	L1	L2	
Trincheras Purple-on-red	1	4	2	2	6	3	2	11	5	6	9	4	6	6	—	1	6	13	2	89
Trincheras Polychrome	—	—	—	1	—	—	—	1	1	1	—	—	—	—	—	—	1	1	—	6
Nogales Polychrome	—	2	—	—	—	—	—	2	2	2	—	—	1	—	—	—	—	—	—	9
Cañada del Oro Red-on-brown	—	1	—	—	—	—	—	—	—	1	4	—	—	—	—	—	2	—	—	8
Cañada del Oro or Rillito Red-on-brown	—	—	—	—	—	1	—	1	1	—	1	—	2	2	—	—	—	1	1	10
Rillito Red-on-brown	—	—	—	—	—	—	—	1	—	—	—	—	—	—	—	—	—	—	—	1
Rillito or Rincon Red-on-brown	—	—	—	—	—	—	—	—	—	2	—	—	—	—	—	—	—	—	—	2
Rincon Red-on-brown	—	—	—	—	—	3	—	2	5	4	1	—	3	3	1	—	1	1	1	25
Rincon or Tanque Verde Red-on-brown	—	—	—	—	—	1	—	—	2	2	1	—	—	1	—	1	—	—	—	8
Tanque Verde Red-on-brown	—	—	—	—	1	—	—	2	3	—	—	—	—	1	—	—	—	—	—	7
Gila Butte Red-on-buff	—	—	—	—	—	—	—	—	1	—	—	—	—	—	—	—	—	—	—	1
Gila Butte or Santa Cruz Red-on-buff	—	—	1	—	1	—	—	1	1	1	—	—	—	—	—	—	—	—	—	5
Santa Cruz Red-on-buff	—	—	—	—	1	—	—	—	—	—	—	—	—	—	1	—	—	1	—	3
Sacaton Red-on-buff	—	—	—	—	—	—	—	1	—	1	—	—	—	—	—	—	1	—	—	3
Local red-on-brown	—	3	—	3	—	—	—	8	3	—	—	—	1	—	—	—	—	—	—	18
Local black-on-white	—	—	—	—	—	1	—	—	—	—	—	—	—	—	—	—	—	—	—	1
Local black-on-red	—	—	—	—	—	—	—	—	—	—	1	—	—	—	—	—	—	—	—	1
Local black-on-brown	—	—	—	—	—	—	—	—	1	—	—	—	—	—	—	—	—	—	—	1
Total	1	10	3	6	9	9	2	30	25	20	17	4	13	13	2	2	11	17	4	198

Key: L = level

Figure 9. Feature 41, a rock cluster, in Test Pit 58.

exposed at the base of Level 2 (Figure 9). No ash or char-coal flecking was observed in association with these rocks. The fill among the rocks was indistinguishable from the Unit II sediments, which encapsulated the feature. The rocks were angular to subangular but did not show any other evidence of direct exposure to fire. It is likely, how-ever, that the angularity of the rocks was the result of thermal shock. Level 3 exposed the outer margin of a pit house, later identified as Feature 15. The northern half of the test pit was outside the edge of the pit house, and Level 3 revealed the native noncultural subsoil (Unit III). The southern half of the test pit intersected the floor of Feature 15 at approximately 15 cm below the contact of Units II and III.

Test Pit 60

Because TP 58 was not entirely within the outline of pit house Feature 15, a second 1-by-1-m test pit, TP 60, was placed on the south side of ASM Trench 2 to obtain another sample of the deposits above the floor. Four levels reaching a maximum depth of 57 cm were excavated. The floor of the pit house was exposed at the base of Level 4.

Test Pit 71

During mechanical removal of Unit II deposits to the west of pit house Features 15 and 16, a remnant of a pit house, Feature 43, was exposed. The visible portion included the entryway and the hearth. Red ware and red-on-brown ce-ramics that were identified in the field as potentially early were observed in the sediments mechanically removed just above the floor. Because this area represented one of the deepest exposures of Unit II, and because early red ware was observed, a 2-by-2-m test pit, TP 71, was excavated in undisturbed deposits just northwest of the hearth in Fea-ture 43. Four levels were excavated for a total depth of 70 cm. Given the long sequence of midden accumulation and the temporal range represented in this test pit, all of the unpainted body sherds and flaked stone artifacts were se-lected for detailed analysis.

Test Pit 103

TP 103 was a 1-by-1-m excavation unit placed above the floor of pit house Feature 44. The burned roof fall and floor of Feature 44 were exposed during mechanical stripping.

This test pit was excavated in four 10-cm-thick levels to a maximum depth of 40 cm. Level 1 represented the uppermost disturbed sediments. Levels 2, 3, and 4 were arbitrary divisions within the Unit II deposits located above the pit house floor. Level 4 was enriched with dark gray ash, charcoal flecks, and fragments of charred wood representing the remains of the superstructure.

Test Pit 108

TP 108 was a 1-by-1-m excavation unit placed on the north side of ASM Trench 1 above the floor of pit house Feature 5. This test pit was excavated in four levels to a maximum depth of 52 cm. Level 1 consisted of the uppermost loose sediments of Unit I, and Levels 2 and 3 were excavated into the general cultural deposit of Unit II. The lower half of Level 3 was dark gray and contained abundant ash and charcoal. This lower level is interpreted as the fill and roof fall of pit house Feature 5.

Test Pits 291 and 293

TP 291 was a 1-by-1-m excavation unit placed on the north side of ASM Trench 3 above a human burial, Feature 213, which had been exposed in the sidewall of this trench. The purpose of this test pit was to obtain a controlled sample of the cultural deposits overlying this burial. For the sake of expediency, only two levels were excavated to a maximum depth of 54 cm. A rock cairn overlying the skeletal remains was exposed at the bottom of Level 2. TP 293 was a rectangular extension of TP 291 excavated to expose the outline of Feature 213.

Stripping Units

Stripping units were large excavation areas where the sediments above archaeological features were removed with a backhoe. The purpose of excavating the stripping units was to quickly remove the sediments that overlay and obscured the outlines of the pit houses while monitoring backhoe operations and collecting artifacts from the backdirt. Five stripping units were excavated (Figure 10). Each stripping unit began as a standard 10-by-10-m unit, but each was expanded as needed to define the outlines of possible pit structures encountered. Consequently, the sizes and shapes of the stripping units became nonstandardized and irregular.

SU 56 was used to define the outline of pit structure Feature 15 north of ASM Trench 2. The stripping area was located between ASM Trenches 1 and 2 and stretched from the fence separating the Santa Cruz County property from Bird Hill Trailer Park about 12 m to the west. Whereas Feature 15 was found to extend only a few centimeters north of Trench 2, human burials and numerous other pit

features were encountered north and west of Feature 15. SU 56 was excavated 8 m north of ASM Trench 2 to define a possible cemetery area. At the western edge of the stripping unit, we located the eastern edge of several superimposed structures (Feature 212).

SU 57 was used to expose the outline of Feature 16. SU 57 is bounded on the south by ASM Trench 3, on the north by ASM Trench 2, on the east by the property boundary, and on the west by an arbitrary line located approximately 12 m west of the property boundary. The original 10-by-10-m stripping unit was expanded to include a 2-by-7-m area along the northwest edge to define the outline of a possible structure (Feature 43) encountered along its western margin.

SU 80 was excavated to define and expose the western limits of a complex of superimposed structures encountered along the western limit of SU 56 (Feature 212) and to define the southern boundary of Feature 5. SU 80 shared its eastern margin with SU 56.

SU 118 was located north of ASM Trench 1. Initially, SU 118 was used to expose the northern limits of pit structure Feature 5 and was excavated 4.5 m north of ASM Trench 1. The stripping unit was expanded to the east beyond Feature 5 to aid in the identification of the northern limit of Feature 212.

SU 120 was placed over pit structure Feature 21. In the process of removing the overlying sediments to define the outline of Feature 21, a large number of features was discovered. Given the time and funds expended on exhuming human burials, pit house Feature 21 was not excavated.

Structures

Prior to our 1996 excavations, archaeological excavations had located in backhoe trenches 10 features that were identified as probable pit houses. We targeted four of these, Features 5, 15, 16, and 21, in our excavations. During removal of the overburden above and adjacent to these pit house features, 14 additional structures were identified and numbered. The distribution of these structures is shown in Figure 11. Eleven structures were excavated either wholly or in part during the 1996 fieldwork at El Macayo. Summary information on these 11 structures is presented in Table 6. Construction and use dates were assigned to these structures based primarily on their associations with painted ceramic types (Table 7).

General Discussion

Even though the houses at El Macayo were poorly preserved, the architectural details gleaned from these excavations reveal that the houses were constructed in a style characteristic of the pre-Classic Formative period in the

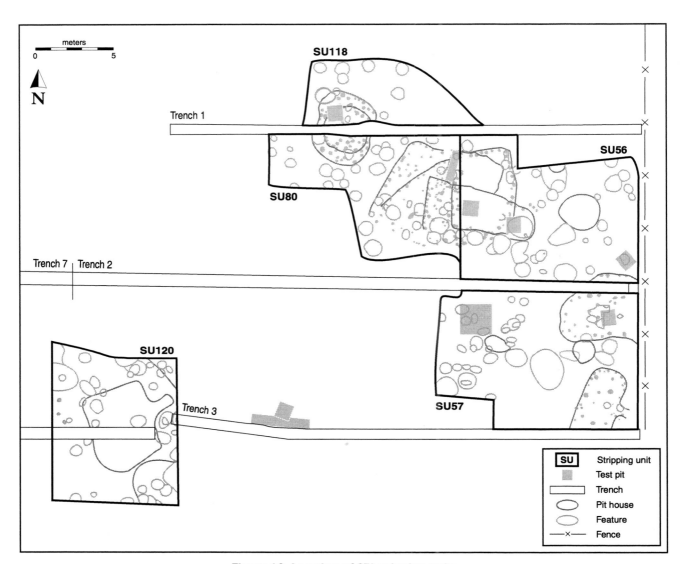

Figure 10. Location of SRI stripping units.

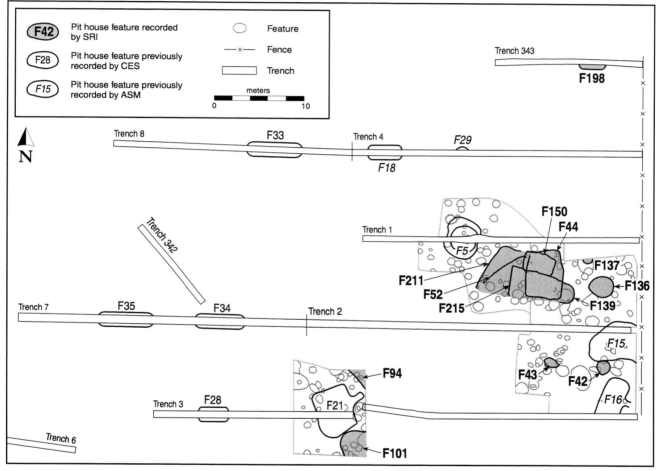

Figure 11. Location of identified pit houses at El Macayo. Structures identified in ASM and CES backhoe trenches are shown in addition to those discovered and excavated during SRI excavations.

Table 6. Summary of Structures Excavated at El Macayo

Feature Number	Age	Orientation	Dimensions (m) (l × w)	Estimated Floor Area (m²)	Shape	Floor Features	Abandonment Mode	Comments
5a	pre-Classic	ESE	4.7 × 3.5	13	oval	hearth (?), pits, postholes	burned (?)	remodeled
5b	pre-Classic	ESE	3.2 × 3.1	8	oval to circular	hearth (?), wall trench, postholes	unburned (?)	remodeled
15	pre-Classic	SE	5.95 × 3.6	17	oval	hearth, postholes	unburned	remodeled
16	pre-Classic	ESE	4.9 × 2.5	10	subrectangular	hearth, pit, postholes	unburned	trough-shaped vessel and sherd disc on floor
42	pre-Classic	?	1.6 × 1.4	2	oval	wall trench	unburned	granary (?)
43	pre-Classic	E	?	?	?	hearth	unburned	house remnant
44	pre-Classic	E	5 × 3.5	14	subrectangular	hearth, ash pit, postholes	burned	floor assemblage
52	pre-Classic	SE (?)	?	?	?	hearth, postholes	unburned	house remnant
139	pre-Classic	?	? × 2.35	?	oval	postholes	unburned	underlies Feature 44, over pit Feature 203
150	pre-Classic	?	? × 3.4	?	subrectangular	postholes	unburned	under Feature 44, cut by Feature 215
211	pre-Classic	SE (?)	?	?	subrectangular	postholes	unburned, cut by Feature 52	
215	pre-Classic	?	? × 3.4	?	subrectangular	postholes, pits	unburned	intrudes Feature 150, underlies Feature 44

Table 7. Summary of Identified Painted Pottery Types from Pit Houses at El Macayo

Pottery Type	Feature 5			Feature 15			Feature 16		F 43	Feature 44		F 139	F 150	F 212	Total
	FIII/RFL	PH FIII	Subfloor Pit FIII	Floor	PH FIII	Subfloor FIII	FIII	PH FIII	FIII	FIII/RFL	Floor	FIII	FIII	PH FIII	
Trincheras Purple-on-red	28	4	3	—	—	4	6	2	—	15	—	10	5	13	90
Trincheras Polychrome	—	—	—	—	—	—	—	—	—	—	—	—	—	1	1
Nogales Polychrome	2	—	—	—	—	—	1	—	—	1	—	2	—	—	6
Cañada del Oro Red-on-brown	—	1	—	—	—	1	—	—	—	—	—	—	—	—	2
Cañada del Oro or Rillito Red-on-brown	2	1	1	—	—	—	2	—	—	—	—	—	1	1	8
Rillito Red-on-brown	1	—	—	—	—	—	—	—	—	—	—	—	—	—	1
Rillito or Rincon Red-on-brown	—	—	—	—	—	—	1	—	—	—	—	—	—	—	1
Rincon Red-on-brown	2	1	—	—	1	—	1	—	—	4	—	3	—	—	12
Rincon Black-on-brown	—	—	—	2	—	1	—	—	—	—	—	—	—	—	3
Rincon or Tanque Verde Red-on-brown	—	1	—	—	—	—	—	—	—	—	—	1	—	—	2
Tanque Verde Red-on-brown	—	—	—	—	—	—	—	—	—	—	1	—	—	—	1
Local red-on-brown	—	—	—	1	—	—	—	—	—	—	—	1	—	—	2
Local black-on-red	—	—	—	—	—	—	—	—	1	—	—	—	—	—	1
Estrella Red-on-gray (incised)	—	—	—	—	—	—	1	—	—	—	—	—	—	—	1
Gila Butte or Santa Cruz Red-on-buff	—	—	—	—	—	1	—	—	—	1	—	—	—	—	2
Sacaton Red-on-buff	—	—	—	—	—	—	—	—	—	—	—	1	—	1	2
Dos Cabezas Red-on-brown	—	—	—	—	—	—	—	—	—	1	—	—	—	—	1
Encinas Red-on-brown	—	—	—	—	—	—	—	—	—	1	—	—	—	—	1
Total	35	8	4	3	1	7	12	2	1	23	1	18	6	16	137

Key: F = feature; PH = posthole; RFL = roof fall

Sonoran Desert. This architectural style is generally characterized as a brush-and-earth structure constructed within a shallow pit, and having a vestibule entryway. Floor plans are most often subrectangular to elliptical, with the hearth located just inside the entryway. Examples from various sites in southern Arizona, including those in the Nogales area, are shown in Figure 12, and an artist's reconstruction is shown in Figure 13. Some details, such as the depth of the house pit, roof support pattern, and extent to which the house pit was integrated as part of the structural walls, vary considerably from house to house. This style has been referred to generally as a Hohokam house-in-a-pit (Haury 1976), but variations in architectural details and the distribution of similar structures across a large portion of southern and southeastern Arizona suggest that this style may encompass more than a single type of house and that it may be inappropriate to attribute this style to a single archaeological culture. The architectural characteristics of the El Macayo houses are pieced together below to provide a generalized discussion of the architectural style.

Construction began with the excavation of a house pit. The depth of this pit varied, ranging from a few centimeters to as much as perhaps half a meter below the prehistoric surface. The depth of the pit was likely determined by a number of variables, which may have included the time of year that the house would be occupied, the depth necessary to reach a substratum suitable for use as a floor, the hardness of the soil, and the intended use and permanence of the structure. Second, a series of upright posts were positioned along the inside margin of the house pit as the principal structural elements for the walls. These posts were usually anchored in individual postholes, but often they were set in a continuous trench or within postholes within a trench. Third, a layer of brush thatch was attached to the upright posts. Next, a roof was constructed. The roof of the structure was probably constructed of materials similar to those of the walls. The weight of the roof was borne, in part, on the exterior wall supports and two upright posts located within the house floor along the longitudinal midline. Finally, the pole framework and brush shell were covered with a layer of mud or adobe.

The central interior feature in most pit structures was the hearth, which was located along the entryway axis and slightly offset from the center toward the doorway. Not all structures had hearths, however. By definition, the presence of a hearth is considered an indication that a structure was intended for residence. The absence of a hearth is conventionally interpreted as indicating that the structure was more likely used for storage and other nonresidential activities. Hearths could be informal or formal. Informal hearths typically appear as slight indentations in the floor or as oxidized sediments within the native subsoil. Formal hearths take the form of a shallow to deep basin lined with a thick adobe plaster. The floor area around hearths prepared in this manner was frequently plastered, as well. The rims of the hearth often were elevated slightly above the floor, with the bowl extending slightly below floor level. In addition, pit structures could include other interior features, such as subfloor storage pits. The hardness of the subsoil may very well have influenced the depth of the house pit, as well as the manner in which the floor was prepared. In locations where there was a hard substratum, such as a caliche layer, a durable floor surface could be achieved by leveling and smoothing the surface created during the house pit excavation. In contrast, in locations where the substratum was softer, the floor surface may have been created by adding a layer of more durable materials over the natural substratum.

A particularly interesting floor treatment that has been documented in the southern Southwest is the construction of raised floors and elevated platforms (Deaver 1998; Di Peso 1956; Haury 1932; Seymour 1990). These built surfaces were constructed of poles and brush and were elevated on stone or wood piers set into the ground. It is likely that these low platforms were covered with woven mats or blankets to create a comfortable walking or sleeping surface. Some of these wooden constructions covered the entire floor area, except for the plastered area around the hearth, and were certainly elevated floors. Others covered only a portion of the floor area and may have been partial floors or sleeping platforms.

Feature 5

Feature 5 (Figure 14) was the remains of a pit structure identified by Gardiner and Huckell (1987:Table 1) in ASM Trench 1. They suggested that this structure may have burned. Given the opportunity to recover a well-preserved artifactual and botanical collection indicative of the activities in the house at the time the house was destroyed by fire, we included this structure in our data recovery plan. The excavation of interior features revealed two episodes of remodeling, designated Features 5a and 5b (Figure 15). No strong evidence exists for which remodeling event occurred first, although there is weak evidence that Feature 5a may be the later construction. Two pits (Features 5.03 and 5.06), associated with Feature 5a, intrude into the encircling groove that defines Feature 5b (see Figure 15). This stratigraphic relationship, if we assume that Features 5.03 and 5.06 were actually part of Feature 5a, indicates that Feature 5b predates Feature 5a. Feature 5a is an enlarged structure, as indicated by a circular arrangement of postholes just inside the house pit outline. Evidence of an earlier period of construction, Feature 5b consists of a 10–16-cm-deep trench with postholes.

Excavation Methods

This structure was sectioned by ASM Trench 1. A 1-by-1-m test pit (TP 108) was excavated on the north side of Trench 1

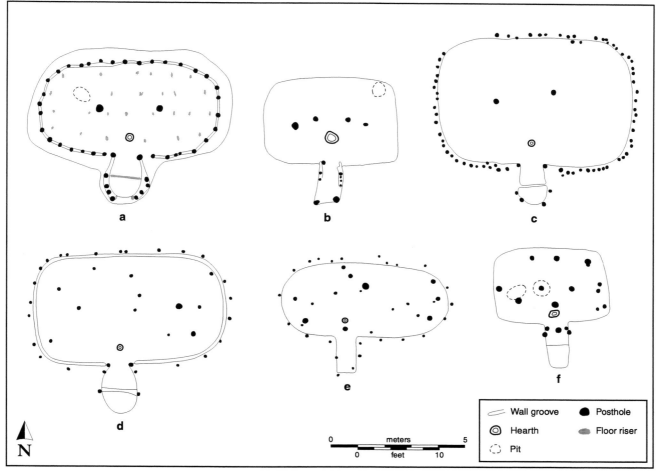

Figure 12. Examples of the pre-Classic period shallow brush-and-earth structure from selected sites across southern Arizona, which are roughly coeval with the occupation at El Macayo:
(a) Feature 8 (Sacaton phase) from Scorpion Point Village (Deaver 1998:Figure 80.8a);
(b) Feature 100 (Rincon phase) from Badger Hole Ranch Ruin (excavated by SRI);
(c) House 6:10 G (Sacaton phase) from Snaketown (Gladwin et al. 1937:Figure 24);
(d) House 3:8 I (Sacaton phase) from Snaketown (Gladwin et al. 1937:Figure 22);
(e) House 2:8 I (Santa Cruz phase) from Snaketown (Gladwin et al. 1937:Figure 28);
(f) House 15 (Cerros phase) from San Simon Village (Sayles 1945:Figure 20).

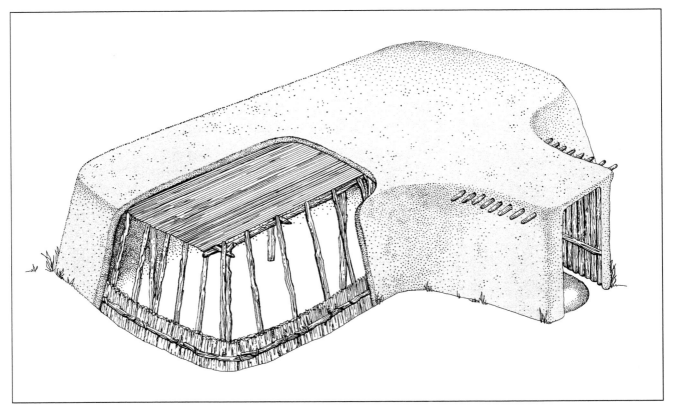

Figure 13. Artist's reconstruction of the brush-and-earth structure.

near the estimated center of the structure (see Figure 14). This test pit provided a controlled sample of the deposits overlying the pit house floor. After excavation of the test pit was completed, the remaining overburden deposits were mechanically removed with a backhoe to define the structure's outline. After stripping, it was apparent that the ASM trench had bisected the house. The remnants of two hearths were observed in the trench walls (see Figure 14). Each half of the house was excavated separately. The remaining fill of the pit house in each half was removed in one level to the floor of the structure. The maximum thickness of the remaining fill was approximately 15 cm in the northwest corner of the house.

Samples of the sediment from each half were collected for macrobotanical analysis of the flotation remains. Once the floor was exposed, numerous interior features were evident. The presence of these features suggested at least two construction episodes. Because of the number of interior features and considerable disturbance to the floor by rodents, no sediment samples were collected for pollen extraction. All interior features were investigated. Features that were interpreted as postholes were excavated only deep enough to confirm that they were postholes and not rodent burrows. Larger interior features, which appeared to be storage pits, were excavated in their entirety. Artifacts recovered from postholes and wall trenches were collected

as a single recovery space. Artifacts recovered from excavations of each of the larger floor pits were segregated by pit.

Fill

The sediments overlying the structure were typical Unit I and II deposits, as described for exploratory TP 108. The lower 10–15 cm of fill immediately above the floor was enriched organically with dark gray ash and numerous charcoal flecks. This organically enriched sediment was designated Stratum IIa. The ashy character of the deposit, the charcoal flecks, and the evidence of light oxidation of the floor were consistent with the inference that the house had burned. The dark gray ashy fill most likely represented the remains of the burned superstructure. No large pieces of charcoal that could be identified as architectural timbers were present, however.

The house pit was excavated prehistorically into the unprepared soft calcic horizon (Unit III). The rather soft and friable floor surface was designated Stratum IIb. In several places, patches of oxidized sediment, attributable to the destruction of the house by fire, were noted. No floor artifacts were observed. The fill of interior features was most similar to the Unit II sediments above the pit house fill, which lacked the organic enrichment, and was designated collectively Stratum IIc.

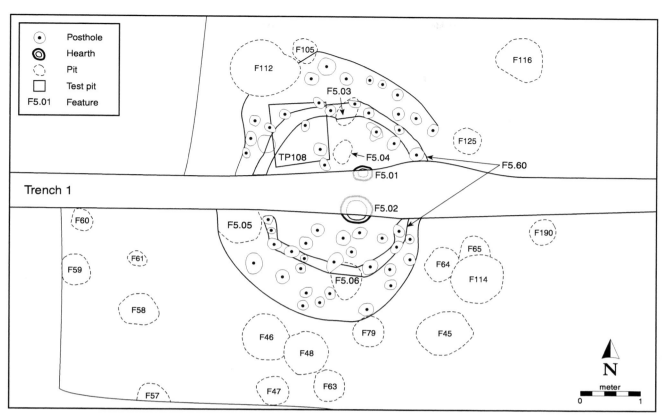

Figure 14. Plan view of Feature 5.

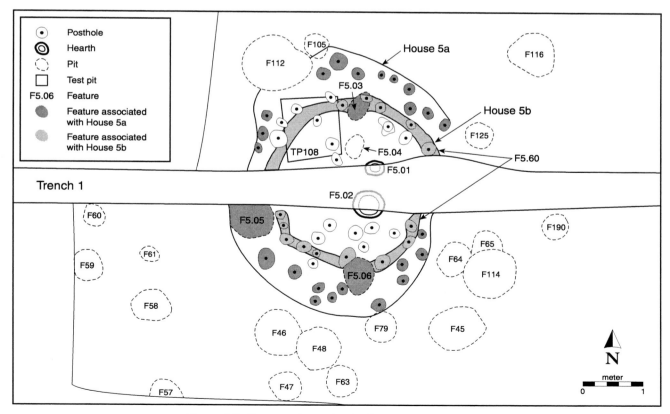

Figure 15. Construction episodes (a and b) of Feature 5.

Interior Features

The intramural features discovered included two hearths (Features 5.01 and 5.02), a 10–15-cm-wide trench (Feature 5.60), four medium to large pits (20–40 cm in maximum horizontal dimension), and 51 small pits (less than 20 cm in maximum horizontal dimension) that are interpreted as postholes.

One of the medium to large floor pits, Feature 5.05, is outside the wall of Feature 5b and is clearly associated with Feature 5a. Pits 5.03 and 5.06 intrude into the wall trench (Feature 5.60) that defines Feature 5b. These two pits may be postabandonment intrusions into the house, or, if associated with Feature 5, they are probably part of construction episode 5a. These two pits provide weak evidence that Feature 5a may represent the final remodeling episode.

Construction

The house pit was excavated prehistorically into the natural slope of Unit III solely for the purpose of leveling the floor. As a consequence, the upslope side of the house (western edge) was excavated approximately 15 cm into the upper part of Unit III, and the downslope side (eastern edge) was flush with the upper surface of Unit III. The northern, southern, and western margins were identified easily. The eastern margin of the structure, however, was not obvious because of the shallow excavation of the house and the natural slope of the underlying Unit III soil unit.

Based on the posthole pattern, we infer that the walls of both structures were constructed of upright posts set around the perimeters of the two floor areas. The wall posts of the smaller structure (5b) appear to have been anchored within a narrow trench that encircled the floor area. Although unobserved, it is reasonable to assume that the remainder of the outer shell was constructed of smaller timbers and brush, covered with earth or adobe. No oxidized adobe was observed in the fill of the structure. The roof support pattern is obscured by the many interior features, but it is likely that some of the postholes inside the encircling wall posts helped to support the roof. The locations of the two hearths suggest that the entryway probably faced to the east. Unfortunately, the suspected location of the entryway was removed in 1987 by ASM Trench 1. The floor of the structure was the bottom of the house pit excavation into the calcic horizon (Unit III). It was soft, fragile, and uneven, with variations in elevation up to 12 cm. Some of this variation may be due to postabandonment rodent and root disturbances. The floor surface does, however, appear to have been purposely elevated around the hearths. The hearths were all but destroyed by ASM Trench 1; the remaining fragments suggest that these were shallow, adobe-lined basins.

Dating

Painted ceramics are the only available evidence from which we can deduce the age of Feature 5. Ceramics recovered from Feature 5, the lowest level of TP 108, and a stratigraphically later pit (Feature 112) span a long period from approximately A.D. 800 to 1150, but careful evaluation suggests that Feature 5 was probably abandoned during the interval between A.D. 800 and 1050.

Identified decorated pottery types from Feature 5 (see Table 7 and TP 108, Level 3, in Table 5) are dominated by Trincheras Purple-on-red. This type and its companion types, Nogales Polychrome and Trincheras Polychrome, are poorly dated pottery types that are usually found associated with contexts dating between A.D. 800 and 1050 (the Hohokam Colonial and early Sedentary periods) (see Deaver 1984:372). The Santa Cruz series (Tucson Basin) pottery types identified indicate a possible age range of A.D. 800–1150. Colonial period types (Cañada del Oro Red-on-brown and Rillito Red-on-brown) are most common, but Sedentary period types (Rincon Red-on-brown and Rincon or Tanque Verde Red-on-brown) also were found. The dominance of the Colonial period types supports the A.D. 800–1050 age range associated with the Trincheras series types, but suggests a slightly more restricted date of A.D. 800–950. Only 12 identified pottery sherds were recovered from the pit, Feature 112, that intrudes into the northwest corner of Feature 5. The types recovered from this pit include Trincheras Purple-on-red (n = 8), Trincheras Polychrome (n = 1), Nogales Polychrome (n = 1), and Rincon Red-on-brown (n = 2). The inventory of pottery types present may not be representative, given that so few sherds were recovered, but the absence of Colonial period types in the fill of this pit and their presence in Feature 5 suggest that Feature 5 was occupied during a time equivalent to the Hohokam Colonial period. Given the available ceramic evidence, the dating of Feature 5 can conservatively be placed at A.D. 800–1050, but a more tightly drawn estimate would place the occupation of this house between A.D. 800 and 950.

Feature 15

This pit structure (Figure 16) was identified at the far eastern end of ASM Trench 2 (Gardiner and Huckell 1987:Table 1). Feature 15 was selected for excavation because of its proximity to Feature 16 (see below). The 1996 excavations at El Macayo confirmed that this feature was in fact a structure, but it was not clearly defined on all sides. The back wall and sidewalls were well defined where the house pit had been dug into the upslope side of Unit III. The front wall, however, was indistinct. This house was built in a single construction and use episode, but it appears to have been constructed over a suite of other features. Because we did not fully define the complete series of superimposed features and because of subsequent rodent burrowing and root disturbances, we were unable to clearly define the front wall and entryway of the structure.

Excavation Methods

Two 1-by-1-m test pits (TPs 58 and 60) were excavated above this structure to sample the overlying cultural deposits. TP 58 exposed the exterior wall of Feature 15, but most of the test unit was outside the structure. TP 60 was excavated to augment the sample fill deposits recovered by TP 58. The remaining sediments overlying the structure were removed with a backhoe to the level where the house pit was visible at the contact of Units II and III. Because there was no evidence that the house had burned, the remaining fill was removed manually to expose the floor but was not screened. All visible interior features were excavated and screened. The artifacts from postholes were collected as a unit and not identified to individual postholes. A subfloor test pit was placed near the center of the house where the excavated postholes exposed cultural deposits below the floor. The test unit exposed at least three pit features and other cultural deposits that predate the construction of the house. Although documented, none of the earlier features was completely excavated.

Fill

The fill of the house and postholes was undifferentiated from the Unit II deposits that covered the house. The hearth was filled with a whitish gray, ashy deposit.

Interior Features

Twenty-nine features that were inferred to relate to the construction and use of this structure were identified. The features include the hearth (Feature 15.01) and 28 postholes. The hearth was a shallow basin in the floor of the structure. It was prepared only in the sense that it was built into the floor plaster covering the earlier features. No archaeomagnetic dating sample was collected, because the floor matrix was not sufficiently well fired to provide reliable dating results.

Construction

The house pit was excavated into the Unit III calcic horizon only deep enough to level the floor. The back wall and the back portions of the sidewalls were defined by the pit edge. The arrangement of postholes is not clear, but there is evidence that the outer walls were supported by upright posts set into postholes positioned around the perimeter of the floor. We infer that brush and earth were probably used to finish out the wall construction. Several postholes were found throughout the center of the floor area, but there is no pattern to their arrangement. Some of these may have been roof support posts, and others may have supported elevated floor platforms.

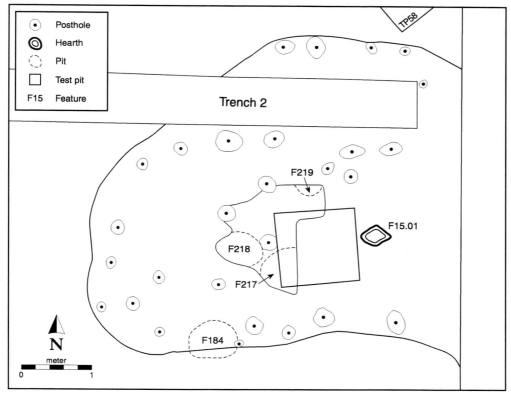

Figure 16. Plan view of Feature 15.

Dating

Pit house Feature 15 was constructed on top of deposits relating to earlier use episodes. Rodent activity resulted in the exposure of cultural deposits below the floor in the central part of the structure. Limited excavations near the center of the pit house revealed two rock-filled pits (Features 217 and 218), which were probably hearths, and another pit (Feature 219) beneath the floor. Few artifacts were recovered from Feature 15, and the hearth was not suitably well fired for archaeomagnetic dating. The identified painted sherds from TPs 58 and 60 and the various deposits related to Feature 15 indicate a broad range of A.D. 800–1150 for the occupation and abandonment of this house.

Feature 16

This pit structure was identified originally in ASM Trench 3 (Gardiner and Huckell 1987:Table 1). Based on Gardiner and Huckell's comments and illustrated cross section, this structure apparently was destroyed by fire. Consequently, this house was targeted for excavation because it had the potential to yield a well-preserved artifactual and botanical record reflecting the age during which it was occupied. Next to Feature 5, Feature 16 is one of the better-preserved structures excavated in 1996 (Figure 17). It has a subrectangular plan, with a vestibule entryway oriented to the southeast.

Excavation Methods

Because of the inexperience of the backhoe operator with archaeological excavations, the balk from which we planned to extract our sample of the overburden deposits was destroyed. In addition, the operator removed most of the upper part of this structure. Only about 2 cm of fill was left intact. This thin layer of fill was removed manually and screened. Visible interior features were excavated, and the fill was screened.

Fill

Gardiner and Huckell (1987:Table 1) described the fill of this structure as a gray-brown, ashy, silty sand with some clay and charcoal flecks. They also observed a chunk of roof fall in a floor pit that is most likely one of the two main roof supports. The small amount of fill that remained after backhoe excavations was typical of the Unit II cultural horizon at the site.

Interior Features

Interior features identified include a hearth (Feature 16.01), a pit (Feature 16.02), and 29 small pits interpreted as postholes. The hearth was offset slightly from the longitudinal axis of the structure but was in line with the entryway. The hearth was a shallow pit in the floor lined with a clayey sandy plaster. It had been extensively disturbed by rodents, and archaeomagnetic sampling was not possible. A pit (Fea-

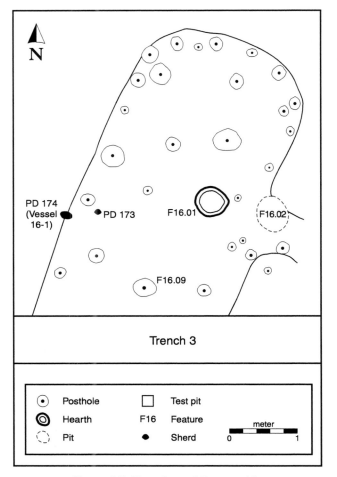

Figure 17. Plan view of Feature 16.

ture 16.02) was identified in the corner of the structure where the entryway and the house joined. Although it was assigned a feature number subordinate to the pit house, the location of the pit in the entryway is suggestive of post-abandonment disturbance. Fifteen postholes were arranged around the perimeter of the house floor. The main posts of the exterior walls probably were set into these postholes. The remaining 14 postholes were scattered across the floor. Two of these (Features 16.09 and 16.30) are likely the postholes in which the main roof supports were anchored. This conclusion derives first from the observed depth of these postholes relative to the other postholes and second from observations made elsewhere in the desert Southwest about the location of the main roof supports relative to the position of the hearth and entryway.

Construction

The house pit was excavated into Unit III. Unlike the other structures exposed in 1996, the house pit was excavated deep enough into Unit III that the pit outline was visible on all sides. The house pit was probably about 20 cm deep, according to measurements provided by Gardiner

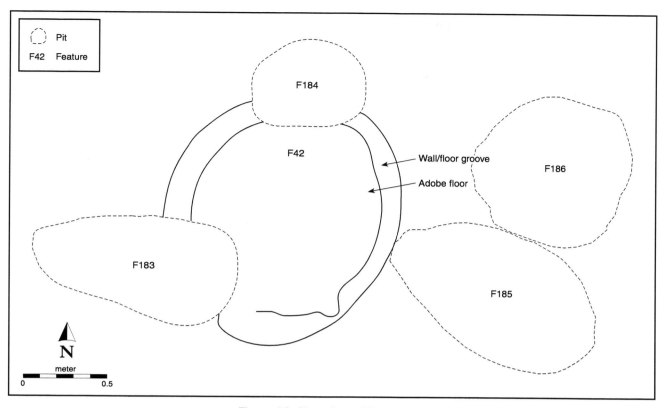

Figure 18. Plan view of Feature 42.

and Huckell (1987:Table 1). A vestibule entryway was observed, but it could not be excavated fully because it extended beyond the boundaries of the Santa Cruz County property.

The walls probably were constructed of upright wooden posts set into the postholes around the perimeter of the floor. We concluded that the roof was internally supported on two upright posts on either side of the hearth. The remainder of postholes in the floor area do not show a clear pattern. These may have been for supplemental roof supports or may have been associated with an elevated floor or platform.

The house pit was excavated into the native Unit III substratum. Whether this soil was used as part or all of the living surface in this house is problematic. Only a small area around the hearth was plastered, with a thin grayish brown clayey material. The remainder of this surface showed signs of oxidation that probably resulted from the fire that destroyed the structure, but it was not plastered. As mentioned above, some of the additional postholes in the floor area may have been used to construct an elevated floor over some or most of the structure. Although not conclusive, the additional postholes in the floor area and the restriction of plastering to a small area around the hearth are similar to characteristics of other structures of comparable age and architectural style in central and southern Arizona that have stronger evidence of elevated floors (Deaver 1998).

Dating

Very few artifacts were recovered from the shallow (2-cm-deep) fill of this structure. Fourteen identified painted sherds were recovered from the house and posthole fill. These types indicate a broad temporal range of A.D. 650–1150, spanning from the middle Hohokam Pioneer period (Estrella Red-on-gray) through the Sedentary period (Rincon Red-on-brown). A trough-shaped plain ware bowl, Vessel 16-1 (PD 174), and a worked sherd disk (PD 173) were found on the floor. Given the small number of sherds and the characteristic mixing of the cultural deposits, we can conclude only that Feature 16 was a pre-Classic period structure.

Feature 42

Feature 42 (Figure 18) is an unusual feature discovered near Feature 15. It is an extraordinarily small (2-m^2) puddled-adobe floor surrounded by a narrow trench. We infer that the narrow trench was used to support some type of superstructure. Given the small size of the floor remnant, we infer that this may have been a small storage structure, perhaps a granary. The floor was discovered during shovel skimming after mechanical removal of the overburden deposits. Only a thin layer of sediments remained above the floor. Most of the artifacts associated with this feature were recovered

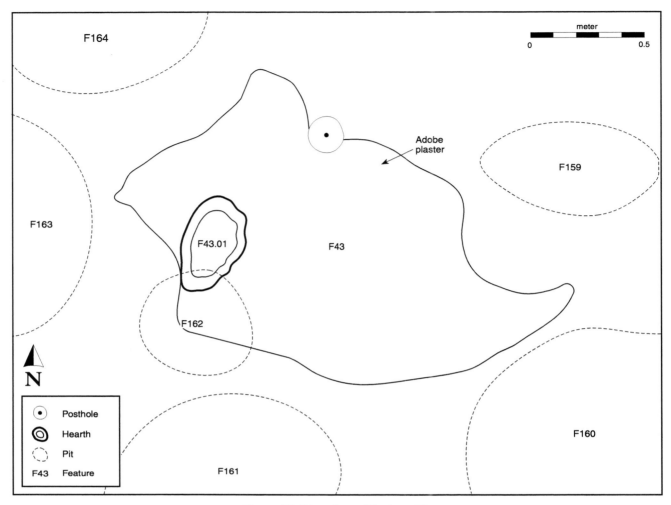

Figure 19. Plan view of Feature 43.

from the wall trench. Feature 42 was intruded into by two later pits, Features 183 and 184, which were not excavated.

Feature 43

Feature 43 (Figure 19) is a small remnant of a deeply buried structure discovered along the western margin of SU 57. Only a small area of plaster surrounding the hearth was found. The structure is in an area with numerous other features, and the remainder of the house cannot be discerned.

Excavation Methods
The plastered surface surrounding the hearth was discovered during shovel skimming after mechanical stripping. A grab sample of artifacts was recovered from the thin layer of fill remaining above and surrounding the hearth. A red ware and a broadline-style red-on-brown sherd were observed in the grab sample. The field identification of these sherds suggested that this was an early structure. A

2-by-2-m test pit, TP 71, was located in the remaining balk just northwest of the hearth to obtain a sample of the deposits above this floor remnant.

Fill
The fill above the floor was indistinguishable from the Unit II sediments.

Interior Features
The only floor feature identified was the hearth, Feature 43.01. The hearth was excavated into the underlying Unit III substratum and was lined with a 1–1.5-cm-thick adobe plaster coating. The bottom and south side of the hearth were badly disturbed by rodents.

Construction
The manner in which the floor around the hearth was prepared is consistent with the architectural style of pit structures found at sites in the southern Southwest. An apron of a thick, fine-grained plaster surrounded the hearth and

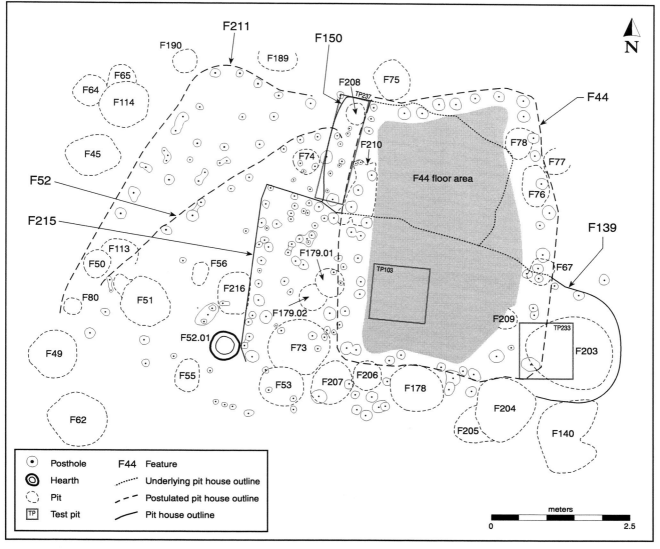

Figure 20. Plan view of Feature 212, a complex of superimposed pit houses.

extended to the east. The edges of this plastered area were badly eroded and intruded on by other pits.

Dating

Based on the thickness of the sediments above this floor remnant and the numerous pits intruding through the floor remnant, we inferred that this house dates early in the site occupation sequence. An archaeomagnetic sample taken from the hearth failed to return viable results (Appendix G). There is a weak temporal trend evident in the distribution of identified painted sherds from TP 71 (see Table 5). Sedentary period pottery types (Rincon Red-on-brown and Sacaton Red-on-buff) were found in all levels. In contrast, the Colonial period pottery type, Cañada del Oro Red-on-brown, was found only in the lowest two levels, and the Classic period pottery type, Tanque Verde Red-on-brown,

only in the uppermost two levels. By the most conservative method, Feature 43 is assigned broadly to the span A.D. 800–1150. However, the distribution of the oldest and youngest types in TP 71 suggests that Feature 43 may be no younger than A.D. 950.

Feature 212

Feature 212 (Figure 20) is not a single construction unit. Instead, this feature number was assigned to a complex of superimposed architectural units. It was not possible to associate all postholes and pits in the various floors with discrete construction episodes; therefore, all postholes were assigned to Feature 212. Pits were given independent feature numbers. Based on the observed house remnants and the definable patterns in the postholes, we concluded that Feature 212 encompasses the remains of no less than six independent construction episodes. Each of these construction episodes was assigned independent feature numbers (in numeric order, Features 44, 52, 139, 150, 211, and 215). These construction episodes are described below in chronological order from youngest to oldest. Based on superpositioning we can define the following chronological sequences, from oldest to youngest: 211, 52, 150, 215, 44; and 139, 44. The chronological relationship of Feature 139 to all other features except Feature 44 cannot be determined.

The spatial limits of the complex, which measures 9.7 by 8.5 m, were exposed by the backhoe. The remainder of the fill was removed manually to expose the floor surfaces and interior features. Given the extensive superpositioning of features and our inability to distinguish the fill of one structure from that of another, most of the fill was not screened. However, when fill could be related to a given structure, that fill was screened. Ultimately, fill associated with three of the six structures was identified and sampled. After the occupation surfaces were exposed, numerous small and large pits were visible. Small pits (less than 20 cm in diameter) were presumed to be postholes indicative of the various construction episodes. All of the potential postholes were excavated. Elsewhere on the site where postholes were associated with a specific construction episode, they were treated as a single recovery unit, and sediments and artifacts were collected in bulk samples. However, because the postholes associated with Feature 212 could not always be associated with a particular construction episode, postholes were assigned individual provenience numbers, and artifacts were collected accordingly. A few of the larger pits were excavated. All fill from these pits was screened, and artifacts and ecofactual samples were collected. These pits are described individually. Each of the identified construction episodes is described below under a separate heading.

Feature 44

Feature 44 (Figure 21) is the latest of the construction episodes encompassed by Feature 212. This structure burned with several ground stone artifacts present on the floor. The presence and outline of this structure were identified initially by the distribution of these artifacts and the pattern of dark gray ash and charcoal that represented the remains of the burned superstructure. An arrangement of postholes was identified later that demarcated the northern and eastern sides of the structure. A corresponding arrangement of postholes on the southern and western sides of the pit house could not be discerned. Consequently, the area of the structure cannot be estimated accurately.

Excavation Methods. Feature 44 was discovered during mechanical stripping. The backhoe exposed several large ground stone artifacts associated with a lens of dark gray ash and charcoal. A dark gray ashy layer representing the roof

fall was visible in the balk profile. A sample of the overburden deposits from the surface to the floor of Feature 44 was obtained from TP 103.

Fill. The roof fall was a fine, dark gray, silty sand with charcoal flecks.

Interior Features. Two interior features, a hearth (Feature 44.01) and an ash-filled pit (Feature 44.02), are associated with the structure. Several postholes surrounding the northern and eastern margins of the floor probably are associated with this structure. Because of the intensive rebuilding in this location, it is not possible to positively identify the series of postholes that formed the western and southern walls. All of the postholes have been numbered subordinate to Feature 212.

The hearth was a shallow, straight-sided basin measuring approximately 25 cm in diameter and 9 cm deep. The sides of the hearth were plastered with a strong, sandy plaster that was 4–5 cm thick. This plaster was well fired from use, and an archaeomagnetic dating sample was collected from this fired plaster. Immediately behind the hearth was a shallow oval pit filled with ash. The ash had accumulated several centimeters above the floor and had spread as much as 10–15 cm beyond the limits of the pit. The sidewalls of the ash pit, as well as the floor beneath the ash, were lightly oxidized, suggesting that the ash was deposited while still hot.

Construction. It is likely that Feature 44 was built in a house pit, but this pit, which would have been excavated into the Unit II horizon, was undetectable. The postabandonment fill above the roof fall zone was indistinguishable from the sediments into which the house pit had been excavated.

Description of the physical evidence for the placement of construction elements is hampered by the multiple construction episodes. The arrangement of postholes along the north and eastern margins of the floor suggests the location of walls for this structure. The house had an unplastered dirt floor. The floor was observed as a compaction layer beneath the ashy roof fall zone. The floor was not sufficiently different from the underlying sediments to permit identification of interior postholes. The only evidence of plaster was found around the hearth.

Dating. Feature 44 is the latest in the series of six structures collectively identified as Feature 212. Identified painted pottery types from TP 103 (see Table 5) provide a general date range of A.D. 800–1300. A single sherd of Tanque Verde Red-on-brown recovered from the floor may suggest that the house dates to the Classic period (ca. A.D. 1150–1300), but this single sherd is inconclusive. An archaeomagnetic dating sample was collected from the hearth. The date obtained from this sample is A.D. 1005 (1150) 1245 (see Appendix G). The midpoint of this date suggests that this house was abandoned near the end of the pre-Classic period.

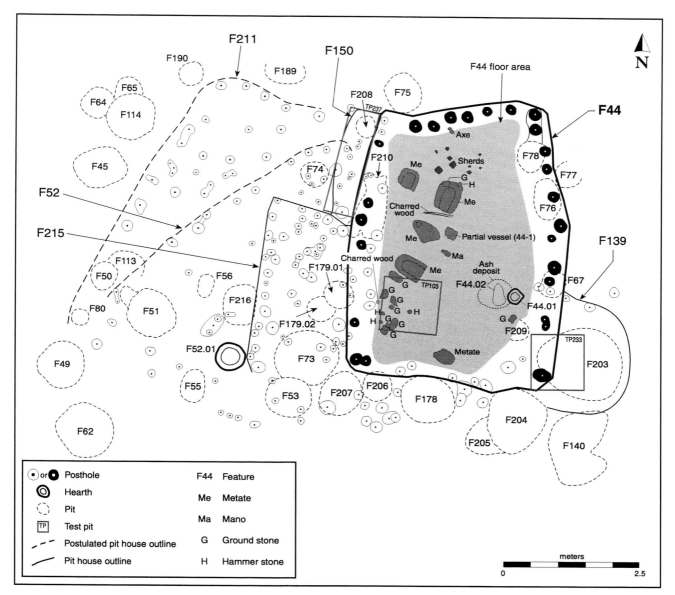

Figure 21. Plan view of Feature 44.

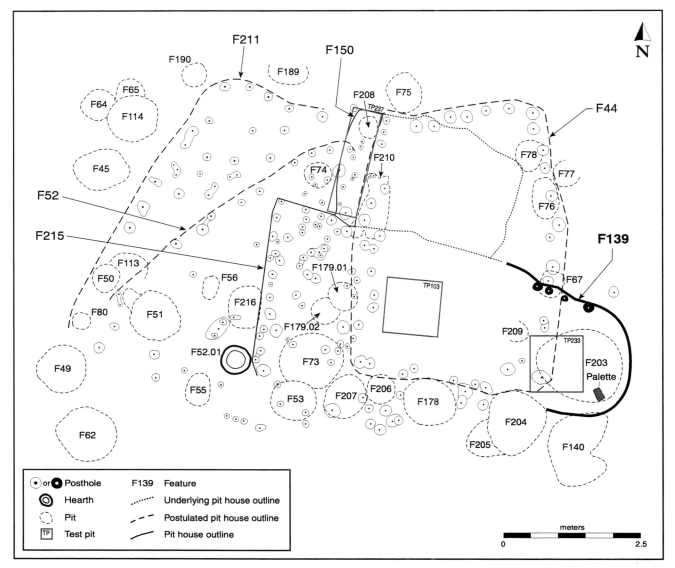

Figure 22. Plan view of Feature 139.

Feature 139

This structure (Figure 22) is the remains of a pit structure partially underlying Feature 44. The eastern portion of the house pit was visible and was excavated. The northern pit wall of Feature 139 aligns and connects with the northern pit wall of Feature 215. Because the southern wall of Feature 139 did not align with the southern wall of Feature 215, it was not possible to ascertain whether Feature 139 and Feature 215 were the same structure.

Excavation Methods. The eastern edge of Feature 139 was first observed along the western margin of SU 56. After the remainder of Feature 212 was exposed, the portion of Feature 139 that extended beyond Feature 44 was excavated. Because of uncertainty as to what the feature represented, the area excavated was designated TP 233. The test

pit revealed the pit walls of Feature 139 and the remaining edge of the floor of Feature 44. The test pit coincided with the area of the feature that was excavated. The fill was removed in a single, 20-cm-thick layer to the floor, and the observed postholes were excavated. Data on artifacts recovered from this test pit are presented in the tables under "Feature 139, fill." Postholes were assigned interior feature numbers subordinate to Feature 212. Four postholes along the northern pit walls were the only features that could be associated with the construction and use of Feature 139. A large pit, Feature 203, was observed within the exposed floor area. This pit was covered by remnants of the floor plaster of Feature 139 and thus clearly predates the structure. We did not excavate this pit in its entirety but obtained a small grab sample of artifacts from the upper portion.

Fill. The fill of this structure was the undifferentiated Unit II deposit.

Interior Features. Four postholes (Features 212.528, 212.529, 212.530, and 212.531) along the northern house pit are the only features that can be associated unambiguously with the construction and use of this structure. A pit in the floor of the house (Feature 209) may be associated with the floor or may be a postabandonment intrusion.

Construction. Feature 139 was constructed in a pit that had been excavated some 14–25 cm into the Unit III horizon. The floor was a brown, clayey sand plaster. The floor plaster partially covered a large pit, Feature 203, beneath the floor.

Dating. Feature 139 is superimposed by Feature 44 and is clearly a pre-Classic period structure. The archaeomagnetic date of Feature 44 places an upper limit for the dating of Feature 139 at about A.D. 1150. A rectangular palette with a raised carved border (PD 382) was found on the floor of this structure (see Chapter 4). The style of this palette is typical of the Hohokam Colonial and Sedentary periods, but the poor quality of the carving is more suggestive of the Sedentary period (Haury 1976:286). The 18 identified painted ceramics from the fill (see Table 7) are consistent with this general age. Trincheras Purple-on-red (n = 10) and Rincon Red-on-brown (n = 3) are the most common types. Based on the earlier cited work of Deaver (1984) in the Santa Rita Mountains, the co-occurrence of these two types may indicate a relatively short span of about A.D. 950–1050. Considering all lines of evidence but relying on the overlap in the ages of Trincheras Purple-on-red and Rincon Red-on-brown, we suggest that Feature 139 probably dates to a period coeval with the early part of the Hohokam Sedentary period between A.D. 950 and 1050.

Feature 215

Feature 215 (Figure 23) is a house in the middle of the six-episode series attributed to Feature 212.

Excavation Methods. The fill of Feature 215 was removed by the backhoe. The structure was not recognized until an abrupt rise in the Unit III horizon that represents the western pit edge of this structure was observed. Because of the disturbance to the fill of this structure, no controlled collections were made. All postholes and two pits (Features 179.01 and 179.02) were excavated, and the fill was screened. After excavation of Feature 44 was completed, a narrow trench was excavated to define the northern edge of this pit structure. No artifacts were recovered.

Fill. The fill of Feature 215 was the undifferentiated Unit II horizon characteristic of the site.

Interior Features. Numerous postholes and pits were discovered in the fill of this structure. Many of these features probably relate to postabandonment activities in the area. A series of postholes were identified as the remains of the western wall of this structure.

Construction. The house was constructed in a pit that was 5–10 cm deep. This house pit intruded below the floors of Features 52, 150, and 211. The superstructure appears to have been constructed of a series of upright posts set around the perimeter of the floor.

Dating. Feature 215 is clearly later than Features 150, 52, and 211 and is earlier than Feature 44. The chronological relationship between Features 215 and 139 was not established. The house pit excavations for these two structures intersect on their northern margins. The midpoints of the archaeomagnetic dates of Features 44 and 52 indicate a maximum and minimum age range for Feature 215 of A.D. 950–1150.

Feature 150

Feature 150 (Figure 24) is a remnant of a pit house. The southern half of this house was destroyed when Feature 215 was built. Feature 44 was subsequently constructed over the fill of Features 150 and 215. The stratigraphic relationship of Feature 150 and Feature 139 was not established.

Excavation Methods. A 1-by-2-m test pit (TP 237) was used to expose the floor of this structure. The limits of this test pit were the western and northern pit edges of Feature 150, the pit edge of Feature 215, and the western definable limit of Feature 44. Only one 13-cm-thick level was excavated, extending from the top of the house pit to the floor. The sediments removed were screened. Data on artifacts recovered from this test pit are presented in the tables under "Feature 150, fill."

Fill. The fill of Feature 150 was undifferentiated Unit II sediments.

Interior Features. Several postholes and two large pits (Features 208 and 210) were discovered in the floor. Poor preservation prevented us from determining whether these pits were associated with the use of the structure or had penetrated the floor at some later time.

Construction. The house pit was excavated approximately 30 cm into Unit III. The Unit III substratum was used as the floor. There was no other evidence of formal preparation of the floor.

Dating. The six identified painted sherds from the fill (see Table 7) are not conclusive evidence for dating this structure, but they generally are consistent with the age determined from stratigraphic relationships with other construction events. By virtue of its stratigraphic position, Feature 150 is clearly a pre-Classic period structure. Feature 150 can best be dated using the archaeomagnetic dating of Features 44 and 52, which stratigraphically bracket this house. These archaeomagnetic dates provide maximum and minimum estimates of A.D. 950–1150, which is the same span assigned to Feature 215 above. Because Feature 150 is earlier than Feature 215, we suspect that the true age of Feature 150 is in the earlier portion of this date range.

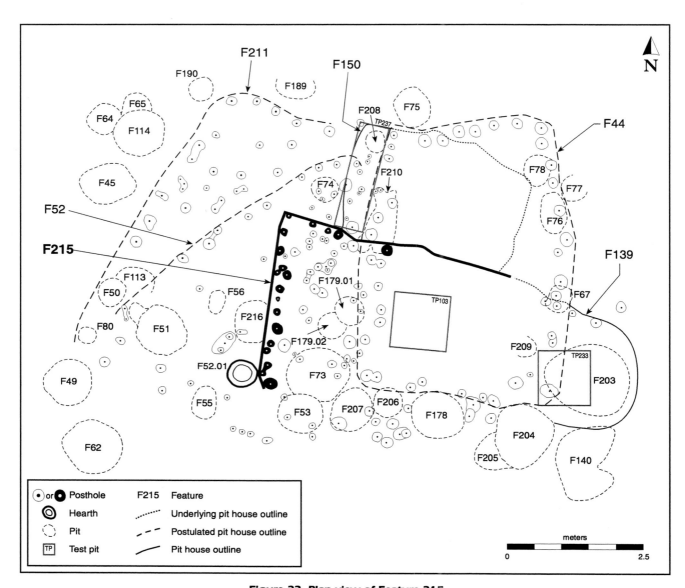

Figure 23. Plan view of Feature 215.

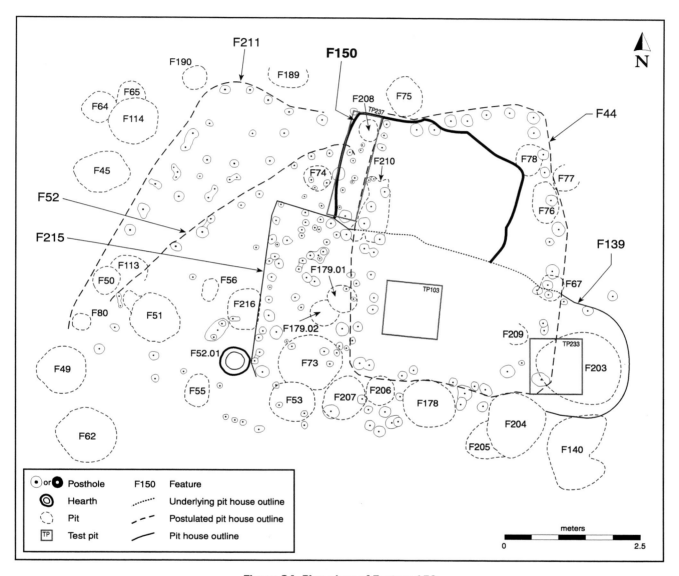

Figure 24. Plan view of Feature 150.

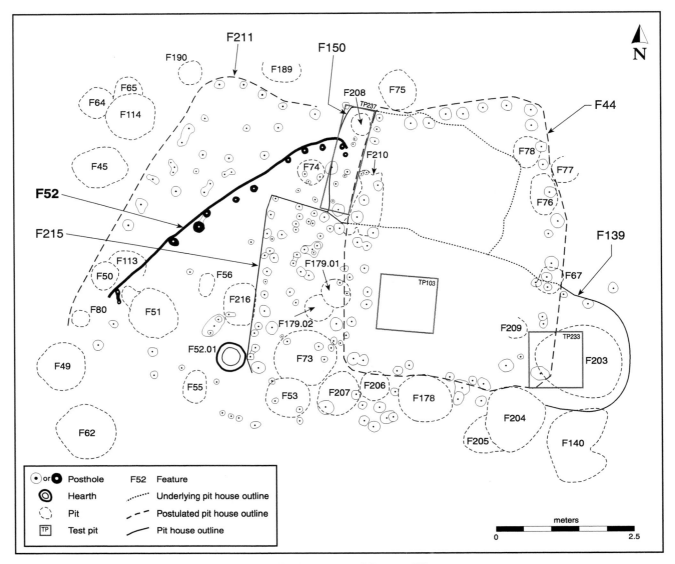

Figure 25. Plan view of Feature 52.

Feature 52

This structure (Figure 25) was discovered during the excavation of SU 80 and was observed as a large, relatively level expanse of floor surrounding a hearth (Feature 52.01).

Excavation Method. All of the fill was removed by backhoe. Postholes and other pit features observed within the defined floor area were excavated, and all fill from these features was screened.

Fill. The fill of the structure was undifferentiated Unit II sediments.

Interior Features. An informal hearth, several postholes, and three pits were associated with Feature 52. The hearth appeared as a circular area of ash, about 50 cm in diameter, excavated into Unit III. The Unit III sediments were oxidized around the perimeter of the ash. This hearth was not clay-lined and had been heavily disturbed by rodents.

The postholes assigned to this structure do not form a clear alignment. They were associated with the structure because they follow a slight ledge in the surface of Unit III. Three pits, Features 51, 55, and 56, were excavated. It is unclear whether these are pits associated with the use of the floor or represent postabandonment activities.

Construction. The house was constructed in a shallow pit. The remnants of this pit had a maximum depth of 9 cm. The floor of the structure was the unprepared surface created by the house pit excavation into Unit III. No other direct evidence of house construction was observed.

Dating. The assignment of calendrical dates to Feature 52 is based on its stratigraphic position relative to the other structures and an archaeomagnetic dating sample collected from the hearth (Feature 52.01). Feature 52 was relatively early in the Feature 212 construction sequence. Our interpretation is that after Feature 52 was abandoned, it was partially destroyed by the construction of Feature 150. Subsequently, both Features 52 and 150 were partially destroyed by the construction of Feature 215. Feature 44, the last house in the sequence, overlies the remnants of Features 150 and 215. Thus, it is clear that Feature 52 is earlier than Feature 44.

The painted ceramics and archaeomagnetic date from Feature 44 (see above) indicate that this structure was abandoned near the end of the pre-Classic period, around A.D. 1150. This is a minimum age for Feature 52. Only six identified painted ceramics were recovered from Feature 150 (see Table 7). These are Trincheras Purple-on-red (n = 5) and Cañada del Oro Red-on-brown (n = 1) sherds. Although few in number, the age of these ceramics corresponds with the documented age of Feature 44.

An archaeomagnetic dating sample was collected from the hearth, Feature 52.01. A date of A.D. 930 (950, 975) 1020 was obtained from this structure (see Appendix G). The midpoint of this date range is earlier than the date obtained from the hearth in Feature 44. In addition, statistical comparison of the archaeomagnetic pole locations indicates that the hearth in Feature 52 was fired at a point in time significantly different from when the hearth of Feature 44 was fired (see Appendix G). Based on the ceramics and archaeomagnetic dates, we conclude that Feature 52 was abandoned during a period coeval with the latter part of the Hohokam Colonial period.

Feature 211

This structure (Figure 26) was demarcated by a series of postholes that followed a slight depression in the Unit III horizon and surrounded a relatively level surface area.

Excavation Methods. The floor of this structure was exposed by the backhoe. No artifacts were collected from the fill. The postholes along the perimeter of the floor area were excavated as part of Feature 212. All fill from these postholes was screened. In addition, two pits, Features 50 and 80, at the southern end of the western margin, were excavated. The fill of these pits was screened.

Fill. The fill of Feature 211 was the undifferentiated Unit II sediments characteristic of the site.

Interior Features. The only features that could be attributed to the floor of this structure were a series of postholes along the western and northern margins.

Construction. The house pit had been excavated only deep enough to level the floor. It reached a maximum depth of 20 cm at the northwestern corner and a minimum depth of 5 cm where it could still be detected. The posthole pattern suggests a brush-and-earthen superstructure with a series of posts set upright in holes around the floor perimeter providing the framework of the walls.

Dating. The age of this structure is unknown. In the relative sequence of construction episodes that make up

Feature 212, Feature 211 appears to be the earliest structure. The archaeomagnetic date associated with the abandonment of Feature 52 indicates that Feature 211 probably predates A.D. 950–975.

Burials

During the three excavation projects at El Macayo, 15 burials and 4 possible burials were discovered (Figure 27). Prior to the 1996 excavations, five burials had been located. Two of these were cremations, and three were inhumations. Gardiner and Huckell (1987:25–26, Table 1) reported two cremations (Features 1 and 2) and two inhumations (Features 19 and 31). Both cremations were characterized by deposits of ash and calcined bones within shallow pits. One inhumation, Feature 19, was found at the bottom of Trench 4. The top of a human cranium and an associated small plain ware jar were exposed but not exhumed. The other inhumation, Feature 31, was indicated by a fragment of a right upper arm bone recovered from the backdirt of Trench 3. Slawson reported finding an inhumation burial of a young child about 4 months old, accompanied by the remains of a small dog (Feature 32) (Fox 1991:19; Slawson 1991:9–10). This burial had been sealed by the placement of three large, ground basalt slabs over the body. During the 1996 data recovery, 10 additional burials were located and exhumed, and 4 possible burials were identified but not excavated (see Table 3). Eight of those exhumed were human interments, and two were animal interments. We also recovered additional remains of Feature 31 originally discovered by ASM. The eleven burials from which we recovered remains during the 1996 excavations are described below.

Human Burials

Previous excavations in the Nogales area have documented the practice of both cremation (Di Peso 1956; Doyel 1977a; Jácome 1986; Reinhard 1978; Reinhard and Fink 1982) and inhumation (Di Peso 1956; Grebinger 1971b) burial. Including prior excavations at this site (Gardiner and Huckell 1987; Slawson 1991), 11 human inhumations and 2 cremation burials have been documented. Characteristics of all human burials are summarized in Table 8. A summary of the painted ceramics recovered from burial fill is presented in Table 9.

Excavation Methods

The following discussion of the excavation methods pertains only to the nine human inhumations that were encountered during the 1996 excavations. Information about the discovery and treatment of burials in previous excavations is available in Gardiner and Huckell (1987) and Slawson

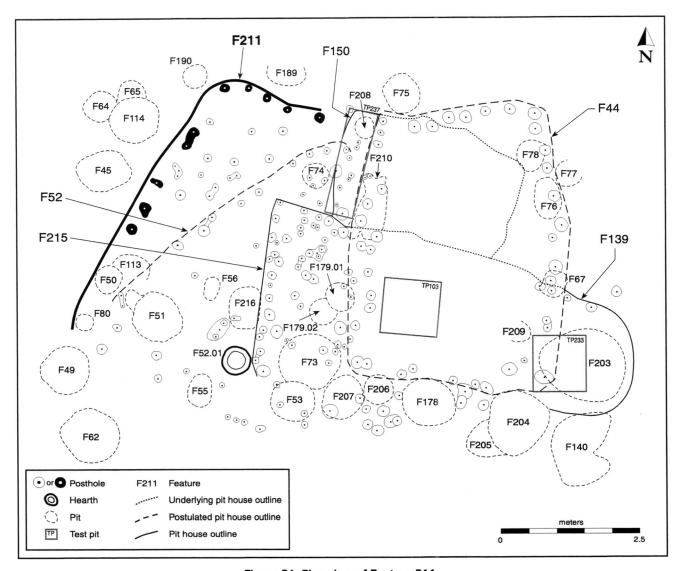

Figure 26. Plan view of Feature 211.

(1991). In the course of removing sediments to expose pit houses and other features, the remains of a number of individuals were encountered. Although it was explicitly not our intent to recover human remains, we were required to exhume those remains that were inadvertently disturbed by data recovery efforts, to treat the deceased with respect and dignity, and to repatriate the remains to the Tohono O'odham as per our BMOA (ASM Agreement on Burial Discoveries: Case No. 95-24; see Appendix H). Only those graves that were disturbed by our excavations were disinterred; the four other features suspected to be graves were left unexcavated and protected.

Each disturbed burial was excavated by a two-person team consisting of an archaeologist and a physical anthropologist. The archaeologist was responsible for observing and recording the archaeological evidence of the mortuary activities and the integrity of the burial deposits. The physical anthropologist was responsible for making osteological observations and taking measurements on the skeletal elements as they were exposed. Most of the skeletal remains were in poor condition; they fragmented and crumbled when exposed to the air and removed from the soil. Consequently, the in situ observations made by the physical anthropologist were vital; most would not have been possible to make on the fragmented skeletal elements after they were removed from the sediment matrix.

All but one of the burials were discovered after the backhoe had removed all of the overlying sediments. We were not able, therefore, to obtain controlled samples of artifacts from the cultural deposits overlying the burials. The only exception was Feature 213. This burial was visible in the sidewall of ASM Trench 3 after we had removed the

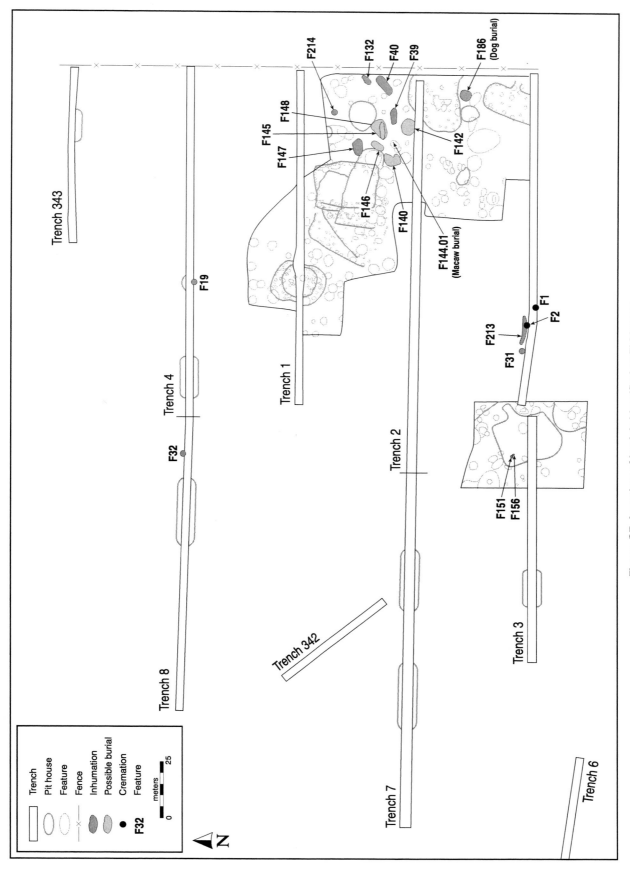

Figure 27. Location of burials identified at El Macayo.

Table 8. Summary Information on Human Burials Excavated at El Macayo

Feature No.	Type	Gender and Age	Body Position	Head Orientation	Rock Cairn	Funerary Items	Comments
1	cremation	indeterminate	n/a	n/a	none	none	28.87 g of calcined bone representing the cranial vault, and long bone fragments (Gardiner and Huckell 1987:25)
2	cremation	indeterminate subadult	n/a	n/a	none	none	28.03 g of calcined bone representing vertebral column, cranial vault, and long bone fragments (Gardiner and Huckell 1987: 25)
19	inhumation	indeterminate	unknown	NE (?)	no	plain ware jar	discovered by ASM in Trench 4; top of the cranium was exposed in trench wall; remains appear to continue to SW beyond trench; unexcavated (Gardiner and Huckell 1987:Table 1)
31	inhumation	indeterminate 5–10 years	unknown	unknown	unknown	unknown	humerous fragment recovered from trench backdirt by SRI refits fragment found by ASM in 1987 (Gardiner and Huckell 1987:26)
32	inhumation	indeterminate 8–16 months	unknown	unknown	yes	none	discovered and excavated by CES (Slawson 1991:9–10); remains of small dog found among remains of child
39	inhumation	indeterminate 3–15 years	flexed (?) on side	E	yes	none	very little bone remaining; body position estimated from position of lower limbs; several medium to large rocks placed over body
40	inhumation	male (?) 45+ years	extended on back	NE	yes	none	
132	inhumation	indeterminate 9–12 months	unknown	SW	no	none	
147	inhumation	indeterminate adult	flexed on right side	E	unknown	none	right femur, tibia, fibula found; body position and orientation estimated from position of leg bones
151	inhumation	indeterminate 5–7 years	flexed on right side	E	no	3 plain ware bowls; 529 shell beads and 508 stone beads	rodent disturbed; overlies Feature 156
156	inhumation	indeterminate 3–9 months	flexed on right side	ESE	no	2 Type 3 shell bracelets; turquoise pendant	rodent disturbed; one shell bracelet found on lower portion of right humerous, another shell bracelet found in rodent disturbance near left humerous
213	inhumation	female 17–25 years	extended on back	E	yes	none	exposed in side wall of trench near where ASM reported Feature 31
214	inhumation	indeterminate subadult	unknown	unknown	yes (?)	plain ware jar	disturbed by backhoe; cranial fragments and partial plain ware jar discovered among several large rocks—perhaps remains of cairn

Table 9. Summary of Identified Painted Pottery Types from Burials at El Macayo

Provenience	Cañada del Oro or Rillito Red-on-brown	Trincheras Purple-on-red	Nogales Polychrome	Total
Feature 31, trench backdirt	1	1	—	2
Feature 39, burial fill	—	1	—	1
Feature 213, burial fill	—	1	1	2
Total	1	3	1	5

trench backfill. A 1-by-1-m test pit (TP 291) was excavated to obtain a controlled sample of artifacts from the overlying cultural deposits. The remaining overburden obscuring the burial pit was removed without screening.

All burial fill was sifted through a sieve with $\frac{1}{4}$-inch wire-mesh screen. In the case of one infant burial, small beads observed near the lower leg of the child and scattered throughout the fill by later rodent disturbance were not recoverable with a $\frac{1}{4}$-inch wire-mesh screen. In this instance, the burial fill was collected and transported to the SRI laboratory, where it was sifted through $\frac{1}{16}$-inch wire-mesh screen. As a result, 1,037 shell and stone beads that accompanied the child were recovered. In addition, samples of the sediments around and beneath the skeletal remains and inside funerary items were collected for palynological analysis.

Burial Fill

With the exceptions of Features 151 and 156, all burial fill removed from the graves was a gray to grayish brown, silty sand indistinguishable from the Unit II cultural horizon. All of the burials except Feature 214 were discovered at the bottom of the Unit II cultural horizon. The human remains were found in shallow pits excavated into the Unit III substratum. It is quite likely that the burial pits had originated at a higher stratigraphic level, but the burial fill could not be distinguished from the Unit II cultural horizon.

Features 151 and 156 were deposited within a previously abandoned pit, Feature 202. Feature 202 was capped with an adobe seal after it was abandoned. Feature 156, the earlier interment, was placed in a small pit excavated into this adobe cap. Feature 151, the later interment, was found resting on top of this adobe cap and was sealed with a 10–15-cm-thick layer of adobe. This adobe was poured directly over the three plain ware vessels that accompanied this individual.

Characteristics of the Burials

The following characteristics of the human burials are summarized from Gardiner and Huckell (1987), Slawson (1991), and Chapter 9. Eight of the inhumations contained individuals younger than 15 years of age (Features 2, 31,

32, 39, 132, 151, 156, and 214; see Table 8). Three of these individuals were infants under 1 year of age. The other five individuals were children older than 3–5 years. Only three burials (Features 40, 147, and 213) were adolescents or adults ranging in age from 17 to more than 45 years old. The relatively larger proportion of subadult individuals, although the sample is small, is consistent with the general pattern of high infant mortality in premodern populations of the Southwest. Also, the remains of a young female (Feature 213) without any observable pathologies or obvious cause of death may attest to the high risk of childbirth among premodern southwestern populations. Possible evidence of anemia was observed on the skeletal remains of one child (Feature 132). Indications of degenerative joint disease were observed on the remains of one of the adult individuals (Feature 40).

Body Position

Body position and orientation were determined for six of the burials, three adults and three subadults (see Table 8). The other burials were too badly disturbed and too fragmentary to determine body position, but orientation was obtained for two of these burials. Two of the adults (Features 40 and 213) were placed in their graves in an extended position, on their backs, with their heads oriented to the northeast and east. The other adult burial (Feature 147) was represented only by the bones of the right leg. Given the position of these leg bones, the body was probably laid in its grave in a flexed position, on its right side, with its head oriented to the east. All three subadult burials (Features 39, 151, and 156) were laid in a flexed position, on their right sides with their heads oriented to the east.

Funerary Offerings

Four individuals (Features 19, 151, 156, and 214) were accompanied by nonperishable artifacts. Additionally, the child in Feature 32 was accompanied by a small dog (Slawson 1991:10) that was probably interred with the child. Gardiner and Huckell (1987:Table 1) discovered a plain ware jar associated with Feature 19. The subadult burial Feature 151 had the largest number of offerings. Three Type I plain ware bowls or scoops (see Chapter 3) were retrieved in the burial fill above and to the side of the body. Pollen washes taken from the interior surfaces of these vessels produced evidence of mesquite and corn pollen. The frequency of these grains suggests that these bowls may have held food offerings (see Chapter 8). One thousand thirty-seven stone and shell beads (see Chapters 4 and 5) were recovered from the burial fill near the lower extremities of the body. Linear alignments of beads were observed in situ beneath the lower right leg. Apparently, these beads were once part of one or more strands encircling the lower right leg. Subsequently, rodent activity resulted in the redeposition of many beads in the burial fill.

The subadult burial Feature 156, which was found beneath Feature 151, was accompanied by shell and turquoise jewelry. Two Type 3 shell bracelets (see Chapter 5) were found with the body. One of these encircled the upper right arm just above the elbow. The other bracelet was found near the lower part of the left upper arm in an area that had been disturbed by rodent activity. Apparently, this child was buried with a bracelet on each upper arm. In addition, a turquoise pendant (see Chapter 4) was found to the side of its head. The location suggests that it was placed on the head rather than around the neck, but it may have been moved by rodent activity.

Subadult burial Feature 214 appears to have been accompanied by a ceramic vessel. This inhumation was located high in the Unit II cultural horizon and, unfortunately, when discovered, had been badly disturbed by the backhoe. A fragment of a Type I plain ware jar (see Chapter 3) was found among several large rocks in the disturbed fill near the cranium.

Manner of Interment

All of the burials except Features 151 and 156 had been placed in pits prepared exclusively for burial of the dead. After the bodies and funerary items had been placed in their graves, the bodies were covered with earth. In most cases, this fill was indistinguishable from the Unit II horizon and probably was the backdirt from the excavation of the grave. Several burials had one or more rocks placed over the body. Feature 213 had the most extensive rock cairn, covering the full extent of the body (Figure 28). The child burial discovered by CES archaeologists, Feature 32, also had a rock cairn, composed of several grinding slabs laid above the body (Slawson 1991:9–10).

Features 151 and 156 were burials in a previously abandoned pit (Feature 202). Feature 156 was the first interment, with the body buried in a small pit dug into the adobe fill of Feature 202. The body of the child in Feature 151 had been placed on top of the adobe cap of Feature 202, and after placement of the body and funerary items, the burial pit had been sealed with a thick layer of adobe. This burial was located near the exterior wall of a pit structure (Feature 21). We did not excavate this structure and thus cannot determine whether Feature 202 was an intramural floor pit into which burials Features 151 and 156 had been placed. It is possible, therefore, that these two children were buried beneath the floor of this structure. The adobe cap may indicate repair to the floor.

Burial Location

Because a systematic effort to locate and excavate burials was not included in our data recovery plan, our understanding of the placement of graves within the settlement is incomplete and complicated by the length of occupation and the frequency of superimposed features. It appears that burials were not interred randomly within the settlement (see Figure 27); a more systematic investigation, however, may find a more dispersed pattern of interment. Except for Features 151 and 156, which may have been buried beneath the floor of a pit structure, the locations of the other burials suggest that there were discrete cemeteries within the village. Work to date at El Macayo indicates that at least three discrete burial locales were present.

Discussion

The predominance of inhumation as a human mortuary practice at El Macayo is the most notable characteristic of the burial collection recovered by SRI. Given the limited extent of the settlement available for our explorations, it is premature to conclude that inhumation was the dominant practice of the settlement. It is important to note, to the contrary, that, except at Potrero Creek (Grebinger 1971b), all human remains reported to date from the upper Santa Cruz River valley (Di Peso 1956; Doyel 1977a; Reinhard 1978; Reinhard and Fink 1982) were cremated, not inhumed. Given the importance of the cremation ritual in Hohokam culture (Gladwin et al. 1937; Haury 1976), we

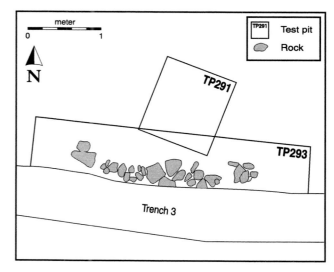

Figure 28. Schematic of burial Feature 213 showing rock cairn placed over body.

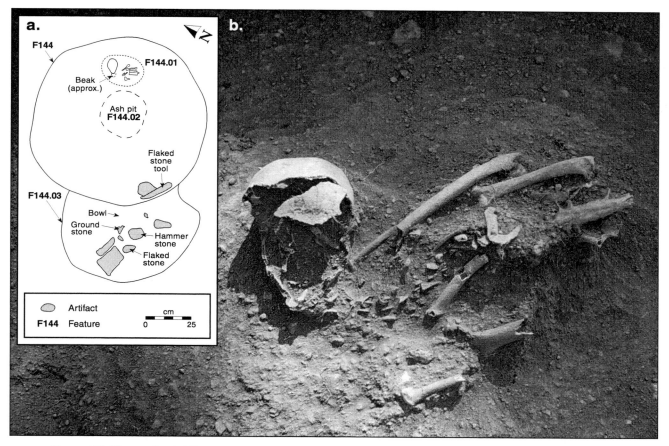

Figure 29. Macaw burial (Feature 144.01): (a) a schematic drawing of Feature 144 showing the location of the macaw burial, (b) photograph of the macaw burial.

suggest that the seeming preference for inhumation burial at these two sites indicates the likely presence of non-Hohokam populations in the upper Santa Cruz River valley.

Animal Inhumations

During the 1996 data recovery program, the inhumations of a military macaw (see Chapter 7) and a dog (see Chapter 6) were discovered. In 1991, CES archaeologists discovered and exhumed the remains of a small dog that accompanied the remains of a small child (Slawson 1991:9–10). The two animal burials discovered in 1996 are described below.

Feature 144.01 (Macaw Burial)
The skeletal remains of a military macaw (Figure 29a, b) were found interred among several human burials and may be part of a small cemetery located immediately north of pit house Feature 15 (see Figure 27). The pit in which the macaw was placed, Feature 144, may have been an abandoned food-processing pit. This pit was discovered during backhoe excavations, and several small pieces of bone were exposed when the feature outline was defined. The backhoe also exposed an intact ceramic bowl (Vessel 144-1; see

Chapter 3) at the western edge of this pit. Based on the small size of the bones and the presence of the bowl, we initially thought that this was a child's burial.

Feature 144 was excavated in the same manner as the human burials. An archaeologist and a physical anthropologist excavated and recorded the burial. During removal of the fill, two notable deposits were observed. First, an ashy deposit isolated within the center of the pit was encountered. This was reminiscent of the filling sequences of several nonburial pits that were excavated within Feature 212 (see below). Second, a ceramic bowl and associated stone tools were found in a separate pit that had intruded on the edge of Feature 144. It became clear that Feature 144, as originally defined, did not represent a single discrete event but was the result of several events. Thereafter, the macaw skeleton was discovered near the eastern edge of Feature 144. As the ashy deposit, the pit containing the bowl and stone tools, and the macaw skeleton were isolated, each deposit was assigned a subordinate feature number. These are shown on Figure 29a.

The macaw was placed in the grave on its back with its head oriented to the north and its beak turned to the west. No funerary objects were associated directly with the macaw, but it is possible that the bowl and stone tools (Feature 144.03) were deposited at the time of burial. The fill of the macaw's burial was indistinguishable from the general fill of Feature 144 and that of Unit II, the general cultural deposit characteristic of the site. The bowl in Feature 144.03 (Vessel 144-1) apparently was manufactured locally and decorated with a simple purple decoration on a light tan slip (see Chapter 3).

Feature 186 (Dog Burial)

The burial of a dog was exposed and disturbed by mechanical excavations just to the south of Feature 15 (see Figure 27). The cranium and much of the upper part of the body were removed by the backhoe. The other skeletal elements were removed, and the remaining burial fill was screened. No grave goods were observed or recovered in the screened deposits. The position of the undisturbed skeletal elements indicated that the body had been positioned on the left side with its head to the south.

Discussion

Animal burials at prehistoric sites are not unusual. Dogs have been found buried alone, as well as with people. Such was the case with Feature 32, discovered by CES archaeologists at El Macayo (Slawson 1991). The macaw burial is more unusual. Importation and trade in macaws and parrots was a well-established practice in prehistory after A.D. 1100 (Hargrave 1970). The fact that macaws are frequently found as burials indicates that these birds were afforded a certain amount of respect and suggests that they were regarded as prized items (Haury 1976:116). A few scattered skeletal elements of macaws were found at Snaketown in deposits as early as the Sweetwater phase and perhaps even as early as the Estrella phase (Haury 1976:116; McKusick 1974), but no burials were found. These specimens represent the earliest evidence of the trafficking of macaws. Although, we cannot assign a calendrical date for the macaw interment at El Macayo, the available dating evidence suggests that this portion of the settlement was occupied before A.D. 1150. Based on the predominance of the Hohokam Colonial and Sedentary period pottery, we suggest that the interment took place sometime within the A.D. 800–1150 span.

Nonarchitectural and Nonburial Features

In accordance with our work plan (Chapter 1), data recovery emphasized the investigation of architectural features. Several nonarchitectural and nonburial features were excavated, however, in the course of excavating test pits, pit structures, and burials. The features excavated are listed and

described in Table 10, and their locations are shown in Figure 30. Because the excavation of these features was not within the primary scope of the data recovery plan, there was no attempt to select an excavation sample that would be representative of the variation observed among nonarchitectural and nonburial features. The features that were excavated were selected only because of their positions relative to architectural or burial features. Two types of features were excavated: a cluster of pebbles (Feature 41), and pit features.

Excavation Methods

Pit features constituted the larger of the two classes of nonarchitectural and nonburial features. All pits were excavated in one of two ways. Most pits were completely excavated, and their fill was sifted through ¼-inch wire-mesh screen. A few of the pit features listed in Table 10, however, were not excavated, but grab samples of associated artifacts exposed in their delineation were recovered.

Fill

As was typical in the 1996 excavations, the fill of most of these nonarchitectural pit features was indistinguishable from the general cultural horizon, Unit II. Four pit features, however, showed a different fill sequence. Features 53, 112, 144, and 178 contained dense ashy deposits. All but Feature 112 had a lower fill indistinguishable from the general Unit II cultural horizon and an upper fill composed mostly of ash. In contrast, Feature 112 had a lower fill (20 cm) of ashy sediments and an upper fill containing sediments indistinguishable from the Unit II cultural horizon. In addition, ash was concentrated in the center of Feature 144. Feature 53 contained discolored and fractured pebbles that indicate the effects of heat alteration. Collectively, the ash deposits and the thermally altered pebbles suggest that these features may have been used as heating or roasting pits. There was, however, no noticeable oxidation of the pit walls or floor.

Feature Characteristics

Feature 41, a pebble cluster, was embedded in the Unit II horizon of TP 60. There was no unambiguous evidence that these rocks were in a pit, but we suspected that at one time they were. The fill among the rocks was indistinguishable from the Unit II cultural horizon above, around, and below the feature. The rocks were angular to subangular in shape, which indicates that they fractured from thermal shock, but there was no evidence of discoloration, ash, or charcoal to indicate that the rocks had been exposed to fire. Nevertheless, the angularity of the rocks is considered sufficient evidence to infer that Feature 41 was a hearth or at least a

Table 10. Characteristics of Nonarchitectural and Nonburial Features

Feature Number	Feature Type	Dimensions (m) (l × w × d)	Fill Characteristics	Comments
45	pit	1.05 × 0.80 × ?	grayish brown silty sand with pebbles	unexcavated, grab sample of artifacts collected during initial exposure
50	pit	0.54 × 0.48 × 0.48	grayish brown silty sand	excavated as part of Feature 212; may be associated with Feature 211
51	pit	0.96 × 0.76 × 0.51	grayish brown silty sand	excavated as part of Feature 212; may be associated with Feature 52
53	hearth	0.88 × 0.78 × 0.34	upper fill: gray to brownish gray, ashy silty sand with pebbles lower fill: brown to dark brown silty sand	excavated as part of Feature 212; probably intrusive into Feature 215
55	pit	0.6 × 0.46 × 0.25	grayish brown silty sand	excavated as part of Feature 212; may be associated with floor of Feature 52
69	pit	0.35 × 0.30 × ?	grayish brown silty sand	unexcavated, grab sample of artifacts collected during initial exposure
73	pit	1.04 × 1.04 × ?	grayish brown silty sand	only partially excavated; part of Feature 212 complex; Feature 53 intrudes upper part of fill; several postholes intrude fill of Feature 73; may be associated with floor of Feature 215
74	pit	0.49 × 0.48 × 0.13	Unit II: grayish brown silty sand	part of Feature 212 complex; may be associated with floor of Feature 150; intruded by several postholes
78	pit	0.60 × 0.48 × 0.25	Unit II: grayish brown silty sand	part of Feature 212 complex; may be associated with Feature 44 floor; located just inside postholes that may have formed Feature 44 east wall; originates at level of Feature 44 floor
80	pit	0.50 × 0.42 × 0.17	Unit II: grayish brown silty sand	part of Feature 212 complex; located along possible wall of Feature 211; intruded by posthole Feature 212-4
105	pit	0.50 × 0.46 × 0.22	Unit II: grayish brown silty sand	intrudes into northwest corner of pit house Feature 5
112	pit	1.20 × 0.98 × 0.51	upper fill: Unit II: grayish brown silty sand lower fill: ashy grayish brown silty sand with large sherds	intrudes into northwest corner of pit house Feature 5; upper fill indistinguishable from Unit II horizon; lower fill has more ash and charcoal flecking
144	pit	1.00 × 0.97 × 0.35	Unit II: grayish brown silty sand with discrete ash deposit (Feature 144.02)	large pit with several associated smaller features; Feature 144.01 is macaw burial placed in Feature 144 fill; Feature 144.02 is ashy deposit near center of Feature 144 fill; Feature 144.03 is small pit adjoining edge
144.03	pit	0.78 × 0.57 × 0.15	Unit II: grayish brown silty sand	small pit adjoining or intruding into edge of Feature 144; pit contained a purple-on-tan bowl (Vessel 144-1) and several stone artifacts
178	pit	0.98 × 0.90 × 0.38	upper fill: ashy grayish brown silty sand lower fill: Unit II: grayish brown silty sand	part of Feature 212
179.01	pit	0.56 × 0.52 × 0.22	Unit II: grayish brown silty sand	part of Feature 212 complex; may be associated with floor of Feature 215; intrudes into pit Feature 179.02
179.02	pit	0.50 × 0.48 × 0.32	Unit II: grayish brown silty sand	part of Feature 212 complex; may be associated with floor of Feature 215; intruded by Feature 179.01

continued on next page

Table 10 (continued).

Feature Number	Feature Type	Dimensions (m) (l × w × d)	Fill Characteristics	Comments
203	pit	1.68 × 1.42 × ?	Unit II: brown to dark brown silty sand	part of Feature 212 complex; pit sealed by floor of Feature 139; partially sectioned by backhoe; not completely excavated; grab sample of artifacts from sidewalls of backhoe excavation
208	pit	0.42 × 0.34 × 0.26	Unit II: grayish brown silty sand	part of Feature 212 complex; in northwest corner of Feature 150 floor; probably associated with Feature 150 floor
210	pit	1.10 × ? × 0.38	Unit II: grayish brown silty sand	part of Feature 212 complex; pit originates in fill below floor of Feature 44 and above floors of Features 150 and 215; several postholes intrude pit fill; pit capped by floor of Feature 44; extends into unexcavated area beneath floor of Feature 44
216	pit	0.56 × 0.48 × 0.07	Unit II: grayish brown silty sand	part of Feature 212 complex; shallow remains of pit in Feature 52 floor; pit may have originated in Unit II above Feature 52

group of rocks that had been used in a hearth and discarded as part of the general site midden.

All of the other nonarchitectural and nonburial pits excavated were oval to round; none were exceptionally elongated. Elongated pits were considered possible burials and were avoided. Three size classes were apparent in the excavated sample. The first size class contains pits with an average diameter of approximately 0.4–0.5 m. The second size class includes pits with an average diameter of approximately 0.7–1.1 m. The third size class has only one member, Feature 203; this pit has an average diameter of more than 1.5 m. A moderately strong correlation between the horizontal and vertical (depth) dimensions of the pits exists ($r = 0.63$).

Dating

Dating of individual extramural features is problematic because of the general lack of chronologically sensitive artifacts or characteristics. The identified painted ceramics from these features are summarized in Table 11. Overall, Trincheras series types dominate the collection from this class of feature. The presence of Santa Cruz and Gila series pottery indicates construction and use during the Colonial and Sedentary periods. Generally, we conclude that these features are part of the pre-Classic period occupation of El Macayo dating to A.D. 650–1150.

Palynological and Macrobotanical Evidence of Pit Use

We did not conduct an exhaustive analysis of palynological and macrobotanical samples taken from the excavated pit features. These features were not within the primary scope of the data recovery plan, and a representative sample of the observable variation in these features was not obtained. Samples of the ashy deposit in Feature 178 were submitted for palynological and macrobotanical analyses (see Chapter 8). The pollen sample was dominated by Chenopodium-Amaranthus (cheno-am) pollen types. The only macrobotanical remains recovered from this deposit were grass stems and small fragments of hardwood that may be mesquite. The mesquite wood probably represents the fuel wood that produced the ash. The grass stems and cheno-am pollen may represent the materials being cooked, additional fuel materials, or unintentional deposits resulting from human disturbance of the local environment. The high percentage of cheno-am pollen recovered from pit features, however, is comparable to the high proportions of cheno-am pollen recovered from the floor surface and the ground stone artifacts in pit house Feature 44. Collectively, these data suggest economic use of these plants.

Discussion

Based on variations in size, filling history, content, and what is known about similar features at other contemporaneous settlements, we suggest that these pits represent a multitude of uses from exterior cooking hearths to food-processing and storage pits. There is also evidence that many of these features may have been used for different purposes at different times during their existence and after their abandonment. Supporting this claim are the notable variations in the fill strata and the reuse of Features 144 and 203 for burials. We do not have the necessary supporting data to evaluate whether the different sizes or shapes of pits correlate with different pit functions.

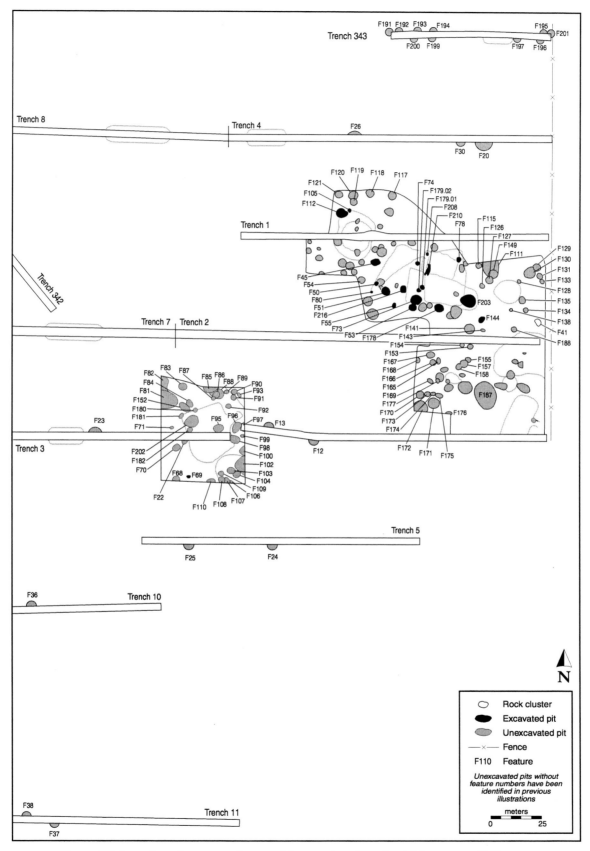

Figure 30. Location of excavated nonarchitectural and nonburial features at El Macayo.

Table 11. Summary of Painted Pottery Types from Pits at El Macayo

Provenience (Pits)	Santa Cruz Series							Gila Series	
	Indet. R/br	Cañada del Oro R/br	Cañada del Oro or Rillito R/br	Rillito or Rincon R/br, Style A	Rincon R/br, Indet. Style	Rincon R/br, Style C	Tanque Verde Blk/br	Indet. R/b	Sacaton R/b
Feature 45	—	—	—	—	—	—	—	—	—
Feature 50	1	—	—	—	—	—	—	—	—
Feature 51	—	—	—	—	—	—	—	—	—
Feature 53	—	—	—	—	—	—	—	—	1
Feature 78	1	—	—	1	—	—	—	—	—
Feature 112	5	—	—	—	2	—	—	—	—
Feature 144	1	—	3	—	—	—	—	2	—
Feature 178	—	—	—	—	—	1	—	—	1
Feature 179	—	—	—	—	—	—	—	—	—
Feature 179.02	—	1	—	—	—	—	—	—	—
Feature 203	1	—	1	—	—	—	—	—	—
Feature 208	1	—	1	—	—	—	—	—	—
Feature 210	2	—	—	—	—	—	1	—	—
Total	12	1	5	1	2	1	1	2	2

Note: Blk/br = Black-on-brown; Blk/red = Black-on-red; Indet. = Indeterminate; P/red = Purple-on-red; R/b = Red-on-buff; R/br = Red-on-brown.

Table 11 (continued).

Provenience (Pits)	Trincheras Series				Local (?) Series		San Simon Series	Total
	Trincheras (Nonspec) P/red	Trincheras (Spec) P/red	Trincheras Polychrome	Nogales Polychrome	R/br	Blk/red	Dos Cabezas or Pinaleno R/br	
Feature 45	1	—	—	—	—	—	—	1
Feature 50	—	2	1	—	1	—	—	5
Feature 51	1	1	1	—	—	3	—	6
Feature 53	—	1	—	—	—	—	—	2
Feature 78	1	—	—	—	—	—	—	3
Feature 112	5	3	1	1	—	—	—	17
Feature 144	4	2	1	—	—	—	1	14
Feature 178	1	—	—	—	—	—	—	2
Feature 179	—	1	—	—	—	—	—	2
Feature 179.02	—	—	—	—	—	—	—	1
Feature 203	—	—	—	—	—	—	—	1
Feature 208	1	—	—	1	—	—	—	4
Feature 210	—	—	—	—	—	—	—	4
Total	14	10	4	2	1	3	1	62

Key: Blk/br = Black-on-brown; Blk/red = Black-on-red; Indet. = Indeterminate; P/red = Purple-on-red; R/b = Red-on-buff; R/br = Red-on-brown.

THREE

Ceramics at El Macayo

Robert A. Heckman

The ceramics recovered from El Macayo were quite diverse. The painted ceramics were an eclectic lot comprising several series that collectively were produced within a broad geographical zone. Several painted sherds that did not conform to published typological descriptions also were recognized. These ceramics may represent the local production of painted wares influenced by contemporaneous traditions characteristic of adjoining regions. This diversity also was recognized in the plain ware ceramics.

Three objectives guided the El Macayo ceramic analysis. The first objective was to document the geographical diversity represented by the ceramic collection. This diversity provides information about the direction and extent of regional interaction between the people living at El Macayo and peoples living in outlying regions. The second objective was to obtain chronological information by identifying ceramic types and forms that serve as markers for particular periods of time. The third objective was to document the stylistic, formal, and technological variability observed in the ceramic collection.

The ceramics collected from El Macayo total 6,617 sherds and seven vessels (Table 12). Not all sherds are equivalent in the amount of information they may contribute toward accomplishing the objectives; therefore, the ceramic collection was sampled. The collection was initially sorted into painted sherds (rim and body), unpainted body sherds, and unpainted rim sherds. The unpainted categories included both plain wares and red wares. No attempt was made during initial sorting to segregate red wares from the remainder of the unpainted sherds. Counts and weights of sherds were taken at this time to provide an assessment of the collection size so that we could select a representative sample. Painted sherds and the unpainted rim sherds possessed the greatest potential for information. Because of this, all painted sherds (n = 624) and all unpainted and red-slipped rim sherds (n = 330) were analyzed. Unpainted body sherds have more-limited information potential, and the analysis was restricted to a sample of 822 sherds.

Because of the extensive mixing of the deposits across the site, the ceramic collection was analyzed at the site level rather than at the feature level. Temporal associations among the ceramics are defined solely on the basis of ceramic style, rather than contemporaneity based on stratigraphy or location within the fill of a particular feature.

Ceramic attributes recorded during the analysis, as well as tables presenting the raw ceramic data, are presented in Appendix C. The painted ceramics are summarized in Table 13. The results of the analysis of the unpainted body sherds are presented in Table 14. Characteristics of the seven reconstructible vessels are presented in Table 15.

Painted Ceramics

All painted ceramics from the El Macayo collection were assigned to typological categories based on the diagnostic attributes observable on the specimen (see Table C.1). Sherds were placed within Colton's (1955) ceramic series (see Table 13), proposed for the southern deserts, for three reasons: (1) most of the sherds fall into a category most readily labeled the Trincheras series, (2) Colton's series provide a framework within which to fit technological and regional categories of pottery, and (3) labeling red-on-brown pottery as part of the Santa Cruz series alleviates the problems associated with using the term Tucson Basin red-on-brown—that is, the potentially false implication that this pottery was manufactured only in the Tucson Basin. Hohokam Buff Ware is labeled Gila series pottery to follow this classificatory system. The only other formal group of painted pottery present in the collection is the San Simon series of red-on-brown pottery, which also falls neatly into Colton's classificatory system. During the analysis, a group of sherds was observed that resembled some types within the Santa Cruz series, but exhibited a consistent set of

Table 12. Summary of the Ceramic Collection from El Macayo, by Provenience

| Provenience | Painted | | Unpainted | | | | | | Total |
| | | | Textured | Plain | | | Red-Slipped | | |
	Sherd	Vessel	Body	Rim	Body	Vessel	Rim	Body	
General site									
Surface	1	—	—	—	—	—	—	—	1
Trench									
TR 343	6	—	—	7	27	—	—	—	40
Stripping units									
SU 56	38	—	—	12	116	—	—	1	167
SU 57	34	—	—	11	142	—	—	—	187
SU 80	6	—	—	4	33	—	—	—	43
SU 118	1	—	—	2	13	—	—	—	16
SU 122	6	—	—	11	65	—	—	—	82
Test pits									
TP 58	17	—	—	8	162	—	—	—	187
TP 60	34	—	—	20	384	—	—	—	438
TP 71	121	—	—	70	816	—	1	2	1,010
TP 103	47	—	—	23	328	—	—	—	398
TP 108	15	—	1	6	121	—	—	1	144
TP 291	26	—	—	10	288	—	—	—	324
Pit houses									
Feature 5									
Fill/roof fall	53	—	—	30	520	—	1	—	604
Posthole fill	11	—	—	5	123	—	—	—	139
Pit fill	5	—	—	1	66	—	—	—	72
Feature 15									
Floor	4	—	—	2	15	—	—	—	21
Posthole fill	3	—	—	—	13	—	—	—	16
Subfloor fill	11	—	—	6	87	—	—	—	104
Feature 16									
Fill	19	—	—	14	213	—	—	—	246
Floor	—	—	—	—	—	1	—	—	1
Posthole fill	2	—	—	2	11	—	—	—	15
Feature 42									
Fill	—	—	—	—	5	—	—	—	5
Floor groove fill	—	—	—	1	19	—	—	—	20
Feature 43									
Fill	1	—	—	1	2	—	—	—	4
Feature 44									
Roof fall	40	—	—	16	503	—	—	—	559
Floor	1	—	—	3	7	1	1	—	13
Hearth fill	—	—	—	—	3	—	—	—	3
Ash pit fill	—	—	—	—	1	—	—	—	1
Feature 139									
Fill	19	—	—	9	173	—	—	—	201
Feature 150									
Fill	9	—	—	5	56	—	—	1	71
Feature 212									
Posthole fill	21	—	—	12	225	—	2	—	260

| Provenience | Painted | | Unpainted | | | | | | Total |
| | | | Textured | Plain | | | Red-Slipped | | |
	Sherd	Vessel	Body	Rim	Body	Vessel	Rim	Body	
Pits									
Feature 45	1	—	—	—	—		—	—	1
Feature 50	5	—	—	2	64	—	—	—	71
Feature 51	6	—	—	1	174	—	—	—	181
Feature 53	2	—	—	1	48	—	—	—	51
Feature 55	1	—	—	—	10	—	—	—	11
Feature 69	—	—	—	—	24	—	—	—	24
Feature 73	—	—	—	—	4	—	—	—	4
Feature 74	—	—	—	—	2	—	—	—	2
Feature 78	2	—	—	1	10	—	1	—	14
Feature 80	—	—	—	—	4	—	—	—	4
Feature 105	1	—	—	—	8	—	—	—	9
Feature 112	16	—	—	6	186	—	—	—	208
Feature 144	14	1	—	3	176	—	—	—	194
Feature 178	2	—	—	2	56	—	—	—	60
Feature 179	3	—	—	4	44	—	—	—	51
Feature 203	1	—	—	—	14	—	—	—	15
Feature 208	4	—	—	—	14	—	—	—	18
Feature 210	4	—	—	1	49	—	—	—	54
Feature 216	—	—	—	—	19	—	—	—	19
Human burials									
Feature 31									
Trench backdirt	7	—	—	4	101	—	—	—	112
Feature 39									
Burial fill	1	—	—	—	34	—	—	—	35
Feature 40									
Burial fill	—	—	—	—	14	—	—	—	14
Feature 147									
Burial fill	—	—	—	1	2	—	—	—	3
Feature 151									
Burial fill	—	—	—	2	12	—	—	—	14
Disturbance	1	—	—	—	10	—	—	—	11
Funerary offering	—	—	—	—	—	3	—	—	3
Feature 156									
Burial fill	—	—	—	1	—	—	—	—	1
Feature 213									
Burial fill	2	—	—	4	41	—	—	—	47
Feature 214									
Funerary offering	—	—	—	—	—	1	—	—	1
Total	624	1	1	324	5,657	6	6	5	6,624

Table 13. Painted Ceramics from El Macayo

Ceramic Type	n	% of Subtotal	% of Total Painted
Local red-on-brown	32	80.0	5.1
Local black-on-red	5	12.5	0.8
Local black-on-brown	2	5.0	0.3
Local black-on-white	1	2.5	0.2
Subtotal	40	100.0	6.4
Gila Series			
Estrella Red-on-gray (incised)	1	1.3	0.2
Gila Butte Red-on-buff	2	2.6	0.3
Gila Butte or Santa Cruz Red-on-buff	8	10.4	1.3
Santa Cruz Red-on-buff	7	9.1	1.1
Sacaton Red-on-buff	12	15.6	1.9
Indeterminate red-on-buff	32	41.6	5.1
Indeterminate buff (no paint)	15	19.5	2.4
Subtotal	77	100.0	12.3
Santa Cruz Series			
Cañada del Oro Red-on-brown	16	6.6	2.6
Cañada del Oro or Rillito Red-on-brown	25	10.3	4.0
Rillito Red-on-brown	4	1.7	0.6
Rillito or Rincon, Style A Red-on-brown	5	2.1	0.8
Rincon Red-on-brown, Style B	2	0.8	0.3
Rincon Black-on-brown, Style B	3	1.2	0.5
Rincon Red-on-brown, Style B or C	4	1.7	0.6
Rincon Red-on-brown, Style C	6	2.5	1.0
Indeterminate Rincon Red-on-brown	40	16.5	6.4
Rincon, Style C or Tanque Verde Red-on-brown	11	4.5	1.8
Tanque Verde Red-on-brown	12	5.0	1.9
Tanque Verde Black-on-brown	1	0.4	0.2
Indeterminate Tucson Basin red-on-brown	113	46.7	18.1
Subtotal	242	100.0	38.8
San Simon Series			
Dos Cabezas Red-on-brown	1	20.0	0.2
Dos Cabezas or Pinaleno Red-on-brown	1	20.0	0.2
Encinas Red-on-brown	1	20.0	0.2
Indeterminate red-on-brown	2	40.0	0.3
Subtotal	5	100.0	0.8
Trincheras Series			
Trincheras Purple-on-red (specular)	129	49.6	20.7
Trincheras Purple-on-red (nonspecular)	100	38.5	16.0
Trincheras (Altar) Polychrome	12	4.6	1.9
Nogales Polychrome	13	5.0	2.1
Nogales Polychrome (white slip, purple paint only)	4	1.5	0.6
Nogales Polychrome (white slip, red paint only)	2	0.8	0.3
Subtotal	260	100.0	41.7
Total decorated	624	100.0	100.0

Table 14. Analyzed Unpainted Ceramics from El Macayo

Sherd Type	Unknown Red Ware	San Francisco Red	Type I Plain	Type II Plain	Type III Plain	Type IV Plain	Textured (Engraved)	Indet. Unpainted	Total
Rim sherds									
Bowls									
Hemispherical	5	—	1	3	—	—	—	—	9
Subhemispherical	1	—	12	22	1	—	—	—	36
Indeterminate	—	—	7	36	6	—	—	—	49
Jars									
Neckless	—	—	4	6	—	—	—	—	10
Flare-rim	—	—	10	25	3	—	—	—	38
Indeterminate	—	—	11	119	8	1	—	—	139
Other									
Beaker	—	—	1	—	—	—	—	—	1
Scoop	—	—	2	—	—	—	—	—	2
Miniature neckless jar	—	—	—	1	—	—	—	—	1
Indet. vessel form	—	—	4	40	—	1	—	—	45
Subtotal, rim sherds	6	0	52	252	18	2	0	0	330
Body sherds	4	1	16	512	25	4	1	259	822
Total	10	1	68	764	43	6	1	259	1,152

Note: Indeterminate unpainted = indeterminate plain ware in the database (see Appendix C). These sherds are too small to classify.

technological characteristics that distinguished them. These sherds were set aside, analyzed separately as a group, and labeled local ceramics (e.g., local red-on-brown).

Trincheras Series

Although this pottery is well represented in the archaeological record in northern Sonora and southern Arizona, it remains poorly described. In fact, a great deal of confusion surrounds the taxonomic nomenclature of the individual types within the series. Gladwin and Gladwin (1929b) first noted the distinctive purple-painted pottery during their survey of the Papaguería. They initially reported the Trincheras series pottery to be a variant of buff ware, which they termed Sonoran Red-on-buff (Gladwin and Gladwin 1929b:121). Shortly thereafter, Sauer and Brand (1931) encountered the purple-on-red and polychrome pottery during their survey of the (upper) Santa Cruz River valley. They referred to the pottery as Trincheras Ware, thus replacing the Gladwins' term in the literature (Sauer and Brand 1931:107–110). Withers (1941, 1973) provided type descriptions of the Trincheras pottery encountered during his excavations at Valshni Village. In 1955, Colton classified

the pottery within Mogollon Brown Ware and labeled it Trincheras series. This was apparently based on its coiled-and-scraped manufacturing technique as well as the polished-over design, and possibly its stylistic similarities with Mogollon Brown Ware painted ceramics.

Collections of Trincheras pottery have been recorded at several sites in southern Arizona and northern Sonora, including Paloparado (Di Peso 1956:316), La Playa (Johnson 1960, 1963), the Baca Float sites (Doyel 1977a:41–43, 60, 85), Nogales Wash (Jácome 1986:38), AZ DD:7:22 (Whittlesey 1992:39), and the Altar Valley survey (McGuire and Villalpando 1993).

Trincheras series pottery exhibits a great deal of technological and stylistic variability (Figures 31 and 32). Designs are executed in broad-line (see Figure 31a–g) and fine-line (see Figure 31h–o) styles, and show an affinity to Mimbres Mogollon and San Simon series pottery (Haury 1936; Sayles 1945). The series includes a bichrome, purple-painted type that may or may not have a red slip, a polychrome that has red paint in addition to the purple paint, and a polychrome that uses a white slip with purple and red paint. The purple paint can vary from a dull, low-luster purple to a highly specular, almost iridescent purple. Confusion surrounds the nomenclature of these types. Various

Table 15. Reconstructible and Whole Vessels from El Macayo

Characteristic	Vessel 151-1	Vessel 151-2	Vessel 151-3	Vessel 214-1	Vessel 16-1	Vessel 44-1	Vessel 144-1
Feature number	151	151	151	214	16	44	144.03
Feature type	inhumation	inhumation	inhumation	inhumation	pit house	pit house	pit
Context	funerary offering	funerary offering	funerary offering	funerary offering	floor	floor	fill
PD number	246	245	244	75	174	319	300
Catalog number	514	511	508	75	274	363	483
Completeness (%)	100	65	40	60	80	50	70
Ceramic type	Type I plain	Type I plain	Type I plain	Type II plain	Type I plain	Type II plain	local purple-on-tan
Interior finish	HS, fire cloud	HS, fire cloud	HS, fire cloud	HS, fire cloud	HS, fire cloud	HS	slip HS, fire cloud
Exterior finish	HS, fire cloud	HS, fire cloud	HS, fire cloud	HS, fire cloud	HS, fire cloud	HS, fire cloud	HS, fire cloud
Temper	sand	sand	sand	sand	sand	sand/mica, < 50% phlogopite mica	sand/mica, < 50% phlogopite mica
Vessel form	scoop	scoop	indeterminate	mini glob jar	scoop	flare-rim jar	subhem. bowl
Vessel part	n/a	n/a	base/body	rim/body	n/a	rim/body	rim/body
Rim form	direct	direct	indeterminate	slight flare	direct	mod flare	direct
Rim finish	variable	variable	indeterminate	variable	variable	rounded	rounded
Modification	none	none	none	none	none	none	burned
Sherd count	whole	2	1	4	1	10	25
Thickness (mm)	6	6	19	8	6	7	7
Exterior rim diameter (cm)	n/a	n/a	indeterminate	8	n/a	18	23
Interior rim diameter (cm)	n/a	n/a	indeterminate	7.5	n/a	17.3	22.3
Interior throat (cm)	n/a	n/a	indeterminate	5.8	n/a	15	n/a
Exterior throat (cm)	n/a	n/a	indeterminate	6.5	n/a	15.6	n/a
Max. body diameter (cm)	length = 15.2 width = 11.1	length = ? width = 9	indeterminate	12	length = 16 width = 8	38	20
Shoulder height (cm)	n/a	n/a	indeterminate	n/a	n/a	n/a	n/a
Rim height (cm)	n/a	n/a	indeterminate	0.9	n/a	1.8	0
Neck height (cm)	n/a	n/a	indeterminate	1.2	n/a	2.5	n/a
Total height (cm)	7	4.5	4.7	9.8	4.7	indeterminate	7
Volume (ml)	375	indeterminate	indeterminate	indeterminate	indeterminate	indeterminate	indeterminate
Use wear	minimum basal abrasion, interior	none	none	minimum basal abrasion, exterior	none	minimum basal abrasion, exterior	none
Comments	vessel repatriated to Tohono O'odham Nation	vessel repatriated to Tohono O'odham Nation	vessel repatriated to Tohono O'odham Nation	vessel repatriated to Tohono O'odham Nation			quartered design with large, interlocking scrolls

Key: HS = hand smoothed; n/a = not applicable; SP = striated polish; subhem. = subhemispherical

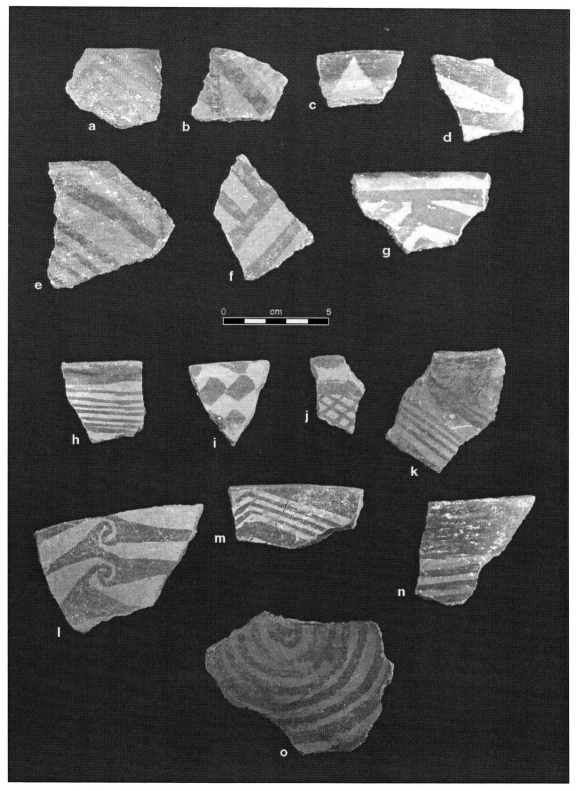

Figure 31. Examples of Trincheras Purple-on-red pottery from El Macayo:
(a–g) broad-line style, (h–o) fine-line style.

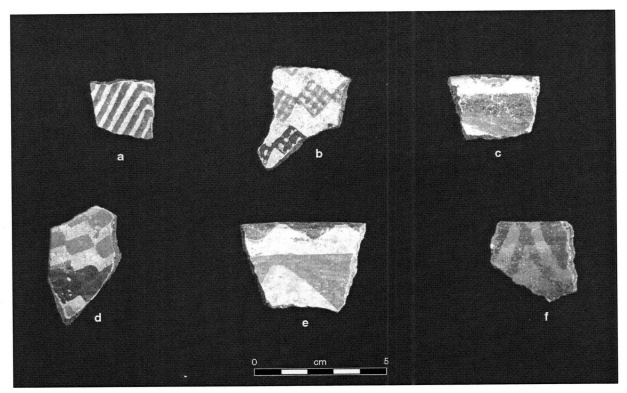

**Figure 32. Examples of Trincheras series polychrome pottery from El Macayo:
(a–e) Nogales Polychrome, (f) Trincheras (Altar) Polychrome.**

type names have been used by different researchers. The result has led to the use of different type names for the same type, as well as the same type name for different types. The typological analysis of the El Macayo collection uses Trincheras Purple-on-red to refer to the bichrome, Trincheras Polychrome to refer to the purple-and-red-painted pottery without a slip, and Nogales Polychrome to refer to the white-slipped pottery with purple and red paint.

Trincheras Purple-on-red

Trincheras Purple-on-red (see Figure 31) is a coarse-sand-tempered and scrape-finished brown ware, characterized by dark, purplish brown paint on a brown to red background. The El Macayo collection contains 229 sherds of this type (see Table 13). The sample exhibits the technological and stylistic variability previously described for this type. The variability in surface color alone has been used by some authors to describe separate pottery types. The greatest proliferation of types was generated by Di Peso (1956) at Paloparado. He separated sherds with a tan base color (Nogales Purple-on-red) from those with a red-slipped background (Trincheras Purple-on-red). Di Peso (1956:361) also defined a type, Ramanote Purple-on-red, that was technologically the same as Trincheras Purple-on-red except for

polishing over the paint and the "crude" execution of the design. Whittlesey (1992:41) split the type into two variants by labeling the red-slipped sherds Trincheras Purple-on-red and the unslipped sherds Trincheras Purple-on-brown. Although the presence or absence of a slip is an important technological aspect of the manufacturing process, the low frequency (n = 37) of sherds exhibiting a red slip precludes definition of a separate type. Instead, the presence or absence of a slip is recorded under surface treatment for each Trincheras Purple-on-red sherd (see Table C.2).

The variability in the paint on Trincheras Purple-on-red has been attributed to technological factors. Di Peso (1956:361), Withers (1973:37), Whittlesey (1992:41) and McGuire and Villalpando (1993:37) recorded specular and nonspecular paint variants of Trincheras Purple-on-red. Several researchers have suggested that grinding the specular hematite to a fine powder, polishing over the painted decoration, or a combination of the two will reduce the specular quality of the paint (Di Peso 1956; Johnson 1960; McGuire and Villalpando 1993; Withers 1973). In the collection of Trincheras Purple-on-red from El Macayo, there appears to be no correlation between nonspecular paint and polishing. An equal number of specular and nonspecular painted decorations are polished over. This suggests that the mineral composition (i.e., iron content and particle size) or the process of grinding the pigment may contribute more to the specular or nonspecular quality of the paint observed by researchers than polishing over the paint.

Vessel Form

The relative proportion of bowl to jar sherds in the collection of Trincheras Purple-on-red sherds from El Macayo is 113 to 116. This nearly equal ratio mirrors Jácome's (1986) findings at the Nogales Wash site. At surveyed or excavated sites in the Altar Valley and Magdalena River valley, the suggested production area for the Trincheras pottery (see Johnson 1960:66), jars outnumber bowls by 3 to 1 (see Gladwin and Gladwin 1929b; Johnson 1960; McGuire and Villalpando 1993; Sauer and Brand 1931). Conversely, sites in southern Arizona that have Trincheras series pottery exhibit the opposite bowl-to-jar ratio. Although Withers (1973) does not quantify the bowl-to-jar ratio, he reported that the great majority of vessels are bowls. Whittlesey (1992:41) indicated that 76 percent of the identifiable sherds were from bowls.

This incongruity recorded for vessel forms may contribute to the interpretation of exchange practices as they pertain to proximity and access to production sources. Whittlesey (1992) suggested that the high ratio of bowls at Arivaca may be a by-product of practical issues related to exchange; that is, bowls are much easier to transport farther distances from the production source than jars. If this hypothesis is correct, then we would expect a decrease in the number of jars as the distance from the production area increases. This may explain the documented regional disparity of bowl-to-jar ratios discussed above. The low frequency of bowls relative to jars in the assumed production area may indicate that bowls were produced largely for the purpose of exchange or export.

Surface Treatment

The exterior surface finish on the Trincheras Purple-on-red jar sherds from El Macayo is striated or uniformly polished on 96.4 percent (n = 107) of those sherds with discernible attributes, whereas the interiors are scraped or wiped on 81.1 percent (n = 90). The El Macayo bowl sherds exhibit striated or uniform polished interiors and exteriors on 93.7 (n = 104) and 94.6 (n = 105) percent, respectively. The application of a red slip was observed on 16.2 percent (n = 37) of the Trincheras Purple-on-red sherds; when present, the slip is a deep terra-cotta red. A great deal of variability was observed in the surface color of the unslipped Trincheras Purple-on-red sherds. The color ranges from a rusty orange or terra-cotta red to a dark or creamy brown.

Design

Little documentation exists on the design universe employed on Trincheras Purple-on-red. The designs are usually constructed of geometric elements with fine- and broadline work. Design elements include crosshatched and solid squares and diamonds, solid triangles pendent from the rim interior and exterior on both jars and bowls, and interlocking scrolls rendered in both positive and negative form. Banded and quartered designs have been documented (see Di Peso 1956:Plate 99a and 99b). The El Macayo collection exhibits all of these design characteristics.

The variability in designs and motifs exhibited on Trincheras Purple-on-red may eventually lead to better temporal refinement within the type. For instance, several of the Trincheras Purple-on-red sherds illustrated by Whittlesey (1992:Figure 14a–h) show striking similarities with the Dos Cabezas, Pinaleño, and Galiuro Red-on-brown sherds illustrated by Sayles (1945:Plates XX–XXII). The ceramic collection from Arivaca, based on associated ceramics, has a strong Colonial component (Whittlesey 1992), which places the occupation of the site within the general period when Dos Cabeza, Pinaleño, and Galiuro Red-on-brown were produced. Previous research indicates that the presence of Trincheras Purple-on-red ceramics is associated with Colonial and, to a lesser degree, Sedentary period Hohokam ceramics (Deaver 1984:370, 1989a:174; Di Peso 1956; Haury 1950; Jácome 1986; Whittlesey 1992; Withers 1973).

Nogales Polychrome (Trincheras Polychrome)

Sauer and Brand (1931:109–110) provided the first description of this type, labeling it Polychrome Trincheras ware. Withers (1941:40–42) used the type name Trincheras Polychrome at Valshni Village. Di Peso (1956:362) called it Nogales Polychrome at Paloparado, as did Jácome (1986:42–44) at the Nogales Wash site, Whittlesey (1992:42) at AZ DD:7:22, and McGuire and Villalpando (1993:39) on their Altar Valley survey. Nogales Polychrome is the preferred name following recent precedents and to avoid confusion with Trincheras (Altar) Polychrome, described below.

Nogales Polychrome has a paste and temper identical to Trincheras Purple-on-red. The type is distinguished by the application of a creamy white slip over the design field and the addition of red paint along with the purple pigment (see Figure 32a–e). Nogales Polychrome (n = 19) constitutes 3 percent of the entire painted ceramics and 7.3 percent of the Trincheras series ceramics in the El Macayo collection. All of the Nogales Polychrome sherds represent bowls. However, 6 of the 19 sherds typed as Nogales Polychrome exhibited either red paint on a white slip (n = 2) or purple paint on a white slip (n = 4). These sherds are small and are presumed to be Nogales Polychrome, based on their technological similarities to sherds that exhibit all three colors (n = 13).

Trincheras Polychrome (Altar Polychrome)

A considerable amount of confusion surrounds the name for this type, because it has been applied to two types of painted pottery. Withers (1941, 1973:47–48) originally defined the type, referring to it as Altar Polychrome. Di Peso (1956:362) and later Johnson (1960) labeled the type Trincheras Polychrome. At Nogales Wash, Jácome (1986:46) refers to the type as Altar Polychrome. This name also was used by McGuire and Villalpando (1993:39). Whittlesey (1992:42–44) chose the label Trincheras Polychrome based on its taxonomic similarities to Trincheras Purple-on-red. Although the rules of taxonomic nomenclature favor Altar Polychrome, Trincheras Polychrome is preferred because of the technological similarities and apparent chronological contemporaneity with Trincheras Purple-on-red. Trincheras Polychrome differs from the purple-painted bichrome only by the incorporation of red paint into the design (see Figure 32f). None of the El Macayo sherds has a red slip applied to the surface. In total, 12 sherds, all from jars, were recovered. Trincheras Polychrome makes up 1.9 percent of the total painted ceramics and 4.6 percent of the Trincheras series (see Table 13). The designs present on the Trincheras Polychrome sherds in the El Macayo collection favor broad zigzag and barbed purple lines, with thinner, straight red lines. Most of the sherds are too small for the overall design layout to be discerned.

Santa Cruz Series

Colton (1955) classified the Tucson Basin red-on-brown ceramic sequence under the Santa Cruz series, within Mogollon Brown Ware. This was largely based on Kelly et al.'s (1978) work at Hodges Ruin. The Tucson Basin red-on-brown ceramic sequence is now typically identified as a regional expression of the Hohokam ceramic tradition. Nevertheless, Colton's Santa Cruz series label was used in this report because these ceramic types were produced along portions of the Santa Cruz River and its tributaries not only in the Tucson Basin, but also apparently in areas outside the basin. At El Macayo, these types are most likely trade wares, although their point of origin cannot be specifically ascribed to the Tucson Basin or surrounding areas. Subsequent temporal and stylistic refinement of the series can be attributed to several researchers (Danson 1957; Deaver 1984; Doyel 1977b; Greenleaf 1975; Wallace 1986).

The published type descriptions of Deaver (1984), Doyel (1977a), Kelly et al. (1978), and Wallace (1986) were followed in the sherd classification. Deaver's (1984) classification of design styles within Rincon Red-on-brown (Styles A, B, and C) was used rather than Wallace's (1986) temporal classification (early, middle, and late) (see Heck-

man and Whittlesey 1999 for a discussion of the two methods). Those sherds lacking sufficient stylistic attributes to be confidently classified to a specific type were identified to more general descriptive categories incorporating two sequential types (e.g., Cañada del Oro or Rillito Red-on-brown; Rincon Style C or Tanque Verde Red-on-brown). Sherds exhibiting technological attributes consistent with the Santa Cruz series, but too small to reveal design attributes, were identified at the ware level only (e.g., indeterminate Tucson Basin red-on-brown).

In the El Macayo collection, Santa Cruz series sherds were almost as common (n = 242) as Trincheras series pottery (n = 260) (see Table 13). The identified types represent the Colonial, Sedentary, and Classic periods of the Tucson Basin cultural phase sequence (Figures 33–35), a period of time spanning 400 years or more. The Santa Cruz series sherds identified at El Macayo exhibit the same technological and stylistic developments documented for these types to the north at Tucson Basin sites. The Colonial period is represented by Caada del Oro Red-on-brown (see Figure 33a–e, h–k) and Rillito Red-on-brown (see Figure 33f, g). These sherds are tempered with a crushed granitic gneiss as is typical for Colonial period Tucson Basin pottery (Deaver 1984, 1988a:147,151, 1989a:172; Heidke 1988: 396). The designs are close emulations of the analogous Gila River series types Gila Butte Red-on-buff and Santa Cruz Red-on-buff (Haury 1937, 1976). The Sedentary and Classic periods are represented by Rincon Red-on-brown (see Figure 34) and Tanque Verde Red-on-brown (see Figure 35), respectively. In the Tucson Basin, there are important technological changes in pottery at the beginning of the Sedentary period (Deaver 1984, 1989b) that are also seen on the Rincon Red-on-brown at El Macayo. The changes that are sweeping the Tucson Basin reach at least as far south as El Macayo. In contrast to the Colonial period types, the Sedentary and Classic period red-on-browns are sand tempered and exhibit greater variation in technical qualities and design execution (compare Figure 34 with Figure 35). One of the outstanding characteristics of the Sedentary period Santa Cruz series pottery is the technological innovation in the pottery craft resulting in the production of red wares, polychromes, and black-pigmented bichromes (Deaver 1984, 1989b) in addition to the red-pigmented bichromes. Two sherds of the black-pigmented ceramic type Rincon Black-on-brown were also identified (Figure 36).

Generally, the sherds classified here as Santa Cruz series would not be technologically or stylistically aberrant if found on any other site farther downstream along the Santa Cruz or in the Tucson Basin. The pots that these sherds represent may have been manufactured at any number of locations, including El Macayo. The actual production source of these sherds will remain unknown until there is additional petrographic and detailed chemical analyses.

Figure 33. Examples of Santa Cruz series Colonial period red-on-brown pottery from El Macayo:
(a–e, h–k) Cañada del Oro Red-on-brown, (f–g) Rillito Red-on-brown.

Figure 34. Examples of Santa Cruz series Rincon Red-on-brown pottery from El Macayo.

Figure 35. Examples of Santa Cruz series Tanque Verde Red-on-brown pottery from El Macayo.

Figure 36. Santa Cruz series Rincon Black-on-brown pottery from El Macayo.

Local Painted Ceramics

In the El Macayo collection, 40 sherds exhibit technological attributes that distinguish them from previously defined types. These sherds are easily distinguished from the well-polished, paddle-and-anvil-finished ceramics represented by the Santa Cruz series and the coiled-and-scraped ceramics of the Trincheras series, although they seem to show affinities to both series. The evidence indicates that vessels were coiled and hand modeled without benefit of the scraping tool or the paddle and anvil. Surface finish is variable. They resemble one another in ceramic paste and other technological characteristics. These ceramics are thought to represent locally produced ceramics that were influenced by northern Santa Cruz series and southern Trincheras series traditions. This, however, has not been evaluated empirically. There is no direct evidence that these presumably local ceramics were, in fact, made at or near El Macayo.

Local Red-on-brown

This category is represented by 32 sherds (Figure 37, see Table 13). A great deal of technological consistency was observed in these red-on-brown sherds (see Appendix C). A coil-and-hand-modeling method of construction was evident on most of the sherds. In general, the bowl exteriors were poorly smoothed prior to tool polishing; coil joints are often visible in the low, unfinished areas. The paste is orange-brown with no slip evident on any of the El Macayo specimens. A sand temper containing varying amounts of

gold mica was used. The red, hematite paint was watery, sometimes poorly bonded, and very thinly applied.

The designs show strong stylistic similarities with Rincon Red-on-brown (compare Figure 37 with Figure 34). Paneled and plaited straight-line designs utilizing rectilinear and curvilinear scrolls, fringe, and solid triangular elements are common. All of the bowl sherds have an interior design. The execution of the design is sloppy and poorly done when compared with Rincon Red-on-brown. Five sherds exhibit stylistic characteristics analogous with those associated with the middle Rincon phase in the Tucson Basin. Nine sherds that were large enough to reveal the design show an "openness" of the design field characteristic of the later part of the Rincon phase. Greenleaf (1975:60) described a late variant of Rincon Red-on-brown at Punta de Agua. Deaver (1984:262) defined Rincon Style C as the stylistic transition between Rincon Style B and the Classic period ceramic style. Wallace (1985:121, 1986:53) also discussed a late Rincon Red-on-brown as "providing the perfect bridge between middle Rincon and Tanque Verde Red-on-brown" (Wallace 1985:121).

Given the stylistic parallels between the local red-on-brown and the middle to late stylistic developments of Rincon Red-on-brown, it is quite possible that this local red-on-brown represents the precursor to Di Peso's (1956:321–323) Ramanote Red-on-brown. The local red-on-brown pottery from El Macayo shares several attributes with Ramanote Red-on-brown, as described by Di Peso. The watery paint and poorly executed designs on Ramanote contrast with Tanque Verde Red-on-brown in the same

Figure 37. "Local" red-on-brown pottery from El Macayo.

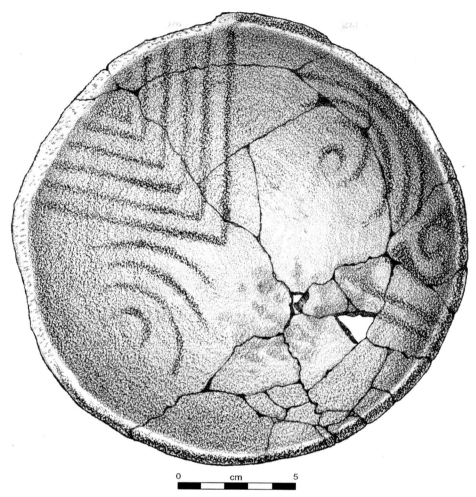

Figure 38. "Local" purple-on-tan bowl (Vessel 144-1) from El Macayo.

manner that the local red-on-brown contrasts with Rincon Red-on-brown at El Macayo. An inspection of the Potrero Creek ceramic collection at ASM revealed that several sherds typed as Rincon Red-on-brown conform in every way to the local red-on-brown recovered from El Macayo. This observation indicates that these apparently local red-on-brown sherds do not represent a phenomenon peculiar to El Macayo.

Local Purple-on-tan

The paste of the partial purple-on-tan bowl (Vessel 144-1) (Figure 38) from Feature 144.03 is identical to the paste of those sherds labeled local red-on-brown (see Appendix C). It is a reddish brown clay with a sand temper containing small amounts of phlogopite mica. The difference is in the paint color and the presence of a slip on the purple-on-tan vessel.

A coil-and-hand-modeled construction technique is implied by the presence of coil joints in the recessed, unpol-

ished areas of the bowl exterior. The interior surface of this bowl has a cream or tan slip and is relatively well polished. The exterior surface is not slipped and is unevenly polished. The interior of the bowl was painted with a powdery specular hematite. The design may have been done in a quartered layout with poorly executed, curvilinear, interlocking scrolls in each quarter. The specular hematite pigment, design motifs, and layout are reminiscent of Trincheras Purple-on-red.

Previous work in Nogales at AZ EE:9:68 by Reinhard (1978) revealed several cremations. Two vessels, each associated with a cremation, were described as local variants of Trincheras Purple-on-red (Reinhard 1978:237). These vessels correspond closely with the purple-on-tan vessel found at El Macayo.

Local Black-on-red

Five sherds from two bowls of a heretofore unidentified black-on-red pottery were recognized in the collection (see

Figure 39. "Local" black-on-red bowl sherd from El Macayo.

Appendix C). The temper is composed of sand with quartz and small amounts of phlogopite mica. These sherds are unique within the El Macayo collection in some technological aspects. The vessel walls are uniform in thickness and well finished. All of the sherds have an interior and exterior red slip. The slip is hard and is highly polished. The slip, in color and appearance, has affinities to the Santa Cruz series red ware (Rincon Red) as well as Papaguería red wares (e.g., Sells Red and Valshni Red). The surface treatment differs on the two bowls represented. The subhemispherical bowl (Figure 39) exhibits zonal polishing striations around the painted surfaces. The other sherd is polished over the paint.

The paint is a dark, blackish brown, mineral pigment. Both vessels have interior designs. The subhemispherical bowl is large enough to provide information about the design structure. These sherds have a thin line painted midway down the interior of the vessel, with large, solid diamonds centered along the band at regular intervals. This simple banded design is similar to Trincheras Purple-on-red, although the elements may be unique.

Local Black-on-brown

Two sherds were placed in this category based on the black paint used in the design. Unfortunately, these sherds are too small to offer any further identification other than their technological similarity with the local red-on-brown sherds. The use of the black pigment is suggestive that these sherds may be local copies of Rincon Black-on-brown.

Local Black-on-white (cf. Santa Cruz Polychrome)

A single bowl sherd, with an interior design, was placed in this category (Figure 40a). This sherd has a crazed, white-slipped interior surface decorated with a black paint. The interior surface is well polished, whereas the exterior surface is not. In general, it is technologically similar to Santa Cruz Polychrome except for the presence of phlogopite mica within the sand temper and the use of only black paint rather than both black and red pigments. The sherd is too small to provide any information about the overall design or for one to conclude that it is not a polychrome. The characteristics of this sherd also correspond to Danson's (1946:29–30) description of Canelo Brown-on-yellow, which he suggested was related to Santa Cruz Polychrome.

Gila Series

The Gila series represents Hohokam Buff Ware as defined by Haury (1937:169–229). The pinkish red paste and the distinctive schistose tempering material made it easily distinguishable from the red-on-browns in the El Macayo collection. Hohokam Buff Ware has a limited frequency at El Macayo (see Table 13). Most sherds are not identifiable to specific types, but exhibit technological attributes consistent with buff ware pottery (Haury 1937, 1976). Even though there are only a few buff ware sherds (n = 77), those that are typeable (n = 30) represent a long period of time. The identified types at El Macayo represent the middle

Figure 40. Miscellaneous sherds from El Macayo: (a) "local" black-on-white
(cf. Santa Cruz Polychrome), (b) Estrella Red-on-gray (incised), (c) unknown engraved
brown ware, (d) Dos Cabezas Red-on-brown, (e) Encinas Red-on-brown.

Pioneer, Colonial, and Sedentary periods. This time period overlaps with that indicated by the Santa Cruz series, but extends back to the middle Pioneer period (A.D. 650–675), as indicated by the presence of Estrella Red-on-gray (incised) (see Figure 40b). Examples of Colonial and Sedentary period buff ware sherds are shown in Figure 41.

San Simon Series

The San Simon series was originally defined by Sayles (1945) based on his work at San Simon Village. The series falls within the rubric of Mogollon Brown Ware (Colton 1955). A total of five sherds were classified to this series. One sherd (see Figure 40d) was identified as Dos Cabezas Red-on-brown (Sayles 1945:42). Another was classified as either Dos Cabezas or Pinaleño Red-on-brown based entirely on the presence of thinner line work. This is a typological ambiguity and does not represent a transitional piece (see Whittlesey et al. [1994:68] for a discussion on collapsing the two types into a single broad-line red-on-brown). A third sherd (see Figure 40e) was identified as Encinas Red-on-brown (Sayles 1945:32). Two other sherds

were identified within the series, based on their technological attributes, but are too small to be identified as to type.

Plain Ware Ceramics

The variability found in the plain ware ceramics of the Santa Cruz River valley has long posed typological problems for researchers. Kelly et al. (1978:69) described the plain ware at Hodges Ruin as "too diverse to be included under one caption." Greenleaf (1975:54) expressed the same frustration at Punta de Agua. Di Peso (1956:297–300) used the type-variety approach to describe plain ware and defined type names for plain ware ceramics encountered at Paloparado. Some researchers have attempted to quantify the variation found within the plain ware ceramics of the Santa Cruz River valley without the inherent constraints of a type-variety classificatory label. The alternative approach has been to record technological variation among the collection of sherds and to identify natural patterns in this variation. This strategy has been used by Deaver (1984),

Figure 41. Gila series Hohokam Colonial and Sedentary period red-on-buff pottery from El Macayo:
(a–h) Santa Cruz Red-on-buff, (i) Sacaton Red-on-buff.

Wallace (1985), Heidke (1986), Jácome (1986), and Whittlesey (1987), among others. The plain ware at El Macayo exhibits the same diversity observed by other researchers for plain wares within the Santa Cruz River valley. This analysis uses a descriptive typological approach similar to that followed by Deaver (1984), Wallace (1985), Heidke (1986), Jácome (1986), and Whittlesey (1987). The objective was to define typological categories that represent natural patterns in the plain ware technology. In the following discussion, these site-specific technological and descriptive types are correlated with previously defined plain ware types and their associated cultures.

Plain ware is a subclass of unpainted pottery (see Table 14). These are sherds that exhibit no evidence of surface decoration of any kind—no painting, no texturing, and no slipping. Among the unpainted ceramics sampled from El Macayo, 557 body sherds and 324 rim sherds are identified as plain wares. The following discussion of plain wares is based on this sample of sherds. The remainder of the unpainted ceramics are either red wares or textured, both of which are described separately below. The sherds were

divided into four categories, Types I–IV, based on observed technological variation. Sherds smaller than a quarter dollar were lumped together as indeterminate unpainted. The rim sherd sample includes all rims that were recovered from the excavations at El Macayo (see Table C.4). The body sherd sample derives from a collection of 822 unpainted body sherds from TP 71 (see Table C.5). These 822 body sherds represent a sample of approximately 10 percent of the unpainted body sherds. Of the unpainted body sherd sample from TP 71, 259 sherds are classified as indeterminate unpainted, because they are too small for reliable classification. These indeterminate unpainted body sherds are not considered in the following discussions or in calculating the relative proportions of the plain ware types to one another.

Type I (Local)

The sherds, reconstructible vessels (Vessels 151-2, 151-3, 16-1), and whole vessel (Vessel 151-1) in the Type I category are distinguished by a hand-modeled construction

Figure 42. Type I plain ware trough-shape vessel from El Macayo (Vessel 16–1).

technique. This method of construction leaves the interior and exterior of the vessels unfinished, with extremely irregular surfaces (Figure 42). The paste may have been derived from an alluvial soil, which is characterized by a high organic content and homogeneity of the nonplastic inclusions. The paste color is dark brown to grayish brown on some of the burned specimens. The tempering consists of small, gravel-size, angular quartz particles approximately 1–2.5 mm in size. Based on this "expedient" ceramic technology, and the general presumption that most plain ware is locally produced, the Type I plain ware is inferred to represent a local manifestation. Type I makes up 3 percent of the plain ware body sherds and 16 percent of the rim sherds (see Table 14). Four of the seven reconstructible or whole vessels from the El Macayo excavations are Type I plain ware (see Table 15).

A wide variety of vessel forms is represented in the rim sherds and vessels (see Table 14). Vessel forms represented in the rims include bowls (subhemispherical and hemispherical), jars, neckless jars, beakers, and scoops. The

bowl-to-jar ratio (1 to 1.3) in the Type I rim sherds indicates a relatively equal proportion of bowls and jars. Three out of the four Type I vessels are simple scoop forms; one is a long, narrow, trough-shaped vessel (see Figure 42). The remaining Type I vessel is indeterminate as to vessel form.

Type II (Local)

Type II plain ware is a heterogeneous lot of pottery. This type is distinguished from Type I based on the use of a more uniformly textured sand temper and better-smoothed surfaces. The paste is light brown to orange-brown, soft and friable to medium hard, and subangular. The potters used a sand temper, with abundant quartz and varying amounts of phlogopite mica, probably derived from an igneous or metamorphic parent material. The gravel temper so evident in Type I is absent in Type II plain ware. The surface finish is variable. Hand-smoothed surfaces have an uneven, sandy feel. Those sherds from tool-polished vessels also are uneven, and coil joints were observed in the low, unpolished areas. Several sherds exhibit what appear to be anvil marks on the interior. These characteristics indicate that some of these sherds originated from vessels constructed using a coil-and-hand-modeling technique similar to Type I; whereas other sherds originated from vessels probably constructed by the paddle-and-anvil technique. These latter sherds, in general, have a uniform tool-polished exterior surface finish. Although this category of plain pottery is generally better manufactured and finished than Type I, there appears to be a continuum between Types I and II.

Type II is the largest plain ware category, making up 92 percent of the plain ware body sherds and nearly 78 percent of the rim sherds (see Table 14). Two reconstructible vessels, a miniature jar (Vessel 214-1) and a flare-rim jar (Vessel 44-1), were placed in the Type II category (see Table 15). As with Type I, a wide variety of vessel forms was identified in the Type II rim sherds. These include bowls (subhemispherical and hemispherical), jars, neckless jars, and miniatures. The jar rim sherds outnumbered the bowl rim sherds by a ratio of 2.5 to 1.

The El Macayo Type II plain ware closely resembles, technologically, Di Peso's (1956:297–300) description of Ramanote and Paloparado plain wares. No attempt was made to separate the sherds representing coiled-and-scraped, hand-smoothed vessels (e.g., Ramanote Plain) from those exhibiting tool polishing (e.g., Paloparado Plain). The Type II category includes sherds exhibiting both finishing techniques, as well as a minority of sherds exhibiting evidence of paddle-and-anvil construction. Di Peso's distinction between Ramanote and Paloparado Plain has been questioned by some researchers as representing intratype variability that may relate to functional differences (Brown and Grebinger 1969:190). It was extremely difficult to separate, with any confidence, these two manufacturing techniques in the sample from El Macayo. An attempt to do so would have left most of the material in an indeterminate category. Two Type II sherds are coiled and scraped in the same manner and have scored interiors similar to the Type III plain ware.

Type III (Trincheras Plain)

Type III plain ware should be considered synonymous with Trincheras Plain. This is the companion plain ware to the Trincheras Purple-on-red and Nogales Polychrome pottery. Type III is distinguished from Types I and II by a coiled-and-scraped finish evidenced by obvious scoring on the interior of jars. The paste and temper are the same as those used to make Trincheras Purple-on-red. This type makes up 4 percent of the body sherds and nearly 6 percent of the rim sherds (see Table 14). The possibility that

these sherds represent undecorated portions of Trincheras Purple-on-red vessels cannot be ignored, nor can it be demonstrated.

Type IV (Gila Plain)

The Type IV plain ware corresponds to the published descriptions of Gila Plain (Haury 1937, 1976). This highly micaceous pottery exhibits polishing striations and fire clouds, thus distinguishing it from the other plain ware encountered in the sample. This type makes up less than 1 percent of the body sherds (n = 4) and less than 1 percent of the rim sherds (n = 2) (see Table 14).

Other Ceramic Wares

Red Ware

The inventoried and analyzed red ware from the El Macayo collection numbers only 11 sherds (see Tables 14 and C.3). This sample includes two sherds from the unpainted body sherd sample from TP 71, three sherds discovered during the analysis of the painted sherds, and six sherds included in the sample of unpainted rim sherds. Given the small number of sherds and the haphazard character of the sampling, these sherds may not be representative of the total range of variation in the red wares.

These sherds exhibit a great deal of technological heterogeneity. Only one sherd was assigned to a specific type, San Francisco Red. The identification was based on the presence of interior and exterior deep red slip and a highly lustrous polish. The paste of this sherd was similar to that for the San Simon series red-on-browns. The remaining red ware was classified as "unknown red ware." These sherds are highly variable and do not conform to any previously described red ware types. All have sand or sand with mica temper. All but one of these sherds are bowls. The bowl sherds have interior and exterior polished red slips, and the jar sherd has an exterior slip only. Slips exhibit allover, uniform polishing or striated polishing. Three of these sherds have a paste similar to that of the Type II plain ware, which suggests that these may be local red wares.

Textured Ware

A single jar sherd with exterior texturing was observed among the ceramic collection (see Figure 40c). This sherd was extracted from the collection during the preliminary sorting and counting of the ceramic collection and is not part of the analyzed sample of unpainted body sherds from TP 71. The sherd is small. The textured pattern consists of a series of closely spaced parallel vertical lines engraved on the exterior of the vessel immediately below the neck. It is clear that the texturing was done after firing. Because there are no known analogues for engraved ceramics from southern Arizona, this sherd may derive from a southern Mexican pottery tradition. Sauer and Brand (1931:111) described a "crudely incised ware" found throughout northeastern Sonora. They never explicitly stated whether the "incisions" were made before or after firing, but the El Macayo sherd fits their description.

Concluding Remarks

The El Macayo ceramics represent a heterogeneous collection that spans a significant period. The identified painted pottery types indicate occupation during the A.D. 650–1150 period. The presence of ceramics representing the Gila River, Trincheras, Tucson Basin, and northern Mexican culture areas suggests a great deal of regional interaction through all phases of the occupation. Locally manufactured, painted ceramics appeared sometime during the Sedentary period (e.g., the red-on-brown sherds with stylistic affinities to Rincon Red-on-brown). The identification of these locally produced ceramics is based primarily on their distinctive technological attributes. The stylistic expressions on the local ceramics appear to be closely related to the "intrusive" types (e.g., Rincon Red-on-brown and Trincheras Purple-on-red). The possibility that these local ceramics represent a "hybrid" of ceramic traditions should be considered (for a detailed discussion of local adoption of a foreign ceramic tradition, see Zedeño 1994).

The plain ware from El Macayo is technologically diverse. Several manufacturing techniques were employed. Archaeologists in the Southwest generally assume that plain wares were produced at a household level, largely for personal consumption. Archaeologists also assume that manufacturing technology is a conservative tradition passed on from one generation of potters to another. Should these assumptions be true, the plain wares suggest that the residents of El Macayo were ethnically diverse. The hypothesis of ethnic coresidence could also explain the diversity found in the painted ceramics. Unfortunately the nature of the deposits, as mixed, at El Macayo preclude us from identifying distinctive ceramic associations that may be further evidence of ethnically distinct groups occupying the same settlement.

Stone Artifacts

Anthony Della Croce

The goals of the lithic analysis were to (1) describe the flaked and ground stone collections recovered from the 1996 excavations at El Macayo, (2) obtain information about flaked stone manufacture and use at the site, and (3) provide temporal and cultural information about the site. Lithic technological evidence, in the form of reduction strategies and raw-material selection, stylistic attributes, and the functional interpretation of formal tools, was used to address broader issues of cultural affiliation and subsistence activities at the site.

The 1996 lithic artifact collection from El Macayo includes 1,343 pieces of debitage, 16 cores, 234 pieces of shatter, 22 tools (hammer stones and bifaces), and 608 ground stone artifacts (including ornamental beads), totaling 2,223 items (Table 16). All of the flaked stone tools and ground stone artifacts were examined, but the debitage was sampled. Of the 1,343 pieces of debitage collected, 762 pieces (57 percent) from selected test pit, pit structure, and pit proveniences were analyzed.

Of the three archaeological projects at El Macayo, the data recovery program in 1996 by SRI recovered the largest number of stone artifacts (see Gardiner and Huckell 1987, Slawson 1991). Further, because few prehistoric archaeological sites in the upper Santa Cruz River valley have been investigated, the lithic collection from this long-lived village site provided an important opportunity for observing potential differences in the manufacture and use of flaked and ground stone artifacts relative to other localities. In particular, we wanted to know if the stone artifacts from El Macayo could shed light on the cultural affinity of its residents as members of the Trincheras or Hohokam culture.

Methods

Flaked stone and ground stone artifacts were analyzed separately. Flaked stone artifacts were sorted first as either debitage or tools. Debitage was subsequently sorted as either unmodified flakes, shatter, or cores. Tools were sorted as bifacially flaked artifacts (bifaces, projectile points) or as "other" tools (drills, scrapers, knives, hammer stones, etc.). Ground stone artifacts were sorted as either utilitarian or nonutilitarian items. Thereafter, class-specific observations were made on each lithic category. All of the data recorded for each flaked stone core and tool are presented in tables in this chapter. Summary data are presented for the debitage and shatter (see Tables D.1 and D.2, for additional information) and for the ground stone artifacts (see Table D.3).

Flaked Stone Analysis

Given the relatively small number of flaked stone items selected for analysis (n = 762), individual flake analysis (IFA) was used to classify the collection. This method was favored over mass analysis (or flake aggregate analysis [FAA]), because it provides a more detailed characterization of the reduction method (e.g., hard hammer, soft hammer, bipolar) and the reduction strategy (primary, secondary, or tertiary). Reduction method and strategy, as well as stylistic variability inherent in formal tools, are useful attributes for describing patterned variation among lithic artifacts (at both the intersite and intrasite levels) and are best discerned by recording a series of flake attributes rather than only a few attributes.

When lithic collections are small or when the research questions demand the level of detail provided by IFA, IFA is the preferred analytic method. With IFA, each flake is examined for a number of morphological and technological characteristics that can be used profitably to address questions of subsistence orientation and cultural affiliation, among other topics.

Table 16. Summary of Stone Artifacts from El Macayo, by Provenience

Provenience	Flaked Stone					Ground Stone	Total
	Bifaces	Cores	Debitage	Shatter	Tools		
General site							
Surface	—	—	—	—	—	1	1
Stripping units							
SU 56	—	—	6	—	—	2	8
SU 57	—	—	20	—	—	5	25
SU 80	—	—	—	—	—	3	3
SU 118	—	—	—	—	—	3	3
SU 122	—	—	1	—	—	5	6
Test pits							
TP 58	—	—	31	—	—	1	32
TP 60	—	—	87	17	—	—	104
TP 71	1	6	163	73	1	6	250
TP 103	1	—	62	18	2	2	85
TP 108	—	—	31	6	1	1	39
TP 291	—	—	68	—	1	—	69
Pit houses							
Feature 5							
Fill/roof fall	2	2	115	43	—	1	163
Posthole fill	—	—	144	—	1	—	145
Subfloor pit fill	—	—	4	3	—	—	7
Feature 15							
Floor	—	—	3	—	—	—	3
Posthole fill	1	—	6	—	—	—	7
Subfloor fill	—	—	19	—	—	—	19
Feature 16							
Fill	—	—	27	10	1	2	40
Posthole fill	—	—	5	—	—	—	5
Feature 42							
Floor groove fill	—	—	2	—	—	—	2
Feature 44							
Roof fall	1	1	80	28	—	4	114
Floor	—	—	—	—	5	52	57
Ash pit fill	—	—	2	1	—	—	3
Feature 139							
Fill	1	—	2	—	—	—	3
Floor	—	—	—	—	—	1	1
Feature 150							
Fill	—	—	37	—	—	—	37

Provenience	Flaked Stone					Ground Stone	Total
	Bifaces	Cores	Debitage	Shatter	Tools		
Feature 212							
Posthole fill	—	—	129	—	1	2	132
Pits							
Feature 50	—	—	10	5	—	—	15
Feature 51	—	1	37	5		1	44
Feature 53	—	2	15	5	—	—	22
Feature 55	—	—	5	—	—	—	5
Feature 73	—	—	3	—	—	—	3
Feature 74	—	—	1	—	—	—	1
Feature 78	—	—	4	—	—	—	4
Feature 80	—	—	5	—	—	—	5
Feature 105	—	—	8	—	—	—	8
Feature 112	—	3	43	8	—	1	55
Feature 144	—	1	43	3	1	2	50
Feature 178	—	—	6	3	—	1	10
Feature 179	—	—	16	6	—	—	22
Feature 208	—	—	10	—	—	1	11
Feature 210	—	—	25	—	—	—	25
Feature 216	—	—	6	—	—	—	6
Human burials							
Feature 31							
Trench backdirt	—	—	24	—	—	2	26
Feature 40							
Fill	1	—	3	—	—	—	4
Feature 151							
Fill	—	—	7	—	—	—	7
Rodent disturbance	—	—	3	—	—	—	3
Funerary offering	—	—	—	—	—	508	508
Feature 156							
Funerary offering	—	—	—	—	—	1	1
Feature 213							
Fill	—	—	24	—	—	—	24
Nonhuman burials							
Feature 186							
Fill	—	—	1	—	—	—	1
Total	8	16	1,343	234	14	608	2,223

In contrast, when lithic collections are large, time is limited, or research questions are more general, FAA is appropriate. With FAA, fewer attributes (such as size distribution, flake shape, and raw material) are recorded. The results of FAA have been successfully applied to the study of lithic reduction strategies at a site, flake distribution, and even taphonomic processes occurring at given sites. Additionally, the results of FAA tend to be more empirical or "interpretation-free" (e.g., size sorting) than IFA, because attributes such as flake type, cortical coverage, or edge damage are somewhat subjective and can vary from one lithic analyst to another (see Ahler 1989 for a full discussion of FAA).

The individual flake attributes recorded for debitage were raw-material type (sourcing and procurement strategies), exterior cortical coverage (reduction intensity), size (reduction intensity), flake type (reduction strategy), striking platform type (reduction strategy), flake completeness (reduction technique), heat damage, and evidence of utilization (subsistence). These attributes were selected as the most informative traits for determining flaked stone reduction strategies at the settlement. Tools, defined as those flaked stone artifacts exhibiting secondary retouch, were sorted into two categories: bifaces and other tool forms. At El Macayo, the bifacial category comprised projectile points and bifaces, while the "other" category included scrapers, hammer stones, knives, and drills. In general, projectile points are the most culturally diagnostic class of flaked tools and were used at El Macayo, as elsewhere, for making inferences about cultural affiliation. The sample of other flaked tools (n = 5, excluding hammer stones) was too small to address questions concerning subsistence activities.

Morphological attributes of bifaces (e.g., notching, base type, and metric data) were used to compare these tools with bifaces typical of the Hohokam and Mogollon traditions. In addition, raw material used in the production of bifaces was recorded to help distinguish local items from exchange items. Steepness of edge angle was an important attribute recorded for scrapers, given that edge angle can be correlated with different subsistence tasks. Finally, the weight of hammer stones was recorded as an indicator of lithic reduction strategy because of the possible relationship between hammer stone mass and primary versus secondary reduction techniques (Whittaker 1994).

Ground Stone Analysis

The ground stone collection was analyzed primarily for information on subsistence. Attributes related to morphology or intensity of use were recorded for each artifact. Morphological traits recorded included overall artifact shape, raw-material type, presence of pigments, and evidence of heat treatment, modification, or damage. Evidence of intensity of use included texture of the use surface, degree of manufacture and use-related shaping, and any indication that the item had been used multiple times.

Ground stone artifacts unrelated to subsistence activities also were recovered from El Macayo. These are referred to as "nonutilitarian" ground stone and are potentially sensitive to stylistic variation indicative of cultural affiliation. These items were classified on the basis of morphology and were compared with similar artifacts found at Hohokam and Trincheras sites.

Results

Descriptive results are listed in tabular form for each analytical class. Interpretations from these data, as they apply to particular research topics, are offered for each table. Flaked stone debitage, cores, and shatter are used to infer lithic reduction strategies. Flaked stone tools are used to address cultural affiliation. Ground stone items can shed light on subsistence and cultural affiliation. Table 16 provides counts of the lithic artifacts recovered from El Macayo. These counts are summarized in Table 17.

Flaked Stone

Debitage

The data in Table 18 indicate that the debitage retrieved from the 1996 excavations at El Macayo is typical of the "expedient flake reduction technology" found throughout the Southwest (Parry and Kelly 1987). High percentages of relatively small, whole, tertiary flakes (i.e., with little or no cortex) with single-faceted platforms suggest a cultural preference for the manufacture of unmodified flakes as functional implements. As with previous investigations at El Macayo, the 1996 debitage analysis revealed a common pattern of on-site core reduction to produce flakes (Gardiner and Huckell 1987; Slawson 1991).

The debitage from El Macayo contrasts with debitage recovered in Tucson Basin Hohokam sites in one important aspect. El Macayo produced a relatively high percentage of bifacial-thinning flakes in contrast to Tucson Basin sites. This class of debitage is often found in very small amounts at Hohokam sites from other regions. The decrease from the Archaic to the Formative period in the production of bifacial-thinning flakes has been correlated with a decreased reliance on hunting and an increasing commitment to agriculture (Schott 1986).

Table 17. Summary of the Lithic Collection

Major Class & Subclass	n	%
Flaked stone		
Debitage (sampled)	762	46
Shatter	234	14
Core	16	1
Biface	8	1
Other tools	14	1
Subtotal	1,034	63
Ground stone		
Utilitarian	92	6
Nonutilitarian	516	31
Subtotal	608	37
Total	1,642	100

Additionally, five pressure flakes were identified. Pressure flakes are rarely found at Formative period sites. It is possible that more-abundant and better-quality chert was available in the Nogales areas and that prehistoric knappers were able to produce more-refined tools as a consequence of this resource opportunity.

Despite evidence of bifacial reduction at El Macayo, it was not reflected in the number or variety of bifaces recovered. None of the bifaces collected from the site differs significantly in form from those recovered in the Tucson Basin. Those that do differ are small and probably were manufactured from a single flake. The use of flakes rather than cores to manufacture bifaces suggests that less time was expended in the manufacture of projectile points. It is difficult to reconcile this finding with the fact that large bifacial-thinning flakes—often associated with the manufacture of more-complex tool forms—were recovered in the collection.

Table 18. Attributes Recorded on Debitage from El Macayo

Attribute	n	%	Attribute	n	%
Flake type			Completeness		
Primary	47	6	Whole	419	55
Secondary	91	12	Split	43	6
Tertiary	404	53	Proximal	82	11
Bifacial thinning	37	5	Distal	40	5
Pressure flake	5	1	Fragmented	178	23
Indeterminate	178	23	Total	762	100
Total	762	100			
			Size		
Cortical coverage			1–3 cm	219	29
0%	561	74	3–5 cm	428	56
1–90%	151	20	5–7 cm	90	12
90%	50	6	7–10 cm	25	3
Total	762	100	10–15 cm	—	—
			Total	762	100
Platform type			Utilization		
Cortical	96	13	Utilized	39	5
Single facet	388	51	Unutilized	723	95
Double facet	9	1	Total	762	100
Multifaceted	9	1			
Bifacial thinning	37	5	Heat		
Pressure flake	5	1	Heated	724	95
None	218	29	Not heated	38	5
Total	762	100	Total	762	100

Table 19. Debltage by Raw Material
and Edge Damage

Material	n	%	Edge Damaged	
			n	%
Aphanitic igneous	170	22	6	15
Chalcedony	5	1	1	3
Chert	364	48	22	56
Gypsum	2	< 1	—	—
Mineral quartz	9	1	1	3
Metamorphic	66	9	2	5
Phaneritic igneous	11	1	—	—
Quartzite	14	2	—	—
Rhyolite	114	15	7	18
Sandstone	4	< 1	—	—
Vesicular basalt	3	< 1	—	—
Total	762	100	39	100

Chert (48 percent) was the most common raw-material type identified in the 1996 El Macayo debitage sample (Table 19), followed by aphanitic igneous rock (22 percent), rhyolite (15 percent), and a variety of other rock types (15 percent). Interestingly, chert was recovered in higher percentages than typically encountered at Tucson Basin Hohokam sites. In contrast, the most common lithic manufacturing materials in the Tucson Basin are rhyolites and aphanitic igneous materials. The recovery of vesicular basalt debitage at El Macayo is likely the result of ground stone manufacture.

The frequency of edge damage covaried with the frequency of raw-material type: the most frequently encountered raw-material types (chert, rhyolite, and aphanitic igneous rock) were also those most extensively used. These cherts and igneous rocks likely were obtained from riverbeds emanating out of the nearby Patagonia, Tumacacori, and Santa Rita Mountains (Drewes 1972). In general, raw-material selection indicates that local lithic resources were preferred over those derived from farther away—a pattern that seems to be typical of the Formative period throughout southern Arizona.

Cores

As with the debitage sample, rhyolites, various igneous rocks, and cherts made up most of the material types in the collection of cores (Table 20). The reduction activities, as reflected by directionality, size, and weight, appear to have been extensive. More than half of the cores weighed less than 100 g or showed multidirectional flake removal. In addition, cores were used repeatedly to produce flakes; few specimens had fewer than three flakes removed from them.

This pattern of intensive use of raw materials differs from those patterns seen at other Formative period sites in the Southwest. Generally, cores at Hohokam sites exhibit less-intensive use. The high intensity documented at El Macayo may be a result of the high quality of the lithic material rather than the shortage of adequate local material. This, however, is a tentative hypothesis, as the sample size is small (n = 16).

Shatter

Shatter was analyzed to assist in the identification of raw materials and reduction technologies used at the settlement. Raw-material percentages generally mirror the patterns observed in the debitage and cores (Table 21). The high ratios of unmodified flake debitage to shatter (greater than 3:1) and of secondary and tertiary flakes to primary flakes (nearly 10:1) at El Macayo suggest that the initial stage of stone tool manufacture (i.e., primary reduction) took place at locations some distance from the pit house features.

Hammer Stones, Bifaces, and Other Flaked Tools

The 14 flaked stone tools and eight bifaces listed in Table 16 were classified by the flaked stone reduction technology used in their manufacture. These include nine hammer stones (shaped through use), eight bifacially retouched pieces, and five unifacially retouched pieces. In the following discussion, the unifacial and bifacial tools are described functionally as knives, drills, scrapers, and projectile points.

The nine hammer stones recovered from El Macayo (Table 22) are neither culturally distinctive nor functionally diagnostic. They are, however, large and heavy. All nine weighed more than 300 g, and five weighed well over 500 g. Such large hammer stones are usually employed for the removal of large flakes (Whittaker 1994), although this notion is based primarily on present-day experimental studies. Five hammer stones, all weighing more than 400 g, were recovered from the floor of Feature 44, possibly indicating a lithic reduction or tool storage area.

Two unifacially flaked artifacts are classified as scrapers (Figure 43d, e; see Table 22). These are steep-sided, and one has noticeable protrusions. These may have been used in plant-processing activities. Alternatively, as Jobson (1986) has shown, such tools are ideal for the butchering of small mammals, particularly rabbits. The steep-sided "working end" of these implements quite effectively severs ligaments and muscle from bone. A third tool, made from a triangular chert flake, is classified as a scraper/drill (see Figure 43c). The pointed tip exhibits flaking that may have resulted from

Table 20. Attributes Recorded for Cores

PD No.	Size Class [a]	Material	Type	Flake Scars (n)	Use Wear?	Weight (g)	Comments
74	2	rhyolite	flake core	5	no	64.1	
74	> 3	rhyolite	flake core	4	no	76.3	
74	> 3	rhyolite	multidirectional	> 5	no	324.4	failed
78	2	rhyolite	multidirectional	> 5	no	53.2	exhausted
78	> 3	chert	unidirectional	2	no	151.8	failed
73	> 3	quartzite	unidirectional	2	no	117.4	
134	2	aphanitic igneous	unidirectional	> 5	no	64.7	
134	> 3	chert	unidirectional	2	yes	47.7	
219	2	chert	unidirectional	3	yes	35.2	
258	> 3	chert	multidirectional	> 5	no	39.2	
286	> 3	phaneritic igneous	multidirectional	3	no	198.1	
286	> 3	chert	multidirectional	> 5	no	204.9	heavy rind
294	> 3	aphanitic igneous	unidirectional	3	yes	115.0	
177	> 3	rhyolite	multidirectional	4	no	120.1	
177	> 3	quartz	unidirectional	3	no	50.6	
177	2	chert	multidirectional	> 5	no	19.3	exhausted

Key: PD = provenience designation
[a] Size classes are as follows: 1 = 0–1 cm; 2 = 1–2 cm; 3 = 2–3 cm.

Table 21. Shatter by Raw Material

Material	n	%
Aphanitic igneous	73	31
Chalcedony	3	1
Chert	127	54
Mineral quartz	2	1
Metamorphic	2	1
Phaneritic igneous	3	1
Rhyolite	15	7
Vesicular basalt	9	4
Total	234	100

Table 22. Characteristics of Flaked Stone Tools from El Macayo

PD No.	Tool Type	Material	Retouch Method	Length of Retouched Margin (mm)	Heat Treated?	Length (cm)	Width (cm)	Thickness (cm)	Weight (g)
293	drill	chert	bifacial	1–5	no	3.3	0.8	0.6	1.7
110	hammer stone	quartzite	n/a	n/a	no	n/a	n/a	n/a	324.7
297	hammer stone	quartzite	n/a	n/a	no	n/a	n/a	n/a	826.8
106	hammer stone	quartzite	n/a	n/a	no	n/a	n/a	n/a	908.1
312	hammer stone	quartzite	n/a	n/a	no	n/a	n/a	n/a	521.8
316	hammer stone	quartzite	n/a	n/a	no	n/a	n/a	n/a	931.8
324	hammer stone	mineral quartz	n/a	n/a	no	n/a	n/a	n/a	447.6
314	hammer stone	quartzite	n/a	n/a	yes	n/a	n/a	n/a	412.4
313	hammer stone	quartzite	n/a	n/a	no	n/a	n/a	n/a	615.7
464	hammer stone	quartzite	n/a	n/a	no	n/a	n/a	n/a	683.2
194	knife	chert	bifacial	1–5	no	4	1.1	1	4.3
169	scraper	rhyolite	unifacial	> 5	no	5.3	3.9	2.1	44
107	scraper	chert	unifacial	> 5	no	4.7	3.8	2.1	41.3
78	scraper/drill	chert	unifacial	1–5	no	3.5	2	0.8	5

Key: n/a = not applicable; PD = provenience designation

Figure 43. Flaked stone tools from El Macayo:
(a) knife (Catalog No. 208),
(b–c) drills (Catalog Nos. 171 and 87),
(d–e) scrapers (Catalog Nos. 272 [d] and 123 [e]).

use as a drill. The opposite end has been unifacially retouched, creating a steep-angled, slightly concave edge.

Two other flaked tools were recovered (see Figure 43a, b; see Table 22). A long sliver of chert has bifacial retouch along one margin and is interpreted as a knife (see Figure 43a). The other tool is a long, thick, bifacially retouched piece of chert that is interpreted as a drill (see Figure 43b). The cortex remains along the full length of one side.

Eight artifacts were recovered that are classified as projectile points (Figure 44; Table 23). All were finished items. Two are merely tip fragments. Seven were made from chert, and the other from a translucent chalcedony. The points recovered from El Macayo appear to have been produced from single flakes. None were produced from biface preforms. All are small, and none resemble Archaic projectile points. These points demonstrate variability in manufacturing technique and quality of workmanship. Most of the points appear to have been manufactured expediently. This is characteristic of collections from Formative period sites in the Southwest. Three of the projectile points shown in Figure 44 (a, b, e) were rather crudely made. The other three points (see Figure 44c, d, f) and the two biface fragments not illustrated (see Table 23) exhibit better-quality workmanship. The blade of one projectile point (see Figure 44a) was shaped by unifacial retouch, but the stem and base were shaped using bifacial retouch. Crudely retouched and unifacially retouched projectile points were observed among

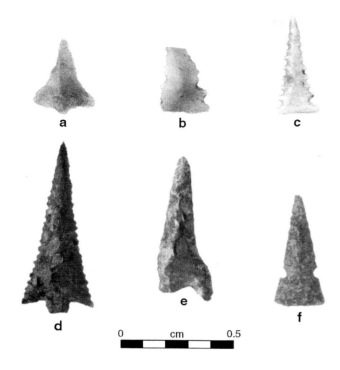

Figure 44. Projectile points from El Macayo: (a) Catalog No. 468, (b) Catalog No. 343, (c) Catalog No. 88, (d) Catalog No. 196, (e) Catalog No. 240, (f) Catalog No. 311. Note that Catalog No. 468 is unifacially flaked and all others are bifacially flaked.

those recovered at middle Formative period sites in the Santa Rita Mountains (Rozen 1984:475, 479).

Traditionally, projectile points have been used as culturally diagnostic artifacts. Although this is a small collection, it exhibits a wide variety of forms. Five "types" are evident. Similar points have been found at sites in the Santa Rita Mountains (Rozen 1984), the Tucson Basin (Kelly et al.

1978), and at Snaketown (Haury 1976; Sayles 1937), and, as such, most of the projectile points can be classified as "Hohokam." Several of the salient characteristics are triangular serrated blades (see Figure 44b–d), straight and concave bases (see Figure 44b, c, e, f), and short stems (see Figure 44a, d).

The projectile point shown in Figure 44a is interesting in its crudeness and expediency of manufacture. As noted above, it is essentially a triangular-shaped flake that has been minimally retouched. In its stylistic characteristics, it is analogous to Rozen's (1984:475–479, Figure 5.11a–m) Type 1 point. A similar style of points has been found at other sites in the Tucson Basin (Kelly et al. 1978:90, Figure 6.6j, l, Figure 6.7a–d, i–l) and at Snaketown (Sayles 1937: Plate XCIa). These points are found most often in Colonial period deposits (ca. A.D. 800–950) (Rozen 1984:479).

The projectile points shown in Figure 44 (b, c) show similar stylistic characteristics, but are technologically quite different. Both points have triangular serrated blades with straight bases. One point (see Figure 44b) is a triangular flake that has been minimally retouched; the other (see Figure 44c) appears to have been shaped more carefully. They are stylistically analogous to Rozen's (1984:480–481, Figure 5.12a–i) Type 3. Similar styles also have been found at Snaketown (Haury 1976:Figure 14.39b; Sayles 1937:Plate LXXXVe–h).

The projectile point shown in Figure 44d is more formally manufactured than the others. Of particular note, it has a formal stem. The base of the stem has snapped off, and we cannot be sure of the shape, but with the narrow stem and long triangular blade, it recalls proto-Mogollon and Mogollon point styles (Haury 1986:175, Figure 9.14; Wheat 1955:127–130, cf. Figure 9f). This point is also similar to Rozen's (1984:483, Figure 5.12q) Type 10 style, but the latter does not have a serrated blade. Other points of similar style have been found at Ventana Cave (see Haury

Table 23. Characteristics of Bifaces and Projectile Points

PD No.	Type	Material	Notch	Base	Length (cm)	Width (cm)	Thickness (cm)	Weight (g)	Comments
134	biface	chert	n/a	n/a	1.7	1.4	0.4	0.7	tip, manual break
105	biface	chert	n/a	n/a	0.9	1.5	0.3	0.4	tip, use break
78	point	chalcedony	n/a	flat	2.2	0.9	0.2	0.2	Hohokam style
135	point	chert	stemmed	concave	3.5	1.2	0.6	1.1	Hohokam/Mogollon style
189	point	chert	n/a	concave	3	1.2	0.5	1.4	Hohokam style
219	point	chert	n/a	n/a	1.5	1.1	0.3	0.4	Hohokam style
255	point	chert	side notched	flat	2.5	1.1	0.3	0.5	Desert Side-notched style
235	point	chert	stemmed	concave	1.7	1.3	0.3	0.4	Hohokam style

Key: n/a = not applicable; PD = provenience designation

1950:297, Plate 22) and at Snaketown (cf. Haury 1976: Figure 14.39h; Sayles 1937:Plate XCIf). Although the point style is suggestive of a Mogollon heritage and is clearly stylistically different from the other five points illustrated in Figure 44, it cannot be unequivocally classified as a Mogollon point.

The projectile point shown in Figure 44e is also crude. This specimen appears to be asymmetrical, but the shape may be the result of breakage and reworking. It is similar to a point style identified at Snaketown (Haury 1976:Figure 14.39i). This point may have originally had two tangs, one of which has broken off, on either side of a short stem. The example from Snaketown also shows a similar breakage pattern.

The final projectile point style (see Figure 44f) is loosely referred to as the Desert Side-notched style. It is similar to Rozen's (1984:480–481, Figure 5.12j) Type 4 style. This style is characterized by side-notched, triangular blades and straight, concave, or convex bases. This style became more common in the later part of the Sedentary period, perhaps after A.D. 1000, and persisted through the Classic period until about A.D. 1450 (Kelly et al. 1978:90–91, Figure 6.6a–d). Similar examples are found at most sites of comparable age throughout the Southwest. This style is so widespread and generalized that it is not culturally diagnostic.

Discussion

The flaked stone artifacts recovered from El Macayo are consistent with what would be expected from a Middle Formative period site. Prehistoric knappers manufactured flaked stone tools expediently; few items were formally retouched. The principal tool was an unmodified flake removed from a stone core derived from locally available materials. There is a slightly higher proportion of chert and other siliceious rocks in this collection than at sites in the Tucson Basin. This may simply be a reflection of the fact that these materials are slightly more abundant in the local fluvial gravels than elsewhere downstream. There is also evidence of a bifacial reduction technique among the debitage, but there were no finished tools that were manufactured using bifacial reduction. The projectile points exhibit a wide range of technical expertise. Some are minimally shaped, again reflecting expediency in their manufacture. Others, however, show a better command and control of the knapping methods. Regardless of the quality of the workmanship, the stylistic attributes are characteristic of point styles attributed to the Hohokam culture of southern Arizona. The conformity to stylistic modes appears to have been of greater importance than technical quality. Only one point is suggestive of a Mogollon stylistic tradition, but similar forms have been found at Hohokam sites elsewhere.

Ground Stone

In total, 608 pieces of ground stone were collected. This collection contains 46 utilitarian artifacts identifiable to a functional class, 9 utilitarian artifacts of unknown function, and 516 nonutilitarian artifacts (Table 24). In addition, 37 andesite spalls were found associated with a metate from Feature 44. Although no attempt was made to reconstruct this specimen, it is clear that these spalls were pieces of a single item of ground stone that detached when the pit house burned.

Utilitarian Ground Stone

Sixteen metates and two grinding slabs were recovered during the excavations. Nine of these were too fragmentary to classify to a specific type. The remainder were classified as trough metates (n = 1), basin metates (n = 4), grinding slabs (n = 2), and flat metates or grinding slabs (n = 2). Six metates came from the floor of pit house Feature 44: two flat metates or grinding slabs, three basin metates, and one trough metate with one end open. Only the trough metate has extensive signs of working and shaping. All of the metates and grinding slabs were made from fine- to medium-textured igneous rocks, including unspecified igneous rock

Table 24. Ground Stone Artifacts from El Macayo

Artifact Class & Type	n	Percentage by Class
Utilitarian ground stone		
Metate	16	17.4
Mano	24	26.1
Polishing stone	1	1.1
Axe	2	2.2
Grinding slab	2	2.2
Architectural	1	1.1
Indeterminate	9	9.8
Spall	37	40.2
Subtotal	92	100.1
Nonutilitarian ground stone		
Palette	2	0.4
Pendant	2	0.4
Bead	511	99.0
Pendant/bead preform	1	0.2
Subtotal	516	100.0
Total	608	

a   b

0   cm   5

**Figure 45. Three-quarter-grooved axes from El Macayo:
(a) Catalog No. 324, (b) Catalog No. 84.**

(n = 10), granite (n = 7), and andesite (n = 1). There is no indication of raw material preferences in the manufacture of particular types of metates or grinding slabs.

Twenty-four manos were recovered from the excavations. These are classified as hand stones (n = 1), basin manos (n = 9), probable mano (n = 9), flat mano/hand stone (n = 3), indeterminate mano/hand stone (n = 1), and indeterminate (n = 1). As with the metates, there was a preference for igneous stones—granite (n = 6) and unspecified igneous (n = 18).

Two three-quarter-grooved axes were recovered from the site (Figure 45). One was recovered from Feature 44 (see Figure 45a), and the other was found in TP 71 (see Figure 45b). The working bit of the axe from TP 71 is still quite sharp, as if it was not used before it was discarded. Also collected from TP 71 was an elongated rectangular stone that was pecked and polished on all six facets (Figure 46a). It may have been used for either polishing or hide processing.

Nonutilitarian Ground Stone

Three forms of nonutilitarian ground stone artifacts were recovered from El Macayo: palettes, beads, and pendants. Two palettes were recovered. One complete, unburned specimen (see Figure 46c) was recovered from the floor of Feature 139. It has a decorated raised border typical of Hohokam palettes (see Haury 1937). However, unlike typical Hohokam palettes, this artifact was fashioned from sandstone and not slate. It may be a local product. Regardless, it was manufactured and decorated in typical Hohokam fashion. The border is decorated with incised zigzag chevron motifs. The other palette was recovered from TP 71 (see

Figure 46b). Although it is much smaller (5.6 by 4.8 cm), it too has a raised border, although the border is undecorated.

In total, 511 beads were recovered from the 1996 excavations at El Macayo. All but three of these were found in a single inhumation burial (Feature 151) (Figure 47). All of the stone beads were made from argillite and are very small (all less than 4 mm in diameter, with most around 2 mm). Another similar argillite bead was recovered from the fill of Feature 144. All of the argillite beads appear to have been perforated by reaming with a thin, sharp object. Microscopic examination revealed a "rifling" scar in the hole of each bead.

Two other isolated beads were recovered at El Macayo. One is a turquoise disk bead similar to the argillite beads in form, but slightly larger (Figure 48b). This bead was recovered from the fill of a posthole in Feature 212. The other bead was a square, columnar bead recovered from TP 71 (Figure 48d). This bead is made of steatite and was biconically drilled.

Two pendants were recovered. A turquoise pendant (see Figure 48e) was found associated with the burial of a child, Feature 156. It was a flat pendant, ground to a subtriangular form. It was suspended by means of a perforation near the top. The other pendant was ground from a quartz crystal into a prismatic shape with an encircling groove near one end (see Figure 48c). The piece still retained some exterior cortex and, therefore, may be unfinished. This pendant was recovered from the backdirt of Trench 2 near two burials (Features 31 and 213) and two cremations (Features 1 and 2).

Finally, a worked piece of turquoise was recovered from Feature 112 (see Figure 48a). It is a small sub-triangular form similar to the turquoise pendant (see Figure 48e). It is ground and polished on both sides and on the edges, but is not perforated. It may be an unfinished bead or small pendant.

Discussion

The ground stone collection from El Macayo is small, and is dominated by artifacts recovered from only a few contexts. This collection, therefore, may not be representative of the ground stone assemblage for the settlement or for the region. The mano-metate milling set, the minimal shaping of metates, and the predominance of basin metates and grinding slabs suggest a milling technology geared toward the processing of small-grained plant resources, similar to subsistence practices during the earlier Archaic period. Coarse-textured, open-ended trough metates made from vesicular basalt are not represented. Most of the manos were classified as types suitable for basin metates (hand stones and basin manos). However, there were also many flat-bottomed, well-shaped examples (probable manos, flat mano/hand stone forms) that are typically associated with trough

Figure 46. Nonutilitarian ground stone artifacts from El Macayo:
(a) elongated, rectangular stone (Catalog No. 85), (b–c) palettes (Catalog Nos. 84 and 471).

metates rather than the convex-bottomed forms typically associated with basin metates. The presence of only one trough metate is perhaps the result of limited sampling or selective curation by the former residents of El Macayo when they abandoned the village or by those who came later. Given that Gardiner and Huckell (1987:23) recovered numerous examples of trough metates in their excavations at El Macayo, we suspect selective curation.

In the case of the other ground stone artifacts, the two palettes are characteristically Hohokam in their style. The three-quarter-grooved axes cannot be definitively assigned to the Hohokam, because Mogollon-style axes are also three-quarter grooved. The beads and pendants recovered do not have any stylistic attributes that are culturally diagnostic, but they do attest to patterns of exchange and the

acquisition of status or ornamental items. The argillite, the turquoise, and the steatite used for the square tubular bead are not locally available.

Conclusions

The principal goals of this analysis were to characterize the stone tool technology and to gather information that may inform on subsistence practices and the question of cultural identity. As noted, the flaked stone collection is standard with respect to most Formative period sites in the Southwest. The inhabitants of El Macayo practiced an expedient

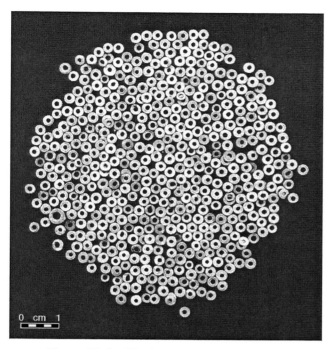

Figure 47. Argillite beads from Feature 151
at El Macayo.

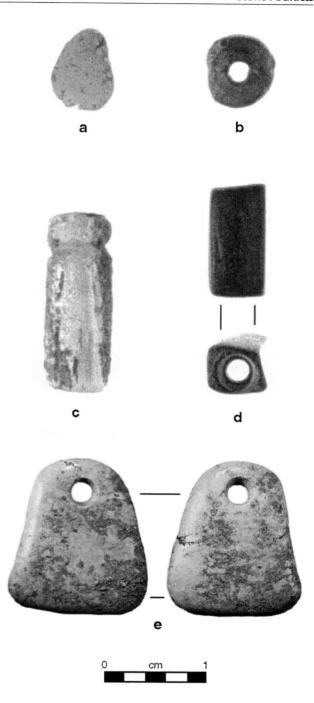

Figure 48. Nonutilitarian ground stone artifacts from
El Macayo: (a) turquoise bead or teseré (Catalog
No. 448), (b) turquoise disk bead (Catalog No. 710),
(c) crystal pendant or "plummet" (Catalog No. 290),
(d) rectangular, tubular steatite bead (Catalog No. 84),
(e) turquoise pendant (Catalog No. 525).

lithic technology utilizing unmodified or minimally modi-fied flakes as tools. There are more bifacial-thinning flakes present than expected at Formative period sites. This sug-gests that bifacial reduction was a component of the lithic tradition during the Formative period in the Nogales area. The use of bifacial-manufacturing technology, however, is not apparent in the finished tools. Consequently, its pres-ence may be a function of the slightly greater use of fine-grained cherts at sites south of the Tucson Basin than at contemporaneous sites to the north. This probably does not reflect a cultural preference, but rather the local geologic conditions and immediate access to these raw materials in the fluvial gravels of the Santa Cruz River. The variable character of the flaked stone tradition is clearly visible in the technology of the projectile points. Some points show a well-controlled knapping technique; others show little con-cern for technique, but emphasize the expedient production of a useful form of projectile point.

The stone tools suggest a diet consisting of milled grains (either cultivated or gathered) and hunted game charac-teristic of Formative period settlements. The morphology of the grinding implements suggests that there may have been an emphasis on the milling of small native grains in addition to the milling of maize.

The culturally diagnostic characteristics of the stone artifacts, particularly the projectile points, palettes, and axes, are few in number. With the exception of a single point that resembles a Mogollon-style projectile, most are similar to Hohokam artifacts in style. The relationship of these artifacts to stone artifacts of the Trincheras culture is unresolved.

FIVE

Shell Artifacts
Beads by the Hundreds

Sharon F. Urban

O nly a small number of excavations have been reported for the Nogales area, and few have produced prehistoric shell artifacts. Prior to data recovery at El Macayo, only four of the eight reported excavation projects in the area resulted in the recovery of shell (Grebinger 1971a; Jácome 1986; Reinhard 1978; Reinhard and Fink 1982). The 1996 excavations at El Macayo resulted in the recovery of 555 specimens, representing four shell genera, in the form of unworked shell, worked shell, ornaments, and utilitarian items. Most of the shell artifacts (n = 529) were beads associated with an infant burial (Feature 151). Shell artifacts were recovered from three excavation contexts: test pits, stripping units, and features. Although not large, the El Macayo collection is substantial in its relative size and diversity, and the total number of recovered items is far greater than that reported for any other site in the Nogales area.

Shell Identification

Genera and Sources

Of the four genera recovered from the 1996 excavations at El Macayo, only one is a freshwater variety—*Anodonta californiensis* (Table 25). Bequaert and Miller (1973:220–223) report that this edible variety of freshwater clam lives in free-flowing streams and is present in the Santa Cruz River. *Anodonta* shell typically measures 8 by 4 cm, is very thin, and exhibits a nacreous interior. When dry, the material is very fragile. Four pieces of this shell were recovered at El Macayo.

The three remaining genera are marine shell, likely derived from the Gulf of California. These three are *Glycymeris* sp., *Pecten vogdesi*, and *Spondylus princeps* (see Table 25). *Glycymeris* is a thick, orbicular shell commonly found in prehistoric sites of the Greater Southwest. Eighteen specimens were identified. Fanlike *Pecten* (scallop) was represented by one specimen, and spiny *Spondylus* (thorny oyster) was represented by two specimens. One of the *Spondylus* specimens was indistinguishable from a possible *Chama* shell.

In addition, 530 specimens could not be identified to a particular genera because artifact manufacture removed the distinctive attributes required to make a positive identification. These specimens are likely to be either *Glycymeris* or *Dosinia* (genus), judging from their sturdy nature and the identification of similar shell artifacts found elsewhere.

Artifact Types

The 555 shell specimens can be placed into one of four artifact classes: unworked shell, worked shell, ornaments, and utilitarian items (Table 26). Unworked shell has not been modified. Worked shell is any piece of shell that shows some evidence of human alteration, such as grinding, drilling, or cutting. Ornaments are finished shell artifacts that are presumably used for personal adornment. Finally, utilitarian items are finished shell artifacts that are presumably used for domestic functions.

Only one item was not worked. Five specimens were worked but are either fragmentary or unfinished. Five hundred forty-eight specimens were considered ornaments. Five types of ornaments were identified. Most were disk (n = 379) or bilobed (n = 151) beads (Figure 49). The

Table 25. Summary of Shell Genera Present at El Macayo, by Provenience

Provenience	Anodonta	Glycymeris	Pecten	Spondylus	Spondylus/Chama	Unknown	Total
TP 60	—	1	—	—	—	—	1
TP 71	—	3	1	—	1	—	5
TP 103	—	3	—	—	—	—	3
SU 57	1	—	—	—	—	—	1
SU 122	—	1	—	—	—	—	1
Feature 5	1	2	—	—	—	—	3
Feature 15	—	1	—	—	—	—	1
Feature 44	—	2	—	—	—	—	2
Feature 51	1	—	—	—	—	—	1
Feature 112	1	—	—	—	—	—	1
Feature 151	—	1	—	1	—	529	531
Feature 156	—	2	—	—	—	—	2
Feature 178	—	2	—	—	—	—	2
Feature 179	—	—	—	—	—	1	1
Total	4	18	1	1	1	530	555

Table 26. Shell Artifact Types, by Genera

Artifact Type	Anodonta	Glycymeris	Pecten	Spondylus	Spondylus/Chama	Unknown	Total
Unworked shell	1	—	—	—	—	—	1
Worked shell	3	1	1	—	—	—	5
Shell ornaments							
Bilobed beads	—	—	—	—	—	151	151
Disk beads	—	—	—	—	—	379	379
Bracelet	—	14	—	—	—	—	14
Bracelet/pendant	—	2	—	—	—	—	2
Pendant	—	—	—	1	—	—	1
Disk bead/pendant	—	—	—	—	1	—	1
Utilitarian shell							
Needle	—	1	—	—	—	—	1
Total	4	18	1	1	1	530	555

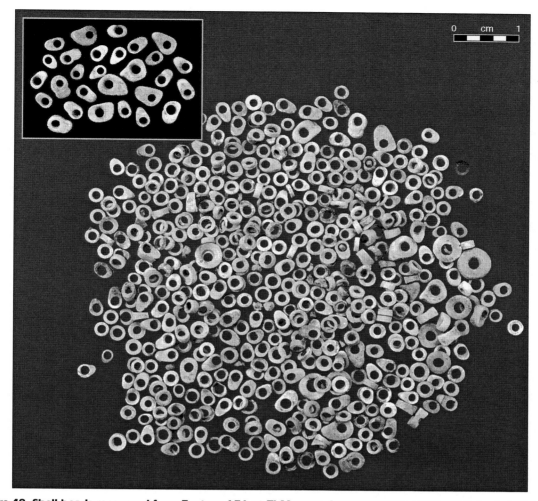

Figure 49. Shell beads recovered from Feature 151 at El Macayo. Inset provides detail of bilobed shell beads.

remaining specimens were bracelets (n = 14), bracelet/pendants (n = 2), pendants (n = 1), or disk bead/pendants (n = 1). Examples of bracelets and a bracelet/pendant are shown in Figure 50. Bracelet/pendants are artifacts that resemble bracelets, but are perforated on the umbo. These items could have been suspended from a cord and worn as a pendant, or worn as a bracelet with other items suspended from them. Also, one pendant was recovered from the excavations (Figure 51). Finally, one item was identified as a needle.

Presumably, shell bracelets were worn as wrist or upper arm circlets. The bracelets were further classified to specific types following Haury's (1976:313) typology. Type 1 bracelets have thin bands (width = 2.5–4.0 mm, thickness = 2.0–4.0 mm) and extensively reduced umbos. Four Type 1 bracelets were recovered. Type 2 bracelets are characterized by medium-width bands (width = 4.0–6.0 mm, thickness = 4.0–5.0 mm). At Snaketown, approximately half of the Type 2 bracelets were perforated (Haury 1976:313). Five Type 2 bracelets were identified in this collection. The

two bracelet/pendants identified in the collection have medium-width bands and may be perforated Type 2 bracelets. Type 3 bracelets have wide bands (width = 6.0–10.0 mm, thickness = 5.0–17.0 mm). Five Type 3 bracelets were identified in the collection. Two bracelets and one of the bracelet/pendants were complete (see Figure 50).

The Provenience of Shell Artifacts

Table 25 summarizes the contexts from which shell artifacts were recovered in the 1996 excavations at El Macayo. Nine specimens were recovered from three test pits, two specimens were located in two stripping units, and the remainder (n = 544) were retrieved from nine excavation features.

TP 60 produced one piece of shell, a Type 1 *Glycymeris* bracelet fragment. TP 71 yielded five pieces of shell that included one Type 2 and two Type 3 *Glycymeris* bracelet

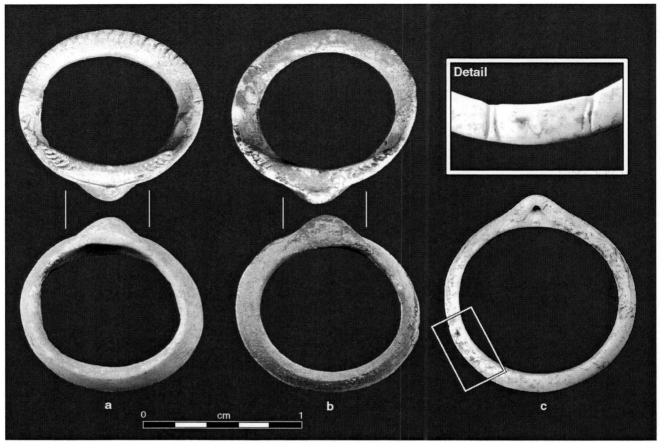

Figure 50. Shell bracelets and bracelet/pendant:
(a–b) Type 3 shell bracelets found on the upper arms of burial Feature 156 (Catalog Nos. 530 and 531)
(scale = 10 cm), (c) Type 2 shell bracelet/pendant from Feature 15, with detail of carving (Catalog No. 260).

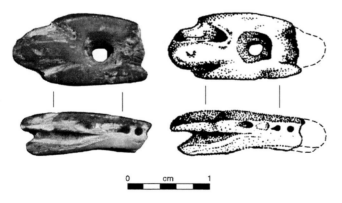

Figure 51. Bird/snake pendant from Feature 151
(Catalog No. 519).

fragments, one worked specimen of *Pecten vogdesi,* and one *Spondylus* or *Chama* disk bead or pendant. Finally, TP 103 yielded three pieces of shell—one Type 1 *Glycymeris* bracelet fragment, one Type 3 *Glycymeris* bracelet fragment, and one *Glycymeris* worked item that may have been a reworked bracelet fragment.

A single worked *Anodonta* shell was collected from the backdirt of SU 57. A Type 2 bracelet/pendant of *Glycymeris* shell was recovered from SU 122. The piece is crescent-shaped in plan; both ends were broken prehistorically, and no further modifications were attempted. The umbo was perforated.

Feature 5, a pit house, yielded three shell artifacts. One is a piece of worked *Anodonta* from the medial portion of the valve, which has cut and ground edges. The second specimen is a band section of a Type 2 *Glycymeris* bracelet. The last specimen is a *Glycymeris* needle, probably manufactured from a broken bracelet. One end is tapered from grinding and use wear. The opposite end is broken on the transverse axis; a V-shaped notch is visible.

Feature 15, a pit house, produced one shell specimen, a complete Type 2 *Glycymeris* bracelet/pendant with a drilled umbo (see Figure 50c). Two sets of two parallel lines (both U- and V-shaped grooves) are visible on the band.

Feature 44, a pit house, yielded two shell artifacts, both fragments of Type 2 *Glycymeris* medial-band bracelets.

A single piece of worked *Anodonta* was recovered from Feature 51, a pit. The sliver-thin specimen was removed from the body of the *Anodonta* shell and has one ground edge.

An unworked specimen of *Anodonta* shell was found in Feature 112.

Five hundred thirty-one pieces of shell were recovered from the excavation of a child burial, Feature 151. Of these, 529 pieces were shell beads (see Figure 49) recovered from deposits around and beneath the right lower leg of the child. These beads most likely were part of one or more anklets consisting of at least 151 bilobed beads (see detail in Figure 49) and 378 disk beads. Two other pieces of shell were recovered from the fill around and above the child's body and were not offerings placed with the child's remains. One of these pieces is a small fragment of the medial band of a Type 1 *Glycymeris* bracelet fragment. The other piece is a fragment of a pendant made from *Spondylus princeps* (see Figure 51). The pendant appears to have been constructed from the hinge or hinge tooth of the shell and has a biconical drill hole; the opening on the outer (convex) surface is larger than the opening on the inner (concave) surface. In plan view, the pendant appears to be the abstract form of a bird (cf. Haury 1976:Figure 15.17i) formed by cutting and grinding. The pendant has also been carved on the sides. In profile, the specimen resembles the head of a snake (see Figure 51).

Two complete Type 3 *Glycymeris* bracelets were found with another child burial, Feature 156 (see Figure 50a, b). Both bracelets were made from juvenile-age specimens, and are small and particularly suitable for a young child. One bracelet was found in situ on the upper right arm positioned just above the elbow. The other bracelet was recovered near the disturbed bones of the upper left arm and may have been in a similar position on the left arm (see Chapter 2).

Two *Glycymeris* bracelet fragments were recovered from Feature 178, a pit. Both are medial portions of the bands. One, a Type 1 bracelet, is grayish and heat-crazed on the exterior surface. The other specimen, a Type 2 bracelet, is an almost translucent gray-brown.

A white disk bead with a central, straight-sided perforation was recovered from Feature 179, a pit. The specimen is quite thin and has a perforation that is somewhat large for its overall size.

Discussion

Although small by southwestern standards, the shell collection from El Macayo is rather diverse in the number of genera and artifact forms. Aside from the 530 bilobed and disk beads from a single context (Feature 151), the 25 remaining specimens derive from four separate shell taxa and represent at least four artifact types. The relatively small size of the collection and the overall absence of unworked shell and manufacturing debris indicate that the prehistoric inhabitants were primarily consumers, rather than producers, of finished shell objects. Furthermore, none of the artifacts exhibit the elaborate and intricate workmanship seen on some artifacts found at larger settlements.

Artifact Identification

The presence of *Anodonta* indicates prehistoric use of locally available freshwater shell, in addition to marine shell. Two of the three marine genera (*Pecten vogdesi* and *Spondylus princeps*), although not rare, are uncommon in prehistoric sites of the Greater Southwest. *Glycymeris*, on the other hand, is recovered commonly from Formative period sites in the Southwest. Unusual at El Macayo is the absence of *Olivella* (olive) shell, which also is common at southwestern sites from the Archaic period onward.

Shell was recovered in unworked, worked, and finished forms (both complete and fragmentary). Only one piece of unworked shell was recovered. The presence of worked shell suggests that ornament and tool manufacture may have occurred at El Macayo. The presence of two kinds of beads (bilobed and disk), bracelets, two types of pendants (bracelet-type and carved zoomorphic and geometric forms), and a needle lends support to the argument that the settlement functioned as a residence where a full range of activities was carried out.

The beads, bracelets, and pendants recovered from El Macayo are common shell artifact forms recovered in the southern Southwest. The sewing needle, however, is not. Broken shell bracelet fragments were probably fashioned into needles or awls, but they are not often found.

Three of the five specimens of worked shell are *Anodonta*. Given that freshwater *Anodonta* clam shell can be obtained locally, is best worked when fresh, and does not transport well, an argument for on-site manufacture could be advanced. Their limited numbers, however, suggest that El Macayo was not a center for exporting *Anodonta* artifacts.

Artifact Provenience

The number of shell artifacts recovered is somewhat deceiving because the total of 555 items includes 529 beads that may have been a part of a single strand of beads. Nevertheless, shell artifacts from El Macayo, although not numerous, were common. Shell artifacts were recovered from every excavation context: test pits, stripping units, pits, pit houses, and burials. Artifacts associated with burials include two Type 3 *Glycymeris* bracelets that probably were worn on the upper arms of a deceased child and the 529 beads found near another child's ankle. Shell recovered from pre-Classic period Hohokam burial contexts is rare, and the recovery of unburned grave offerings with inhumations is even more unusual. No shell artifacts were found with the other burials at El Macayo. The remainder of the shell artifacts recovered from test pits, stripping units, pits, and pit houses were part of the general midden accumulation characteristic of the site. Most of these artifacts were fragmentary.

Comparison and Conclusion

Since 1966, nine excavation projects have been reported for the Nogales area (Table 27). Shell artifacts were recovered from five of these projects: Potrero Creek (Grebinger 1971b), the Nogales cremations (Reinhard 1978), the Nogales Wash site (Jácome 1986), and two projects at El Macayo (Gardiner and Huckell 1987; and this report). Neither the 1976–1977 (Reinhard and Fink 1982) nor the 1997 (Lynn S. Teague, personal communication 1997) excavations of cremations at the St. Andrew's site yielded shell.

Similarly, no shell artifacts were recovered from the limited excavations at the Buena Vista Ranch site (Neily 1994) or at one of the limited excavations at El Macayo (Slawson 1991).

With a total of 562 specimens recovered from the 1987 and 1996 excavations, the El Macayo collection clearly is the largest to date from the Nogales area. Second to El Macayo in shell frequency is the Potrero Creek site (Grebinger 1971b) with more than 210 specimens of shell, 146 of which are disk beads from one location (data on file in the archives of ASM).

The Potrero Creek shell represents at least eight genera (*Anodonta, Glycymeris,* Oliva [?], *Olivella, Pecten circularis* and *P. vogdesi, Spondylus,* and *Vermetis*), plus an unknown type. Artifact categories include unworked shell, miscellaneous worked materials, and ornaments (bracelets, rings, beads, and pendants). Shell was found in houses, in extramural contexts, and with burials. Shell artifacts were found with the human inhumations but were not found with the human cremations. Burial 2 had one *Glycymeris* ring fragment. Burial 6 contained 146 disk beads of an unknown marine shell. Burial 9 had one disk bead of an unknown genera. Burial 33 contained a pendant fragment (probably of *Anodonta*). Another burial (number not noted) had a *Glycymeris* bracelet fragment located near the nose. Three cremations were located at the site as well, but none had associated grave goods.

The Nogales Wash site also yielded at least seven genera (*Anodonta, Argopecten, Cerithium, Conus, Glycymeris, Haliotis,* and *Laevicardium*). Artifacts include unworked pieces, ornaments (bilobed, disk, and whole shell beads; bracelets; pendants; and rings), and utilitarian items (awls). Thirteen cremations and one inhumation were located at this site. No shell items were associated with any of the human inhumations, but a few were found with cremations.

Table 27. Summary of Previous Archaeological Projects in the Nogales Area and the Number of Shell Specimens Recovered

Site Name	Site Number (ASM)	Excavation Date	Reference	Shell Specimens Recovered (n)
Potrero Creek	AZ EE:9:53	1966	Grebinger 1971a, 1971b	210+
Nogales Cremations	AZ EE:9:68	1967	Reinhard 1978	16
St. Andrew's Church	AZ EE:9:67	1976–1977	Reinhard and Fink 1982	—
St. Andrew's Church	AZ EE:9:67	1997	Teague, personal communication 1997	—
Nogales Wash site	AZ EE:9:93	1982–1983	Jácome 1986	59
El Macayo	AZ EE:9:107	1987	Gardiner and Huckell 1987	7
El Macayo	AZ EE:9:107	1991	Slawson 1991	—
El Macayo	AZ EE:9:107	1996	this report	555
Buena Vista Ranch	AZ EE:9:151	1993	Neily 1993	—

The shell collections from El Macayo, Potrero Creek, and Nogales Wash sites are comparable. All have a diverse set of both genera and artifact types, and all yielded shell artifacts in association with human burials. Of particular interest are shell artifacts associated with the inhumation burials from El Macayo and the Potrero Creek site, noteworthy because funerary offerings are rarely associated with pre-Classic period inhumation burials in southern Arizona. Shell artifacts were similarly recovered with cremated human remains (Jácome 1986; Reinhard 1978). Whether this practice can be attributed to prescribed burial practices of distinctive social or cultural groups in the Nogales area as markers of status or ethnicity cannot be determined at this time. It is important, however, to note that this discovery was not unique to a single site.

In conclusion, the shell collection from El Macayo is significant. It adds detail to our interpretations of shell procurement and manufacture and our understanding of artifact diversity in southern Arizona. Furthermore, it may provide important evidence of the distinctive cultural practices in the Nogales area.

SIX

Faunal Remains

Marcy H. Rockman & Steven D. Shelley

This chapter describes all faunal materials recovered from the 1996 excavations at El Macayo, except for the interred skeletal remains of a macaw (Feature 144.01). This uncommon find is described in Chapter 7. Marcy Rockman contributed the following section on unworked faunal remains; Steven Shelley, the section on bone tools.

Unworked Faunal Remains

A total of 409 unworked faunal specimens (excluding 274 bones from the macaw burial [Feature 144.01]) was recovered (Tables 28 and 29). The collection is dominated by small- to medium-size mammals but also includes two species of reptiles, six varieties of bird, and several specimens of larger artiodactyl and artiodactyl-size mammals. A canid burial (Feature 186) found during excavations accounts for nearly half of the specimens in the collection.

Methods

All of the faunal specimens were identified by means of comparison with the National Park Service (NPS) faunal collection currently curated at ASM. Specimens were classified according to the scheme developed for the Marana Platform Mound site (Szuter and Bayham 1984). This scheme includes coding for taxon and size class, element, fragmentation, degree of epiphyseal fusion, burning, weathering, rodent and carnivore gnawing, and evidence of cultural modification. A listing of identified taxa is given in Table 29. A brief discussion of taphonomic characteristics is followed by a discussion of each of the represented classes.

Taphonomy

Preservation of the collection is generally good, although most of the specimens are fragmentary. Only a small portion of the specimens (14.7 percent) are complete. The remaining specimens display old breaks (40.8 percent), recent breaks (27.1 percent), a combination of old and recent breaks (15.4 percent), and indeterminate breakage (2.0 percent). As a result, nearly half of the collection (47.9 percent) could be identified only to class and size grade. An additional small percentage (2.7 percent) is unidentifiable or identifiable only to size grade.

Evidence of weathering and other postdepositional surface damage is relatively minor. Most of the collection (89.5 percent), irrespective of fragmentation, is in good to excellent condition. A small percentage (3.2 percent) displays a slight amount of surface cracking, and four specimens (1.0 percent) display deep cracking or have lost large portions of the cortical surface. An additional 24 specimens (5.9 percent) display a medium gray, muddy clay coating. The coating cannot be removed by brush but does not adversely affect the identification of the specimens. Extent of weathering could not be determined for two very small fragments (0.5 percent).

Similarly, rodent and carnivore gnawing have had a minimal impact on the collection. Thirteen specimens (3.2 percent) display gnawing damage, 12 from rodent gnawing and 1 from a carnivore-type puncture. The lack of carnivore damage is interesting, given the relatively large number of canid-size animals represented by the collection. Gnawed specimens are predominantly artiodactyl or large mammals (38.5 percent of the gnawed collection) and *Sylvilagus* sp. (23.1 percent), which suggests that these specimens are possibly discarded food remains, as discussed further below.

Table 28. Summary of the Faunal Collection from El Macayo

Provenience	Mammalia	Aves	Reptilia	Unidentified	Total
Stripping units					
SU 56	1	—	—	—	1
SU 57	3	1	—	—	4
SU 80	1	1	—	—	2
SU 118	1	—	—	—	1
SU 122	2	—	—	—	2
Test pits					
TP 58	2	1	—	2	5
TP 60	—	—	1	—	1
TP 71	12	2	—	—	14
TP 103	5	—	—	—	5
TP 291	6	—	—	1	7
Pit houses					
Feature 5	31	—	—	2	33
Feature 15	1	—	—	1	2
Feature 16	7	—	—	—	7
Feature 44	20	5	1	—	26
Feature 139	8	—	—	1	9
Feature 212	10	3	—	2	15
Pits					
Feature 50	1	—	—	—	1
Feature 51	1	—	—	—	1
Feature 53	17	—	—	—	17
Feature 55	1	—	—	—	1
Feature 105	2	—	—	—	2
Feature 112	9	—	—	—	9
Feature 144	—	—	—	1	1
Feature 179	2	—	—	—	2
Feature 203	1	—	—	—	1
Feature 208	1	—	—	—	1
Feature 210	6	—	—	—	6
Burials					
Feature 40: human burial	12	—	—	—	12
Feature 151: human burial	25	—	—	1	26
Feature 186: dog burial	191	1	—	—	192
Feature 213: human burial	3	—	—	—	3
Total	382	14	2	11	409

Table 29. El Macayo Faunal Collection

Taxa	NISP	% of Total NISP	MNI
Reptilia			
Kinosternidae (musk and mud turtles)	1	0.2	
Gopherus agassizii (desert tortoise)	1	0.2	1
Aves			
Anatidae (swans, geese, and ducks)	1	0.2	
Buteo jamaicensis (red-tailed hawk)	1	0.2	1
cf. *Callipepla squamata* (scaled quail)	1	0.2	
Gallus gallus (domestic chicken)	1	0.2	1
cf. Columbidae (pigeons and doves)	1	0.2	
cf. Cuculidae (cuckoos, roadrunners, and anis)	1	0.2	
Unidentified bird, size unknown	3	0.7	
Small bird (quail/rail)	1	0.2	
Medium bird (crow/raven/hawk)	2	0.5	
Large bird (turkey/eagle)	2	0.5	
Mammalia			
Leporidae (rabbits and hares)	4	1.0	
cf. Leporidae	3	0.7	
Lepus sp. (jackrabbit)	3	0.7	
Lepus californicus (black-tailed jackrabbit)	12	2.9	2
Sylvilagus sp. (cottontail)	9	2.2	
Rodentia	30	7.3	
Geomyidae (pocket gophers)	7	1.7	
Cricetidae (New World mice and rats)	1	0.2	
Ondatra zibethicus (muskrat)	3	0.7	1
cf. *Ondatra zibethicus* (muskrat)	1	0.2	
Canidae (doglike and foxlike mammals)	1	0.2	
Canis sp. (dog, coyote, wolf)	92	22.5	
cf. *Canis* sp.	13	3.2	
Felidae			
cf. *Felis rufus* (bobcat)	1	0.2	
Artiodactyla (even-toed ungulates)	13	3.2	
cf. *Antilocapra americana* (pronghorn)	1	0.2	
Unidentified mammal	18	4.4	
Very small mammal (rodent-size)	20	4.9	
Very small/small mammal	3	0.7	
Small mammal (rabbit-size)	17	4.2	
Small/medium mammal	4	1.0	
Medium mammal (coyote-size)	90	22.0	
Medium/large mammal	27	6.6	
Large mammal (deer- to bison-size)	9	2.2	
Unidentified faunal bone			
Unidentified specimen	3	0.7	
Very small/small animal	2	0.5	
Small animal	2	0.5	
Small/medium animal	4	1.0	
Total number of specimens	409	99.3[a]	

Key: MNI = minimum number of individuals; NISP = number of identified specimens
[a] Percentage total does not equal 100 because of rounding.

Most of the collection (90.7 percent) was recovered in association with features. Evidence of cultural modification, particularly burning, and evidence of cutting or butchering are discussed below in the discussions of identified classes.

Identified Taxa

Reptilia

Two specimens belong to the class Reptilia. One is a longbone of a member of the family Kinosternidae, which includes musk and mud turtles, and the other is a segment of a posterior portion of a plastron of a *Gopherus agassizii*, a desert tortoise. Both Kinosternidae and *G. agassizii* currently range in southeastern Arizona within the elevational range of El Macayo (Stebbins 1954:167, 180). Kinosternidae includes thoroughly aquatic species (Stebbins 1954:169), and the specimen may derive from a population in nearby Nogales Wash. *G. agassizii* inhabits a wider range of environments, including washes, sandy and gravelly flats, and hillsides (Stebbins 1954:180), several of which are found at El Macayo. The Kinosternidae specimen was recovered in association with Feature 44; the *G. agassizii* was not associated with any features. Neither specimen displays burning or evidence of cultural modification, and it is possible that they represent noncultural intrusions into the archaeological deposits.

Aves

A total of 14 specimens belong to the class Aves. Six of the specimens are identifiable to the level of family and below, five specimens are identifiable to size grade, and the remaining three are not identifiable as to family or size (see Table 28). The identified families include Anatidae (swans, geese, and ducks), Columbidae (pigeons and doves), and Cuculidae (cuckoos, roadrunners, and anis). Identified genus and species include *Buteo jamaicensis* (red-tailed hawk), *Callipepla squamata* (scaled quail), and *Gallus gallus* (domestic chicken). With the exception of *G. gallus*, all of the represented taxa are known to migrate through southeastern Arizona and are expected components of avian collections in the region surrounding El Macayo (American Ornithologists' Union 1975). None of the identified specimens display burning or evidence of cultural modification. All of the specimens, however, except *B. jamaicensis,* were recovered in association with features and may represent food remains. Most of the specimens identified to size class also were recovered in association with features. The shaft of one longbone displays a patch of charring, which suggests that avian species did contribute to the prehistoric diet at El Macayo. *G. gallus* is an Old World species introduced

to the area after European contact. The *G. gallus* specimen is heavily weathered and likely represents a recent addition to the site.

Mammalia

A total of 382 specimens belong to the class Mammalia. Of these, 194 specimens are identifiable to the level of order and below; the remaining 188 specimens are identifiable only by size. The primary identified taxa include Leporidae, Rodentia, Canidae, Felidae, and Artiodactyla.

The Leporidae specimens include *Lepus* sp., *Lepus californicus* (black-tailed jackrabbit), and *Sylvilagus* sp. (cottontails). The *L. californicus* specimens include elements from at least two individuals; number of individuals was not calculated for the other two taxa, as they were not identified to a distinct species. One *Lepus* sp. longbone displays a charred patch. The *Sylvilagus* sp. specimens include a blackened mandible and also display a high degree of gnawing damage (30 percent of identified *Sylvilagus* sp. specimens). All three taxa are represented predominantly by hind limb and mandible elements. This differential representation of elements, combined with the scattered evidence of charring, may indicate use of Leporidae populations as a prehistoric food source. Additionally, the gnawing damage on the *Sylvilagus* sp. specimens may be in part a result of exposure as food remains. A very similar element representation is also seen, however, in the Rodentia specimens (discussed below). Leporidae populations are common in the vicinity of El Macayo and are expected components of both noncultural and cultural faunal collections. In the absence of evidence of working and more-extensive charring, and given the generally low overall representation in the collection, it is possible that the differential element representation is a result of natural formation processes (see Schiffer 1987). It is possible then that Leporidae did not constitute a substantial portion of the prehistoric diet of the occupants of El Macayo.

The Rodentia specimens include four elements of *Ondatra zibethicus* (muskrat), as well as members of Geomyidae (pocket gophers), and Cricetidae (New World mice and rats) families. *O. zibethicus* is currently known to range in the lower reaches of the Colorado River in western Arizona and in the vicinities of the Gila River and the White Mountains (Cockrum 1960:211). It is possible that its range prehistorically may have extended into the upper reaches of the Santa Cruz drainage. The taxa Geomyidae and Cricetidae have a considerable range throughout the American Southwest (Hall and Kelson 1959) and may become part of the archaeological record through cultural or natural processes. All three taxa are represented predominantly by hind limb elements and mandible fragments. None of the Rodentia specimens display evidence of burning or working, and it is suggested that the differential element representation is a result of sampling or natural formation processes, and that Rodentia was not an integrated portion of the prehistoric diet.

The Canidae specimens include one specimen identified as *Canis* sp. (dog, coyote, and wolf), one identified as Canidae, and a collection of 104 *Canis* sp. specimens recovered from a burial context. The nonburial specimens include a distal humerus and a metatarsal, each from a mature individual. Both specimens are in good condition and show no evidence of burning or other cultural modification.

The burial collection includes one moderately complete mature individual, with representation of most elements except for the skull. The specimens are in good condition, with little to no surface damage, but with some patches of the gray clay staining as described above. Nearly half of the skeletal elements are complete. Most of the rest of the elements show recent breaks or a combination of new and old breaks. Gnawing was observed on two elements, one with rodent damage and the other with carnivore puncture damage. None of the elements show evidence of burning or other modification. Previous investigations at El Macayo yielded a canid in association with the burial of a small child (Slawson 1991:10). Canidae species, particularly *Canis latrans*, range throughout Arizona. This collection and previous associations, however, suggest that the *Canis* sp. collection was not part of the diet, but rather may have served another purpose.

Other specimens included with the *Canis* sp. burial are 85 specimens identified as medium-size mammals, one specimen of *Lepus californicus*, one of a small mammal, and one of a small bird. The medium mammal specimens are very similar to the *Canis* sp. specimens and likely represent additional portions of that individual.

A single specimen is identified as a vertebrae of a *Felis rufus* (bobcat). The specimen is not burned or worked, though it was recovered in association with a feature. *F. rufus* ranges throughout Arizona (Cockrum 1960:247) and may represent a noncultural inclusion in the collection.

Artiodactyla includes one specimen identified as *Antilocapra americana* (pronghorn) and 13 specimens identified solely as Artiodactyla. An additional 9 specimens are classified as large mammal, and 27, as medium to large mammal. Collectively, these specimens display most of the evidence of cultural modification noted in the collection. Most of the specimens are limb bone shafts and fragments, and fragments of antler or horn cores. Four of the Artiodactyla specimens and seven of the mammal specimens are burned, including two of the antler or horn core fragments. One large mammal specimen displays a single knife mark, and three additional specimens display breakage patterns that suggest cultural modification (after Lyman 1994:319). Additionally, five specimens, two of which are burned,

display rodent gnawing. As noted with respect to the *Sylvilagus* sp. specimens, given the overall low degree of gnawing in the faunal collection, concentration of gnawing damage on two taxa may indicate that these specimens were food remains. Several artiodactyl species range locally, including *A. americana* (Hall and Kelson 1959). Previous investigations have identified specimens of *Odocoileus virginianus* (white-tailed deer) (Gardiner and Huckell 1987:26), and it is likely that both species (*A. americana* and *O. virginianus*) contributed to the prehistoric diet.

Bone Tools

During the excavations at El Macayo, five pieces of worked faunal bone were recovered. The recovery context, descriptions, and other observations on the artifacts are presented in Table 30. The kinds of tools represented in this small collection are those typically found at Formative period habitation sites. Three of the five pieces of worked bone were identified as the tips of bone awls. Another piece is a fragment of a deer antler tine and may be a flaking tool for working stone. The final piece is a small bird bone that appears to have a worked tip and may have been used as a needle for delicate work.

Based on the wear patterns observed on the bone awls, we speculate that these awls were used for basket weaving and leather working. Two of the awl tips were short and blunt with longitudinal striations with a slight lateral twist near the end. These are inferred to have been basketry awls. The other tip was more tapered and more pointed. This tip did not exhibit striations but was well polished and may have been used in leather working.

Summary

A wide range of species inhabits the region surrounding El Macayo, and this diversity is reflected in the faunal remains recovered from excavated contexts. Evidence of cultural modification, particularly burning and butchering, suggests that prehistoric faunal procurement was focused on Artiodactyla species, as well as some Leporidae species, particularly *Sylvilagus* sp. The few fragmentary bone tools recovered appear to be related to leather working, basket weaving, and the manufacture of stone tools, which are all activities expected at a settlement such as El Macayo.

Table 30. Bone Tools from El Macayo

Tool Type	Catalog Number	Prov.	Burned?	Element	Artifact Description
Awl	46	TP 60	yes	mammal longbone?	tip of awl; rounded, blunted tip, diagonal and longitudinal striations, possible polish; probably used in basketry manufacture
Flaker	70	TP 71	no	deer antler tine	possible flaker; tip worn, entire tool is weathered; several areas of rodent gnawed "chisel-like" marks
Awl	83	TP 71	no	mammal longbone?	tip of awl; long, slender cylindrical tip; tip highly polished; possibly used for hide manufacturing, or on some other soft material
Awl	466	F 139	no	cf. proximal radius medium-large mammal	manufactured using bone splinter; has series of five deep cut marks on end that may have been functional rather than manufacturing; proximal end modified and slightly weathered; tip is rounded and polished, has faceted point; probably a basketry awl
Needle?	478	F 144	no	small bird radius	very small and delicate, may have a worked tip; definitely not a basketry awl, if it is a tool; must have been for very fine and delicate work, perhaps for threading beads

Osteological Description and Observations on the Macaw Skeletal Remains

Steven D. Shelley

One of the remarkable finds during the excavations at El Macayo was a macaw burial (Feature 144.01). The cultural practices associated with the interment are discussed in Chapter 2. This chapter describes the skeletal remains and discusses the significance of this find in relation to other macaw burials found in the southwestern United States.

The macaw was tentatively identified as a juvenile military macaw (*Ara militaris*) and was estimated to be about 8 weeks old. The specimen is unusual in at least three ways. First, the individual is young. In Hargrave's (1970:53, Table 10) comparative study of Mexican macaws from sites in the Greater Southwest, none of the individuals for which an age could be determined was as young as the individual found at this site. Second, the individual is a member of a rarely identified species. Hargrave (1970:53) recorded 145 individual macaws from the Greater Southwest, of which only one was a military macaw; the other 101 specimens identified to species were scarlet macaws (*A. macao*). Finally, macaw remains of any kind are rare in southern Arizona. Consequently, the discovery and description of this individual is important.

Identification and Description of the Skeletal Elements

The skeletal elements present include major portions of the skull, axial skeleton, and wings (Table 31). The identifica-

tion of the elements, species, and age were made with reference to Hargrave (1970), with additional reference to other sources such as Gilbert et al. (1981) and McKusick (1974). The overall condition of the skeletal elements was good, with most or all of each bone present. Some of the bones were damaged during excavation, as evidenced by fresh breaks. The elements present indicate that the entire bird was interred at one time. The presence of numerous tracheal rings indicates that the bird was buried in the flesh. Parts of the skeleton were missing from the elements recovered. In particular, most of the major leg and foot elements were missing, although a few of the phalanges were recovered. According to the burial description (see Chapter 2), the pit in which the macaw was buried may have been disturbed by rodents. The leg elements may have been moved upward into the overlying cultural deposits that were removed before discovery of the pit. Some of the bones had old breaks that probably occurred after the individual was interred.

Despite the generally good condition of the remains, species identification remains tentative because most of the diagnostic bone elements were either missing or the relevant portions were damaged. The distal part of the premaxilla (beak) was broken, although the overall shape was most similar to the military macaw. Likewise, the distal half of the cranium was missing, although the basiotemporal plate characteristics were most like the military macaw, as illustrated by Hargrave (1970). The quadrate characteristics also follow Hargrave's military macaw characteristics. The shape of the distal condyles on the femur (Figure 52) matched those of the military macaw (McKusick 1974:283). The basihyal-basibronchial bone was most

Table 31. Skeletal Elements from the Macaw Burial at El Macayo

Element	Condition	Comments
Head and neck		
Cranium	partial	posterior third fused to foramen magnum; rest of skull missing except for 14 fragments, mostly from the vault; basiotemporal plate characteristics most similar to *Ara militaris*; age juvenile?
Premaxilla	partial	most diagnostic characteristics broken; tip of beak missing, as is the proximal portion; overall shape most similar to *A. militaris*
Mandible	partial	distal end broken
Right quadrate	complete	quadrate most like *A. militaris*
Left quadrate	complete	quadrate most like *A. militaris*
Basihyal-basibronchial	complete	most characteristic of *A. macao*
Tracheal rings		33 complete, 26 fragments
Atlas	complete	spinous process missing
Cervical vertebra	complete	8 total
Cervical vertebra	partial	1 fragment
Body		
Left scapula	partial	distal end broken
Right scapula	partial	distal end broken
Sternum	partial	only sterno-coracoidal process and rib facets from left side present
Rib	partial	13 fragments, mostly proximal portions
Sternal rib	complete	3 total
Sternal rib	partial	6 fragments
Thoracic vertebra	complete	6 total
Left coracoid	complete	part of the sterno-coracoidal process of the sternum still attached to coracoid
Right coracoid	complete	
Pelvis	partial	proximal vertebra not completely fused
Wings		
Right humerus	partial	proximal half only; proximal head most like *A. militaris*
Left humerus	partial	shaft is complete; proximal and distal heads partially broken
Right ulna	complete	1 condyle missing on distal head
Left ulna	complete	distal end broken and healed; shaft roughened
Left radius	partial	proximal two-thirds present (old break); shaft slightly twisted
Right radius	complete	
Left carpometacarpus	partial	proximal head and distal half; medial section missing
Left wing phalanx 2 (Digit 2)	complete	
Left pollex	complete	
Legs		
Left femur	complete	femoral head broken; lateral condyle matches McKusick's (1974) definition for military macaw
Foot phalanx 1 (Digit 1)	complete	
Foot phalanx (ungual: Digit 1)	complete	1
Foot phalanx 3 (Digit 3)	partial	proximal half
Tail		
Caudal vertebra	complete	2 total
Pygostyle	complete	

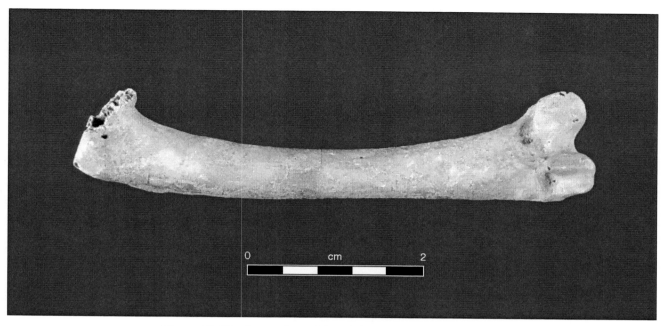

Figure 52. The femoral condyles of the macaw from El Macayo.

similar to the military macaw. Overall, the evidence supports identification of the specimen as a military macaw.

The age of this specimen can be established with confidence as a juvenile of 7–8 weeks. This determination was based on the fusing of all but one of the sacral vertebra (Figure 53). According to Hargrave's (1970) data, the sacrum of a juvenile bird fuses when the bird is about 8 weeks old. Also according to Hargrave (1970:4), only the posterior third of the cranium is fused around the foramen magnum, whereas the remainder of the cranium is composed of thin plates. In this macaw, only the posterior half of the cranium was present (see Table 31), and most of the cranial vault was broken into several pieces. In living birds, the sternum is still cartilaginous at 7 weeks (except at the sternal rib attachments), while the pelvis is completely ossified. In the El Macayo macaw, only a portion of the sternum around the sacral vertebra attachments was present. The condition of these bones in the macaw also supports a determination of juvenile age because thinly ossified bones would have broken easily, and cartilage would not have been preserved.

Pathologies

Pathologies were noted on the left ulna and left radius (see Table 31). The left ulna was broken by a greenstick fracture, which subsequently healed (Figure 54). The left radius was noticeably twisted and flattened, a deformity almost certainly related to the event that caused the break in the ulna.

It is possible that this break was intentional; it may have been done to handicap the bird's ability to fly. However, if the wings of macaws were broken regularly to prevent them from flying, this practice should have been observed on many of the macaws thus far recovered, which has not been the case. Of the 145 individuals in Hargrave's (1970) survey, 68 (47 percent) displayed pathologies to the bones. These pathological conditions reflected normal accidents or were attributed to dietary deficiencies. There was no evidence of deliberate mutilation, such as breaking a wing to inhibit flight (Hargrave 1970:53).

A review of Hargrave's (1970) data on pathologies also revealed that the ulnae had a disproportionately high number of pathologies. To explore whether a pattern in the pathologies exists, Hargrave's data were analyzed. First, the data were classified by major body part (Table 32). These included the wings (from the humerus to the phalanges), skull (including the premaxilla and mandible), body, and legs. Second, the ulnae were separated from other wing elements to test for a specific pattern of pathologies to the ulna. As Hargrave often does not list the exact elements present, the data were organized by body part. Each of these categories is mutually exclusive. When at least one element displayed a pathology, the entire body part was classified as having a pathology. Because the table is based on body parts, individual bones were included as representing the entire body. In most cases, however, the data were derived from macaw burials where numerous elements representing multiple parts of the body were recovered.

A chi-square (x^2) test was performed on the distribution of pathologies shown in Table 32. The x^2 statistic

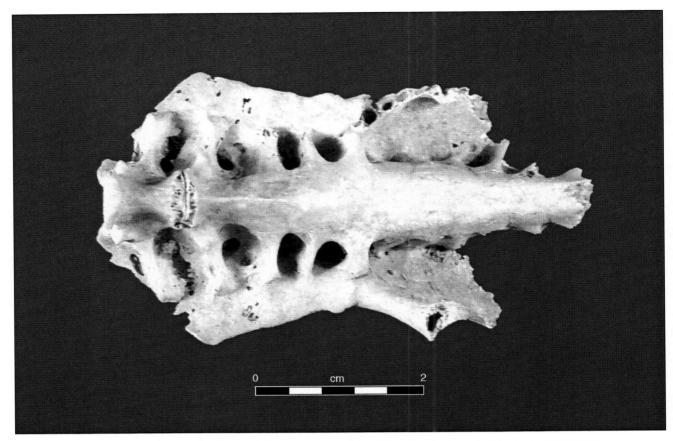

Figure 53. The sacral vertebrae of the macaw specimen. Note the fusing of all but one vertebrae.

showed a significant difference in the pattern of pathologies (x^2 = 54.61591, df = 4, p = 0.001). Ulnae were by far the most likely body part to exhibit a pathology. The most common pathology was a roughening of the ulna, which was caused by stress to the wing. McKusick (1974:280–281) noted that there were 133 cases of roughened ulnae at Casas Grandes and suggested that this may have been caused by plucking secondary feathers. This explanation, however, does not fit the evidence for the macaw at El Macayo, because it probably had either no feathers or, at most, undeveloped feathers. Also, plucking would not have caused the greenstick fracture noted on this bird. This fracture had time to heal, so it clearly would have occurred when the bird was too young to have had feathers. Thus, it appears that the pathologies present on the wing of this specimen were not caused by plucking.

Of the 20 individuals in Hargrave's (1970) study where both ulnae were present, six cases had only one ulna roughened and 14 had both ulnae roughened. In addition, pathologies to the other wing elements were often accompanied by this type of pathology to the ulna, usually on the same wing. Some of the ulnar roughening noted on these birds may have been the result of plucking, but it seems that some other action resulted in this damage. Perhaps the application

of an external device to prevent captive birds from flying was the cause of this pathology. For example, the binding of the wing below the humerus would result in stress that would cause the type of roughening seen on the ulnae. In addition, it would explain the presence of greenstick fractures on the wing as the unintentional result of the bird struggling against this restraint. It would also explain why the pathologies to other wing elements often accompany the roughening of the ulnae.

Discussion

At the time that Hargrave published his study, only two macaws had been unearthed in the desert Southwest outside the Mimbres area: one was from the Gatlin site near Gila Bend and the other from the Reeve Ruin on the lower San Pedro River east of Tucson. A summary of faunal remains from sites excavated since that time (Szuter 1990) includes only three additional macaws, all of which are from Snaketown. In addition, all previously known macaws in the desert region, and all but one from the southwestern United

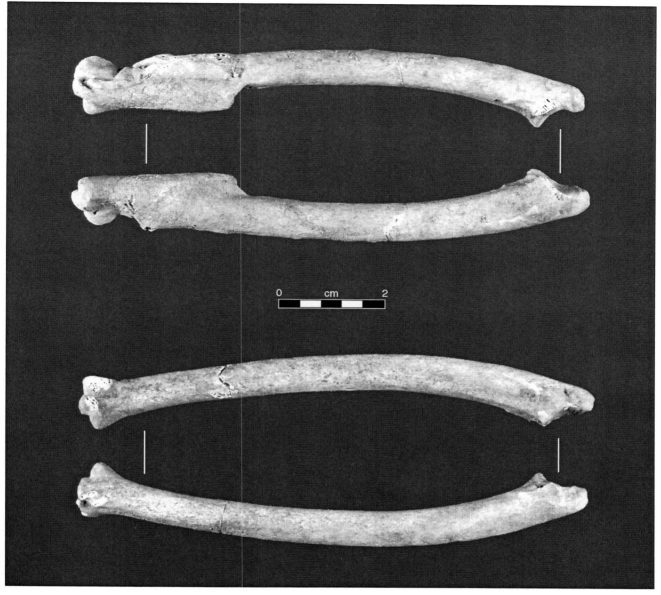

Figure 54. The ulnae of the El Macayo macaw specimen. Note the healed break of the left ulna.

Table 32. Distribution of Pathologies in Macaw Body Parts

Body Part	Pathology Present	No Pathology	Total
Ulna	36	30	66
Other wing bone	13	60	73
Skull	8	71	79
Body	11	54	65
Legs	8	63	71
Total	76	278	354

Note: From Hargrave 1970

States, have been identified as scarlet macaws (*A. macao*). The El Macayo specimen is certainly an important discovery, and it is only the second military macaw (*A. militaris*) documented for the southwestern United States. The only other military macaw was found at the Galaz Ruin (see Hargrave 1970:Table 9). Furthermore, this unusually young specimen is one of the few macaws that date before A.D. 1150. Most macaws from archaeological contexts have been dated to the late A.D. 1100s or later. The dating of the El Macayo specimen is based on indirect evidence—the general assessment of the age of the cultural deposit overlying the burial. The dominance of pre-Classic period ceramic types in this deposit suggests that the El Macayo specimen was interred before A.D. 1150 (see Chapter 2). This would make this find one of the earlier occurrences of macaw in the southwestern United States.

The distribution of scarlet macaws across the southwestern United States appears to be the result of widespread trade (Hargrave 1970:53). This conclusion is drawn from a convergence of three key pieces of evidence. First, the dominant species of macaw found in the Southwest, the scarlet macaw, is native to the tropical lowland areas of eastern Mexico. Second, only three of the 117 macaw specimens in Hargrave's (1970:53) study that were identifiable as to age actually were of breeding age (4 years of age or older). Third, none of the specimens aged by Hargrave were nestlings (0–6 weeks old) or juveniles (7 weeks–4 months old). The youngest macaws documented by Hargrave were 4–11 months old (1970:53, Table 10). Considering the native distribution of scarlet macaws, the absence of macaws of breeding age, and the absence of nestlings or juveniles, the evidence is compelling that macaws were not bred in the southwestern United States, but rather were distributed through extensive trade networks. The closest documented find of breeding-age macaws is the site of Casas Grandes in northern Chihuahua (McKusick 1974).

The El Macayo specimen may have been acquired through the same trade networks responsible for the distribution of scarlet macaws, but the known native distribution of the military macaw and the age of the El Macayo specimen suggest an alternative explanation. In contrast to the distribution of the scarlet macaw, the military macaw is found in arid and semiarid regions of pine and oak forests up to 8,000 feet as far north as central Sonora, Mexico (Hargrave 1970:10). This places the known range of military macaws close to southern Arizona. Young military macaws generally do not leave the nest for at least 3 or 4 weeks after they are born, and they are not flight-worthy at 8 weeks of age. The El Macayo specimen, therefore, was possibly born in captivity either at El Macayo or at a location not more than a few weeks journey away.

The juvenile stage is a critical point in macaw development for the capture and taming of young birds not born in captivity (McKusick 1974). At about 7 weeks, the beak is sufficiently ossified to help the bird move about its nest. At this age, the bird is virtually naked. By 8 weeks of age, the beak and the skull are sufficiently ossified to permit climbing and other activities using the beak and feet. The wings are developing, and the bird's characteristic features are becoming evident. Despite its rapid development, a young, only partially feathered bird is susceptible to respiratory illness brought about by chilling. While capture and transport of a young flightless bird at this stage would be ideal, the risk of death due to respiratory illness is high.

The death of the macaw at a young age provides a strong piece of evidence that this site was occupied during the summer. According to Peter Siminski, the general curator at the Arizona-Sonora Desert Museum (personal communication 1996), military macaws are seasonal breeders that breed and hatch young in the late spring, around April or May. Our juvenile macaw, therefore, would have died in mid to late summer, probably in late June or July. Because the bird was buried in the flesh, the site must have been occupied during the summer. Finally, unless military macaws ranged farther north during prehistoric times, the presence of this bird suggests that people were clearly moving between what is now central Sonora and the Nogales area.

Archaeobotanical Materials

Analyses of Pollen and Flotation Samples*

Richard G. Holloway

Ten samples for pollen extraction and analysis, six samples for flotation analysis, and two samples for botanical identification were sent to Quaternary Services. These samples were taken from the excavation at El Macayo by SRI. The site is situated at an elevation of 1,146 m (3,760 feet) AMSL on patented county land within the City of Nogales, Santa Cruz County, Arizona. The modern vegetation of the site is dominated by numerous grasses. Isolated mesquite trees (*Prosopis juliflora* var. *velutina*) grow on the flatter portions of the project area, and their numbers increase to the west, where the hillslope steepens.

Methods and Materials

Palynology Methods

Chemical extraction of pollen samples was conducted at the Palynology Laboratory at Texas A&M University, using a procedure designed for semiarid southwestern sediments. The method, detailed below, specifically avoids use of such reagents as nitric acid and bleach, which have been demonstrated experimentally to be destructive to pollen grains (Holloway 1981).

From each pollen sample submitted, 25 g of soil were measured and used as a standard subsample unit. Prior to chemical extraction of the pollen grains, three tablets of concentrated *Lycopodium* spores (Batch 307862, Department of Quaternary Geology, Lund, Sweden; 13,500 ± 500 marker grains per tablet) were added to each subsample. The addition of marker grains permits calculation of pollen concentration values and provides an indicator for accidental destruction of pollen during the laboratory procedure.

Four of the pollen samples submitted for analysis consisted of pollen washes of artifacts—three from plain ware vessels and one from a painted purple-on-tan bowl. The wash and residue collection procedure was conducted by personnel at SRI. Loose dirt adhering to the interior surface of the artifact was brushed off lightly. The interior surface then was washed with distilled water. Thereafter, the surface was washed with a 10 percent solution of hydrochloric acid (HCl), followed by a second wash with distilled water. The liquid portions of all three washes were combined in a single container and sent to Texas A&M University for extraction. The pollen wash samples were centrifuged to consolidate the particulate fraction, and the supernatant liquid was discarded. These samples were then processed according to the protocol described below.

The samples were treated with 35 percent HCl to remove carbonates and to release the *Lycopodium* spores from their matrix. After the acid was neutralized with distilled water, the samples were allowed to settle for at least three hours before the supernatant liquid was removed. Additional distilled water was added to the supernatant, and the mixture was swirled and allowed to settle for five seconds. The suspended fine fraction then was decanted through 150μ mesh screen into a second beaker. This procedure, repeated at least three times, removed lighter materials, including pollen grains, from the heavier fractions. The fine material was concentrated by centrifugation at 2,000 revolutions per minute (RPM).

The fine fraction was treated with concentrated hydrofluoric acid (HF) overnight to remove silicates. After the acid was completely neutralized with distilled water, the

* Originally published as Quaternary Services Technical Report Series No. 96-021, in November 1996; edited for style and grammar for this publication.

samples were treated with a solution of Darvan and sonicated in a Delta D-9 Sonicator for 30 seconds. The Darvan solution was removed by repeated washing with distilled water and centrifuged at 2,000 RPM until the supernatant liquid was clear and neutral. This procedure removed fine charcoal and other associated organic matter and effectively deflocculated the sample.

The samples were dehydrated in glacial acetic acid in preparation for acetolysis. Acetolysis solution (acetic anhydride:concentrated sulfuric acid in a 9:1 ratio) was added to each sample following Erdtman (1960). Centrifuge tubes containing the solution were heated in a boiling water bath for approximately 8 minutes and then cooled for an additional 8 minutes before centrifugation. The acetolysis solution was removed with glacial acetic acid followed by a distilled water rinse. Centrifugation at 2,000 RPM for 90 seconds dramatically reduced the size of the sample without removing any fossil palynomorphs.

This procedure was followed by heavy-density separation using zinc bromide ($ZnBr_2$), with a specific gravity of 2.00, to remove much of the remaining detritus from the pollen. The light fraction was diluted with distilled water (10:1) and concentrated by centrifugation. The samples were washed repeatedly in distilled water until neutral. The residues were rinsed in a 1 percent solution of potassium hydroxide (KOH) for less than 1 minute, which was effective in removing most of the unwanted alkaline soluble humates.

The material was rinsed in ethanol (ETOH) stained with safranin-O, rinsed twice with ETOH, and transferred to 1-dram vials with tertiary butyl alcohol (TBA). The samples were mixed with a small quantity of glycerine and allowed to stand overnight for evaporation of the TBA. The storage vials were capped and sent to Quaternary Services for analysis. The capped vials were returned to SRI at the completion of the project.

A drop of the polliniferous residue was mounted on a microscope slide for examination under an 18-by-18-mm cover slip sealed with fingernail polish. The slide was examined using 200× or 100× magnification under an aus-Jena Laboval 4 compound microscope. Occasionally, pollen grains were examined using either 400× or 1,000× oil immersion to obtain a positive identification to the family or genus level.

Abbreviated microscopy was performed on each sample, in which either 20 percent of the slide (approximately four transects at 200× magnification) or a minimum of 50 marker grains was counted. If warranted, full counts were conducted by counting to a minimum of 200 fossil grains. Regardless of which method was used, the uncounted portion of each slide was completely scanned at a magnification of 100× for larger grains of cultivated plants such as *Zea mays* and *Cucurbita,* two types of cactus (*Platyopuntia* and *Cylindropuntia*), and other large pollen types, such as

members of the Malvaceae or Nyctaginaceae families. Because corn pollen was very common in many of these samples, corn grains were tabulated during the scans only if an unequal distribution of this taxon was observed on the microscope slide.

For those samples warranting full microscopy, a minimum of 200 pollen grains per sample were counted as suggested by Barkley (1934)—a procedure that allows the analyst to inventory the most common taxa present in the sample. All transects were counted completely, resulting in various numbers of grains counted beyond 200. Pollen taxa encountered on the uncounted portion of the slide during the low-magnification scan were tabulated separately.

Total pollen concentration values were computed for all taxa. The percentage of indeterminate pollen also was computed. Statistically, pollen concentration values provide a more reliable estimate of species composition within the collection. Traditionally, results have been presented by relative frequencies (percentages) where the abundance of each taxon is expressed in relation to the total pollen sum (200+ grains) per sample. With this method, rare pollen types tend to constitute less than 1 percent of the total collection. Pollen concentration values provide a more precise measurement of the abundance of even these rare types. The pollen data are reported here as pollen concentration values using the following formula:

$$PC = \frac{K \times \Sigma_p}{\Sigma_L \times S}$$

Where: PC = pollen concentration
K = *Lycopodium* spores added
Σ_p = fossil pollen counted
Σ_L = *Lycopodium* spores counted
S = sediment weight

The following example should clarify this approach. Taxon X may be represented by a total of 10 grains (1 percent) in a sample consisting of 1,000 grains, and by 100 grains (1 percent) in a second sample consisting of 10,000 grains. Taxon X is 1 percent of each sample, but the difference in actual occurrence of the taxon is obscured when pollen frequencies are used. The use of pollen concentration values is preferred because it accentuates the variability between samples in the occurrence of the taxon. The variability, therefore, is more readily interpretable when comparing cultural activity to noncultural distribution of the pollen rain.

The pollen concentration values for pollen wash samples were calculated using a modification of the above formula. This modification involved the substitution of the area washed (in cm^2) for the sediment weight (S) variable in the denominator from the above equation, because the sample was in liquid form. The resulting concentration value is thus expressed as estimated grains per cm^2. The resulting pollen concentration values from pollen wash samples are treated independently of those from soil samples in the results and discussion sections, although the data are presented with the other samples in the tables. The use of pollen concentration values from these particular samples is preferred, as explained above, in order to accentuate the variability between pollen wash samples. The use of the area washed also provides a mechanism for the comparison of calculated pollen concentration values between artifacts.

Variability in pollen concentration values can also be attributed to deterioration of the grains through natural processes. In his study of sediment samples collected from a rockshelter, Hall (1981) developed the "1,000 grains/g" rule to assess the degree of pollen destruction. This approach has been used by many palynologists working in other contexts as a guide to determine the degree of preservation of a pollen assemblage and, ultimately, to aid in the selection of samples to be examined in greater detail. According to Hall (1981), a pollen concentration value below 1,000 grains/g indicates that forces of degradation may have severely altered the original assemblage. However, a pollen concentration value of fewer than 1,000 grains/g can indicate restriction of the natural pollen rain. Samples from pit structures or floors within enclosed rooms, for example, often yield pollen concentration values below 1,000 grains/g.

Pollen degradation also modifies the pollen assemblage because pollen grains of different taxa degrade at variable rates (Holloway 1981, 1989). Some taxa are more resistant to deterioration than others and remain in assemblages after other types have deteriorated completely. Many commonly occurring taxa degrade beyond recognition in only a short time. For example, most (about 70 percent) Angiosperm pollen has either tricolpate (three furrows) or tricolporate (three furrows each with pores) morphology. Because surfaces erode rather easily, once deteriorated, these grains tend to resemble each other and are not readily distinguishable. Other pollen types (e.g., cheno-am) are so distinctive that they remain identifiable even when almost completely degraded.

Pollen grains were identified to the lowest taxonomic level whenever possible. Most of these identifications conformed to existing levels of taxonomy, with a few exceptions. For example, cheno-am is an artificial, morphological category that includes pollen of the family Chenopodiaceae (goosefoot) and the genus *Amaranthus* (pigweed), which are indistinguishable from each other (Martin 1963). All members are wind-pollinated (anemophilous) and produce very large quantities of pollen. In many sediment samples from the American Southwest, this taxon often dominates the collection.

Pollen of the Asteraceae (sunflower) family was divided into four groups. The high-spine and low-spine groups were identified on the basis of spine length. High-spine Asteraceae contains those grains with spine length greater than or equal to 2.5μ, while the low-spine group has spines less than 2.5μ long (Bryant 1969; Martin 1963). *Artemisia* pollen is identifiable to the genus level because of its unique morphology; it possesses a double tectum in the mesocopial (between furrows) region of the pollen grain. Pollen grains of the Liguliflorae also are distinguished by their fenestrate (windowlike openings) morphology. Grains of this type are restricted to the tribe Cichoreae, which includes such genera as *Taraxacum* (dandelion) and *Lactuca* (lettuce).

Pollen of the Poaceae (grass) family are generally indistinguishable below the family level, with the single exception of *Zea mays,* identifiable by its large size (ca. 80μ), relatively large pore annulus, and internal exine morphology. All members of the family contain a single pore, are spherical, and have simple wall architecture. Only complete or fragmented grains containing this pore were tabulated as members of the Poaceae.

Clumps or aggregates of four or more pollen grains (anther fragments) were tabulated as single grains to avoid skewing the counts. Pollen aggregates from archaeological contexts are interpreted as evidence of the presence of flowers at the sampling locale (Bohrer 1981). This enables the analyst to infer possible human behavior.

Finally, pollen grains that were in the final stages of disintegration but retained identifiable features, such as furrows, pores, complex wall architecture, or a combination of these attributes, were assigned to the indeterminate category. The potential exists to miss counting pollen grains without identifiable characteristics. For example, a severely deteriorated pollen grain may have no distinguishing feature and, therefore, may resemble many spores. Pollen grains and spores are similar in size and are composed of the same material (sporopollenin). To avoid counting spores as deteriorated pollen, only those grains containing identifiable pollen characteristics were assigned to the indeterminate category. Thus, the indeterminate category contains a minimum estimate of degradation for any assemblage. When the percentage of indeterminate pollen is between 10 and 20 percent, relatively poor preservation of the assemblage is indicated. When the percentage of indeterminate pollen is greater than 20 percent, however, severe deterioration is likely.

In those samples where the total pollen concentration values are approximately at or below 1,000 grains/g and the percentage of indeterminate pollen is 20 percent or greater, counting was terminated at the completion of the abbreviated microscopy phase. In some cases, the collection was so deteriorated that only a small number of taxa remained. Statistically, the concentration values may have exceeded 1,000 grains/g. If the species diversity was low (generally these samples contained only pine, cheno-am, members of the Asteraceae [sunflower] family, and indeterminate category), counting also was terminated after abbreviated microscopy, even if the pollen concentration values slightly exceeded 1,000 grains/g.

Flotation Methods

Sediment samples were processed for flotation analysis and macrobotanical identification by SRI personnel. The entire sample submitted for analysis was treated using water separation. The initial volume of material was measured and recorded, and then screened to remove the larger particles. The screened material was examined separately but was not subject to water separation. The material passing through this screen was placed in a modified flotation device for the physical flotation. The light fraction was collected and dried separately. After drying completely, the material was placed in labeled, zipper-locked plastic bags and sent to Quaternary Services for analysis. The heavy fraction also was collected, air dried, and placed in labeled, zipper-locked plastic bags, but was retained by SRI.

Upon arrival at Quaternary Services, the contents of the light fraction were measured (volume) and then examined using a Meiji stereoscopic zoom microscope (7–45× magnification). Wood charcoal specimens were examined using a modification of the snap method of Leney and Casteel (1975) to expose fresh transverse surfaces. These are necessary because soil particles often fill the vessel elements of the wood charcoal, obscuring the characteristics necessary for identification. Identifications of wood charcoal and seed materials were based on published reference materials (Martin and Barkley 1961; Montgomery 1977; Panshin and de Zeeuw 1980; Schopmeyer 1974), as well as comparisons with modern reference specimens.

Results

For ease of comparison, Table 33 contains a list of the scientific and common names of various taxa used in this report. Table 34 reports the raw pollen counts, and Table 35 reports the calculated pollen concentration values from these samples. Table 36 contains the results of the flotation analysis. Table 37 presents the raw counts for pollen grains identified in the low-magnification scan and the adjusted pollen concentration values for these types. The results of both the pollen and flotation analyses are presented below by feature.

Pollen from Features

Feature 15.01

Pollen (Catalog No. 263) and flotation (Catalog No. 262) samples were taken from a hearth feature (Feature 15.01) within pit house Feature 15. The pollen collection contained 1,620 grains/g total concentration (see Table 35). The collection was dominated by cheno-am pollen (1,009 grains/g), with large amounts of high-spine (245 grains/g) and low-spine (153 grains/g) Asteraceae pollen. Poaceae pollen (61 grains/g) was moderate, with traces of *Pinus* pollen (31 grains/g) and a fairly significant amount of *Prosopis* pollen (31 grains/g). Additional Prosopis grains (n = 4) also were identified in the low-magnification scan (see Table 37).

The flotation sample contained unidentified hardwood charcoal and unidentified conifer (cf. *Juniperus*) charcoal (see Table 36). Uncharred plant debris, insect parts, and snail remains also were present. The charcoal fragments were very tiny, and more than 95 percent of the collection was uncharred.

Feature 43.01

This was a hearth feature within pit house Feature 43. The pollen sample (Catalog No. 323) contained only 44 grains/g total concentration, and the type identifications were based on a pollen sum of only 5 grains. Cheno-am pollen and high-spine Asteraceae pollen were the only taxa present.

The flotation sample (Catalog No. 322) contained only 15 ml of light fraction, and more than 90 percent of the material was uncharred. The charcoal fragments were very tiny and could be identified only as hardwood charcoal or possible conifer wood charcoal.

Feature 44

Three pollen and three flotation samples were analyzed from pit structure Feature 44. Two samples, one pollen and one flotation, were obtained from the hearth (Feature 44.01). Another two samples, one pollen and one flotation, were obtained from an ash pit (Feature 44.02) located immediately adjacent to the hearth. A composite pollen sample was collected from the floor of this pit house. The sediment that makes up this sample was obtained from beneath floor-contact artifacts. A flotation sample of the roof fall stratum immediately above the floor also was analyzed. This flotation sample was a composite of roof fall deposits from across the entire structure area.

Feature 44.01
The pollen sample from the pit house hearth (Catalog No. 385) contained 2,986 grains/g total concentration (see Table 35). The sample was dominated by cheno-am (2,668 grains/g) pollen. Moderate amounts of both high- (64 grains/g) and low-spine (95 grains/g) Asteraceae pollen were present, in addition to traces of *Pinus* (64 grains/g) pollen. Small amounts of non-*Opuntia* Cactaceae and Brassicaceae (32 grains/g each) pollen also were present.

Table 33. Scientific and Common Names of Plant Taxa Observed at El Macayo

Scientific Name	Common Name
Amaranthus	pigweed
Asteraceae	composite family
High-spine Asteraceae	pollen morphological group, spines > 2.5μ
Low-spine Asteraceae	pollen morphological group, spines < 2.5μ
Artemisia	sagebrush
Liguliflorae	pollen morphological group, fenestrate pollen
Brassicaceae	mustard family
Carya	pecan, hickory
Cheno-am	pollen morphological group, members of Chenopodiaceae and genus *Amaranthus*
Chenopodiaceae	goosefoot family
Cichoreae	tribe of Asteraceae, heads composed entirely of ligulate flowers
Cucurbitaceae	gourd family
Cylindropuntia	subgenus of *Opuntia*, cholla cactus
Indeterminate	pollen morphological category, beyond identification
Juniperus	juniper
Lactuca	lettuce
Lycopodium	club moss
Nyctaginaceae	desert four-o'clock family
Onagraceae	evening primrose family
Opuntia	prickly pear or cholla cactus
Pinus	pine
Platyopuntia	subgenus of *Opuntia*, prickly pear cactus
Poaceae	grass family
Prosopis	mesquite
Quercus	oak
Sphaeralcea	globe mallow
Taraxacum	dandelion
Zea mays	corn

The flotation sample (Catalog No. 384) contained 60 ml of light fraction, and more than 90 percent of the material was uncharred (see Table 36). Most of the charred material consisted of charcoal fragments, although a few pieces of *Prosopis* charcoal also were present. In addition, insect remains and uncharred plant debris were present.

Feature 44.02
The pollen sample from the ash pit (Catalog No. 390) contained 2,337 grains/g total concentration (see Table 35). The sample was dominated by cheno-am (1,932 grains/g) pollen with a moderate to high amount of low-spine Asteraceae and *Artemisia* (125 grains/g each) pollen. A trace of Nyctaginaceae pollen (31 grains/g) also was present.

The flotation sample (Catalog No. 389) contained 80 ml of light fraction, but more than 90 percent of the material was uncharred. The charred materials consisted of generally small and very friable charcoal fragments. A few pieces

were identifiable as *Prosopis*. A small charred fragment of an unknown seed type also was present, but because of its fragmentary nature, it has not been identified. In addition, a single grass stem was present.

Composite Samples from House Floor and Roof Fall
The composite pollen sample from the floor (Catalog No. 730) contained 2,580 grains/g total concentration (see Table 35). Cheno-am (2,250 grains/g) pollen dominated the sample, with low to moderate amounts of low-spine Asteraceae (30 grains/g) and *Artemisia* (90 grains/g) pollen. Poaceae (60 grains/g) pollen was moderate, with a trace of *Pinus* (60 grains/g) pollen. A small number of cheno-am pollen aggregates also were present. One grain each of *Onagraceae, Prosopis,* and *Sphaeralcea* were observed in the low-magnification scan (see Table 37).

The composite flotation sample from the roof fall zone (Catalog No. 731) consisted of the light fraction recovered

Table 34. Pollen Grain Counts for Plant Taxa Observed in Palynological Samples from El Macayo

Cat. No.	Feature No.	Type	Pinus	Prosopis	Brassicaceae	Poaceae	Cheno-am	Cheno-am Aggregate	High-Spine Asteraceae	Low-Spine Asteraceae	Artemisia	Cactaceae	Nyctaginaceae
263	15.01	pit house hearth	1	1	—	2	33	—	8	5	—	—	—
323	43.01	pit house hearth	—	—	—	—	4	—	1	—	—	—	—
385	44.01	pit house hearth	2	—	1	—	84	—	2	3	—	1	—
390	44.02	pit house ash pit	—	—	—	—	62	—	—	4	4	—	1
730	44	pit house: composite floor	2	—	—	2	75	2	—	1	3	—	—
484	144.03	painted bowl PW	1	1	1	—	51	—	4	4	—	—	—
510	151	plain ware PW (indet. vessel form)	—	—	—	—	4	—	1	—	—	—	—
513	151	plain ware scoop PW	—	2	—	—	—	—	—	—	—	—	—
516	151	plain ware scoop PW	3	1	—	—	6	—	—	—	—	—	—
537	178	extramural pit	2	—	—	—	57	—	—	2	—	—	—

Table 34 (continued).

Cat. No.	Feature No.	Type	Indeterminate	Zea mays	Sum	% Indeterminate	Concentration	Marker	Lyco Added	Weight/Area	Transect	Total Transects	Mark/Slide
263	15.01	pit house hearth	3	—	53	5.66	1,620	53	40,500	25	8	26	172
323	43.01	pit house hearth	—	—	5	0.00	44	184	40,500	25	4	24	1,104
385	44.01	pit house hearth	1	—	94	1.06	2,986	51	40,500	25	6	25	213
390	44.02	pit house ash pit	4	—	75	5.33	2,337	52	40,500	25	6	26	225
730	44	pit house: composite floor	1	—	86	1.16	2,580	54	40,500	25	4	24	324
484	144.03	painted bowl PW	1	—	63	1.59	58	173	40,500	254	4	25	1,081
510	151	plain ware PW (indet. vessel form)	—	—	5	0.00	17	203	40,500	60	4	20	1,015
513	151	plain ware scoop PW	—	—	2	0.00	9	175	40,500	50	4	24	1,050
516	151	plain ware scoop PW	—	2	12	0.00	8	372	40,500	167	4	25	2,325
537	178	extramural pit	1	—	62	1.61	1,702	59	40,500	25	6	24	236

Key: PW = pollen wash; Marker = *Lycopodium* spores counted; *Lyco Added* = *Lycopodium* spores added; Mark/Slide = Marker grains/slide
Note: Number is total pollen grains observed for each taxon in the 200+ grain count and the low-magnification scan.

Table 35. Pollen Concentration Values for Plant Taxa Observed at El Macayo

Cat. No.	Feature No.	Type	Pinus	Prosopis	Brassicaceae	Poaceae	Cheno-am	Cheno-am Aggregate	High-Spine Asteraceae	Low-Spine Asteraceae	Artemisia	Cactaceae	Nyctaginaceae	Indeterminate
263	15.01	pit house hearth	31	31	—	61	1,009	—	245	153	—	—	—	92
323	43.01	pit house hearth	—	—	—	—	35	—	9	—	—	—	—	—
385	44.01	pit house hearth	64	—	32	—	2,668	—	64	95	—	32	—	32
390	44.02	pit house ash pit	—	—	—	—	1,932	—	—	125	125	—	—	125
730	44	pit house: composite floor	60	—	—	60	2,250	60	—	30	90	—	31	30
484	144.03	painted bowl PW	1	1	1	—	47	—	4	4	—	—	—	1
510	151	plain ware PW (indet. vessel form)	—	—	—	—	13	—	3	—	—	—	—	—
513	151	plain ware scoop PW	—	9	—	—	—	—	—	—	—	—	—	—
516	151	plain ware scoop PW	2	1	—	—	4	—	—	—	—	—	—	—
537	178	extramural pit	55	—	—	—	1,565	—	—	55	—	—	—	27

Table 35 (continued).

Cat. No.	Feature No.	Type	Zea mays	Total Pollen Grains Counted	% Indeterminate	Total Pollen Concentration	Grains/Artifact	Marker	Lyco Added	Weight/Area	Transect	Total Transects	Mark/Slide	Est. Max. Potential Concentration
263	15.01	pit house hearth	—	53	5.66	1,620	—	53	40,500	25	8	26	172	9.40
323	43.01	pit house hearth	—	5	0.00	44	—	184	40,500	25	4	24	1,104	1.47
385	44.01	pit house hearth	—	94	1.06	2,986	—	51	40,500	25	6	25	213	7.62
390	44.02	pit house ash pit	—	75	5.33	2,337	—	52	40,500	25	6	26	225	7.19
730	44	pit house: composite floor	—	86	1.16	2,580	—	54	40,500	25	4	24	324	5.00
484	144.03	painted bowl PW	—	63	1.59	58	14,749	173	40,500	254	4	25	1,081	1.50
510	151	plain ware PW (indet. vessel form)	—	5	0.00	17	998	203	40,500	60	4	20	1,015	1.60
513	151	plain ware scoop PW	—	2	0.00	9	463	175	40,500	50	4	24	1,050	1.54
516	151	plain ware scoop PW	1	12	0.00	8	1,306	372	40,500	167	4	25	2,325	0.70
537	178	extramural pit	—	62	1.61	1,702	—	59	40,500	25	6	24	236	6.86

Key: PW = pollen wash; Marker = *Lycopodium* spores counted; *Lyco Added* = *Lycopodium* spores added; Mark/Slide = Marker grains/slide.
Note: Pollen concentrations have been rounded to nearest whole number; therefore, sum may not equal total pollen concentration.

Table 36. Results of the Analysis of Macrobotanical Samples from El Macayo

Cat. No.	Fea. No.	Feature Type	Sample Type	Vol. (liters)	Light Fraction (ml)	Recovery (%)	Charcoal	Wood	Seeds	Contaminants	Other	Notes
262	15.01	pit house hearth	flotation	4	50	1.25	CF, hardwood; conifer, cf. *Juniperus*			ucpd, S, I		CF very tiny; > 95% uncharred
322	43.01	pit house hearth	flotation	3.3	15	0.45	CF; cf. conifer, tiny; hardwood, tiny			ucpd, I, S		CF very tiny; > 90% uncharred
384	44.01	pit house hearth	flotation	3.4	60	1.76	CF; *Prosopis*			ucpd, I		CF very tiny; > 90% uncharred
389	44.02	pit house ash pit	flotation	4	80	2.00	CF; *Prosopis*		1 small, broken, unknown fragment	ucpd	grass stem	CF very tiny, friable; > 90% uncharred
731-346	44	pit house: composite roof fall	flotation	4	100	4.00	CF; conifer, cf. *Juniperus*			ucpd, I, S		CF all conifer charcoal
731-344	44	pit house: composite roof fall	flotation/botanical		40		CF; *Prosopis*	*Juniperus*		ucpd		CF all hardwood; large charcoal all *Prosopis*
731-333	44	pit house: composite roof fall	flotation/botanical		20		CF; *Quercus*					
367	44	pit house roof fall—beam	botanical						*Juniperus*			
378	44	pit house roof fall—beam	botanical					*Juniperus*				charred wood
536	178	extramural pit	flotation	4	30	0.75	CF; hardwood; cf. *Prosopis*			ucpd, I	2 grass stems	CF very tiny; > 90% uncharred

Key: CF = charcoal fragments; cf. = compares favorably; I = insect parts; S = snail remains; ucpd = uncharred plant debris

Table 37. Pollen Taxa Observed in Low-Magnification Scan

Cat No.	Feature No.	Feature Type	Pinus	Prosopis	Onagraceae	Cactaceae	Sphaeralcea	cf. Carya
263	15.01	pit house hearth	—	4	—	—	—	—
323	43.01	pit house hearth	—	—	—	—	—	—
385	44.01	pit house hearth	—	—	—	—	—	—
390	44.02	pit house ash pit	—	—	—	—	—	—
730	44	pit house: composite floor	—	1	1	—	1	—
484	144.03	painted bowl PW	8	5	—	1	—	—
510	151	plain ware PW (indeter. vessel form)	—	2	—	—	—	—
513	151	plain ware scoop PW	1	5	—	—	2	1
516	151	plain ware scoop PW	—	—	—	—	—	—
537	178	extramural ash pit	—	—	—	—	—	—

from flotation of the sediments that made up the roof fall deposit (Catalog No. 346), as well as larger pieces of charcoal that had been collected originally as two separate macrobotanical specimens (Catalog Nos. 333 and 344) (see Table 36). The three component samples contained different plant taxa. The light fraction (Catalog No. 731-346) consisted of *Juniperus* charcoal. The light fraction also contained insect and snail remains, along with uncharred plant debris. One of the macrobotanical specimens (Catalog No. 731-344) consisted of *Prosopis* charcoal and charred *Juniperus* wood. The other macrobotanical specimen (Catalog No. 731-333) contained *Quercus* wood charcoal. These charcoal pieces were large. Additionally, two specimens of charred wood were submitted for identification; both represent the remains of a partially charred architectural timber. Both samples (Catalog Nos. 367 and 378) were identified as *Juniperus*.

Feature 178

This feature was an extramural pit. Pollen (Catalog No. 537) and flotation (Catalog No. 536) samples were collected from an ashy deposit that composed the upper fill of the pit. The pollen sample contained 1,702 grains/g total concentration (see Table 35). Cheno-am (1,565 grains/g) pollen again dominated the sample. A moderate amount of low-spine Asteraceae pollen (55 grains/g) also was present. *Pinus* pollen was present but in trace amounts.

The flotation sample contained only 30 ml of light fraction (see Table 36). This sample consisted primarily of hardwood charcoal fragments. A few of the larger specimens compared favorably to the anatomy of *Prosopis* but, because of their size, could not be positively identified. Two charred grass stems also were present.

Pollen Washes from Artifacts

A pollen wash (Catalog No. 484) was obtained from the interior of a purple-on-tan painted bowl (Vessel 144-1) recovered from an extramural pit, Feature 144.03. Based on the pollen concentration values (see Table 35), the artifact contained a total of 14,749 pollen grains, with an average of 58 grains/cm². The sample was dominated by cheno-am pollen (47 grains/cm²). Both high-and low-spine Asteraceae pollen were present in the same amounts (4 grains/cm²). *Pinus, Prosopis,* and Brassicaceae pollen also were present (1 grain/cm²). Additional grains of *Pinus* (n = 8), *Prosopis* (n = 5), and *Cactaceae* (n = 1) were identified in the low-magnification scan (see Table 37).

The remaining three pollen washes were in association with Feature 151, a human burial. These samples (Catalog Nos. 510, 513, and 516) were obtained from the interiors of three plain ware vessels. Catalog No. 510 from Vessel 151-3 contained 998 pollen grains on the artifact (17 grains/cm²). The pollen assemblage was based on a count of only 5 grains (see Table 35). Cheno-am (13 grains/cm²) and high-spine Asteraceae pollen (3 grains/cm²) were the only taxa present in the pollen count. Two *Prosopis* pollen grains were later identified in the low-magnification scan (see Table 37). Catalog No. 513, from a plain ware scoop (Vessel 151-2), contained a total of 463 grains (9 grains/cm²). The identified sample of taxa was based on a pollen sum of only 2 grains, both of which were *Prosopis*. *Pinus* (n = 1), *Prosopis* (n = 5), *Sphaeralcea* (n = 2), and the nonnative *Carya* (n = 1) pollen grains were identified in the low-magnification scan (see Table 37). Catalog No. 516, from another plain ware scoop (Vessel 151-1), contained a total of 1,306 grains on the artifact (8 grains/cm²). Small amounts of *Pinus* (2 grains/cm²), cheno-am (4 grains/cm²), *Prosopis*

(1 grain/cm^2), and *Zea mays* pollen (1 grain/cm^2) were present.

Discussion

The pollen collections are noteworthy for their low overall pollen concentration values. These low values are indicative of a sparse desert scrub plant community that produces relatively little pollen. *Pinus* pollen was present in 7 of 10 samples, although the pollen concentration values were extremely low. The low pollen concentration values for this taxon (less than 64 grains/g) indicate that *Pinus* was not present in the immediate vicinity of the site, but rather was introduced via long-distance transport. *Pinus* produces pollen in structures called strobili that are found in clusters of 5–7 on the terminal branch ends. Each strobilus of *Pinus* produces in excess of 1,000,000 pollen grains that are wind dispersed. Thus, pollen production in *Pinus* is enormous, and it is not uncommon for pine pollen to be present, even though the taxon is absent from the community. In an investigation of surface pollen frequencies from southern Alberta, Canada, Holloway (1984) found *Pinus* pollen present in quantities greater than 15 percent from vegetational stands located more than 150 miles away from the nearest pine source.

The other arboreal taxa present in these samples was *Prosopis* (mesquite). Pollen from this taxon was present in a sample from the hearth of a pit structure, Feature 15.01 (Catalog No. 263). The roofs and walls of a pit structure would have blocked the normal pollen rain. The presence of this taxon within an architectural structure might indicate its deposition by a cultural vector, perhaps brought in with potential fuel sources.

Prosopis also was identified in all of the pollen washes from ceramic vessels (see Tables 34 and 37). *Prosopis* pollen is wind and insect pollinated and generally produces relatively few pollen grains per anther, especially when compared with other arboreal taxa. Thus, the presence of *Prosopis* pollen, even in low concentration values, usually indicates a much greater presence. This is not unexpected in these samples, because *Prosopis* is present in the immediate vicinity. The presence of *Prosopis* on the interior of the three pottery vessels strongly suggests that this is the result of a cultural vector. This taxon is present on all three vessels associated with burial Feature 151. This is suggestive that *Prosopis* pollen may have been used in some type of burial ritual. Alternatively, the pollen may have been deposited inadvertently during the burial preparation.

A single grain of *Carya* (pecan, hickory) pollen was recovered from the pollen wash (Catalog No. 513) of one of the vessels (Vessel 151-2) associated with burial Feature 151. *Carya* is not native to Arizona, although *Carya* orchards are present nearby. The presence of this taxon is undoubtedly the result of modern contamination. The context of this single grain was from a burial, and it is possible that the pollen may have been deposited onto the vessel during excavation or incorporated into the burial sediments by rodents. Elsewhere, I have noted the presence of nonnative taxa (e.g., *Ulmus*) correlated with burial contexts (Holloway 1996). Given the presence of only a single grain, the mechanism responsible for the deposition of this taxon cannot be clearly defined.

Brassicaceae pollen was recovered from two samples: one from the hearth in pit structure Feature 44 (Catalog No. 385) and the other from a painted bowl recovered from Feature 144.03 (Catalog No. 484). Brassicaceae pollen is insect pollinated, and consequently, its presence strongly suggests a cultural vector for deposition. This may indicate cultural use of members of this family (such as tansy mustard), or it may indicate the presence of other native members of this family.

The pollen wash samples contained a number of potentially economic pollen taxa. Non-*Opuntia* Cactaceae pollen (Catalog No. 484), *Sphaeralcea* (Catalog No. 513), and *Zea mays* (Catalog No. 516) pollen were present from these contexts (see Tables 34 and 37). The taxa, however, appeared to be restricted to individual ceramics. Because the ceramics were generally associated with burial contexts, it is interesting to speculate that these vessels may have contained different materials. The pollen concentration values are very low for these economic taxa, which are represented by only 1 or 2 grains. Given the low pollen concentration values, it appears that these vessels contained various plant parts (such as fruits or stems) and that the pollen was introduced by adhering to other plant materials, rather than that the vessels contained pollen per se. The presence of these pollen taxa may indicate ritual use of these plants during the burial activities.

The presence of *Zea mays* pollen is particularly interesting. *Zea mays* pollen (2 grains) was present only from a single artifact, one of the plain ware scoops (Vessel 151-1). If we are correct in inferring that the corn pollen was deposited into the scoop while adhering to other plant parts, then this suggests that unprocessed corn materials were present and available locally, despite the low frequency of pollen.

Although macrobotanical remains of corn were absent from the flotation samples examined, corn remains were recovered from an earlier study. Gardiner and Huckell (1987) reported the presence of charred cupules, glumes, or chaff from two pit features (Features 13 and 17). Feature 17 was a pit feature located just west of Feature 15. Feature 13 was a bell-shaped pit located just west of Feature 2 and the inhumation burial Feature 31. The presence of these corn remains indicates that cob materials likely were being used as a fuel source (Gardiner and Huckell 1987). With the recovery of both macrobotanical and pollen remains from this site, and given the time period involved (Sedentary Hohokam), it is likely that corn was grown locally.

Sphaeralcea (globe mallow) and Onagraceae (evening primrose) pollen also were present from the floor of pit structure Feature 44. Given their low concentration values, it appears that the pollen of these plants was introduced with other plant materials brought into the structure.

The flotation samples, unfortunately, contained only a single, unknown seed fragment that was present from the ash pit, Feature 44.02, associated with the hearth in the pit structure (Catalog No. 389). The remainder of the macrobotanical materials recovered consisted of wood charcoal and charred wood. Most of these materials consisted of *Prosopis* charcoal, which is not surprising given its presence in the area. *Juniperus* charcoal and small fragments of conifer charcoal were present from both Features 15.01 (Catalog No. 262) and 43.01 (Catalog No. 322). *Prosopis* charcoal was present from Features 44.01 (Catalog No. 384), 44.02 (Catalog No. 389), and 178 (Catalog No. 536).

The architectural timbers from Feature 44 were identified as *Juniperus* (Catalog Nos. 367 and 368; see Table 36). A composite sample from the roof fall of Feature 44 also was submitted. This composite sample (Catalog No. 731) contained *Juniperus, Prosopis, Quercus,* and conifer wood charcoal, as well as *Juniperus* wood. This suggests that the superstructure from Feature 44 was constructed of at least three taxa. These taxa indicate a preference for hard, durable wood for house construction. *Juniperus* probably composed the largest elements of the roof, and *Prosopis* and *Quercus* likely were used for the smaller roof elements. All of these taxa likely were available locally.

Summary and Conclusions

Based on the results of the high-magnification pollen counting (see Tables 34 and 35) and the low-magnification scanning for species with potentially economic uses (see Table 37), 14 taxa were identified from the analyzed pollen samples. Only one unquestionably domesticated taxon,

Zea mays, was recovered. The most ubiquitous taxon was cheno-am (9 of 10 samples) followed by *Pinus* (7 of 10 samples), *Prosopis* (6 of 10 samples), low-spine Asteraceae (6 of 10 samples), and high-spine Asteraceae (5 of 10 samples). The remainder had ubiquity values of either 2/10 (*Artemisia*, Brassicacae, Cactaceae, Poacea, and *Sphaeralcea*) or 1/10 (Nyctaginaceae, Onagraceae, and *Zea mays*). One grain of *Carya* pollen was observed in the low-magnification scan of one of the pollen washes. This is a nonnative species, and its presence attests to the potential for postdepositional disturbance and mixing of the archaeological deposits.

The results of the palynological analyses reveal a background pollen assemblage indicative of a sparse, desert-scrub-type community. *Pinus* pollen is present, but only as the result of long-distance transport. The composite pollen sample from the floor of Feature 44 contained a few pollen types that are known to have been used economically by historical-period Native American groups in southern Arizona and may have been similarly used prehistorically. The pollen wash samples contained a few additional economic taxa, with the distribution suggesting that these vessels may have held separate materials such as cactus, mallow, and corn materials. The pollen concentration values obtained from these pollen wash samples indicate that the vessels probably did not contain pollen offerings per se, but rather contained plant remains on which plant pollen adhered. These remains were likely part of a burial ritual.

Macrobotanical remains recovered from this site included charred fuel wood, charred architectural timber, and charred seeds and grass stems. At least three kinds of wood are represented: *Prosopis, Juniperus,* and *Quercus.* In addition, specimens identified only as hardwood type and conifer type were recovered.

The dominant charcoal type was *Prosopis,* which is present locally today. The dominance of *Prosopis* charcoal suggests that it was locally abundant during the occupation of the settlement. The macrobotanical evidence from Feature 44 suggests that the framework of the house was constructed of *Juniperus, Prosopis,* and *Quercus. Juniperus* likely was used for the larger beams, with the other taxa used for secondary beams and closing material.

Osteology and Pathology of the Human Skeletal Materials

Juerena R. Hoffman

Nine inhumations as well as isolated bones were recovered from El Macayo by SRI (Table 38). These human remains were analyzed following their removal from the excavation units. Most of the remains represent subadult individuals less than 15 years of age.

Following cleaning and reconstruction, the remains from each feature were inventoried, assessed for age and sex, measured, and evaluated for the presence of pathologies. The data collected correspond to recommendations by Buikstra and Ubelaker (1994). Data were recorded on forms developed by Cindy G. Condon and Keith W. Condon for use during the excavation of a historical-period cemetery in Dallas, Texas, with revisions by this author. Standard methods for age determination used in this study include dental maturation (Schour and Massler 1944; Ubelaker 1984), epiphyseal union (Krogman 1978), diaphyseal length (Maresh 1955; Ubelaker 1984), the morphology of the auricular surface of the ilium (Lovejoy et al. 1985), and dental attrition (Scott 1979; Smith 1984). Osteometrics collected (Table 39) correspond to those of the Tennessee data bank (Moore-Jansen et al. 1994), with additional subadult osteometrics as suggested by Fazekas and Kosa (1978) for fetal remains. Because of the poor preservation of the two adults, only a few nonmetric traits could be scored (Table 40).

Determination of biological sex for the adults is severely limited by poor preservation, especially of the skull and innominates. For two of the adults (Features 213 and 40), however, sufficient morphological characteristics are observable for possible sex determination.

Feature Descriptions

Feature 31

Sex: Not determinable.
Age: 5–10 years old, based on the size of the humerus shaft.

This humerus midshaft fragment fits to the left subadult humerus fragment recovered by ASM in 1987 (Gardiner and Huckell 1987). Together, they represent the almost complete right humerus of a subadult individual between the ages of 5 and 10 years.

Feature 39

Sex: Not determinable.
Age: 3–15 (probably 6–8) years old, based on fusion of the lumbar vertebral arches and the lack of fusion of the hand phalanges (Krogman 1978).

This feature represents a poorly preserved child whose arms and upper thorax were not recovered. Age estimation is limited by the absence of teeth and the lack of complete diaphyses. Recovered elements include portions of the frontal, right parietal, and ethmoid bones; the left ilium; left and right femurs, tibiae, and fibulae; one hand phalange; three lumbar vertebrae; and at least five ribs. No pathologies were observed on the recovered elements. The cranial fragments are too eroded to observe pathologies.

Table 38. Summary of Human Burials and Isolated Remains from El Macayo

Feature Number	Age at Death	Sex	Description
31	5–10 years	not determinable	left humerus fragment recovered
39	3–15 years	not determinable	poorly preserved subadult lacking dentition
40	45+ years	possible male	osteophytic lipping observed on the vertebrae and ribs
132	9–12 months	not determinable	unremodeled porotic hyperostosis observed on the parietals and occipital; eye orbits not recovered
147	adult	not determinable	right femur, tibia, and fibula recovered
151	5–7 years	not determinable	the first cervical vertebra exhibits nonfusion of the anterior portion
156	3–9 months	not determinable	possible unremodeled periostitis observed on the basilar portion of the occipital bone
213	17–25 years	possible female	poorly preserved cairn burial
214	subadult	not determinable	one cranial bone fragment
SU 122	not determinable	not determinable	one burned longbone fragment
5 (N2 L1 RFL)	not determinable	not determinable	one burned longbone fragment

Table 39. Osteometrics (in mm) for Human Remains Recovered from El Macayo

Osteometric	F 39	F 40	F 132	F 147	F 151	F 156	F 213
Length of lesser wing of sphenoid [a]						R: 19	
Width of lesser wing of sphenoid [a]						R: 14	
Length of basilar occipital [a]			17			15	
Width of basilar occipital [a]			24			17	
Width of lateral occipital [a]			L: 27				
Length of zygomatic [a]						R: 29	
Width of zygomatic [a]						R: 26	
Length of mandible [a]						R: 42	
Width of mandible [a]						R: 21	
Length of half mandible [a]						R: 62	
Length of humerus [a]					L: 143 R: 142	L: 72	
Circumference of humerus [b]		L: 66			L: 30 R: 31	L: 22 R: 22	R: 59
Width of distal end of humerus [a]				L: 25	L: 30 R: 28	L: 20 R: 18	
Length of radius [a]					L: 113 R: 113	R: 60	
Length of ulna [a]					L: 124 R: 125	L: 67 R: 68	
Physiological length of ulna [b]		R: 198					
Length of clavicle [a]					L: 76		
Circumference of clavicle [b]		L: 33					
Length of scapula [a]					L: 70		
Width of scapula [a]					L: 54		

Feature 40

Sex: Possible male, based on the overall robusticity of the longbones, relative narrowness of the sciatic notch, and the narrow, curved sacrum.

Age: 45+ years old, based on a composite estimate from the left and right auricular surfaces, which exhibit significant density and macroporosity with lipping at the apex (Lovejoy et al. 1985).

This poorly preserved and fragmented adult is represented by portions of the frontal, parietals, occipital, temporals, mandible, left sphenoid, and hyoid. Fragments of the left and right scapulae, clavicles, humeri, ilia, ischia, femurs, tibiae, and fibulae are present, along with the right radius and ulna. The hands are represented by the left and right naviculars, right lunate, left triquetral and pisiform, left and right lesser multangulars, capitates, hamates, right MC-I, left MC-V, and eight phalanges. Foot elements include the left and right tali, calcanei, left navicular, left and right cuneiform III and cuboids, right MT-II and MT-III, left and right MT-IV and MT-V, six phalanges, and one sesamoid bone. Also identified were 6 cervical vertebrae, 10 thoracic vertebrae, 4 lumbar vertebrae, the sacrum, 12 left ribs, and 11 right ribs. Only two right mandibular incisors (Nos. 25 and 26) are present. Neither exhibits shoveling. Dental attrition is moderate (Smith 1984) (Stages 5 and 6).

Mild osteophytic lipping, indicating degenerative joint disease, is observed around the glenoid fossa of the right

Osteometric	F 39	F 40	F 132	F 147	F 151	F 156	F 213
Width of ilium [a]					L: 65		
Length of ischium [a]					L: 40	R: 21	
Width of ischium [a]						R: 14	
Length of os pubis [a]					L: 31	L: 21	
Length of sacrum [b]		98					
Breadth of sacrum [b]		112					
Length of femur [a]					L: 192 R: 192		
Diameter of femoral head [b]		L: 44			L: 21		
Femur subtrochanteric anteroposterior diameter [b]				R: 24	L: 13 R: 14	R: 10	
Femur subtrochanteric mediolateral diameter [b]				R: 29	L: 19 R: 21	R: 11	
Femur midshaft anteriolateral diameter [b]	L: 17 R: 18				L: 10 R: 10	R: 8	
Femur midshaft mediolateral diameter [b]	L: 16 R: 16				L: 12 R: 12	R: 8	
Circumference of femur [b]	L: 55 R: 55				L: 38 R: 40	R: 25	
Width of distal end of femur [a]					L: 41		
Length of tibia [a]					L: 163 R: 163		
Circumference of tibia at nutrient foramen [b]	L: 65 R: 67	L: 84 R: 85			L: 41 R: 39		
Tibia anteroposterior diameter at nutrient foramen [b]	L: 22 R: 23	L: 31 R: 32			L: 12 R: 12		
Tibia mediolateral diameter at nutrient foramen [b]	L: 17 R: 18	L: 21 R: 22			L: 12 R: 11		
Length of fibula [a, b]		L: 319			L: 156 R: 159		

Key: F = feature; L = left; R = right
[a] Fazekas and Kosa 1978
[b] Moore-Jansen et al. 1994

Table 40. Nonmetric Traits Observed among Adult Burials from El Macayo

Trait	Feature 213	Feature 40
Os coronal		L: 1
Parietal notch bone		R: 1
Asterionic bone		R: 1
Os lambdoid		R: 2
Inca bone		1
Auditory exostosis		R: 1
Foramen ovale incomplete		L: 1
Patent foramen spinosum		L: 1
Post-condylar canal patent		R: 2
Divided hypoglossal canal	L: 1	R: 1
Atlas: lateral bridging		R: 1
Atlas: posterior bridging		R: 1
Cervical 3: accessory transverse foramen		L: 1
Cervical 5: accessory transverse foramen		R: 1
Cervical 6: accessory transverse foramen		L: 1
Humerus: septal aperture	R: 1	R: 1
Inion hook		1
Incisal shoveling	2	1
Incisal rotation	1	
Molar enamel extensions	2	

Key: 1 = trait absent; 2 = trait present; L = left; R = right
Note: Traits not observable are not included.

scapula. In addition, moderate to heavy lipping is observed on the superior and inferior surfaces of the anterior body surfaces of the fifth and sixth cervical vertebrae, as well as mild to moderate osteophytic development on the superior and inferior articular facets. The thoracic vertebrae show moderate to heavy lipping on the anterior bodies, as well as mild to moderate lipping on the transverse processes and rib articulations. The first sacral vertebra exhibits mild lipping along the anterior edges of the auricular surfaces. Various ribs exhibit osteophytic lipping corresponding to that seen on the articular facets of the thoracic vertebrae. Left ribs 1, 10, and 2, and right rib 12 exhibit mild to moderate lipping at the head. Several ribs from each side show mild to heavy lipping around the tuberosity. There is no evidence of inflammatory or developmental pathologies.

Feature 132

Sex: Not determinable.

Age: 9–12 months old, based on dental development (Schour and Massler 1944; Ubelaker 1984) and supported by fusion of the thoracic vertebral arches (Krogman 1978).

The recovered bone elements include the right parietal, occipital, temporals, left and right scapulae, left humerus, right ulna, one hand phalange, two foot phalanges, two cervical vertebrae, seven thoracic vertebrae, five left ribs, and five right ribs.

Pathologies observed on this relatively poorly preserved subadult are unremodeled porotic hyperostosis lesions on the left and right parietals, the occipital squamous, and the right temporal bone. The orbits were not recovered. In addition, possible remodeled periostitis is observed on the left lateral portion of the occipital and on the left and right scapulae on the posterior blade, inferior to the spinous process.

Feature 147

Sex: Not determinable.
Age: Adult, based on size of the recovered longbone shafts.

Only the right femur, tibia, and fibula shafts were recovered. Erosion of the shaft surfaces prevents pathology determination.

Feature 151

Sex: Not determinable.
Age: 5–7 years old, based on dentition (Schour and Massler 1944; Ubelaker 1984) and supported by the diaphyseal age (Weaver 1977).

This exceptionally well-preserved subadult is mostly complete except for the cranium. It was previously disturbed by rodent activity and probably by Feature 156. The recovered elements include maxillary teeth (Nos. 3, 8–11, and 14). The mandible is complete with erupted teeth (Nos. 19, K–T, and 31) and unerupted teeth (Nos. 18, 20–29, and 31). Also recovered are the hyoid elements, scapulae, clavicles, humeri, radii, ulnae, ilia, ischia, os pubes, femurs, tibiae, fibulae, right calcaneus, left and right MC-I, one MC-II, one MC-III, left and right MC-IV, left and right MC-V, and 12 phalanges (hand). Seven cervical vertebrae, 10 thoracic vertebrae, 4 lumbar vertebrae, 10 left ribs, 9 right ribs, and the gladiolus also are represented.

The only inflammatory pathologies observed are healed periostitis on the left and right tibiae and the right fibula. The first cervical vertebra exhibits an unusual developmental defect. The anterior portion of the vertebra is unfused, and there is evidence that more than one center of ossification was present in this anterior area of the C-1 vertebra.

Feature 156

Sex: Not determinable.
Age: 3–9 months old based on dentition (Schour and Massler 1944; Ubelaker 1984) and supported by diaphyseal age (Maresh 1955; Weaver 1977).

This very well-preserved infant was disturbed by rodent activity. Despite this disturbance, the remains are mostly complete, with recovery of the left and right frontals, parietals, occipital, right temporal, right zygomatic, right maxilla with deciduous teeth Nos. A–C, right mandible with deciduous teeth Nos. R–T, deciduous mandibular teeth Nos. M–Q, left and right sphenoids, and horns of the hyoid. Postcranial elements recovered include the humeri, radii, ulnae, right ilium, right ischium, left os pubis, femurs, right tibia, right capitate, left and right MC-I, left and right MC-II, left MC-III, left MC-V, nine phalanges (hand), two phalanges (foot), one cervical vertebra, five thoracic vertebrae, five lumbar vertebrae, one sacral vertebra, six left ribs, and four right ribs. The only pathology observed is possible periostitis on the ectocranial side of the occipital basilar portion.

Feature 213

Sex: Possible female, based on the general gracility of the longbones.
Age: 17–25 years old, based on the partial fusion of the iliac crest and of the annular rings of the vertebrae and the non-fusion of the sternal end of the clavicle (Krogman 1978).

This is a poorly preserved individual, previously damaged by trenching that removed a portion of the south side of the cairn burial. Elements recovered include portions of the parietals, occipital, temporals, left zygomatic, maxilla, mandible, and hyoid. Fragments of left and right scapulae, left clavicle, right humerus, radius, ulna, and ilium, ischium, left os pubis, tibia, and fibula were recovered. In addition, the right greater multangular, MC-I, MC-II, MC-III, one phalanx (hand), right calcaneus, two phalanges (foot), five cervical vertebrae, eight thoracic vertebrae, four lumbar vertebrae, four sacral vertebrae, six left ribs, four right ribs, and the gladiolus were recovered. The dentition is represented by teeth Nos. 2–5, 7–11, 29, and 30. The recovered maxillary incisors (Nos. 7–10) are shoveled. Dental attrition of the incisors is moderate (Smith 1984) (Stages 4 and 5); the posterior dentition is more heavily worn (Scott 1979) (Stages 6–9). No pathologies were observed on the recovered bones.

Feature 214

The only skeletal element recovered from this individual is an uncremated cranial fragment. This individual was a subadult human.

Additional Remains

Stripping Unit 122

A burned longbone fragment of indeterminate species was recovered from SU 122. Because it was burned, it is not attributable to either of the unburned inhumations, Features 151 and 156, discovered and exhumed within SU 122.

Feature 5

A burned longbone fragment was recovered from the roof fall level of Feature 5, a pit house. No diagnostic features were present to determine conclusively whether or not this was a human bone.

Test Pit 291

Seven fragments of burned bone weighing 6 g were recovered from the overburden above Feature 213. This is in the general vicinity where Gardiner and Huckell (1987:25–26, Table 1) discovered and exhumed two cremations, Features 1 and 2. These few pieces of burned bone may be related to those previously discovered cremations.

Summary

The sample of individuals represented by these burials, although it cannot be considered entirely representative of the prehistoric population from which it is derived, corresponds to certain patterns established from other prehistoric southwestern burial samples. The disproportionate number of subadults is indicative of the high infant mortality rates exhibited by premodern populations. Likewise, the presence of a possible young female (Feature 213) who exhibits no evidence of pathologies or external cause of death may be attributable to the high risks of childbirth for women prior to the middle of the twentieth century.

The subadults exhibit few pathologies overall. However, one burial (Feature 132) exhibits unremodeled porotic hyperostosis on the ectocranial surfaces of the right parietal and of the occipital (the eye orbits were not recovered, so no corroborating observation of cribra orbitalia can be made). Porotic hyperostosis is considered indicative of anemia of various etiologies. Current theory attributes such anemia to a wide range of causes, including nutritional iron deficiency as a result of high cereal or grain diets, high parasite loads that drain the body of nutrients (especially iron), and genetic anemias such as thalassemia and sickle-cell (Stuart-Macadam 1985). In the case of Feature 132, a 9–12-month-old child, an additional cause may be weaning stress or the poor health and nutrition status of the nursing mother. As with any subadult under 1 year old, such pathologies provide indirect evidence of the mother's health status.

Comparison of the diaphyseal lengths of Feature 151 and 156 to the standards of Ubelaker (1984) and Maresh (1955) shows a growth curve pattern similar to that reported for other samples: the younger infant (Feature 156) corresponds well to both samples for length of diaphyses compared to dental maturation, and the older child (Feature 151) shows good correspondence for diaphyseal age with Ubelaker's prehistoric Native American sample but is aged at least 1.5 years too young (3.5 years old) when compared to Maresh's modern whites from Ohio. Most children will be born with very similar longbone lengths, and differences in length probably begin to become apparent only as the first year is attained and nutritional stress causes a slowing of growth in children. This observation also illustrates the need to compare skeletal samples with similar samples (as determined by chronological, environmental, and ethnic variables), especially for discussions of subadult age based on skeletal (rather than dental) indicators.

Osteophytic lipping observed on the male (Feature 40) is possibly the result of years of manual labor that produced joint strain, eventually leading to degeneration of the joint surfaces. The mild lipping of the anterior rim of the glenoid fossa of the right scapula is also likely due to mechanical stress at that joint. Unfortunately, neither the articulating humeral head nor the left glenoid fossa and humeral head were recovered. The presence of mild to heavy lipping in the axial skeleton is consistent with that of an individual over the age of 40 years.

Overall, the skeletal remains of the reported sample of individuals are consistent with previously reported prehistoric southwestern burial samples in both age distribution and presence of pathologies. Aside from the developmental defect of the first cervical vertebrae observed on Feature 151, the El Macayo burial sample exhibits no extraordinary traits.

Evaluation, Summary, and Conclusion

Carla R. Van West & William L. Deaver

A data recovery program was undertaken at the archaeological site of El Macayo (AZ EE:9:107) in Nogales, Arizona, between April 16 and May 23, 1996, by a crew of three to four SRI archaeologists and a physical anthropologist supervised by William Deaver. The work was undertaken to mitigate anticipated impacts to an important National Register of Historic Places (NRHP)–eligible village site occupied more or less continually from about A.D. 650 to 1150. The archaeological investigations were funded by Santa Cruz County to fulfill preservation requirements prior to the construction of a baseball field and exercise path on and near the prehistoric village.

Based on the sample of structures identified previously by ASM and CES (Gardiner and Huckell 1987; Slawson 1991), four structures—Features 5, 15, 16, and 21—were targeted for excavation. These structures were selected for the following reasons. First, Features 5 and 16 had indications that they had burned upon abandonment and offered the possibility of recovering artifactual collections that would provide a momentary view of the settlement's history and yield well-preserved subsistence remains. Second, Feature 15 was selected because of its proximity to Feature 16. Preliminary data suggested that Features 15 and 16 represented contemporaneous structures and may offer a glimpse of the site's spatial and organizational structure. Third, Feature 21 was selected because it was located near the edge of the settlement and possessed characteristics that suggested it was more formally constructed than the other structures. Thus, it might provide additional information on site structure, chronology, and cultural affiliation.

By the end of the 28 days of fieldwork, a total of 177 features had been exposed, identified, and mapped. Of these 177, 11 pit structures, 11 burials, 19 pits, and 1 miscellaneous feature had been fully or partially excavated and are described in this report. As planned, the pit structures Features 5, 15, and 16 were excavated, but Feature 21 was left unexplored because of the number of burials encountered and the need to record and remove them. An additional eight pit structures, however, were investigated (Features 42–44, 52, 139, 150, 211, and 215).

One objective of an archaeological excavation is to unearth new evidence that will inform upon past lifeways and cultures. Another objective, however, is to evaluate the effectiveness of data recovery techniques and ascertain whether alternative methods and techniques would have been more appropriate. The data recovery plan constructed for the 1996 investigations of El Macayo employed a backhoe to remove the thick layer of sediments that overlay the buried pit houses. This was done to quickly reach the structural fill and architectural features and to recover as much cultural information as possible. Previous experiences with pit houses have taught us that this is an effective strategy when the color and texture of the buried structural fill is different from the native subsoil into which structures were constructed. This was indeed the case at this site, but three unanticipated factors limited the success of this approach.

The first factor related to the techniques of the backhoe operator. Although a skilled operator, the individual was not experienced with archaeological excavations, where the machinery is used to strip large, shallow areas just to the level where subsurface anomalies (i.e., features and other evidence of cultural behavior) appear. As a result, mechanical actions destroyed or altered some features that were contained within the overburden deposits and disturbed the upper parts of certain features and deposits that were at the bottom of this unit.

A second factor that limited our success with mechanical excavations related to the behaviors practiced by the prehistoric inhabitants of El Macayo. Because the terrace on which the settlement was located slopes from west to east, many of the house floors were excavated 10–15 cm below the top of the calcic horizon on the upslope side but were flush with the top of the calcic horizon on the downslope side. In a number of cases, sediments were removed in level cuts, resulting in the destruction of the upslope construction features and fill directly above the floor.

Finally, the third factor related to the processes that led to the creation of the archaeological record. As work progressed, it became clear that the house pits excavated prehistorically for these pit structures had been dug only deep enough to reach a consistent level in the underlying Unit III calcic soil. The houses themselves, however, were located largely in what would become the lower portions of Unit II. Given the complex history of building and rebuilding that took place on the terrace, it is not surprising that superimposed features and remodeling events often obscured the outlines of the targeted structures.

In retrospect, an alternate strategy for excavating a site similar to this would be to employ a larger manual labor force and broadside the excavation areas in arbitrary levels, systematically screening selected excavation units. Because it is easier to control manual excavation, particularly along the vertical dimension, we would have had a greater chance of defining and documenting the stratification of features that was no doubt present. This technique would, however, cost more (and perhaps take more time) than using a backhoe to remove overburden deposits.

Despite these problems, we still obtained important information about this settlement and gained insight into the history of settlement in the Nogales area. Our program of data recovery at El Macayo augments a small but growing data set on the archaeological remains of this poorly understood geographic area. In the following section, we summarize our results and compare them with data and patterns observed at other sites in the Nogales area where data recovery has been reported. Our discussion is organized by the research themes presented in Chapter 1.

El Macayo and Middle Formative Period Occupation in the Nogales Area

Chronological Issues

In an effort to refine a local chronological sequence for the Nogales area, we attempted to assign calendar dates to chronometrically sampled features, establish construction sequences for particular loci within the site, and suggest a general site occupation sequence by combining these results with those inferred for time-diagnostic artifacts. Unfortu-

nately, few features yielded organic materials that could be subjected directly to absolute dating methods, and considerable reuse and superpositioning of architectural features frequently obscured stratigraphic relationships. Consequently, we relied heavily on the associations of painted ceramics to suggest use dates for various features. For the most part, these painted sherds derived from Trincheras series, Santa Cruz (Tucson Basin) series, and Gila series vessels that we assume were whole or otherwise usable items obtained through prehistoric exchange, gift giving, and inheritance.[1] Use dates assigned to features and occupational surfaces, therefore, were assigned on the basis of these intrusive types. The intrusive types themselves have been dated by their co-occurrence elsewhere with Anasazi and Mogollon pottery types, which, in turn, have been dated by their association with tree-ring-dated contexts.

Painted ceramic types recovered from the Santa Cruz County portion of El Macayo suggest that occupation began at least by A.D. 750 (and possibly as early as A.D. 650), and could have persisted as late as A.D. 1450 (Figure 55); however, the number of sherds dating to before A.D. 750 and after A.D. 1200 were notably few. Archaeomagnetic dating of two hearths (Features 43 and 44) confirms that the site was occupied in the late tenth and middle twelfth centuries A.D. Ceramic evidence further suggests that the site was largely abandoned by the beginning of the thirteenth century A.D. It is important to note, however, that if we learn from future archaeological studies that painted ceramics were not used in the Nogales area for culinary and funerary purposes after A.D. 1150 or 1200 and that only local plain wares were manufactured and used after that time, then our suggested dates for the duration of occupation and site abandonment will have to be revised. Similarly, if it were possible to conduct excavations on the portions of El Macayo not owned by Santa Cruz County, and if data recovery indicated the presence of a late village component to the east, we would also have to revise our settlement chronology to acknowledge the history and direction of settlement growth.

El Macayo and Its Temporal Relationship to Other Settlements in the Nogales Area

The method of assigning occupation dates to features and sites on the basis of intrusive pottery types, as well as temporally diagnostic projectile points or architectural characteristics, is standard practice in the upper Santa Cruz River valley. Few radiocarbon dates or archaeomagnetic dates have been obtained from professionally investigated sites, and as a result, most Formative period sites are dated by the presence, absence, or abundance of cross-dated painted ceramics (Table 41). The wide occupational ranges given for Formative period sites in the Nogales area reflect the low temporal resolution afforded by this reliance on cross-dated ceramics (Figure 56).

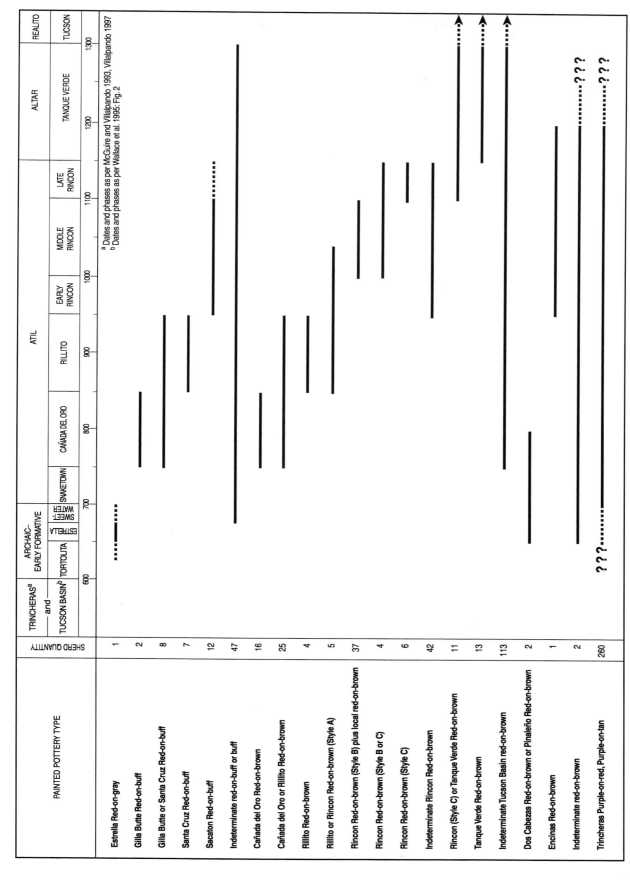

Figure 55. Manufacture and use dates by phase for painted pottery types recovered from El Macayo.

Table 41. Sources of Data Used to Date Formative Period Sites in the Nogales Area

Site Name	ASM Site No.	[14]C	Archaeomagnetic Dating	Ceramics	Projectile Points	Architectural Attributes
Arivaca site	AZ DD:7:22	x	x	x		
Baca Float site	AZ DD:8:127		x	x		
Buena Vista Ranch site	AZ EE:9:151			x		
Cemetery Ridge site	AZ DD:8:122		x	x		
El Macayo	AZ EE:9:107		x	x	x	
Nogales Wash site	AZ EE:9:93			x	x	
Paloparado	AZ DD:8:2 and 12			x	x	x
Potrero Creek site	AZ EE:9:53			x		x
South River Road site	AZ EE:9:117	x	x	x	x	x
Tinaja Canyon site	AZ DD:8:128			x	x	

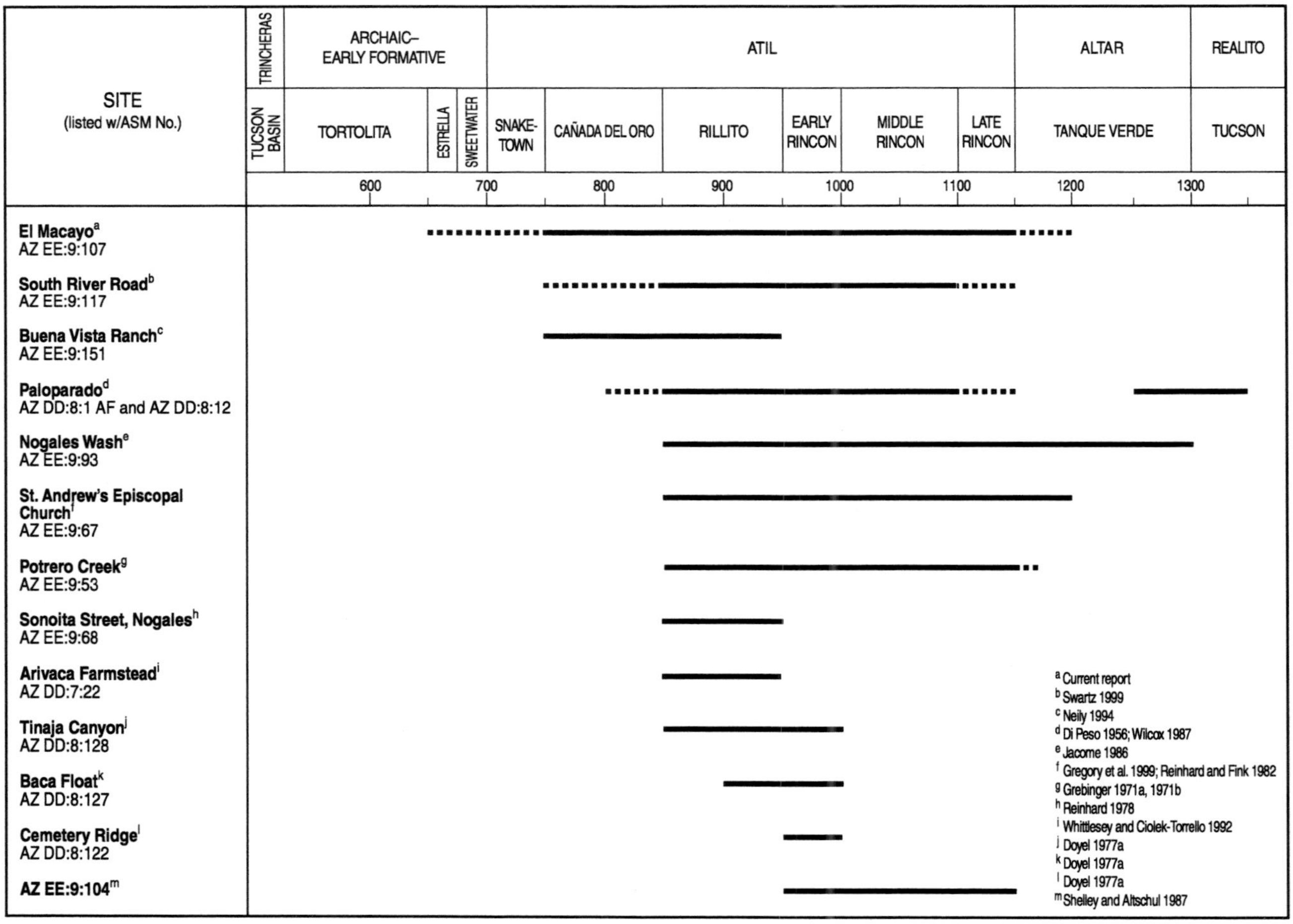

Figure 56. Occupation dates inferred for Nogales-area sites.

Examination of Figure 56 in conjunction with a reading of the original reports suggests the following. First, the presence of early intrusive types at sites such as El Macayo, Potrero Creek, and Nogales Wash hints at the presence of an Early Ceramic period occupation in the Nogales area, but it has not been recognized as such because unambiguous material culture signatures have yet to be defined. Second, the primary occupation of all but one of the sites reported to date dates to A.D. 750–1150, whereas the primary occupation of Paloparado dates to post-1150. Scant evidence, in the form of ceramics, of a post-1150 occupation in Nogales exists: a few sherds of Tanque Verde Red-on-brown recovered from El Macayo, Nogales Wash, Potrero Creek, and the Saint Andrew's Episcopal Church site. Finally, three sites stand out by virtue of the length of their primary occupation and the number and variety of features recovered from excavation: El Macayo, Paloparado, and Potrero Creek. Each appears to have been a place of persistent and extensive settlement over many centuries. Each is located on a low terrace above the confluence of two drainages adjacent to sizable patches of high-quality arable land.

Within a 3-mile radius of El Macayo are 28 sites recorded in the ASM site files (Table 42). Ten of these are historical-period resources (the Santa Cruz County Courthouse and the Old Nogales City Hall and Fire Station, both listed in the NRHP; Pete Kitchen's Ranch; a structure thought to be associated with Pete Kitchen's Ranch; two distinct locations of the 1916–1917 National Guard Camp; a historical road segment; a segment of a historical railroad route; a mid-twentieth-century vernacular house; and a trash dump) and 18 are prehistoric resources (seven habitation sites, three cemeteries, five lithic procurement and -processing locations, one agricultural site, and two sites of unknown function).

Of the seven prehistoric habitation sites, four have been investigated through testing or more-complete data recovery and are archaeologically contemporaneous. These include the Potrero Creek site (Grebinger 1971a, 1971b); the Saint Andrew's Episcopal Church site (Gregory et al. 1999; Reinhard and Fink 1982), which is believed to be a northern portion of the Potrero Creek site; the Nogales Wash site (Jácome 1986); and El Macayo (Gardiner and Huckell 1987; Neily and Euler 1987; Slawson 1991; this report). Each of these four has produced human cremations and inhumations. The remaining three habitation sites (AZ EE:54, 104, 155) are known only through surface survey but appear to date to the pre-Classic period, as well.

The three sites recorded as prehistoric cemeteries have received only minor attention to date: the Sonoita Street site (Cummings, additional site information, 1928, 1932, ASM[2]; Reinhard 1978; Reinhard and Fink 1982); an unnamed site on the south side of the confluence of Mariposa Wash and Nogales Wash, west of U.S. Highway 89 (AZ EE:9:85) (Goree 1972; site files, ASM); and the Mary Margarite site

(Urban, site files, 1985, ASM), which is a component of a modern cemetery by that name. Each of these may have been part of a residential site, but emergency data recovery undertaken at the Sonoita Street, for example, did not reveal evidence of pit structures or other domestic activity features. A depression that may have represented a pit house was observed at the unnamed site on the south side of Mariposa Wash (Goree 1972). It is unlikely that these three sites were isolated cemeteries; rather, the loci investigated or observed are undoubtedly but portions of three habitation sites that have not yet been documented.

Although dates have not been assigned to the Mary Margarite prehistoric cemetery, Rillito Red-on-brown and Trincheras Purple-on-red ceramics recovered from cremations on Sonoita Street indicate that this was a cemetery used prior to A.D. 1150. Similarly, ceramic vessels recovered from the cremations at the site on the south bank of Mariposa Wash included plain ware and Trincheras series types. These data add support to data gathered from excavated habitation sites suggesting that primary occupation of the Nogales area took place in the A.D. 750–1150 period, a span equivalent to the Hohokam Colonial and Sedentary periods and the Trincheras Atil phase (McGuire and Villalpando 1993; Villalpando 1997).

The remaining eight prehistoric sites are known only through surface remains, and occupation or use dates are not reported in the literature. These include a lithic scatter inferred to be a quarry and processing locale (AZ EE:9:159) (Carpenter and Tompkins 1995), three lithic scatters described as procurement and processing locations (AZ EE:9:141, 142, and 143) (Martynec et al. 1994), and a lithic scatter identified as a limited-activity site (AZ EE:9:173) (Lite et al. 1996). Nearby, at the foot of a low volcanic hill, is another lithic scatter, AZ EE:9:179, that also contains rock piles, a terrace, an agave knife, and other artifactual material inferred to be associated with prehistoric agricultural endeavors. Finally, two sites, AZ EE:9:160 and 173, are sherd-and-lithic scatters of unknown function.

What we may conclude from the foregoing review, then, is that (1) El Macayo was one of a small number of hamlet- or village-size settlements along the major tributaries to the upper Santa Cruz River valley, (2) El Macayo is archaeologically contemporaneous with a number of sites in the near vicinity, and (3) El Macayo is chronologically representative of Middle Formative period occupation in this locality. Ceramically visible occupation in the locality began sometime between A.D. 650 and 750, was most evident between A.D. 750 and 1150, and continued for some time into the Late Formative period (A.D. 1150–1450). Whether El Macayo was indeed abandoned in A.D. 1150–1200 is open to question, given the limitations of our data recovery sample and current dating methods. Still, it seems plausible to us that the residents of this village may have abandoned this settlement and joined other local populations to form a

Table 42. Sites Recorded in the ASM Site Files for Nogales, Arizona

ASM Site No. (AZ EE:9:)	Name	Reference	Site Type	Settlement Function	Size
53	Potrero Creek	Grebinger 1971a, 1971b; Lite et al. 1996; Vivian, site cards, 1966	artifact scatter	habitation	200 × 200 feet
54		Lite et al. 1966; Stone 1995; Vivian and Wrasse, site cards, 1966	artifact scatter	habitation?	100 × 100 feet
67	St Andrew's Episcopal Church	Gregory et al. 1999; Reinhard 1978; Reinhard and Fink 1982	artifact scatter, cremation	habitation and burial	60 × 60 m
68	Sonoita Street	Cummings, additional site info., ca. 1928, 1932, ASM; Reinhard 1978; Reinhard and Fink 1982	cremation	burial	not given
85		Goree 1972	artifact scatter, cremation	burial, habitation ?	not given
88	Pete Kitchen's Ranch	Melot, site cards, 1976; Wilson 1974, NRHP listed in 1975	historical-period structures	historical-period habitation	not given
89	Old Nogales City Hall and Fire Station	NRHP listed in 1980	NRHP-listed historic structure	public buildings	not given
92	Old Santa Cruz Co. Courthouse	NRHP listed in 1977	NRHP-listed historic structure	public buildings	not given
93	Nogales Wash	Jácome 1986; Urban, site cards, 1982	artifact scatter, cremation	habitation, burial	200 × 200 m
102/107	El Macayo	Neily and Euler 1987; Gardiner and Huckell 1987; this report	artifact scatter, cremation	habitation, burial	125 × 70 m?
103	Mary Margarite Cemetery	Urban, site cards, 1985	artifact scatter, cremation	habitation, burial	200 × 400 m
104		Shelley and Altschul 1987	prehistoric artifact scatter and historical period	habitation?	50 × 50 m for prehistoric scatter; 175 × 200 m overall
105		Shelley and Altschul 1987	prehistoric artifacts; historical-period artifact scatter and structure	unknown prehistoric; historical-period habitation	4 × 7 m for prehistoric scatter; 18 × 20 m overall
108	1916–1917 National Guard Encampment	Gardiner and Huckell 1987	artifact scatter; historical-period foundations	20th-century military camp	not given

ASM Site No. (AZ EE:9:)	Name	Site Type	Settlement Function	Size	Reference
109	1916–1917 National Guard Encampment	artifact scatter, foundations, 13 loci	20th-century military camp	350 × 700 m	Gardiner 1987; Gardiner and Huckell 1987; Neily and Euler 1987
110	Thelma Street Dump	artifact scatter	20th-century trash dump	90 × 60 m	Urban, site cards, 1990
141		lithic scatter	procurement and processing	120 × 100 m	Martynec et al. 1994
142		lithic scatter	procurement and processing	40 × 50 m	Martynec et al. 1994
143		lithic scatter	procurement and processing	40 × 80 m	Martynec et al. 1994
155		artifact scatter	habitation	35 × 40 feet	Adams and Hoffman 1995; Stone 1994
159		lithic scatter	quarry and processing	120 × 90 m	Carpenter and Tompkins 1995
160		artifact scatter	unknown	50 × 25 m	Swartz 1995
172		railroad route	New Mexico and Arizona Railroad	200 × 10 feet	Lite et al. 1996
173		artifact scatter	limited-activity site	130 × 90 m	Lite et al. 1996
176		road segment	old Nogales-Tucson Road	6 mi. × 40 feet	Lite 1996a; Lite et al. 1996
177		historical-period house	1940–1960 vernacular	50 × 30 feet	Lite and Palus 1997
179		lithic scatter, rock piles, terrace	agriculture	150 × 120 m	Lascaux 1998

Note: Site cards are on file at the Arizona State Museum, University of Arizona, Tucson.

limited number of large villages elsewhere in the region. This type of demographic reorganization has been widely documented in both the southern and the northern Southwest for this time (Adler 1996; Dean et al. 1994) and is reflected in the archaeological record as changes in settlement location, settlement size, economic focus, and external connections. The site of Paloparado (Di Peso 1956; Wilcox 1987), for example, appears to have been one of these large community centers in the upper Santa Cruz River valley during the Classic period. Radical changes in the scale and organization of settlement as compared with its pre-Classic form suggest that societal transformations sweeping across the Southwest during the thirteenth century were also taking place in the borderlands.

During the pre-Classic period, settlements in the Nogales area coeval with El Macayo included the Potrero Creek and Saint Andrew's Episcopal Church sites to the north and the Nogales Wash, Mary Margarite, and Sonoita Street sites to the south (see Figure 1). Given the low resolution of current dating schemes, we cannot suggest which settlements may have been members of the same community or how many communities were present at any given time. Nonetheless, we can suggest that if there was a Classic period occupation in the immediate Nogales area, and if populations aggregated into fewer but larger residential sites as they did elsewhere in the Southwest, the most promising location for such a center was in the vicinity of the Potrero Creek site, which is located at the confluence of the two largest drainages in the Nogales area in a reach with high-quality arable land and perennial subsurface water. It is likely that in the early Classic period, the residents of El Macayo did reestablish themselves at places of greater economic security at settlements such as Potrero Creek, which may have been the Nogales area equivalent of Paloparado, just 19.6 km (12.2 miles) farther downstream.

Settlement Structure and Intrasettlement Behavior

Prior to our fieldwork, we hoped that our data recovery efforts would expose a sufficiently large portion of the site to reveal a variety of architectural units and extramural features. We wanted to identify intervillage settlement patterns and to deduce the principles and practices that governed the development and use of the settlement over time. Our plan was, first, to describe the various architectural and organizational characteristics and, second, to identify activity areas where evidence permitted. Finally, if chronological and archaeological data permitted, we hoped that we could suggest growth characteristics and patterned changes in intrasettlement behavior through time. Unfortunately, we were not able to strip large areas in the time available to us, few features produced datable remains, and we discovered

that the record of individual architectural features was obscured by frequent remodeling or rebuilding (e.g., Feature 212; see Chapter 2).

As an alternate strategy, we reviewed architectural data, site plan data, and archaeological interpretations of village growth for excavated sites in the Nogales area (Figures 57–62). Table 43 summarizes selected characteristics of house forms, and Table 44 summarizes basic information about the number and type of extramural features recorded at these same sites. Table 45 summarizes burial information. Data presented in these tables were derived from published reports or counted and measured from site maps when not reported. The purpose of this review was to determine whether the architectural forms (e.g., shape, size, orientation, and intramural features) recorded at El Macayo were similar to or different from those recorded at nearby sites and to suggest cultural correspondences or divergences.

Twenty-four pit structures (houses-in-pits) have been recorded on the Santa Cruz County Complex portion of El Macayo (see Table 43 and Figure 11). Of these 24, only five were sufficiently well preserved or investigated to determine their approximate dimensions, shape, and house orientation. All others were encountered in trench profiles, poorly preserved, or otherwise unexplored. Of the five houses, two were rectangular (Features 16 and 44; see Figure 59g, i), two were oval (Features 5a and 15), and one was round (Feature 5b). The oval and rectangular houses generally were about 5 m long and 3 m wide, with vestibule or wall entries, oriented to the east or east-southeast. We were not able to document roof support systems in more than one house (Feature 16; see Figure 59g), but we did record a great number of wall postholes, internal postholes—presumably related to raised platforms, raised floors, and other intramural features—nonthermal pits, and hearths within many structures. Our small sample compares well with the two houses found at Nogales Wash (see Figure 59e, f); most of the 12 structures investigated at Potrero Creek (see Figure 59b); the Type 1, 3, and 5 structures excavated at the pre-Classic component of Paloparado (see Figure 59a); and the three houses excavated at Cemetery Ridge and the Baca Float site (see Figure 59c, d). Our sample differs from the single Arivaca Farmstead site house (see Figure 59k) in that our structures are shallow houses-in-pits rather than surface structures. Our houses are completely unlike the cobble-lined pit structure excavated at the Buena Vista Ranch site (see Figure 59j). Finally, the remains at South River Road are too incomplete to make a comparison (see Figure 59l, m).

Extramural features recorded on the Santa Cruz County portion of El Macayo include 28 thermal and 144 nonthermal pits (including storage pits and postholes), 2 secondary cremations in shallow pits, and 17 inhumation burials, including 1 macaw, 2 dogs, and 3 unexcavated pits inferred to be graves (see Tables 44 and 45). No courtyards were

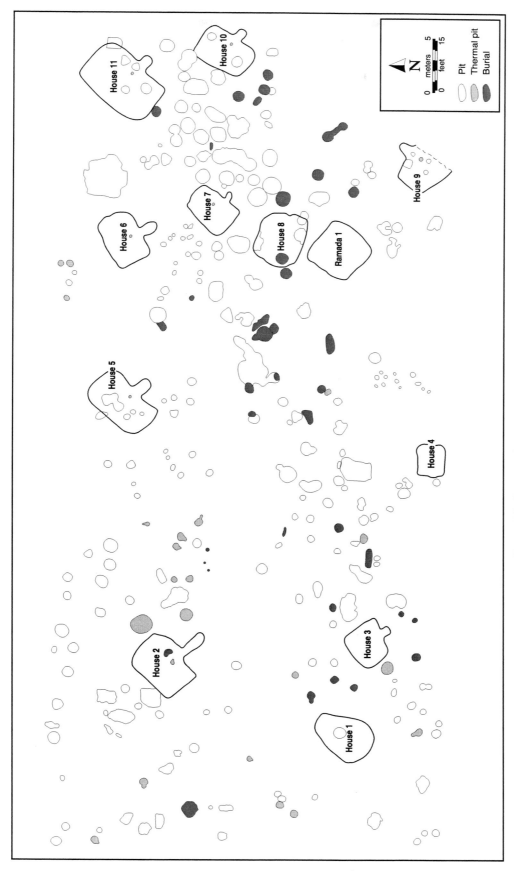

Figure 57. Site plan for the Potrero Creek site.

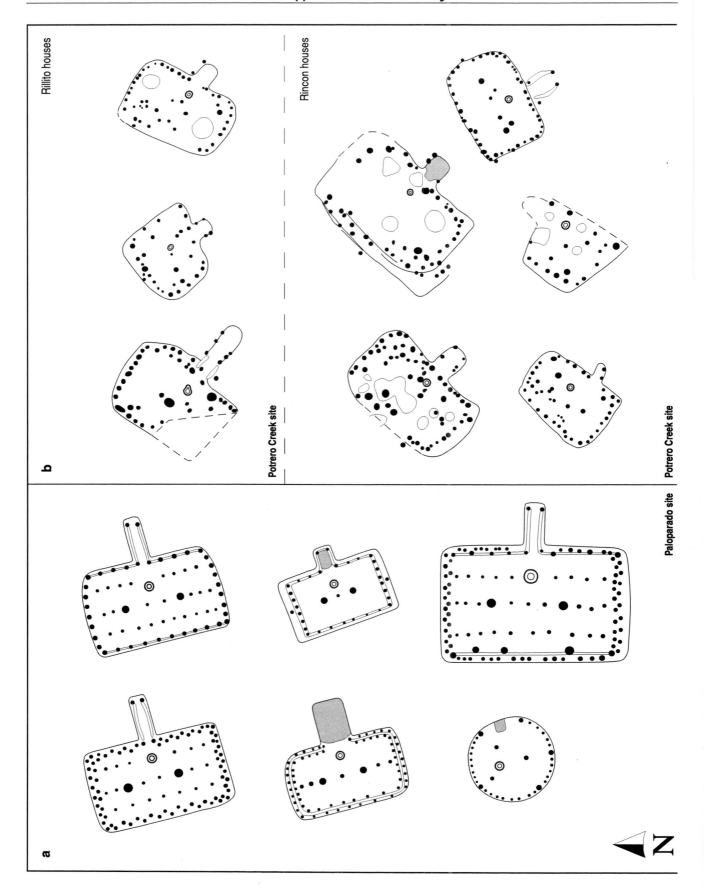

Rillito houses

Rincon houses

Potrero Creek site

Potrero Creek site

Paloparado site

b

a

N

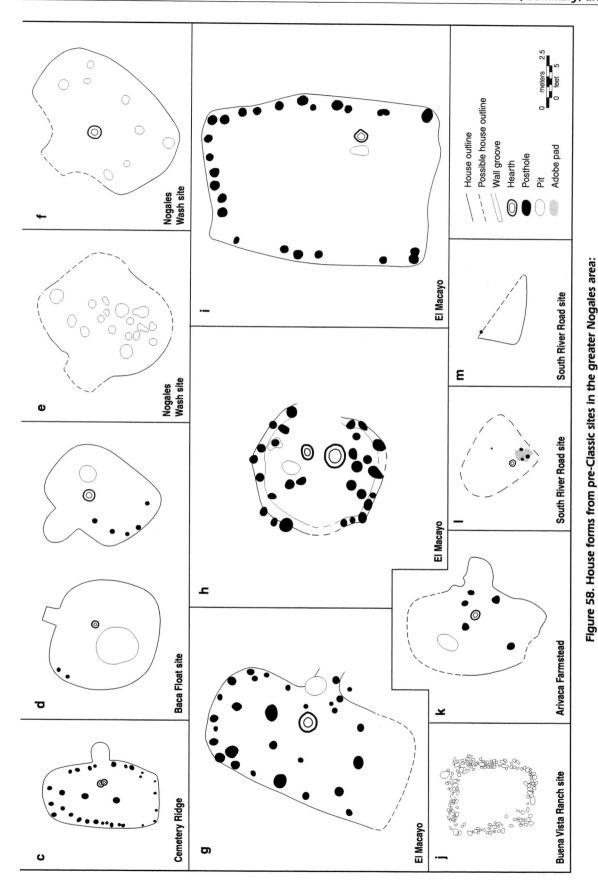

Figure 58. House forms from pre-Classic sites in the greater Nogales area:
(a) after Di Peso 1956:Figure 32; (b) after Grebinger 1971b:Figure 1;
(c) after Doyel 1977a:Figure 4; (d) after Doyel 1977a:Figure 21; (e, f) after Jácome 1986:Figures 4.2 and 4.3;
(g) see Figure 17, this report; (h) see Figure 15, this report; (i) see Figure 21, this report; (j) after Nelly 1994:Figure 11;
(k) after Whittlesey and Ciolek-Torrello 1992:Figure 10; (l) after Swartz 1999:Figure 3.2; (m) after Swartz 1999:Figure 3.1.

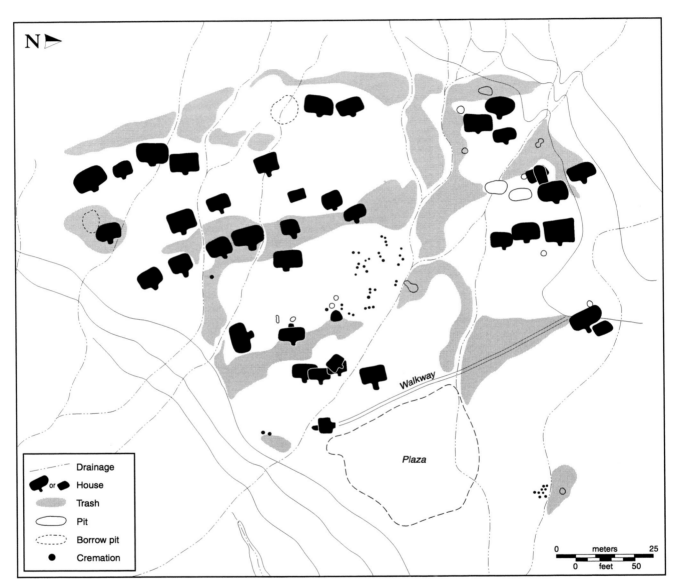

Figure 59. Site plan for the pre-Classic period occupation at Paloparado Ruin (after Wilcox 1987:Figure 3).

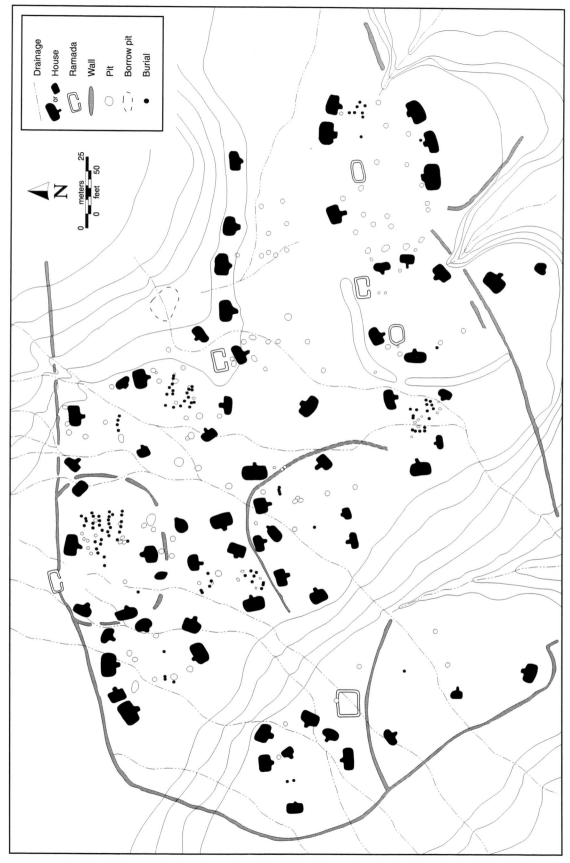

Figure 60. Site plan for the Classic period occupation at Paloparado Ruin, Upper Terrace (after Wilcox 1987:Figure 4).

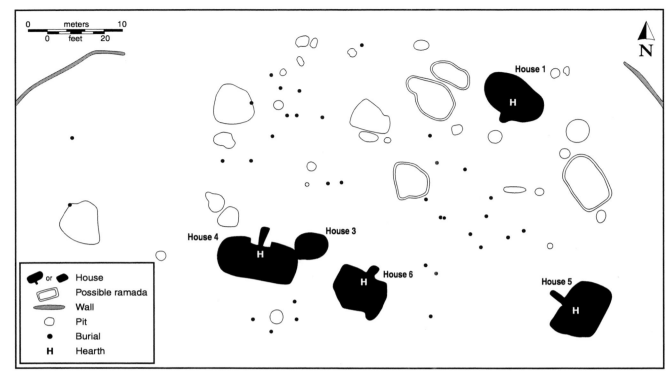

Figure 61. Site plan for the Classic period occupation at Paloparado Ruin, Lower Terrace (after Brown and Grebinger 1969:Figure 1).

identified, nor were borrow pits, trash mounds, or evidence of public architecture or villagewide shared space (e.g., perimeter walls, terraces, banquettes, dance floors, plazas, or ceremonial architecture).

The single site that compares well with El Macayo with regard to the number and ratio of thermal to nonthermal extramural pits is Potrero Creek, just 2.4 km (1.5 miles) to the north (see Figure 57). No other site, including the Rillito-Rincon phase occupation of Paloparado, evidenced a similar number and distribution of extramural pits. Di Peso (1956) recorded only six thermal features and no nonthermal features in pre-Classic Paloparado (see Figure 58). Grebinger (1971b), however, recorded 20 thermal features and 195 nonthermal features associated with the Rillito and Rincon occupations of Potrero Creek. The smaller habitation sites—Cemetery Ridge, Baca Float, Tinaja Canyon, Arivaca Farmstead, Buena Vista Ranch, and South River Road—and the Nogales Wash site did not compare well with El Macayo.

Similarly, the fact that both cremations and inhumations are present at El Macayo (2 cremations to 13 human inhumations and 3 animal inhumations) compares favorably with Potrero Creek (4 cremations to 35 human inhumations), Nogales Wash (12 cremations to 1 human inhumation), and Paloparado (77 cremations to 215 human inhumations and 3 animal inhumations). Mapped distributions of features at El Macayo and Potrero Creek suggest that

both sites contained areas where human and animal burials occurred in groups. The presence of these groups suggests that, during the occupation of these two settlements, there were designated cemetery areas. In the case of El Macayo, our ability to clearly delineate these cemeteries was reduced by the persistent building and superpositioning of houses and other domestic space, but the map of Potrero Creek suggests a similar dedication of space within the village. At Paloparado, most of the cremations were clustered in a single burial area near the only round pre-Classic house, and inhumations were grouped in nine burial areas, each associated with a distinctive Classic period compound.

The contrast in burial practices at Paloparado is very strong and is supported by considerable numbers. Cremations made up 100 percent of the pre-Classic burial population, with inhumation burials entirely restricted to the Classic period occupation. Di Peso (1956:515) recovered 181 human inhumations, 3 animal inhumations, and 2 cremations from the Upper Terrace Classic period occupation (see Figure 60), and Brown and Grebinger (1969:189) recovered 34 inhumations from the Lower Terrace Classic period occupation (see Figure 61). In contrast, the assignment of dates to the burials at El Macayo is weak. Most of the inhumations recovered at El Macayo are thought to date to the pre-Classic because of their proximity to pre-Classic period houses. Of the 13 human inhumations identified at El Macayo, only three (Features 32, 151, and 214) were

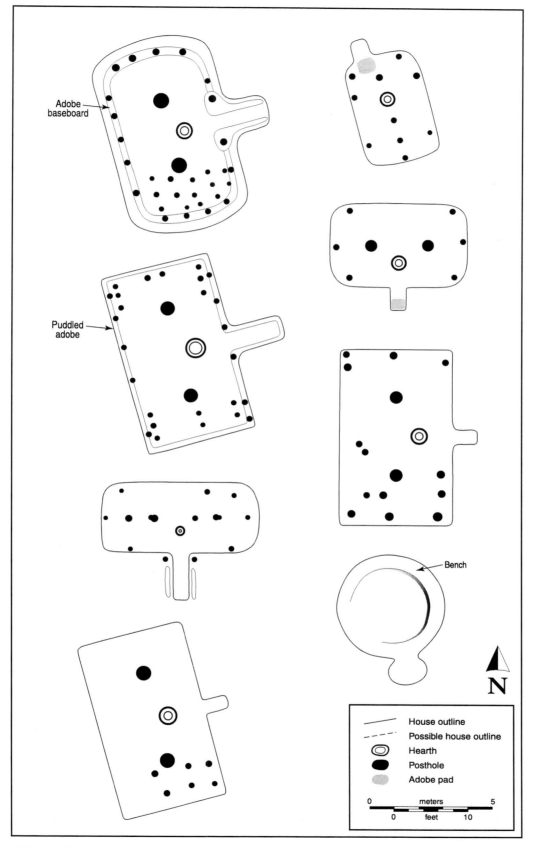

Figure 62. House forms from Classic period Paloparado Ruin (after Di Peso 1956:Figure 13).

Table 43. Selected Architectural and Settlement Data for Nogales-Area Sites

Site [Area m²]/ Feature No./ House Type	Occupation	Feat. Length (m)	Chamber Width (m)	Area (m²)	L:W Ratio	Shape	Entry	Entry Type	Entry Position	Orient.	Hearth	Hearth Type	Hearth Location	Roof Support	Post-holes	Pits
Potrero Creek (2,808 m²)																
House 2	Rillito	5.4	4.1	22.14	1.32	rectang.	yes	vest.	long wall	SE	yes	na	near entry	na	yes	yes?
House 3	Rillito	3.8	3.5	13.3	1.09	square	yes	vest.	long wall	SE	yes	na	near center	na	yes	no?
House 10	Rillito	5.1	3.4	17.34	1.50	rectang.	yes	vest.	long wall	SE	yes	na	near entry	na	yes	yes?
House 5	Rincon	6.2	3.5	21.7	1.77	rectang.	yes	vest.	long wall	SE	yes	na	near entry	na	yes	yes?
House 6	Rincon	4.9	3.2	15.68	1.53	rectang.	yes	vest.	long wall	SE	yes	na	near entry	2-post?	yes	no
House 7	Rincon	4.3	3	12.9	1.43	rectang.	yes	vest.	long wall	SE	yes	na	near center	na	yes	no
House 9	Rincon	5.4	3.8	20.52	1.42	rectang.	yes	vest.	long wall	NE	yes	na	near entry	na	yes	no?
House 11	Rincon	7.6	4.6	34.96	1.65	rectang.	yes	vest.	long wall	SE	yes	na	near entry	na	yes	yes?
House 1	unknown	5.4	4.1	22.14	1.32	oval	no				no			na	yes	yes?
House 4	unknown	3	2.4	7.2	1.25	square	no				no			na	yes	no?
House 8	unknown	4.9	4.1	20.09	1.20	square	no				no			na	yes	yes?
Ramada 1	unknown	6.8	6.2	42.16	1.10	square	no				no			na	yes	yes?
Nogales Wash (5,780 m²)																
Feature 11	late Rillito	6	unk.	unk.	unk.	unk.	unk.	unk.	unk.	unk.	unk.	unk.	unk.	unk.	unk.	yes
Feature 1	Rincon	5.8	5	29	1.16	square	yes	vest.	long wall	NW	no	unk.	unk.	unk.	yes	crem. burial
Feature 2	Rincon	7.2	4.3	30.96	1.67	rectang.	yes	vest.	long wall	NW	yes	unk.	near entry	unk.	yes	no?
Arivaca Farmstead (40 m²)																
Feature 1	Colonial	5	4.38	21.9	1.14	square	yes	vest.	corner	E	yes	plastered	near center	unk.	yes	yes
South River Road (305.5 m²)																
Feature 1	Colonial?	inc.	inc.	inc.	inc.	rectang.	no	unk.	unk.	unk.	unk.	unk.	unk.	unk.	yes	no?
Feature 37	unknown	3.7	3.3	12.21	1.12	unk.	yes?	unk.	unk.	SE?	unk.	plastered	near entry	unk.	yes	yes (intrusive)
Buena Vista Ranch (3,200 m²)																
Feature 5	Santa Cruz	3.18	2.8	8.90	1.14	square	no?	unk.	unk.	unk.	no?	unk.		unk.	yes	yes

Site (Area [m²])/ Feature No./ House Type	Occupation	Feat. Length (m)	Chamber Width (m)	Area (m²)	L:W Ratio	Shape	Entry	Entry Type	Entry Position	Orient.	Hearth	Hearth Type	Hearth Location	Roof Support	Post-holes	Pits
Cemetery Ridge (874 m²)																
Feature 19	Rillito-Rincon transition	4.75	3.25	15.44	1.46	rectang.	yes	vest.	long wall	NW	yes, 2	plastered	near entry	3-post	yes	yes
Baca Float site (258 m²)																
Feature 1	Rincon?	5.6	5.3	29.68	1.06	square	yes	vest.	long wall	NW	yes?	unk.	near center	no	yes	yes
Feature 2	unknown	5.5	5	27.5	1.10	round	yes	vest.	long wall	N-NE	yes	plastered	near center	no	yes	yes (predates house)
Tinaja Canyon (Locus A = 1,200 m²; Locus B = 150 m²)																
Locus A, Feature 3 (PH 1)	Rillito-Rincon transition	5.9	5.2	30.68	1.13	oval	yes	vest.	long wall	W-SW	yes	unk.	unk.	no	no	no
Locus A, Feature 11 (PH 2)	Rillito-Rincon transition	5.1	3.5	17.85	1.46	rectang.	no				no			no	no	no
Locus A, Feature 8	post-Rincon	5.2 diam.		21.24		round	no				no			no	no	no
Locus A, Feature 9	post-Rincon	4.5 diam.		15.9		round	no				no			no	no	no
Locus A, Feature 12	post-Rincon	4.3 diam.		14.52		round	no				no			no	no	no
Locus B, Feature 3	post-Rincon	3.7 diam.		10.75		round	no				no			no	no	no
Locus B, Feature 4	post-Rincon	3.5 diam.		9.62		round	no				no			no	no	no
Paloparado, Upper Terrace (pre-Classic = 18,500 m²; Classic = 58,600 m²)																
Type 1 house (28 examples)	Rillito-Rincon	6.5	4	26	1.63	rectang.	yes	vest.	long wall	E	yes	unplastered	near entry	2-post	yes	no
Type 2 house (8 examples)	Rillito-Rincon	6.5	4.2	27.3	1.55	rectang.	yes	vest.	long wall	E	yes	unplastered	near entry	2-post	yes	no
Type 3 house (3 examples)	Rillito-Rincon	6.1	3.2	19.52	1.91	rectang.	yes	vest.	long wall	E	yes	unplastered	near entry	2-post	yes	no
Type 4 house (3 examples)	Rillito-Rincon	5.1	3.1	15.81	1.65	rectang.	yes	vest.	long wall	E	yes	unplastered	near entry	2-post	yes	no
Type 5 house (1 example)	Rillito-Rincon	3.6 diam.		10.18		round	yes	wall	east wall	E	yes	plastered	center	3-post	yes	no
Ceremonial house (1 example)	Rillito-Rincon	8.8	5.6	49.28	1.57	rectang.	yes	vest.	long wall	E	yes	plastered	near entry	2-post	yes	no
Type 1A house (57 examples)	Classic	8.38	5.05	42.32	1.66	rectang.	yes	vest.	long wall	E	yes	plastered	near entry	2-post	yes	no

Site [Area (m²)]/ Feature No./ House Type	Occupation	Feat. Length (m)	Chamber Width (m)	Area (m²)	L:W Ratio	Shape	Entry	Entry Type	Entry Position	Orient.	Hearth	Hearth Type	Hearth Location	Roof Support	Post-holes	Pits
Type 1B (1 example)	Classic	7.6	4.7	35.72	1.62	rectang.	yes	vest.	long wall	E	yes	plastered	near entry	2-post	yes	no
Type 1C (1 example)	Classic	6.5	2.9	18.85	2.24	rectang.	yes	vest.	long wall	E	yes	plastered	near entry	9-post	unk.	unk.
Type 1D house (1 example)	Classic	7.5	4.4	33	1.70	rectang.	yes	wall	long wall	E	yes	plastered	near entry	2-post	yes	no
Type 2A (3 examples)	Classic	4.8	3.2	15.36	1.50	rectang.	yes	wall	short wall	E	yes	plastered	near entry	3-post	yes	no
Type 2B house (2 examples)	Classic	6.6	4.7	31.02	1.40	rectang.	yes	vest.	long wall	E	yes	plastered	near entry	2-post	yes	no
Type 2C (1 example)	Classic	7.5	4.7	35.25	1.60	rectang.	yes	wall	long wall	E	yes	plastered	near entry	2-post	yes	no
Type 2D house (1 example)	Classic	4.3 diam.		14.52		round	yes	vest.	south wall	S	no			unk.	unk.	unk.
3 ramadas	Classic															
Paloparado, Lower Terrace (2,200 m²)																
House 1 (Type 1C)	Classic	7.5	4.5	33.75	1.67	rectang.	yes	vest.?	long wall	W	yes	na	near entry	na	yes	no?
House 3	Classic	4	3	12	1.33	rectang.	no				no			na	yes	no?
House 4 (Type 1A)	Classic	9	4	36	2.25	rectang.	yes	vest.	long wall	E	yes	na	near entry	na	na	no?
House 5 (Type 1C)	Classic	7	4.5	31.5	1.56	rectang.	yes	vest.	long wall	N	yes	na	near center	na	na	no?
House 6 (Type 1A)	Classic	6	5	30	1.20	square	yes	vest.	long wall	E	yes	na	near entry	na	na	no?
3 ramadas	Classic															
El Macayo (2,500 m²)																
Feature 5a	pre-Classic	4.7	3.5	16.45	1.34	oval	yes	wall?		E-SE	yes	plastered	center	unk.	yes	yes
Feature 5b	pre-Classic	3.2	3.1	8.04	1.03	round	yes	wall?		E-SE	yes	plastered	center	unk.	yes	unk.
Feature 15	pre-Classic	6	3.6	21.6	1.67	oval	no				yes	unplastered	unk.	unk.	yes	unk.
Feature 16	pre-Classic	4.9	2.5	12.25	1.96	rectang.	yes	vest.	long wall	E-SE	yes?	plastered	near entry	unk.	yes	unk.
Feature 18	pre-Classic	unk.	unk.	unk.	unk.	unk.	unk.				unk.			unk.	unk.	unk.
Feature 21	pre-Classic	5 est.	unk.	unk.	unk.	unk.	unk.				unk.			unk.	unk.	unk.
Feature 28	pre-Classic	4 est.	unk.	unk.	unk.	unk.	unk.				unk.			unk.	unk.	unk.
Feature 29	pre-Classic	4.85 est.	unk.	unk.	unk.	unk.	unk.				unk.			unk.	unk.	unk.
Feature 33	pre-Classic	6.5 est.	unk.	unk.	unk.	unk.	unk.				unk.			unk.	unk.	unk.
Feature 34	pre-Classic	7.5 est.	unk.	unk.	unk.	unk.	unk.				unk.			unk.	unk.	unk.

Site [Area [m²]]/ Feature No./ House Type	Occupation	Feat. Length (m)	Chamber Width (m)	Area (m²)	L:W Ratio	Shape	Entry	Entry Type	Entry Position	Orient.	Hearth	Hearth Type	Hearth Location	Roof Support	Post-holes	Pits
Feature 35	pre-Classic	6.0 est.	unk.	unk.	unk.	unk.	unk.				unk.			unk.	unk.	unk.
Feature 42	pre-Classic	1.6	1.4	2.24	1.14	oval	unk.				unk.			unk.	unk.	unk.
Feature 43	pre-Classic	unk.	unk.	unk.	unk.	unk.	yes			E	yes	unk.		unk.	unk.	unk.
Feature 44	pre-Classic	5	3.5	17.5	1.43	rectang.	yes			E	yes	unk.		unk.	yes	ash pit
Feature 52	pre-Classic	unk.	unk.	unk.	unk.	unk.	unk.			E?	yes	unk.		unk.	yes	unk.
Feature 94	pre-Classic	unk.	unk.	unk.	unk.	unk.	unk.				unk.			unk.	unk.	unk.
Feature 101	pre-Classic	unk.	unk.	unk.	unk.	unk.	unk.				unk.			unk.	unk.	unk.
Feature 136	pre-Classic	unk.	unk.	unk.	unk.	unk.	unk.				unk.			unk.	unk.	unk.
Feature 137	pre-Classic	unk.	unk.	unk.	unk.	unk.	unk.				unk.			unk.	unk.	unk.
Feature 139	pre-Classic	unk.	2.35	unk.	unk.	unk.	unk.				unk.			unk.	yes	unk.
Feature 150	pre-Classic	unk.	3.4	unk.	unk.	rectang.	unk.				unk.			unk.	yes	no
Feature 211	pre-Classic	unk.	unk.	unk.	unk.	rectang.	unk.			SE?	unk.			unk.	yes	no
Feature 212	pre-Classic	unk.	na	unk.	unk.	na	na				na			na	yes	yes
Feature 215	pre-Classic	unk.	3.4	unk.	unk.	rectang.	unk.				unk.			unk.	yes	yes

Key: diam. = diameter; est. = estimated; inc. = incomplete (feature only partially preserved); unk. = information unknown (feature not completely excavated, not recovered through test excavations); na = data not available for this report; vest. = vestibule-type entryway

Table 44. Selected Attributes of Extramural Features for Nogales-Area Sites

Site	Thermal Features	Nonthermal Features	Well-Defined Cemetery	Public Architecture	Trash Mounds	Other
Potrero Creek	ca. 20	195	1?	—	unknown	
Nogales Wash	—	7	unknown	terrace	2	
Arivaca Farmstead	2	—	—	—	1	
South River Road	3?	21	—	—	1	
Buena Vista Ranch	—	3	—	—	—	4 petroglyph boulders
Baca Float site	3	8	1	—	1	
Cemetery Ridge	—	1	—	—	—	
Tinaja Canyon	—	4	—	—	—	
Paloparado,						
Upper Terrace, Rillito-Rincon phases	6	—	4	2 (banquette, dance plaza)	yes	borrow pits
Upper Terrace, Classic period	257	11	9	3 (wall, reservoir, terrace)	yes	borrow pits
Lower Terrace	< 20	11+	4	2 (wall, canals)	na	
El Macayo	28	144	1	—	—	—

accompanied by ceramic vessels, and of these, only one burial (Feature 32) was found with 15 plain ware sherds and a single Rincon Red-on-brown (style C) sherd. Features 151 and 214 were accompanied by three plain ware bowls and a plain ware jar, respectively. Published data do not describe the dating of the Potrero Creek burials, but Grebinger nowhere suggests that the 35 inhumations depicted on his site map (1971b:Figure 1) are not coeval with his Rillito and Rincon phase houses. Thus, we are left to conclude that the burials from El Macayo, Potrero Creek, and possibly Nogales Wash date to the pre-Classic period, whereas the burials at Paloparado are most certainly Classic period in age, given the painted pottery types that accompany many of the burials (Di Peso 1956:531–537).

As discussed above, the data recovered from El Macayo did not permit us to discern activity areas within the site or temporal changes in intrasite settlement. Dated features and horizontal exposures were sufficient to infer intrasite settlement patterns at Potrero Creek and Paloparado. We can review conclusions reached by Grebinger (1971b) and Di Peso (1956) regarding settlement growth to suggest what processes may have occurred at El Macayo.

Grebinger's 1971 dissertation on activity structure at the Potrero Creek site derived from a 1966 program of data recovery directed by James Sciscenti of the ASM Highway Salvage Program (see Figure 57). Based on the stripping of that portion of the site, which was within the highway right-of-way (2,808 m^2 of contiguous stripping units), Grebinger concluded that village growth proceeded west to

east. The later, Rincon phase–style houses and most of the burials were clustered in the eastern half of his study area, whereas two of the three earlier, Rillito phase–style houses and the four cremations were in the western half (Grebinger 1971b:37, Figure 1). He conjectured that not all houses were occupied simultaneously, given the existence of two different architectural styles and a broad range of cross-dated intrusive painted ceramics that suggested a 200–500-year occupation. Consequently, he did not discuss the village plan and the internal organization of houses in either rows or clusters. The distribution of various artifact classes (scrapers and plant and animal remains) and extramural features (thermal versus nonthermal pits) suggested separate loci for resource processing and for food cooking.

Di Peso (1956:219–227), in contrast, who investigated a larger settlement and exposed a greater area (58,600 m^2 total, which incorporated a 18,500-m^2 area for the earlier Rillito-Rincon occupation), suggested that the pre-Classic component of Paloparado was spatially organized in five north-south rows of east-facing houses, with a single, larger ceremonial house (House 30-4) located at the northern margin, a communal cemetery located in the center, and a walkway (banquette) and dance plaza located on the far eastern margin of the site (see Figure 58). Di Peso noted that four of the five house types were present throughout the pre-Classic occupation of the site (Types 1, 2, 3, and 5 were used throughout the pre-Classic occupation, but Type 4 appears to have been used late in this pre–A.D. 1150 period [see Figure 59a]). Consequently, no clear pattern as to the

Table 45. Selected Attributes of Burial Features for Nogales-Area Sites

Site	Cremation				Human Inhumation							Animal Inhumation
	Primary	Secondary	Grave Goods	Total	Flexed	Extended	Position Unknown	Orientation	Condition Unknown	Grave Goods	Total	
Potrero Creek	—	1 pit, 3 urns	na	4	24	5	—	1 SE, 2 E, 2 W	6	na	35	—
Nogales Wash	—	urns	in 2	12	na	—	—	—	—	unk.	1	—
Arivaca Farmstead	—	—	—	0	—	—	—	—	—	unk.	0	—
South River Road	—	—	—	0	6 in pit	—	—	—	—	—	6	—
Buena Vista Ranch	—	—	—	0	—	—	—	—	—	—	0	—
Baca Float site	—	—	—	0	—	—	—	—	—	—	0	—
Cemetery Ridge	—	urns	in 15	29	—	—	—	—	—	—	0	—
Tinaja Canyon	—	urns	in 2	3	—	—	—	—	—	—	0	—
Paloparado												
Upper Terrace, Rillito-Rincon phases	—	75	in fewer than 50%	75	—	—	—	—	—	—	0	—
Upper Terrace, Classic period	—	2	na	2	5	113	63	most E	—	in most	181	3 dogs
Lower Terrace	—	—	—	0	3	26	5	most E	—	na	34	—
El Macayo	—	2	unk.	2	4	2	4	5 E, 2 NE, 1 SW	3	in most	13	1 macaw, 2 dogs

Key: na = data not available for this report; unk. = information unknown (i.e., not recovered through test excavations)

167

direction of village growth emerged for the pre-Classic occupation.

Di Peso (1956:118–121; Wilcox 1987) reconstructed the post–A.D. 1150 Classic period occupation of Paloparado as covering a much larger area (see Figure 60). The Classic period occupation was built over the pre-Classic occupation area and extended farther to the north, east, and south. During the Classic period, the village was organized as a series of multiple-household groups within a walled settlement that also contained a reservoir and some artificial terraces. Most of 12 household groups incorporated two to eight houses (averaging six), which were positioned around a common courtyard that contained a variety of extramural features and burial plots. House floor area was considerably larger during the Classic period (a mean of 40.05 m^2 versus a mean of 25.06 m^2 in the pre-Classic), and more houses were present in the village (66 versus 42) (see Figure 62 and Table 43). The low cobble wall that defined the settlement's western, southern, and eastern margin likely served to divert surface runoff and delimit village boundaries; it apparently was not used for defense, however. An additional wall and the construction of an artificial terrace within the village suggested to Di Peso that the dual-division principle might have operated during the Classic period occupation of Paloparado.

What Potrero Creek and Paloparado suggest, then, is that, with a sufficiently large exposure, a clearer understanding of processes of internal differentiation and settlement growth at El Macayo could be obtained. At present, most of the site lies buried under private lands to the east and south of the county complex. We suspect that houses and extramural features dating to the Classic period remain buried in these places. If so, a different interpretation of site occupational history would have to be argued. It might be that El Macayo also grew from west to east like Potrero Creek, and that, like Paloparado, cremations are early and inhumations are late in the occupation of the settlement. At present, however, there is no way to evaluate these ideas without further data recovery on the privately owned portions of the site.

In sum, El Macayo appears to have been a long-lived settlement that was largely occupied during the Middle Formative period and was characterized by a variety of house forms, extramural activity areas, cemeteries, and trash deposits. In comparison to contemporary occupations at the loosely patterned Potrero Creek and formally arranged Paloparado, El Macayo was a loose organization of features and activity spaces. No integrative architecture or evidence of public works has been recovered. Most of the food preparation, cooking, and storage functions took place outside individual houses, the spatial arrangements and interrelationships of which are unknown. Five houses had small floor areas (8.04–21.60 m^2) and probably did not house entire nuclear families. Burials included both secondary cremation burials placed in ceramic vessels within pits and uncremated inhumation burials of humans, dogs, and at least one military macaw. The grouping of inhumations provides the strongest evidence to date for the deliberate partitioning of use space at the settlement.

Subsistence

Macrobotanical, pollen, and faunal remains recovered from El Macayo allowed us to identify some of the plants and animals used by the occupants of this pre-Classic settlement (see Chapters 6 and 8). These data, as well as information on food procurement and -processing equipment (see Chapters 3 and 4), settlement location, and relevant environmental parameters of the Nogales area, shed light on prehistoric subsistence practices and economic adaptations in the upper Santa Cruz River valley. Tables 46 and 47 summarize botanical and faunal data recovered from excavated sites in the Nogales area that provide a context for evaluating prehistoric human-environment relationships in the area.

The Middle Formative period economy of El Macayo, as elsewhere in the southern Southwest (e.g., Bohrer 1981, 1984; Gasser and Kwiatkowski 1991a, 1991b), was based on a generalized foraging-farming subsistence pattern that included wild-plant collecting, hunting and trapping of indigenous animals, and farming. Food remains recovered with pollen, flotation, and macrobotanical samples from prehistoric sites in the Nogales area indicate that grass seeds, nuts, fruits, and leafy greens were important wild foods and that maize, some varieties of beans, and possibly gourds and squashes were cultivated domesticates. Agave, an indigenous plant, was cultivated for its nutritious heart and fibrous leaves and is considered to have been a domesticated plant in southern Arizona by at least the early Classic period (Fish et al. 1992; Gasser and Kwiatkowski 1991a; Van Buren et al. 1992). Animal foods recovered from faunal samples indicate that jackrabbits, cottontails, a variety of rodents, deer, pronghorn, and a few varieties of birds made up most of the hunted and trapped species. Canine bone was recovered from El Macayo and elsewhere, in both burial and nonburial contexts, but evidence of burning or butchering for use as food is generally lacking.

Plants probably contributed more calories to the diet of El Macayo residents than did animal food. Three lines of evidence support this tentative conclusion. First, the flaked stone tools show no indications that hunting was a major activity. Arrow points are rare and were expediently fashioned from crude flakes (see Chapter 4). Second, the faunal evidence reveals a wide variety of animals, but small to medium size mammals, especially jackrabbits, cottontails and rodents, dominate the collection (see Chapter 6). The remains of larger, meatier game animals are relatively

Table 46. Ubiquity of Selected Food Resources for Nogales-Area Sites

| Site | No. of Macrobotanical or Flotation Samples | No. of Pollen Samples | Domesticates | | | | Grains | Oak Acorns | Unld. Legume | Nuts/Seeds | | Black Walnut |
			Maize	Cucurbits	Beans	Agave	Grasses			Mesquite/Palo Verde	Hackberry	
Arivaca Farmstead site	14 F	12	13 F, 11 P	—	—	6 F	—	8 F	1 F	8 P	—	—
Baca Float site	4 F	9	2 P	—	—	—	7 P	—	3 P	—	2 P	—
Buena Vista Ranch	3 F	2	1 P	—	—	—	2 P	—	—	—	—	—
Cemetery Ridge	6 F	7	1 P	—	—	1 P	1 F, 5 P	—	1 P	1 P	1 P	—
El Macayo (SRI)	10 F	10	1 P	—	—	—	2 P	—	—	4 P	—	—
El Macayo (ASM) (Features 13, 17)	2 F	—	2 F	—	—	—	2 F	—	1 F	—	—	—
Nogales Wash	—	—	—	—	—	—	—	—	—	—	—	—
Paloparado												
Pre-Classic period	1 M	—	—	—	—	—	—	—	—	—	—	—
Classic period	21 M	—	6 M	—	1 M	5 M	13 M	—	—	1 M	—	—
Potrero Creek	—	7	4 P	1 P	—	—	—	3 P	—	—	—	present
South River Road (prehistoric)	8 F	2	3 F, 2 P	1 P	—	—	1 F	—	—	—	1 P	—
Tinaja Canyon site	7 F	4	—	—	—	—	—	—	1 P	—	—	—
Total	76	53										

Key: F = flotation sample; M = macrobotanical sample; P = pollen sample

169

Table 46 (continued).

Site	Cacti		Eriogonum: Wild Buckwheat (spring, summer)	Cheno-ams (summer, early fall)	Seasonal Indicator Plants	Cucurbita digitata: Fingerleaf Gourd (summer, fall)	Euphorbia: Spurge (summer)
	Cholla	Prickly Pear			High-Spine Composites: e.g., Sunflower, Aster (spring, summer, fall)		
Arivaca Farmstead site	6 P	—	3 P	1 F, 12 P	12 P	—	1 F, 3 P
Baca Float site	—	—	—	2 F, 9 P	—	—	1 P
Buena Vista Ranch	—	—	—	2 F, 2 P	2 P	—	1 P
Cemetery Ridge	—	—	—	6 F, 7 P	—	—	1 P
El Macayo (SRI)	—	—	—	9 P	—	—	—
El Macayo (ASM) (Features 13, 17)	—	—	—	—	—	—	—
Nogales Wash	—	1 F?	—	—	5 P	—	—
Paloparado							
Pre-Classic period	—	—	—	—	—	—	—
Classic period	—	—	—	present	—	—	—
Potrero Creek	—	—	—	6 P	7 P	—	—
South River Road (prehistoric)	—	1 P	2 P	3 F, 2 P	1 F, 2 P	—	—
Tinaja Canyon site	—	1 F	—	7 F, 4 P	—	—	1 P

Key: F = flotation sample; M = macrobotanical sample; P = pollen sample

Table 46 (continued).

	Seasonal Indicator Plants						
Site	Kallestromia: Arizona Poppy (late summer)	Convolvulaceae: e.g., Morning Glory (late summer)	Nyctaginaceae: e.g., Spiderling (late summer, fall)	Onagraceae: E. Primrose (spring)	Sphaeralcea: Globe Mallow (spring, late summer)	Trianthema: H. Purslane (spring to fall)	Typha: Cattail (moisture)
Arivaca Farmstead site	—	—	11 P	—	1 P	1 F	—
Baca Float site	1 P	—	9 P	—	—	—	—
Buena Vista Ranch	—	—	—	—	—	1 F	—
Cemetery Ridge	—	—	6 P	1 P	2 P	—	—
El Macayo (SRI)	—	—	1 P	—	—	—	—
El Macayo (ASM) (Features 13, 17)	—	—	—	—	—	—	—
Nogales Wash	—	—	—	—	1 F	—	—
Paloparado							
Pre-Classic period	—	—	—	—	—	—	—
Classic period	—	—	—	—	—	—	—
Potrero Creek	—	—	—	—	—	—	6 P
South River Road (prehistoric)	2 P	—	—	—	—	1 F	—
Tinaja Canyon site	1 P	—	4 P	—	—	—	—

Key: F = flotation sample; M = macrobotanical sample; P = pollen sample

Table 47. Frequency of Selected Taxa of Animal Bone in Nogales-Area Sites

Taxa	AF	BF	BVR	CR	EM (SRI)	EM (ASM)	NW	P (PC)	P (C)	PC	SRR	TC	Total	% of Areal Total
Birds[a]	3	—	2	7	14	—	4	—	3	—	—	1	34	2.08
Reptiles[b]	—	1	—	3	2	—	—	—	—	2	2	—	10	0.61
Amphibians[c]	—	—	—	—	—	—	—	—	—	7	—	—	7	0.43
Rodents[d]	1	4	—	1	38	—	7	1	6	15	4	2	79	4.82
Lagomorphs														
Cottontail	5	—	—	4	9	—	14	1	12	13	2	4	64	3.91
Jackrabbit	8	—	—	2	15	—	14	5	49	22	8	1	124	7.57
Indet. leporids	—	—	—	—	7	—	—	—	—	5	—	—	12	0.73
Cervids														
Deer	1	1	3	4	—	1	72	7	47	21	5	10	172	10.50
Mountain sheep	—	—	—	—	—	—	—	—	—	—	—	1	1	0.06
Pronghorn	—	—	—	—	1	—	—	1	30	—	—	—	32	1.95
Indet. artiodactyl	—	2	3	—	13	1	29	—	11	4	24	—	87	5.31
Canids[e]	—	1	—	1	106	—	1	1	8	11	—	—	129	7.88
Other mammals														
Bobcat	—	—	—	—	1	—	—	—	—	1	—	—	2	0.12
Red fox	—	—	—	—	—	—	—	—	—	1	—	—	1	0.06
Gray fox	—	—	—	—	—	—	—	—	3	1	—	—	4	0.24
Javelina	—	—	—	—	—	—	—	—	1	—	—	—	1	0.06
Badger	—	—	—	—	—	—	—	—	1	—	—	—	1	0.06
Skunk	—	—	—	—	—	—	—	—	—	2	—	—	2	0.12
Muskrat	—	—	—	—	4	—	—	—	—	1	—	—	5	0.31
Small	12	—	48	—	44	—	—	—	—	—	13	—	117	7.14
Medium size	12	—	33	—	117	2	—	—	—	—	—	—	164	10.01
Large	5	—	323	—	9	2	—	—	—	—	32	—	371	22.65
Historical-period cow, horse, sheep	—	—	34	—	—	—	—	—	7	—	—	—	41	2.50
Unidentified	—	—	89	—	29	—	56	—	—	—	4	—	178	10.87
Total	47	9	535	22	409	6	197	16	177	107	94	19	1,638	100.00

Key: AF = Arivaca Farmstead site; BF = Baca Float site; BVR = Buena Vista Ranch; CR = Cemetery Ridge; EM (SRI) = El Macayo (SRI); EM (ASM) = El Macayo (ASM) (F 13,17); NW = Nogales Wash; P (PC) = Paloparado (pre-Classic period); P (C) = Paloparado (Classic period); PC = Potrero Creek; SRR = South River Road (prehistoric); TC = Tinaja Canyon site
[a] Birds include quail, hawk, turkey, golden eagle, turkey/eagle, and indeterminate.
[b] Reptiles include box turtle, mud turtle, and desert tortoise.
[c] Amphibians include frog and toad.
[d] Rodents include ground and rock squirrel, pocket gopher, kangaroo rat, pocket mouse, and deer mouse.
[e] Canids include dog and coyote.

scarce. Third, the bones of one of the child burials (Feature 132) exhibited evidence of porotic hyperostosis, a pathology induced by anemia—a frequent condition in populations dependent on maize (El Najjar et al. 1976; Snow 1990; Walker 1985) (see Chapter 9).

Finally, our data suggest that generations of El Macayo residents may have emphasized wild-plant collection over agricultural production. At present, the data are equivocal as to the caloric importance of maize and other domesticates to the overall subsistence base. Although maize was recovered in the two macrobotanical samples taken during the 1987 test excavations at El Macayo (Gardiner and Huckell 1987:24–25), only a single grain of maize pollen was recovered in our 1996 data recovery effort (see Chapter 8). In contrast, ubiquity values for a variety of grasses, leafy plants, and seeds were relatively high. This apparent emphasis on native grasses over cultivated grain is reflected in the grinding equipment used to process small hard seeds. For example, the most common forms of grinding equipment recovered from El Macayo are those types traditionally associated with the milling of native seeds rather than maize—basin-type metates and oval, one-hand basin-type manos (see Chapter 4). Interestingly, Classic period burials at Paloparado were accompanied by ceramic vessels containing panic grass (*Panicum*) and Chenopodium seeds, illustrating the continuing importance of wild seeds and grasses even when we are certain that maize and beans were cultivated. It may well be that the riparian zone, grasslands, and woodlands of the Nogales area were sufficiently rich in native plant food resources that intensive agriculture was either unnecessary or undesirable.

An argument against this interpretation can be made, however. First is the location of the site itself. The fact that El Macayo is located on an elevated Pleistocene river terrace at the confluence of two seasonally flowing streams, which overlooks large patches of high-quality arable land, suggests that the settlement was deliberately situated. This location would have taken advantage of summer floodwater captured from two local watersheds and locally high water tables and subsurface moisture—conditions essential for successfully growing warm-season crops in the southern Southwest. Second is the presence of numerous Formative-type pit structures accompanied by storage pits and dedicated burials areas. This investment in residential architecture and facilities signals at least a seasonal commitment to agriculture. Plant remains indicative of soil disturbance typically associated with fields and irrigation features are present in the El Macayo botanical collections. These include a variety of pollen types attributed to the summer- and early-fall-maturing Chenopodium and amaranth families of plants, which typically volunteer in and near agricultural fields and are opportunistically harvested as they mature. Finally, the small number of botanical samples retrieved from all sites in the Nogales area to date should caution us

not to come to conclusions too quickly concerning diet and economic strategies in upper Santa Cruz River region. Our review indicates that only 76 macrobotanical samples and 53 pollen samples were recovered from the 10 sites excavated between 1956 and 1996 (see Table 46). Clearly, this question will be resolved only with additional excavation and analysis.

Prehistoric Environmental Conditions

The distribution of plants, animals, and arable soils; the availability of potable water and wood for construction, fuel, and light; and the predictability of climatic regimes (especially the timing and the abundance of seasonal precipitation and length of the growing season) are the critical variables for self-sustaining, broad-based, subsistence-type economies. Changes in the availability of or access to these key resources can have profound impacts on the sustainability and resilience of a given economic adaptation. Of particular importance to populations practicing agriculture in the southern Southwest is the distribution of arable land and water, especially along the floodplains of dependable rivers and streams. Stable or aggrading floodplains and alluvial fans; deep, loamy, organically enriched sediments; and a predictable source of water to nourish seedling and growing plants are essential variables for successful floodwater farming of aboriginal crops. In places where irrigation techniques were known and could be implemented, arable soils on older river terraces above the current floodplain could be farmed, as well.

As described in Chapter 1, the site of El Macayo (located at 1,146 m, or 3,760 feet, AMSL) is situated within the Chihuahuan semidesert grasslands of the southern Southwest and northeastern Mexico, but within a 64-km (40-mile) radius of plant and animal resources of four contrasting biotic communities: the Madrean woodland and conifer forests (north, south, east, and west), the Plains grassland (east), and the subtropical Sinoloan thorn scrub (south). The prehistoric village, as mentioned, was located at the base of a low, Pleistocene-age river terrace at the confluence of two streams, Mariposa Wash and Nogales Wash, that were probably dependable sources of surface water during the summer monsoon and winter rainy season. Within a 1-km radius of the village are 23.41 ha (57.85 acres) of high-quality arable soils (Pima and Grabe soils) within the floodplains of the two washes (Figure 63). These soils could have been farmed with either overbank floodwater or irrigation methods during the long potential growing season (220 days from early April to mid-November) when over 60 percent of Nogales's moisture (254 mm, or 10 inches) is delivered during July, August, and September.

Through the historical documentation of environmental change (Brown 1994; Bryan 1925; Cooke and Reeves 1976;

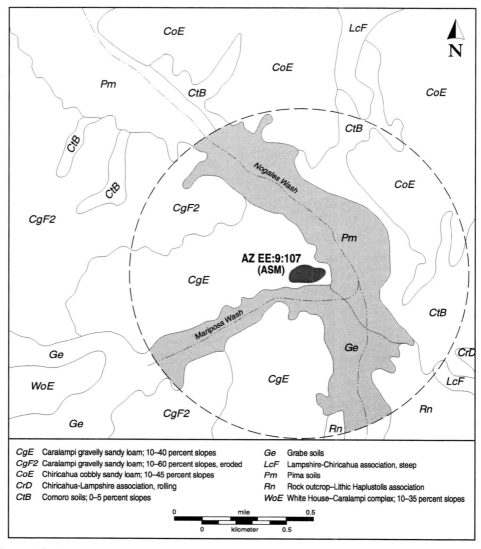

CgE   Caralampi gravelly sandy loam; 10–40 percent slopes
CgF2   Caralampi gravelly sandy loam; 10–60 percent slopes, eroded
CoE   Chiricahua cobbly sandy loam; 10–45 percent slopes
CrD   Chiricahua-Lampshire association, rolling
CtB   Comoro soils; 0–5 percent slopes

Ge   Grabe soils
LcF   Lampshire-Chiricahua association, steep
Pm   Pima soils
Rn   Rock outcrop–Lithic Haplustolls association
WoE   White House–Caralampi complex; 10–35 percent slopes

Figure 63. Distribution of arable floodplain soils within a 1-km radius of El Macayo Village.

Hastings and Turner 1965; Schwalen and Shaw 1957), we have learned that some aspects of physical environment have changed rather dramatically in the last three centuries. Among these are the reduction in number, variety, and distribution of native bunchgrasses and their replacement with modern sod-type grasses, largely in response to overgrazing, fire-suppression, and successful competition from introduced species palatable to cattle, sheep, and horses. The proliferation of certain native plants (e.g., mesquite, cacti, burroweed, and snakeweed) and animals (e.g., mule deer and javelina), and the reduction of certain tree species near settlements, military outposts, and mines used for fuel and construction timber (e.g., oak and juniper) serve as examples of human-induced biotic change.

The greatest change in the physical environment from its pre-Hispanic condition to the late twentieth century, however, is probably that of overall water availability. Certainly,

groundwater pumping, urban growth, and stream entrenchment have significantly altered the obtainability of subsurface and surface flow. Nevertheless, long-term, natural cycles in alluvial water-table levels that influence channel depth and floodplain development or erosion are significant factors in determining the environmental characteristics of the region. For example, a 550-year primary oscillation in alluvial water table levels that is punctuated by a 275-year secondary minimum has been documented for many portions of the American West (Karlstrom 1988). Cyclical natural variations, which are presumably controlled by large-scale climatic variability (Cooke and Reeves 1976; Hirschboeck 1987; Webb and Betancourt 1992) in conjunction with human-induced changes to runoff, streamflow, and groundwater supply, have had profound effects on the carrying capacity of southern Arizona in the last century. We presume that natural variation in and anthropogenic changes to environmental conditions had equally significant impacts on the prehistoric populations of the region.

We surmise that the physical environment around El Macayo was different in two respects from what we see today. First, we suspect that composition of the vegetation was somewhat different. Second, we hypothesize, on the basis of data presented by Karlstrom (1988), and Waters (1987, 1988), that during the time of major occupation at the site (ca. A.D. 850–1150), streams flowed more vigorously, floodplains were generally aggrading or stable, and channels were less entrenched than they are today. We suggest that changes in alluvial geomorphology and ground-water levels served as important and dynamic controls for prehistoric floodwater and irrigation farming in the Nogales area.

Botanical data recovered from our excavations reveal the same type and range of plants species as those that exist currently within the region, but their distribution within the immediate locality may have changed. Among the wood species, for example, represented in our macrobotanical record of the charred plant remains are oak, juniper, and mesquite. Currently, mesquite is the predominant arboreal species in the vicinity of the site, whereas oak and juniper grow only at higher elevations on the slopes of the nearby mountains. Assuming this is not a problem of archaeological sampling, two explanations exist to account for this disjunction. Either juniper and oak were felled on the slopes of nearby uplands and brought back for use as construction timbers, or juniper and oak formerly grew closer to the site during its period of occupation. In support of the latter, we note that Hastings and Turner (1965) have documented significant vegetative change by comparing recent photographs with historical-period photographs of particular southern Arizona landscapes. In so doing, they have observed the widespread upward retreat of the oak-woodland to elevations higher than 1,220 m (4,000 feet) and the replacement of these hardwood stands at lower elevations with mesquite.

Corroborative evidence in support of this environmental change hypothesis exists from the excavations conducted by Whittlesey and Ciolek-Torrello (1992) near Arivaca. There they found that oak and juniper were the sole contributors to wood charcoal recovered from the small farmstead along Arivaca Creek, but that mesquite—a species frequently encountered in the record of prehistoric sites in the Sonoran Desert region—was not present in the macrobotanical record (Huckell 1992). Today, the area around the site supports a thriving mesquite bosque. Although Whittlesey and Ciolek-Torrello reviewed the evidence for changes in the modern distribution of mesquite in the grasslands of southern Arizona, they concluded that culturally conditioned preferences for the selection of oak rather than mesquite was more likely. In contrast, we see their wood charcoal record as complementary to our own. Together, these plant records suggest that the distribution of tree species was somewhat different from what we see today, and that human-induced changes to the grasslands since the historical period have had a profound impact on local vegetation.

The evidence of stronger streamflow, aggrading floodplains, and less entrenched stream channels resides largely in geomorphic data and alluvial chronostratigraphic reconstructions. A macroscale model of floodplain dynamics has been presented by Karlstrom (1988). Mesoscale reconstructions of fluvial processes on the middle Santa Cruz River have been prepared by Haynes and Huckell (1986) and Waters (1987, 1988). Here, we draw first on the Karlstrom macroscale model to portray general trends in alluvial water tables and floodplain processes, and then draw on Waters's (1987, 1988) interpretations for the San Xavier reach of the Santa Cruz River as a proxy for local trends in the upper Santa Cruz River. We recognize, of course, that geomorphic processes vary for different locations within the Santa Cruz River watershed, and that Waters's reconstructions may not fully apply to smaller upland drainages such as Mariposa Wash, Nogales Wash, and Potrero Creek. But until detailed geomorphological studies and chronostratigraphic calibration take place for the Nogales area, we can cautiously apply these nonlocal data and evaluate their local utility. Our purpose in using these data is to correlate streamflow and floodplain availability with settlement patterns. Together, the data presented by Karlstrom and Waters suggest which processes might have been operating when El Macayo and the other pre-Classic settlements in the Nogales area were established, used, and abandoned. They also permit us to speculate as to why certain settlements persisted when others were abandoned.

Briefly, Karlstrom (1988:47, 49, 50) suggested that (1) surface-water flow and water-table levels respond to long-term trends in annual (particularly winter) precipitation, (2) recharge and discharge rates and local threshold values determine the height of the water table and the length and permanence of streamflow reaches, and (3) time lags between precipitation input and hydrological responses are expected and will vary in duration (weeks to decades) from place to place depending on local geomorphic factors. Drawing on data compiled from numerous localities across the western United States, Karlstrom (1988) developed a 2,000-year reconstruction of alluvial water-table fluctuation and floodplain aggradation-degradation cycles for the Colorado Plateau and adjacent regions (Dean 1988:Figure 5.7H, I). Subsequently, Dean (1988) and his colleagues used these data in an integrated adaptation model to suggest when floodplain farming would have been possible and when it would not, and how this environmental condition influenced settlement patterns in northeastern Arizona. Karlstrom's model has been applied to paleoenvironmental data off the Colorado Plateau, as well. For example, Van West and Altschul (1998:350, 355, Table 9.5) used Karlstrom's

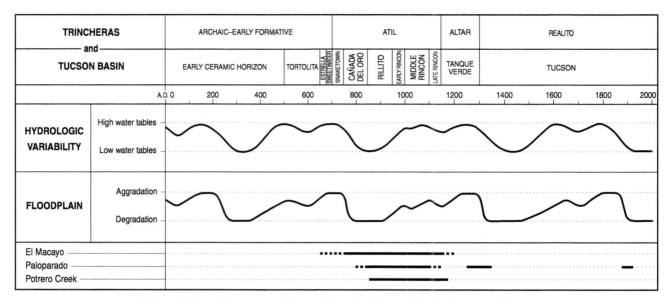

Figure 64. The relationships among inferred floodplain and alluvial water-table history and inferred occupation dates for El Macayo, Potrero Creek, and Paloparado.

data in modeling agricultural strategies and crop productivity in the Lower Verde River valley. Similarly, Van West et al. (2000) used Karlstrom's data in a synthesis of environmental-human interactions in the Lower Tonto Basin–Lake Roosevelt area.

Independently, Waters (1988:216–217) studied the geomorphology of a 15-km reach of the middle Santa Cruz River near San Xavier Mission to infer the history of the river and its floodplain and suggested how these changes influenced Formative-era settlement in that locality. Organic deposits from archaeological features were dated with radiocarbon methods and were used to assign cut-and-fill events along that portion of the river. His research suggested that during the Rillito and early Rincon phases (A.D. 850–1000), the channel was filling, the stream was shallow, and the floodplain was broad, sandy, and appropriate for floodwater farming. Settlements were established adjacent to the floodplain and major washes entering the floodplain, but were situated above areas of active flooding. During the middle Rincon period (A.D. 1000–1100), settlements responded to a period of channel entrenchment by relocating northward to avoid the incipient head-cutting of the stream. During the late Rincon period (A.D. 1100–1150), settlements again shifted, this time eastward in response to discontinuous channel cutting and the continued destruction of arable land. During the Tanque Verde phase (A.D. 1150–1300), settlements grew in number, and some grew in size, likely in response to stabilization and partial filling of the channel and the emergence of a *cienega* environment nearby. The opportunity for a variety of successful agricultural techniques, including ditch irrigation from the *cienega*, dry-farming on small dunes, floodwater on the floodplain, and

ak chin farming of alluvial fans, is hypothesized. Waters suggested that the channel was filled during the Tucson phase (A.D. 1300–1450), and was available for extensive floodplain farming, but that the *cienega* contracted in size and probably was ineffective for ditch irrigation. Finally, entrenchment was initiated again at about A.D. 1450, once again rendering the floodplain unfarmable—a condition, he suggests, that was in part responsible for the abandonment of the middle Santa Cruz River valley.

Figure 64 combines the reconstructions of Karlstrom and Waters and plots the inferred occupation dates for El Macayo, Potrero Creek, and Paloparado. If indeed El Macayo was established between A.D. 650 and 750, then the environmental data suggest that this location was settled at a time when regional water tables were relatively high, and formerly entrenched channels were filling with alluvium. Alternatively, if El Macayo and nearby Potrero Creek were established between A.D. 800 and 900, then both settlements were located along reaches of their respective streams, where regional water tables were at the 550-year low, and channel incision and avulsion of the former floodplain were taking place in vulnerable reaches of the region's major streams. What this suggests to us is that smaller tributaries of the Santa Cruz River, such as Nogales Wash, were fairly resistant to degradation because surface geology likely prevented infiltration and maintained surface flow. That there is still marshland near Potrero Creek today suggests that this is so.

From about A.D. 900 to 1000, Karlstrom's and Waters's data indicate that regional water tables rose, floodplains aggraded, channels filled, and opportunities for floodwater farming were created when reliable but low-discharge summer floods overflowed their shallow banks and could water floodplain fields. It was at this time that most of the pre-Classic settlements in the Nogales area were occupied. A minor period of entrenchment suggested by the Karlstrom model at about A.D. 1000–1050 corresponds to Waters's middle Rincon phase entrenchment. A more formidable period of falling water tables, channel incision, and floodplain degradation, however, began in the early A.D. 1100s at the end of the late Rincon and beginning of the Tanque Verde phase. Waters's dating of the continued erosion of floodplain sediments at this time supports Karlstrom's reconstruction for the early twelfth century. And it is at this time that most pre-Classic settlement in the Nogales area seems to end or at least was reorganized and concentrated in fewer but larger sites. While subsequent Classic period occupation has not yet been documented for Nogales proper, occupation along the main stem of the Santa Cruz River at Paloparado continues or resumes in the A.D. 1200s and early 1300s (Wilcox 1987), likely in response to high water tables and aggrading floodplains. The Classic period appears to end when conditions presumably inimical to irrigation and floodwater agriculture returned by A.D. 1450 or so.

In short, we see a reasonable correspondence between environmental changes on the floodplain and the chronicle of settlement in the Nogales area. But until empirical studies can be conducted to reconstruct local geomorphic history and test the proposition that floodplain history and human history are intimately intertwined, we must consider our correlations as hypotheses.

Cultural Affiliation

Our final areas of inquiry concerned cultural identity and interaction. Despite our best attempts to link patterns in the archaeological record with culturally meaningful behavior, we are unable to assign a cultural label to the people who inhabited the Nogales area in pre-Hispanic times. Unknown and perhaps unknowable are the genetic, linguistic, and "ethnic" markers of these Formative period populations. At present, we consider the Middle Formative period populations of El Macayo to be successive generations of an unnamed local cultural group who had enduring relationships with cultural groups to the north in the Tucson Basin and Gila River and to the southwest in the Rio Altar–Magdelena area of northwestern Sonora.

We, like others before us (e.g., Di Peso 1956; Doyel 1977a, 1977b; Grebinger 1971a; Jácome 1986; Neily 1994; Whittlesey and Ciolek-Torrello 1992; Wilcox 1987), wanted to characterize the identity of the inhabitants of El Macayo and their nearest neighbors and understand how wide were their networks of social and economic interaction. First, we wanted to know if we could consider them to be

Hohokam or Trincheras, or whether their social and economic practices were sufficiently different that we should think of them as a separate indigenous culture, much as the Sinagua are distinct from the Anasazi (Colton 1939, 1946). Second, we wanted to know whether a single cultural tradition, a multiethnic population, or a sequence of homogeneous or heterogeneous populations could be discerned. Finally, we wanted to know if the prehistoric settlements of the Nogales area were peripheral participants of a widespread culture whose center was elsewhere, or whether the Nogales settlements were components of independent communities who interacted with other cultural groups for various reasons at different times.

To make headway on this topic, we need to be clear about what we want to know and what we are able to learn from the archaeological record. Following Rouse (1972:5–6), we can describe group identity or ethnicity as being based on: (1) shared beliefs and activities (i.e., cultural groups, a people with a distinct culture), (2) participation in an integrated system of social institutions (i.e., social groups, a society organized by its social structure), (3) similar morphological and biological characteristics (i.e., morphological groups, races defined by distinct phenotypic and genotypic traits), and (4) membership in the same speech community (i.e., linguistic groups, or speakers of the same language). In our case, we do not have historical records, oral histories, or biological data that unambiguously connect modern populations with prehistoric populations. Neither do we have written records that can tell us what languages were spoken by the prehistoric peoples of the region. What we do have, however, are archaeological features, materials, and the patterning of materiel (Rouse 1972:155) at a variety of scales, both in time and space. What we are attempting to characterize, then, is group identity based on shared beliefs and activities as inferred from the material remains and patterns observed in the archaeological record. In Rouse's terms, we are attempting to identify *cultural groups*.

Hohokam Culture, Trincheras Culture, and Nogales-Area Sites

In the following section, we compare selected pre-A.D. 1150 Formative period Nogales-area traits and patterns to those documented for coeval traits and patterns associated with Gila-Salt, Tucson-Basin, and Papaguería Hohokam and with the Magdalena–Altar Valley Trincheras (Table 48) and briefly evaluate their fit. Finally, we review evidence for intergroup connections based on the presence of nonlocal materials in the inventory of Nogales-area sites and the sharing of culturally specific practices (e.g., Hohokam mortuary customs) and suggest the nature, strength, and significance of those relationships.

For the purposes of this comparison, we assume that the Gila-Salt Basin, Tucson Basin, and Papaguería were, at

Table 48. Selected Traits of Pre-Classic Period Residential Sites for Five Geographic Areas

Site Traits	Gila-Salt Basin (Hohokam)	Tucson Basin (Hohokam)
Key references	Gladwin et al. 1937; Haury 1976	Greenleaf 1975; Kelly et al. 1978
Environmental zone	Sonoran desert scrub, Lower Colorado River subdivision	Sonoran desert scrub, Arizona upland subdivision
Subsistence economy	intensive agriculture, supplemented with wild-plant collecting and hunting	intensive agriculture, supplemented with wild-plant collecting and hunting
Primary agricultural techniques	irrigation, floodwater, *ak chin*	irrigation, floodwater, *ak chin*
House forms	rectangular houses-in-pits, pit houses	subrectangular houses-in-pits and pit houses most common; occasionally square, oval, true rectangular forms
Public/integrative architecture and space	ball courts, plazas, mounds in community centers, crematoria	trash mounds
Private/household architecture and space	domestic courtyard groups, intramural storage, extramural cooking, burial areas	domestic courtyard groups, intramural storage, extramural cooking, burial areas
Local painted pottery	red-on-buff pottery, micaceous schist temper	red-on-brown pottery, sand temper; paddle-and-anvil finish
Local slipped pottery	red-slipped buff ware with smudged interior, micaceous schist or phyllite temper	red-slipped brown ware with sand temper occurs only in Tortolita and Rincon phases
Local unpainted pottery	plain buff wares, micaceous schist or phyllite temper	plain brown wares, sand temper
Projectile points	large array of projectile points, delicate workmanship	large array of projectile points
Flaked stone	few chopping, scraping, and cutting tools	significant array of sawing, hoeing, scraping, and pounding tools
Ground stone	full trough metate, predominate form; slate palette common	full trough metate, well shaped; slate palette common, especially in Colonial period
Carved stone	carved stone bowls and other forms well represented	stone and shell jewelry abundant and elaborate
Jewelry	stone and shell jewelry abundant and elaborate; turquoise present	carved stone and shell well developed
Burial forms	secondary pit and urn cremations predominate	primary and secondary pit and trench cremations and urn cremations; rare inhumations
Other material culture	human and animal figurines common copper bells recovered mosaic and painted plaques (including iron pyrite mirrors) present zoomorphic representations and motifs common and varied (esp. snake and bird)	human and animal figurines present copper bells recovered (rare) mosaic and painted plaques (including iron pyrite mirrors) present zoomorphic representations less common and less varied
Macaws	only one reported, scarlet macaw reported from the Gatlin site (Hargrave 1970)	none reported

Papagueria (Hohokam)	Rios Magdalena and Altar, Sonora (Trincheras)	Nogales Area
Withers 1973	Braniff Cornejo 1992; Johnson 1960:183; McGuire and Villalpando 1993; McGuire et al. 1999; Villalpando 1997	Di Peso 1956; Doyel 1977a, 1977b; Grebinger 1971a, Jacome 1986; Neily 1993; this report
Sonoran desert scrub, Arizona upland and lower Colorado River subdivisions	Sonoran desert scrub, Arizona upland and Lower Colorado River subdivisions	Semidesert grasslands and Madrean Evergreen woodlands
agriculture, wild-plant collecting, hunting	agriculture in riverine areas; opportunistic agriculture elsewhere; wild-plant collecting, hunting	agriculture in riverine areas; opportunistic agriculture elsewhere; wild-plant collecting, hunting
small-scale irrigation, *ak chin*, floodwater	small-scale irrigation, *ak chin*, floodwater	small-scale irrigation, *ak chin*, floodwater, (and possibly dry farming)
rectangular houses-in-shallow-pits or surface structures	pit structures, circular and rectangular rooms (*corrales*), surface structures	rectangular, square, and round houses-in-pits
none reported	*cerros de trincheras* in Altar phase (terraces, walls, public architecture?)	Paloparado notable: dance plaza, banquette, crematoria, communal cemetery
house clusters, extramural cooking, work, and burial areas	Atil and Altar phase traits not fully known; extramural cooking, work, and burial areas	house clusters; outdoor work and cooking areas, burial areas
red-on-brown pottery, sand temper; paddle-and-anvil finish	purple- (or black-) on-red (or -brown) and polychrome pottery; sand-tempered, coil-and-scrape finish	local red-on-brown, purple-on-tan, black-on-red, sand temper
red-slipped brown ware, sand temper (beginning late Colonial period)	red-slipped brown ware, sand temper, coil-and-scrape finish	red-slipped brown ware in Sedentary period, sand temper
plain brown wares, sand temper, paddle-and-anvil finish	plain brown ware, sand temper, coil-and-scrape finish early and paddle-and-anvil finish late	plain brown ware, sand temper
limited variety of flaked stone projectile points	projectile points present, pre-Classic styles not yet defined	projectile points present, pre-Classic style poorly defined
variety of chopping, scraping, and cutting tools	abundance of chopping, scraping, and cutting tools	abundance of chopping, scraping, and cutting tools
slab and basin metate predominate, effigy palette present	trough, basin, and slab metates; slate palette present, but unlike Hohokam palettes	basin-shaped metate predominates, also trough and slab; slate palette present, but uncommon and unlike Hohokam palette
stone and shell jewelry present, but simple	abundant evidence of shell manufacture and use	stone and shell jewelry common
carved stone present but uncommon	carved stone present but uncommon	carved stone present but uncommon
inhumations, flexed (and extended?)	pit and urn cremation predominate, inhumations present	cremations and inhumations (flexed and extended)
none reported	none reported	animal figurine present, rare
none reported	none reported	none reported
mosaic plaque fragment recovered, rare	none reported	mosaic plaque base fragments (2) recovered at Paloparado, rare
zoomorphic representations rare	zoomorphic representations rare (lizards and birds not present; frogs most common)	zoomorphic representations rare; frogs most common
none reported	none reported	only one reported, El Macayo (this report)

various times, the loci of subregional traditions of Hohokam culture whereas the Magdalena–Altar Basin was the center of Trincheras culture. The Hohokam were prehistoric farming peoples who lived in the lower Sonoran Desert portion of the American Southwest, and who, like many of their foraging and farming contemporaries, grew corn, beans, squash, cotton, and agave with floodwater, irrigation, runoff, and dryland methods. During the pre-Classic period, they lived in distinctive forms of houses constructed in shallow pits, usually located with related households in courtyard groupings; manufactured culturally diagnostic red-on-buff or red-on-brown ceramic types and vessel forms; participated in ball court rituals; cremated their dead; and were well-known for the production of carved and etched shell jewelry, turquoise mosaics, slate palettes, pyrite mirrors, clay figurines, and distinctive serrated projectile points. Much has been written about the Hohokam, and descriptions of material culture, architecture, and their economic, political, and social systems can be found in Gladwin et al. (1937), Haury (1976), Doyel (1987), Gumerman (1991), Crown and Judge (1991), Wallace (1997), and Whittlesey (1998) among many other publications. In contrast, the Trincheras culture is poorly known; relatively few programs of systematic study have been conducted, and few reports describing the Formative period archaeology of northwest Sonora have been published. The following briefly summarizes the characteristics of Trincheras culture.

Trincheras culture refers to a prehistoric archaeological culture that emanated out of the Rio Concepción–Rio Magdalena and Rio Altar Valleys of northwest Sonora. Some archaeologists (e.g., Haury 1950; Johnson 1960, 1963) consider Trincheras as yet another regional variant of Hohokam culture, but others (Bowen 1972, 1976; Braniff Cornejo 1992; Di Peso 1979; McGuire and Villalpando 1993) consider it a separate cultural tradition. What is called Trincheras appears to have developed from a Cochise-culture base to which pottery and farming were added to an Archaic-type subsistence economy adapted to wild-plant collection, hunting, and exploitation of marine resources (Bowen 1972, 1976; McGuire and Villalpando 1993:71). Evidence of river irrigation and hillside-terrace farming has been documented in the Altar Valley (McGuire and Villalpando 1993) and along Rio Magdalena near the village of Trincheras and the Trincheras culture type site of Las Trincheras (Fish and Fish 2000). It is most clearly recognizable in the period from A.D. 800 to 1450, but an early ceramic sequence beginning at about 200 B.C. and lasting until about A.D. 800 has been attributed to the Trincheras culture as well (Bowen 1976; McGuire and Villalpando 1993). Archaeologically, its hallmarks are several varieties of purple-painted pottery, settlements and agricultural plots on terraced volcanic hills known as *cerros de trincheras*, and a local emphasis on marine shell procurement from the Gulf

of California, as well as shell jewelry manufacture and export (Villalpando 1997). If its geographic distribution is determined by the joint presence of *cerros de trincheras* and purple-painted pottery, then it extended to the east and south as far as the middle Rio San Miguel, to the west just beyond Caborca on the Rio Concepción (sometimes referred to as the Rio Asunción), and to the north to the middle reaches of the Santa Cruz and San Pedro River valleys (Braniff Cornejo 1992; Downum et al. 1994; Whittlesey 1996).

Few sites attributed to the Trincheras culture have been professionally investigated, and systematic surveys within the Trincheras region have been limited in scope. Consequently, our understanding is derived largely from three sites—the multiple component La Playa site (primarily Late Archaic with a Middle Formative occupation ca. A.D. 800 to 1300; Johnson 1960, 1963; Woodward 1936), Las Trincheras (ca. A.D. 1250–1450; Fish 1998; Fish and Fish 2000; McGuire et al. 1999), and La Proveedora (ca. A.D. 1200–1450; Braniff Cornejo 1992)—and the reconnaissance and intensive surveys reported by Sauer and Brand (1931), Eckholm (1939, 1940, cited in Carpenter and Sanchez 1997), Hinton (1955), Wasley (1968), Bowen (1972, 1976), Braniff Cornejo (1992), McGuire and Villalpando (1993), and Fish and Fish (2000). Among the more recent syntheses that consider Trincheras culture are those prepared by Phillips (1989), Whittlesey (1992, 1996), Fish and Fish (1994), and McGuire et al. (1999).

Three phases attributed to the Trincheras culture have been delimited in the Altar Valley (McGuire and Villalpando 1993; Villalpando 1997:102): Atil (ca. A.D. 700–1150, roughly equivalent to the early portion of Bowen's [1976] Stage 3), Altar (ca. A.D. 1150–1300, equivalent to later portion of Bowen's [1976] Stage 3), and Realito (ca. 1300–1450, equivalent to Bowen's [1976] Stage 4). McGuire and Villalpando (1993:71–72, 86, 87) suggested that the Atil phase, which is equivalent to the Colonial and Sedentary periods in the Hohokam sequence, was marked by the presence of Trincheras Plain (variants 1 and 2) and fine-lined Trincheras Purple-on-red, specular variety, pottery in association with Colonial and Sedentary intrusive pottery types from southern Arizona; cremation burials; small pit houses; a subsistence economy that included agriculture; and a settlement pattern tethered to the Altar River and its major washes. Sites also occur on the *bajada* flanking the river.

The subsequent early Classic period equivalent, the Altar phase, is identified by the presence of Trincheras Plain (variant 2); Trincheras Purple-on-red, non-specular variety; Trincheras Purple-on-brown; Altar Polychrome; Nogales Polychrome; and two local types—Thin Plain and Thin Red-on-brown (McGuire and Villalpando 1993:72). *Cerros de trincheras* appeared during this phase, not later as Bowen (1972) proposed (see also Downum et al. 1994 for a discussion of dating *cerros de trincheras* in southern Arizona). Pit houses continued to be the primary house form. McGuire and Villalpando (1993:86, 87) suggested that the Altar phase is the phase characterized by the highest populations and greatest variety of site types: habitations, rockshelters, plant-processing locations (*hornos*), resource-collecting sites, and ceremonial sites. In the Altar Valley, 11 *cerros de trincheras* date to the Altar phase. Among these is Tio Benino, a hill with more than 40 terraces, which constitutes the largest *cerro* in the valley (McGuire and Villalpando 1993:192–196). During this phase, substantial pit house villages were located in the floodplain, and sites occur in a variety of physiographic settings: floodplain, hill, terrace, plain, and *bajada*.

The late Classic period equivalent, the Realito phase, was characterized by the replacement of Trincheras pottery finished with scraping (Trincheras Plain) by pottery smoothed and finished with a paddle and anvil and later polished (Late Plain and Late Red) (McGuire and Villalpando 1993:72, 87, 88). McGuire and Villalpando suggested that no local pottery was painted during the Altar phase, and only a few decorated types were imported. The intrusive types recovered from Altar phase sites in the Altar Valley are restricted to Gila Polychrome and Ramos Polychrome, which have been recovered in urn cremation contexts. Thin metates (*metates delgado*) and drop-ended manos were exclusive to this phase. Houses continued to take the form of pit structures and were more often on terrace settings than in floodplains. Some habitation sites contain low, oval mounds, in which cremations have been recovered. Less frequent but present are inhumation burials. The overall number and variety of sites decrease (e.g., loss of *horno* sites) in the Realito phase, but site size increases. McGuire and Villalpando (1993:88) noted that Altar phase *cerros de trincheras* are largely abandoned and new *cerros de trincheras* are built in the Realito phase, suggesting that these hill sites served different roles than before. Overall, the material culture resembles late prehistoric assemblages from the Papaguería, Tucson Basin, and San Pedro River valley. Marine shell manufacture and exchange patterns continue.

The following section compares the pre–A.D. 1150 traits of five geographic areas: the Gila-Salt Basin, the Tucson Basin, the Papaguería, the Rios Magdalena and Altar, and the Nogales area.

Archaeological Comparisons

Table 48 suggests more similarities than differences among these five geographic traditions. Each area supported relatively simple agricultural populations where warm-season maize cultivation could be supplemented by the collection of wild plants and the hunting and trapping of indigenous animals. In each area, the larger, more enduring residential settlements occurred along the perennial reaches of major streams, whereas limited-activity sites, representing short-term and seasonal activities to acquire economic resources, were essential components of each geographic system. In addition, houses, storage facilities, and cooking features were of similar design and materials insofar as we can determine from published reports. Further, each area had access to a relatively similar array of trade items and exotics—especially marine shell, turquoise, and extralocal pottery. Finally, it appears that the range and type of basic tools and household items were greatly similar.

Differences among these cultural traditions, on the other hand, seem more a matter of degree than kind. Subsistence strategies, for example, appear to be determined more by hydrology, geomorphology, and resource availability than technological knowledge. However, differences in internal structure of comparable settlements and the settlement type hierarchy, differences in esoteric and nonsubsistence items, and differences in burial customs may indeed suggest important contrasts among these five geographic traditions. The presence or absence of public architecture and integrative space, as well as the existence of distinctive ways of internally partitioning space within the village, suggest underlying differences in the structuring of human relationships that signal the existence of distinct cultural groups. Further, the presence, abundance, and range of certain artifacts thought to represent participation in specific cultural traditions, such as pyrite mirrors, slate palettes, and carved stone censers, do vary from area from area.

The Nogales-area sites in general, and El Macayo specifically, are not identical to the archaeological manifestations of the Gila Basin, Tucson Basin, Papaguería, or poorly documented Trincheras area. With the possible exception of Paloparado, the data retrieved from excavated sites in the Nogales area provide inconclusive evidence for determining cultural identity or affiliation. Environmentally, the Nogales area stands alone; the settlements of the upper Santa Cruz River watershed are within the Chihuahuan grasslands, and all others are within lowland or upland portions of the Sonoran desert scrub. In economic orientation, architecture, site structure, material culture, and mortuary practices, however, it shares selective characteristics with each area. The following paragraphs relate to the recovered remains of El Macayo and explore aspects of those shared activities and cultural behaviors that signal group identity.

Economic Orientation

The floral and faunal remains (see Chapters 6 and 8), as well as the flaked and ground stone collections (see Chapter 4), the investment in architecture and storage (see Chapter 2), and the site location itself indicate that many generations of El Macayo residents were foragers as well as farmers. This pattern was typical for most Formative period populations in the Arizona deserts and had its roots in the subsistence practices of the late Archaic period. There is some evidence, however, to suggest that foraging played a greater role in subsistence endeavors than at contemporary sites in the Tucson or Gila-Salt Basins. The paucity of recovered domesticates and the prevalence of basin-type metates and one-handed manos at El Macayo suggests that a greater emphasis was placed on the procurement and processing of native seeds than on the cultivation of domesticated crops. Should this be true, it could signify that populations in the grasslands of the upper Santa Cruz River valley were economically distinct from their contemporaries in the lower and drier areas around them.

Domestic Architecture

The architecture at El Macayo is typical of the house-in-a-pit style. Although considered typical of Hohokam building practices, it is not exclusively a Hohokam trait. For example, houses built in shallow pits have been found at Formative period settlements in southeastern Arizona that otherwise were considered Dragoon variant (Fulton 1934a, 1934b, 1938; Fulton and Tuthill 1940) or San Simon variant Mogollon sites (Sayles 1945). Similarly, a version of the house-in-a-pit construction technique has been found at late Archaic sites in the Tucson Basin (Mabry 1997) and at Viejo period sites in Chihuahua (Di Peso 1974). In general, these late Archaic and Viejo period structures differ from the houses-in-pits found at El Macayo and at other Formative period sites in southern Arizona in the arrangement and form of interior features. Nevertheless, these Archaic and Formative period structures share the characteristic of having brush-and-pole superstructures anchored inside shallow house pits.

Site Structure

Over its 300–600-year history, El Macayo was characterized by a variety of house forms, extramural activity areas, cemeteries, and trash deposits (see Chapter 2). Although we did not expose a sufficiently large area to see how space was partitioned and use-space arranged, we did note that El Macayo was similar to Potrero Creek in its rather loose organization of features and activity spaces. As in most portions of the southern Southwest, food preparation, cooking, and interment of the dead generally took place outside individual houses, but in our case, the relation of these features to domiciles and household groups remains unknown. The abundance of extramural storage pits at El Macayo (and at Potrero Creek), however, seems to contrast with Gila-Salt, Tucson Basin, and Papaguerían sites, where aboveground, intramural storage was more common. This pattern may indicate that residents were less concerned about exclusive access to food and household resources than elsewhere in the Southwest where space was more deliberately divided and allocated to separate social entities or functions.

Ceramics

Five pottery traditions were present at El Macayo: Gila series (Gila-Salt Hohokam), Santa Cruz series (Tucson Basin Hohokam), San Simon series (San Simon Mogollon), Trincheras (Altar-Magdelena Basin), and what appears to be a local tradition (see Chapter 3). The Gila series Hohokam pottery is technologically and stylistically distinct from the other three series. It is a buff ware with distinctive temper, and it constitutes a minority of the painted pottery (12.3 percent). These items undoubtedly were manufactured in the Salt-Gila area and were transported to the Nogales area. The remaining four traditions, however, are brown wares. We suspect that most of the pottery classified as Santa Cruz series (38.8 percent), San Simon series (0.8 percent), and Trincheras series (41.7 percent) (see Table 13) was made outside of the Nogales area, but we have not conducted studies to demonstrate this. Thus, it is possible that some of this brown ware pottery was manufactured locally. For example, Whittlesey (1992) evaluated the results of a petrographic analysis of sherds from the nearby Arivaca area and concluded that some of the Trincheras-like pottery may have been made locally. Although similar analyses have not yet been conducted on Trincheras pottery from El Macayo, we can suggest, on the basis of macroscopic inspection, that Trincheras pottery was manufactured from raw materials that differ from the pottery made in the Tucson Basin or those we have identified as "locally" made. Furthermore, the Trincheras series pottery was constructed with a different manufacturing technology than any of the other series.

Ceramics attributed to the Trincheras, Tucson Basin, and San Simon traditions are typical of the pottery from these areas. If we had recovered these same sherds from sites in Sonora or in the Tucson Basin, none would have been considered anomalous. In contrast, the "local" pottery of El Macayo is technologically and decoratively different from these two other brown ware traditions and potentially signals something different about the potters who produced it.

Heckman (see Chapter 3) identified several types of locally manufactured pottery at El Macayo; all are sand-tempered brown wares. Collectively they differ from the Trincheras, San Simon, and Tucson Basin tradition pottery in several technological characteristics. In general, these local types appear to be part of a subtradition within the Santa Cruz series that incorporates attributes characteristic of the Trincheras ceramic tradition as well as distinctive qualities presumed to be locally derived. Vessels appear to have been constructed by hand modeling, either as coiled constructions, slabs, or "pinch" pots, and finished by hand without benefit of paddle and anvil or scraping tools. Vessel walls are typically irregular in thickness and poorly smoothed.

Two local plain wares and five local painted variations were recognized in the El Macayo collection. Type I plain ware has coarse temper and is crudely finished (6 percent of all analyzed unpainted sherds and four of six plain ware vessels) (see Table 14). Type II plain ware is similar but has finer temper and is more finely finished (66 percent of all unpainted sherds and two reconstructible vessels).

The five decorative types are red-on-brown (5.1 percent of painted sherds), black-on-brown (0.3 percent), purple-on-tan (one reconstructible vessel), black-on-red (0.8 percent), and black-on-white or polychrome (0.2 percent) (see Table 13). Most of the decorated pieces are painted with a red- or black-firing paint on an unslipped brown background. One restorable bowl (Vessel 144-1) is painted with a purple pigment on a tan, slipped background (see Table 15). The designs on the red-on-brown and the purple-on-tan pieces resemble the designs on the apparently contemporaneous Tucson Basin type, Rincon Red-on-brown. Several sherds representing two black-on-red bowls also are attributed to this local tradition based on technical qualities of the clay body, even though the surface finish on these pieces is exceptional. The fifth painted variation is represented by a single sherd that has a black-pigmented design on a crazed white-slipped background. This piece resembles Santa Cruz Polychrome but is associated with the local tradition based on the presence of large flecks of gold mica in the clay body. In short, the local painted pottery appears to have been a poorly executed attempt at replicating Tucson Basin and Trincheras ceramic types.

Despite the lack of chronometrically dated contexts associated with this local painted tradition, we can say that this pottery does not appear until sometime after A.D. 950. We assign this beginning date—the transition between the Hohokam Colonial and Sedentary periods—to the tradition on the basis of design styles and correlated manufacturing technology. All of the red-on-browns with Colonial-age design styles are executed in a manufacturing technique that is typical for the Tucson Basin. The vessels are well constructed, the surfaces are smoothed, and the temper consists of a crushed-micaceous-metamorphic rock. From these attributes, we might infer that these items were not produced in the Nogales area, but rather were made in the Tucson Basin. Further, the local painted pottery has stylistic attributes that suggest that it generally follows the decorative tradition of the Tucson Basin Sedentary period. The local red-on-browns in Nogales with Sedentary period designs resemble the Tucson Basin Rincon phase red-on-browns. Similarly, the Nogales-area black-on-red sherds have precedents in the Rincon Polychrome–Rincon Red technological tradition of the Tucson Basin.

The ceramic evidence accumulated to date suggests the following. Prior to about A.D. 950, painted pottery was either acquired by trade from the Trincheras and Tucson Basin areas or was made in the Nogales area by potters well trained in the traditions of these two regions. No local painted traditions existed before the Sedentary period. After that time, the importation of painted wares slowed or

stopped altogether, and a distinctly local painted tradition was developed to take its place. This development occurred during the Sedentary period and continued into the Classic period. The Classic period examples of this local series were not present at El Macayo but have been found at Paloparado, where they were identified as Ramanote Red-on-brown (Di Peso 1956).

In this local painted tradition, we see the strongest source of influence to be the Tucson Basin, but some technological and stylistic attributes—primarily the used of coil-and-hand-finishing techniques, paint, and some decorative elements—are suggestive of Trincheras decorative practices. The local sand-tempered plain brown ware tradition suggests an affinity with both Tucson Basin and Trincheras traditions, but distinctive manufacturing techniques set local potters apart from either of these traditions.

Ground Stone
Della Croce (see Chapter 4) observed that the milling collection appeared to be geared toward the processing of small native seeds rather than corn, given the preponderance of basin and slab metates and their associated manos and hand stones. We do not interpret this to mean that corn was not ground on these tools, but rather that the milling tools were not corn-dedicated. Their forms were such that they could be used for a variety of grain sizes. The generalized nature of the grinding tools is suggestive of an economy that regularly used native seeds. Palynological and macro-botanical analyses (see Chapter 8) support this inference. Rather than seeing this aspect of the subsistence economy as a cultural indicator, we suggest that the milling collection reflects the pragmatism of prehistoric peoples to effectively utilize a wide variety of locally available natural resources.

The nonutilitarian ground stone is equally unspecialized. It is largely devoid of cultural information except for one item. The single palette recovered from the floor of a pit house is unquestionably manufactured in the Hohokam style. It was made of a local material, however, and is an indicator that local residents may have practiced Hohokam rituals associated with this artifact form. A second smaller palette was recovered that is ambiguous as to cultural affiliation.

Five hundred fourteen nonutilitarian decorative items also were recovered (see Chapter 4). The majority of the stone beads were argillite and formed a single necklace placed with a child burial (n = 508 beads). The remainder of the stone items represented three small pieces of turquoise (one bead, one bead or pendant blank, and one pendant), one pendant made from a quartz crystal, another argillite bead, and a steatite bead.

Flaked Stone
Della Croce (see Chapter 4) noted that the flaked stone collection is typical of Formative period settlements across

the entire Southwest and was unremarkable in most respects. Differences observed between the El Macayo collection and those recovered in Hohokam sites of the Tucson or Gila Basins included raw material preferences and certain technological attributes. For example, at El Macayo we recovered evidence of the use of fine-grained siliceous rocks and production of bifacial-thinning flakes in quantities higher than those usually observed in comparable Hohokam settlements. What seems to be a cultural preference for chert and other fine-grained stone may in fact be nothing more than its availability in the Nogales area relative to a dearth of this material in the Tucson or Gila Basins. Despite having access to finer-grained raw materials, El Macayo knappers demonstrated no greater skill or care at making flaked stone tools.

With the possible exception of one projectile point, all points were manufactured in styles characteristically found at Hohokam sites in the Tucson and Gila Basins. In every case, they were expediently created from flakes rather than cores; technique was of little consequence. Flakes of fine-grained stone were worked only enough to produce the desired shape. Although function and generalized form over artistry were the desired goals, it is clear that the points recovered from El Macayo were fashioned to reflect Hohokam projectile styles.

Shell and Bone Artifacts

Some 555 shell specimens (see Chapter 5) and five bone tools were recovered from El Macayo (see Chapter 6). The shell objects were manufactured from at least four genera and were fashioned into disk and bilobed beads, bracelets, an animal effigy pendant, and a needle. Given the dearth of manufacturing debris or unfinished pieces, Urban (see Chapter 5) suggests that the residents of El Macayo were consumers rather than producers of shell jewelry. The items were simple in form and of common genera; no suggestion as to place of manufacture was possible.

Finally, the bone items included three awls, a flaker, and a possible needle. Although these items significantly add to our knowledge of material cultural patterns in the Nogales area, none is distinctive as to cultural origin or affiliation.

Mortuary Customs

Of all the cultural markers used by archaeologists to signify group membership, mortuary practices probably are cited most frequently because these rites of final passage are considered to be linked closely with a sense of group identity and are believed to be highly conservative traditions (see Whittlesey [1999] and Woodson et al. [1999] for two recent discussions related to southeastern Arizona).

Two types of burials were encountered at El Macayo (see Chapter 2)—inhumation and secondary cremation. The majority of human and animal remains unearthed at the village were inhumations (13 humans, 2 dogs, 1 macaw). Of the

human inhumations, four were flexed, two were extended, and the remaining seven were either unexcavated or indeterminate. Only two human cremations have been reported to date; both were recovered as isolated features within test trenches (see Table 8).

As discussed earlier, the age of these inhumations is equivocal. Only three (Features 32, 151, 214) of the 11 recorded inhumations were accompanied by ceramic containers (a 1+-year-old, a 5–7-year-old, and a subadult, respectively). Of these three, only one (Feature 32) contained a sherd that was assignable to a specific temporal period (typed as Rincon Red-on-brown, style C). Nonetheless, the burial pits were excavated into the same strata as the pre-Classic period houses at El Macayo and there is evidence that these inhumations are contemporary with these pre-Classic houses. The burials were spatially concentrated and less disturbed by subsequent construction than other portions of the site.

In contrast, the Hohokam of the Gila-Salt and Tucson Basins primarily cremated the dead during the late Pioneer to Sedentary periods. Data for the Papaguería are limited, but Withers (1973) documented a single inhumation in the late pre-Classic period at Valshni Village and Scantling (1940) recorded three inhumations from the Classic period Jackrabbit Village. Burial data are near nonexistent for the Trincheras area in pre-Classic times, but the discovery of both cremations and inhumations has been reported (Bowen 1972; McGuire and Villalpando 1993). Thus, on the basis of this trait alone, we could argue that most of the inhabitants at El Macayo were not Hohokam.

Inhumation is a manner of interment that has great antiquity in southern Arizona and northern Sonora and can be traced back as far as the late Archaic (Huckell 1988, 1995; Mabry 1997; Sayles 1983:129) and continued into the Early Formative period (Woodson et al. 1999). In the Nogales area, both types of burials have been found. Inhumation was the dominant custom at predominantly pre-Classic El Macayo and Potrero Creek (Grebinger 1971b) and in the Classic and early historical occupations of Paloparado (Di Peso 1956; Wilcox 1987). Cremation, however, was the preferred custom in the pre-Classic occupation of Paloparado, at the Cemetery Ridge site, and Nogales Wash, among other sites (Di Peso 1956; Doyel 1977a, 1977b; Jácome 1986; Reinhard 1978; Reinhard and Fink 1982).

As a burial custom, cremation was used by cultures prior to the Hohokam and was never exclusive to the Hohokam. For example, cremation was used by late Archaic and Early Formative period populations in the southern Southwest long before the emergence of the Hohokam as a distinctive cultural entity (Ciolek-Torrello 1995; Dongoske 1993; Haury 1957), and cremation was practiced by other Middle and Late Formative period peoples of the southern Southwest, such as the Trincheras culture (Bowen 1972; McGuire and Villalpando 1993).

If we accept the proposition that burial customs are highly conservative cultural patterns and that they are strongly indicative of cultural affiliation, then we can propose two alternative interpretations for El Macayo specifically and the Nogales area in general. First, if inhumations and cremations co-occur in the pre-Classic period, then we can infer that the Nogales area was home to a multiethnic or multicultural population. Individuals or social groups practicing cremation, and possessing items made or used in the Hohokam heartland (e.g., pottery, stone and shell jewelry of certain types, slate palettes), may have been culturally Hohokam, while other social groups practicing inhumation were not. Furthermore, it is possible that cultural identity could have been manifest at the level of settlement. For example, pre-Classic Paloparado or the Sonoita Street site may have been culturally Hohokam, whereas contemporary Potrero Creek and El Macayo were not Hohokam. Alternatively, if the practice of inhumation largely replaced the practice of cremation in the early Classic period, then we can infer that populations in the Nogales area either reinterpreted the manner in which the deceased needed to be prepared for the afterlife or were replaced by different populations in the post–A.D.1150 period. Too few excavated burials and poor chronological control over those that have been documented limit our ability to determine which possibility is the stronger case.

Summary

Without linguistic, biological, or historical evidence to resolve the question, the assignment of cultural identity must depend on the availability of material evidence. Here we ask, does the material evidence indicate a Hohokam or Trincheras affiliation, or does it represent something else? The collective evidence derived from the archaeological data is equivocal. On the one hand, the predominant house style, projectile point forms, intrusive ceramics, palettes, a liking for shell jewelry, and the practice of cremation burial suggest that Hohokam cultural traditions were well known and practiced. On the other hand, an apparent emphasis on foraging activities, the informality of settlement layouts, the production of local ceramic types using non-Hohokam techniques, the use of a generalized flaked stone industry, and the persistence of inhumation burial customs are suggestive of non-Hohokam cultural patterns. Yet another compelling piece of evidence that at least some of the inhabitants were not Hohokam is the absence of ball courts in upper Santa Cruz River valley.[3] The absence of this signature architectural form suggests that local communities were integrated by a different mechanism than that which signified participation in the Hohokam world and served as a integrative mechanism for contemporary pre-Classic communities in the Tucson and Gila Basins. As to whether the populations of the Nogales area were affiliated with the Trincheras culture is, at present, unknowable. So

little excavation or intensive survey has been conducted that archaeologists simply do not know what type of features, site layouts, material, and cultural patterns characterize this cultural tradition.

In short, we conclude that the data are inconclusive. It is probably neither useful nor necessary to classify the populations of El Macayo as Hohokam, Trincheras, a Hohokam-Trincheras blend, or "other." We do not know if the village was made up of a single ethnic group or was composed of more than one cultural group. Nor are we able to evaluate whether the cultural developments in the Nogales area were peripheral to centers elsewhere. Certainly, they appear to be economically self-sustaining, but whether there was a political or social link with surrounding groups is unclear. For the time being, we suggest that populations of Nogales were local groups who selectively incorporated customs and material items into their own heterogeneous cultural patterns. This "local" culture was no doubt shaped by indigenous and exogenous processes and events over time. Finally, we suggest that by concentrating on the description of local patterns and sequences, we will more likely avoid imposing preexisting and perhaps unsuitable classification schemes that obscure the importance and necessity of local adaptations.

Extralocal Social Interaction and Exchange

Evidence of interregional interaction exists in the presence of items manufactured from nonlocal materials, the presence of an exotic bird species, and in the inferred direction and frequency of contact. Among the more significant items recovered from El Macayo were ceramics believed to have been manufactured outside of the Nogales area, marine shell, turquoise, argillite, and a military macaw recovered from a burial.

Among the painted ceramics recovered from the site were pottery types typically associated with manufacturing locales in southeastern Arizona (San Simon series: 5 sherds, or 0.8 percent of painted), the Tucson Basin (Santa Cruz series: 242 sherds, or 38.8 percent of painted), the Gila Basin (Gila series: 77 sherds, or 12.3 percent of painted), and northern Sonora (Trincheras series: 260 sherds, or 41.7 percent of painted). By virtue of sherd abundance, it would appear that over the life span of the village, contacts were most frequent with the Tucson Basin and Trincheras culture areas. This is not surprising, given that these are the adjacent cultural areas to the north and south. That these two areas in particular were sources of local influence can be seen in the characteristics of decoration and vessel construction and finish on local forms of pottery (see Chapter 3).

At least four genera of marine shell were recovered from El Macayo (see Chapter 5): *Anodonta* (4 specimens),

Glycymeris (18 specimens), *Pecten* (1 specimen), *Spondylus* (1 specimen), either *Spondylus* or *Chama* (1 specimen), and, finally, a shell bead necklace of a sturdy shell likely to be either *Dosinia* or *Glycymeris* (530 specimens). All of these genera are endemic to the Gulf of California and were likely procured there, transported to manufacturing centers elsewhere, and supplied to the inhabitants of El Macayo through a variety of exchange mechanisms. Each of these types has been reported from Rio Magdalena–Altar Valley sites (Bowen 1972; Braniff Cornejo 1992; Johnson 1960; McGuire and Villalpando 1993; Villalpando 1997) and from the Hohokam area (McGuire and Howard 1987; Nelson 1991).

Three pieces of turquoise were recovered from El Macayo (see Chapter 4): a turquoise bead, a bead or pendant blank, and a perforated turquoise pendant. Turquoise occurs in most geological settings where copper ores are present and was mined prehistorically in both the American Southwest and Mexico (Ball 1941; Bartlett 1935, 1966; Blake 1899; Greeley 1987; Harrington 1939, 1940; Harvey and Harvey 1938; Haury 1934; Johnston, 1964, 1966; Jones 1904, 1909; Warren and Mathien 1985; Warren and Weber 1979; Weigand 1982a, 1982b, 1994; Welch and Triadan 1991). Although no turquoise quarries are in the immediate vicinity of Nogales, prehistoric turquoise quarries have been found in a number of localities in Arizona, including the Dragoon Mountains, at the confluence of the Salt and Canyon Creeks, and at Mineral Peak near Kingman (Nations and Stump 1981:185). As with shell, opportunities for expeditions to mine turquoise or to acquire it through down-the-line trade existed for prehistoric populations. Although several techniques are available to source turquoise, we did not attempt this. Given turquoise's long-standing appeal and widespread exchange, its place of origin, subsequent modification, and commodity exchange are not likely to be isomorphic.

A single necklace composed of 508 argillite disk beads was found with the child's burial in El Macayo (Feature 151, see Chapters 2 and 4). We know of no argillite source in the Nogales area, but the closest documented source is the Tucson Mountain Redbed within Saguaro National Monument (Elson and Gundersen 1992). A number of local argillite sources also are present in central Arizona within the Mazatzal Quartzite Formation, but these are farther from Nogales than the Tucson Basin source. Elson and Gundersen (1992:461) suggested that the "Tucson Mountain Redbed argillite appears to be extremely localized, to the extent that it may possibly be monopolizing the southern Arizona argillite trade." As with the shell, we did not attempt to source the argillite beads, but it would be possible to do this and to compare their mineral signatures with those obtained for the Tucson Mountain Redbed source so as to test this hypothesis. For the time being, the likelihood that the argillite beads at El Macayo derived from

a Tucson source supports other data suggesting an enduring relationship with northern populations.

The discovery of a military macaw (*Ara militaris*[4]) was an important and unusual find at El Macayo. Far less common in archaeological sites than the scarlet macaw (*Ara macao*), its tropical lowland relative, the military macaw is a bird native to temperate climates and inhabits semiarid oak and conifer forests of the Sierra Madre of Sonora and Chihuahua at elevations ranging from 1,000 to 2,700 m AMSL. Bullock and Cooper (1999:2) suggested that, given its habitat preference, the prehistoric range of the military macaw could have been as far north as the Mogollon Rim country of central Arizona and the Gila Mountains of west-central New Mexico. In contrast, there are no analogous habitats that could have supported scarlet macaws, who today are endemic to the lowland forests of eastern and southern Mexico below 900 m (Bullock and Cooper 1992:2). Thus, the presence of scarlet macaws in sites within the American Southwest suggests long-distance transport and exchange, whereas the presence of military macaws, particularly in the southern Southwest, might indicate that the colorful birds were captured locally or within forests no more than a few days away. At the present time, we are unable to determine if macaws were a member, albeit a rare member, of the Madrean woodland and forest communities on the mountains surrounding Nogales. That the macaw was an immature bird with what appears to have been a deliberately broken wing (see Chapter 7) and was recovered in a burial, possibly with grave goods (see Chapter 2), suggests that it was obtained at some distance, maimed to keep it from flying, and held in some esteem.

In short, these data indicate that the Middle Formative period populations of El Macayo were in regular contact with populations both north and south of the Nogales area. The most persistent and perhaps more influential contacts were with cultural groups of the Tucson Basin to the north and the Trincheras area to the south. Evidence to support the northern connections resides in the presence and dating of Santa Cruz series pottery types, the emulation of Rincon Red-on-brown style vessels and designs by Nogales potters after the tenth century, and the presence of argillite beads thought to have come from the Tucson Basin. Evidence to support southern connections rests largely in the presence and predominance of Trincheras series pottery types. Although the marine shell was obtained from the Gulf of California, and the turquoise probably was not mined locally, their presence in deposits at El Macayo does not suggest where the centers of production and exchange for these items might have been located. Likewise, the presence of a military macaw hints at connections to the south and southeast, but it is possible that these forest-dwelling birds were living near Nogales in the pre-Hispanic period. Collectively, these data suggest that the Nogales area was involved in regional exchange systems that moved desirable non-subsistence items from their place of origin or production to places of consumption or use. Although distant from large population centers, populations of the upper Santa Cruz watershed were not isolated, and that goods, people, and information likely traveled across ancient transportation routes throughout the southern Southwest.

Conclusion

El Macayo was a prehistoric hamlet or village inhabited by a local culture of forager-farmers who lived at the confluence of two small, but dependable, upland drainages in the Nogales area. The site may have been used as early as the seventh century A.D. but certainly was occupied in the eighth century and again between the mid-ninth and late twelfth centuries. The terrace and ridge upon which El Macayo was situated was a place of persistent, if not continuous, year-round settlement for many generations.

The duration of settlement at El Macayo is impressive. First, the large number of architectural features identified in a relatively small horizontal exposure, as well as the frequency of feature superposition, attests to the continuous building and rebuilding of facilities at this location. Second, the abundance and temporal range of painted ceramics (see Table 13) suggest that this location was occupied for a minimum of 300 and a maximum of 600 years. Third, the placement of a residential site upon and adjacent to a low river terrace at the confluence of two manageable washes with access to excellent soils for agriculture, indigenous riparian resources, and a commanding view of surrounding territory is very suggestive. Such a location would have been advantageous to peoples who relied on the cultivation of crops and the collection of native plants that were growing in these bottomlands. In addition, the settlement was safe from the periodic floods that undoubtedly occurred along the washes, yet it was near the valuable resources of the river and its floodplain. Finally, the residents of the site could have monitored the passage of travelers who may have followed these water courses while en route to places north and south.

The village of El Macayo was in many ways typical of small-scale agrarian settlements everywhere in the southern Southwest during the Middle Formative period. It was an agricultural settlement established at a place that was well positioned to access and control the critical natural resources: soil, water, fuel, building material, native plants, and indigenous animals. Houses, intramural and extramural storage, outdoor cooking features, outside activity areas, cemeteries, and trash deposits indicate that it was the primary abode of many generations of Nogales people. Likely self-sufficient with regard to the basic items of survival, it

nevertheless was connected to places and people far from its immediate territory, and its most enduring connections seem to have been with other cultural groups in the Tucson Basin and the Altar and Rio Magdelena Valleys. Still, the traditions and goods of the Phoenix Basin and Mogollon cultural groups to the northeast were not unknown, and pottery, shell, and other desirable items moved up the rivers and across the passes to the village. Further, the residents of El Macayo enjoyed many of the same items of material wealth and status that settlements larger and more formal enjoyed. The inventory of shell artifacts was amazingly diverse for such a small data recovery effort, and it produced one of the largest collections recovered to date from a site in the Nogales area. Finally, the site contained a military macaw, an item rare in the material inventories of most southwestern sites.

The data recovery program at El Macayo produced a wealth of data concerning Middle Formative period adaptations in the Nogales area. We are fortunate to have had the opportunity to explore one of the last remaining portions of this once extensive site. We hope our work will be seen as a worthy contribution to the archaeology of the upper Santa Cruz River watershed, and we eagerly await the results of ongoing work along the borderlands to shed new light on this poorly known geographic area.

Endnotes

1. If these painted sherds—especially the few examples of early painted types—were not portions of complete specimens but rather were pottery fragments collected elsewhere as mementos by the ancient inhabitants of El Macayo, then our interpretations of settlement occupation will need to be altered.

2. Collections made by Cummings at the Sonoita Street locale in 1928 are stored in the ASM (Mike Jacobs, Curator, ASM, personal communication May 2000). These include 4 nonperishable archaeological objects (1 rectangular stone object, 1 stone object rubbed on several surfaces, 1 rectangular stone slate with incised edges, 1 miscellaneous shell and shell fragments) and 24 whole ceramic vessels. These vessels include Rillito Red-on-brown (1 bowl), Rincon Red-on-brown (1 jar, 1 plate), Santa Cruz Red-on-buff (1 jar), Trincheras Plain? (2 bowls, 2 elongated bowls, and 12 jars), Trincheras Polychrome (1 bowl), Trincheras Purple-on-red (2 jars, 1 seed jar).

3. Two sites in the upper Santa Cruz River area (i.e., from the confluence of Sonoita Creek to its headwaters in the San Rafael Valley) are purported to contain ball courts. One is

the Santa Cruz site in Sonora and the other is a site at the confluence of Sonoita Creek with the Santa Cruz River (Neily 1994:89).

4. Bone samples from this macaw are undergoing DNA analysis by Alan Cooper, Oxford University, and Peter Coo-per, Office of Archaeological Studies, Museum of New Mexico. Confirmation that this individual is indeed a military macaw rather than a scarlet macaw will be forthcoming. Results will be available from SRI after this report is published.

ELEVEN

Management Recommendations

Carla R. Van West

Our 1996 investigations at El Macayo (AZ EE:9:107) indicated that a substantial portion of this prehistoric habitation site remains unexcavated on those portions of the site that are controlled by Santa Cruz County. In a five-week period, we excavated some 400 m^2 of surface area and exposed, identified, and mapped 177 features, including a number of pit structures and human burials (Figures 65 and 66). This 400-m^2 area represents about 16 percent of the 0.62-acre portion of the village that is on Santa Cruz County land. This is only a fraction of what we estimate to have been a village that incorporated some 20–40 acres on the west bank of Nogales Wash during the A.D. 650–1150/1200 period. If cultural features are encountered at a similar density across the as-yet-unexcavated portions of the site, we estimate that some 60+ pit houses and perhaps 30–50 burials are still buried within Santa Cruz County land.

Given the local and regional significance of the site, we suggest that the recommendation made by Slawson (1991:16) to grant archaeological clearance for the area outside that tested by CES in 1991 be modified. Depending on which action the county chooses to pursue, we recommend the following.

Option 1: Avoidance. This is the most conservative and risk-minimizing option and the option we endorse from a preservation perspective. Should Santa Cruz County decide to abandon development plans for this portion of the County Complex parcel, then unexcavated deposits would remain undisturbed, and no further archaeological investigations would be required.

Option 2: Trail system. This is the level of development under which our data recovery plan originally was designed. Should Santa Cruz County decide to build a paved trail system through the site, the level of data recovery conducted by SRI at this time would suffice, and no further costs would be incurred. As we understand it, the trail would

be 10 feet wide and would entail only minimal land-leveling efforts. It is more likely that fill would be brought in to level irregular areas than it would be that excavation machinery would be required to remove high places. Less than a foot of the modern ground surface would be disturbed, and no underground utilities or deep excavations (for example, a toilet facility) would be necessary.

Option 3: Picnic and playground. Should Santa Cruz County decide to construct a picnic area and playground, the level of data recovery conducted by SRI in 1996 *may* be sufficient if land leveling and the subsurface disturbance are minimal. Such a development would likely entail the creation of an access road or path and may or may not require the construction of visitor facilities (e.g., toilets, water fountain, ramadas). A specific development plan and analysis of impacts would have to be prepared before we could recommend that clearance be granted. Again, if proposed developments were to impact the existing site only minimally, then no further archaeological work would be required and no further costs would be entailed by Santa Cruz County for archaeological data recovery. If specific facilities that require excavation and modest land leveling are required, archaeological monitoring at the time of construction may be warranted. Should additional human burials (either cremations or inhumations) be encountered at that time, they would require removal by professional archaeologists.

Option 4: Baseball field. Should Santa Cruz County decide to construct a baseball field and related features and facilities (seating area, rest rooms, parking area, lights, etc.), then additional data recovery may be necessary. The selection of such an option likely would necessitate the cutting and filling of irregular landforms to create a level playing field and a foundation for auxiliary features. Thus, the likelihood of encountering additional cultural deposits, including human burials, is great. Again, a development plan and impact analysis would be required. If subsurface ground disturbance were to be extensive, then excavation of additional portions of the site (as determined by specific site development plans) and recovery of all affected human remains would be necessary. This likely would involve additional archaeological data recovery efforts and additional funds to cover the costs of this work.

Option 5: Construction of buildings. Should Santa Cruz County decide to develop the land for the construction of buildings, then additional data recovery would be necessary. Such an action would definitely require the excavation of foundations for structures and trenches for utilities, as well as significant land leveling. Given the density of subsurface cultural remains, it is almost certain that cultural deposits would be encountered. Such a choice would necessitate additional data recovery. If only 50 percent of the anticipated 60 pit houses and associated features are excavated, additional costs exceeding $450,000 should be expected. This estimate is based on a general rule of thumb for the total costs of excavating, analyzing, and writing up a single pit house in the Tucson Basin: $15,000–20,000 per pit house and associated extramural features.

In sum, if Santa Cruz County selects Option 1 (avoidance) or Option 2 (trail system), no additional costs would be incurred and the total for archaeological data recovery would remain just under $50,000. Depending on the degree of anticipated land modification, selection of Option 3 (picnic area and playground) may also result in no additional costs to Santa Cruz County. If development plans require subsurface excavation in a select number of locations, however, monitoring for human burials may result in additional expenditures, but these costs would be minor. Both Options 4 (ball field) and 5 (building site) would necessitate additional excavation and monitoring for specific areas affected. Costs would increase as the area of land and extent of subsurface disturbance increase.

Figure 65. Aerial view of SRI's 1996 excavation area at El Macayo
(image taken from a blimp-mounted camera by Kurt Brei of Blimp Shots, Inc.).

Figure 66. Aerial view of features excavated by SRI at El Macayo
(image taken from a blimp-mounted camera by Kurt Brei of Blimp Shots, Inc.).

Control of the Archaeological Record
El Macayo Provenience Designation System

William L. Deaver

The primary responsibility of archaeological fieldwork is to maintain control of the spatial dimensions of the archaeological record. To this end, we maintained an inventory of every archaeological recovery space at El Macayo from which we extracted artifacts, shell, faunal bone, botanical samples, soil samples, and about which we made observations and notes. We refer to this inventory as the provenience designation (PD) list. This inventory contains vital information about the archaeological recovery spaces we defined during the excavations including the location, dimensions (length, width, and depth), and the general character of the sample recovered from that space. The PD number is the necessary link that allows us to regroup the information recorded during the various analyses so that we can make inferences about past human behavior.

The raw data from several of the analyses are presented in appendixes that follow. To avoid redundancy, the locational information is not repeated. Each of the these data tables, however, has the PD inventory number that references the archaeological recovery space. The spatial parameters and other characteristics of the archaeological recovery space for each PD number are presented in Table A.1. Each of the categories is described below. As with most lists and databases, the information recorded in the PD inventory is complex, and many of the categories have several possible values. To make the database succinct and more manageable, we use an established system of abbreviations and codes; a listing and explanation for each are attached at the end of Table A.1. Some definitions of these categories are presented below.

Provenience Designation Number: a sequential number between 1 and *n* assigned to a defined unit of space. The space can be as large as an entire site or as small as a single artifact. The space can be two-dimensional, such as the present ground surface or the floor of a house, or it can be three-

dimensional, such as the volume of a backhoe trench, a level, or a stratum. The space can be delimited by nonarbitrary boundaries (a feature), or the space can be delimited by arbitrary boundaries (such as test pits, trenches, and other excavation units). Each PD number refers to one and only one unit of space, but it is possible that one unit of space may have more than one PD if, for example, it was visited twice and different collection strategies were used.

Feature Number: a sequential number between 1 and *n* that refers to what we call an archaeological feature. An archaeological feature is distinguished from other types of archaeological spaces, such as trenches and test pits, by the field interpretation that the vertical and horizontal dimensions of the space in question were established by human or natural forces. Implicit in the designation of a feature is that the boundaries are not arbitrary. In most cases, the feature space represents an archaeological manifestation of a past behaviorally defined space and is the unit of inference. As an example, a pit house is an archaeological feature where the limits are defined by the pit walls and floor. As another example, a wash channel is a feature of the geological landscape that was created by natural forces and that has physically recognizable boundaries. Appendix B provides an excerpt of a comprehensive list of feature and subfeature types available on file at Arizona State Museum (ASM).

Subfeature Number: a sequential number assigned to features that are components of larger features. Certain features, such as a house, are constellations of other features, including floor, hearth, postholes, pits, and other facilities. We use a feature–subfeature numbering system that reflects this intimate relationship among such features. Subfeature numbers are assigned consecutively within the parent feature. For instance, the hearth in pit house Feature 5 is numbered 5.01, and the hearth in pit house Feature 44 is numbered Feature 44.01. Similar to a feature, the boundaries of a subfeature are not arbitrarily defined.

A subfeature must be physically and systemically linked to the suprafeature. As a point of clarification, in a typical case, a trash pit or some other feature intruding into the fill and floor of a pit house is assigned a new feature number because it represents an archaeological event that is systemically unrelated to the house. It is not considered a subfeature of the house into which it intrudes.

Excavation Unit: a coded descriptor of the horizontal space to which the provenience number applies. Typically, an excavation unit is an arbitrarily defined unit of space that we use to maintain horizontal control over the location of artifacts, samples, and other bits of evidence in the absence of features. Trenches and test pits are a common example. Feature spaces and excavation unit spaces are not mutually exclusive, however. In large features, such as pit houses, it is common to define smaller arbitrary units within the house walls to attain finer control over the excavations. In smaller features, such as hearths or postholes, however, the entire feature may be excavated as a single unit, and thus the excavation unit boundaries are coincident with the feature boundaries. In other situations, features are often discovered within arbitrarily defined excavation units so that a later subset of the excavation unit space is redefined as feature space. There is an implicit hierarchical relationship between feature and excavation unit in this system. If a feature number is assigned, the excavation unit must be coincident with or be a subset of the feature space; it cannot refer to a unit of space that is larger than the feature space.

Northing and *Easting:* coordinates of the provenience in a Cartesian coordinate grid superimposed over the site area to map and record the spatial location of features, excavation units, and artifacts. The Northing and Easting are the *y* and *x* coordinates, respectively, within this grid. When only one number is listed, rather than a range of two numbers, the one number refers to the *x* or *y* coordinate at the center of that particular excavation unit or artifact.

Stratum: a soil or sediment accumulation that resulted from human or natural processes and has observable physical properties that distinguish it from other strata. The distinction between stratum and level (below) is the same as between feature and excavation unit. A stratum is not arbitrarily defined. At El Macayo, we identified four main soil units that we designated with Roman numerals I, II, III, and IV. These represent four important episodes of natural

and cultural accumulations of soils and sediments. Within Unit II, which was the culture-bearing horizon, we used lowercase letters (a, b, c, etc.) to designate distinct sediment types.

Stratum Type: this category is a field interpretation of the origins and processes responsible for the deposition of these sediments. For example, a designation as *roof fall* is an inference that the sediments were deposited in their present location by the collapse of the roof and walls of a structure. This designation indicates that the artifacts and other materials recovered within and beneath this layer are implicitly more closely linked to the use of the underlying house floor, than materials in the *fill* above the roof fall.

Level: an arbitrarily defined vertical unit numbered from 1 to *n* from top to bottom. A level may be coincident with a stratum or may be independent of a stratum. Our excavations use both arbitrary and natural vertical units, depending on the overall excavation plan and the objective of the immediate situation. For example, in a stratigraphic test pit in a pit house, the excavation may adhere strictly to arbitrary levels of a given thickness (e.g., 10 cm or 20 cm). The remaining excavation of the house, however, may follow natural depositional units (strata) that were defined from the test pit. Even in a situation where excavations follow natural strata, levels may be employed. If a stratum is excessively thick, such as in the case of a 40-cm-thick deposit at a site where 20 cm is the maximum allowable vertical unit, the stratum may be arbitrarily divided into two levels. Also, because natural sediment deposits can undulate, slope, or be intermittent, the same stratum may not always be encountered at the same depth.

Depth: beginning and ending depths for excavation units measured from a common site datum. All elevations, with a few exceptions, are measured in meters below datum (mbd). The datum elevation is arbitrarily set so that 0 mbd is above all parts of the site. Two trenches and one feature are the exceptions, and were measured in centimeters below surface (cmbs), which is noted on Table A.1.

Recovery Mode: a coded descriptor that indicates the level of recovery effort. During the excavations we may employ several methods for recovering artifacts and samples. In backhoe trenches and stripping units, for example, we often recover grab samples of artifacts or other materials, but in test pits and feature excavations, the sediments are usually screened.

Table A.1. Provenience Designation (PD) List

PD No.	Feature No.	Subfeature	Excavation Unit	Northing	Easting	Stratum	Stratum Type	Level	Depth [a]	Recovery Mode	Date	Comments
1			site	100	100	0	SURF	0	not reported	GS	15 Apr 96	ASM trench
2			TR 1	120.5	100–109	0	TB	1	not reported	INIT	16 Apr 96	ASM trench
3			TR 2	110.5	88–129	0	TB	1	not reported	INIT	16 Apr 96	ASM trench
4			TR 3	100	76–99	0	TB	1	not reported	INIT	16 Apr 96	ASM trench
5			TR 4	131	99–130.5	0	TB	1	not reported	INIT	16 Apr 96	ASM trench
6			TR 5	90	91–117	0	TB	1	not reported	INIT	16 Apr 96	ASM trench
7			TR 6	100	100.2–128.8	0	TB	1	not reported	INIT	16 Apr 96	CES trench
8			TR 7	118.5	75–100	0	TB	1	not reported	INIT	16 Apr 96	CES trench
9			TR 8	138.5	72–98	0	TB	1	not reported	INIT	16 Apr 96	CES trench
10			TR 9	159	72–99	0	TB	1	not reported	INIT	16 Apr 96	CES trench
11			TR 10	84	70–92	0	TB	1	not reported	INIT	16 Apr 96	CES trench
12			TR 11	73	73.5–100	0	TB	1	not reported	INIT	16 Apr 96	CES trench
13			TR 12	105	20	0	TB	1	not reported	INIT	16 Apr 96	CES trench
14	1		FEAT	100	109	II	CULT	0	not reported	DISC	16 Apr 96	ASM feature
15	2		FEAT	101	107.25	II	CULT	0	11.18–11.31	DISC	16 Apr 96	ASM feature
16	3		FEAT	120	103	II	CULT	0	not reported	DISC	16 Apr 96	ASM feature
17	4		FEAT	111	102	II	CULT	0	not reported	DISC	16 Apr 96	ASM feature
18	5		FEAT	120.2	111	II	CULT	0	10.11–10.23	DISC	16 Apr 96	ASM feature
19	6		FEAT	120	116.5	II	CULT	0	not reported	DISC	16 Apr 96	ASM feature
20	7		FEAT	110.5	105	II	CULT	0	not reported	DISC	16 Apr 96	ASM feature
21	8		FEAT	110.5	106.5	II	CULT	0	not reported	DISC	16 Apr 96	ASM feature
22	9		FEAT	120.5	120.5	II	CULT	0	not reported	DISC	16 Apr 96	ASM feature
23	10		FEAT	120.5	123–124.5	II	CULT	0	not reported	DISC	16 Apr 96	ASM feature
24	11		FEAT	120.5	124.75	II	CULT	0	not reported	DISC	16 Apr 96	ASM feature
25	12		FEAT	100	107	II	CULT	0	not reported	DISC	16 Apr 96	ASM feature
26	13		FEAT	101	103	II	CULT	0	not reported	DISC	16 Apr 96	ASM feature
27	14		FEAT	110.5	115–116	II	CULT	0	not reported	DISC	16 Apr 96	ASM feature
28	15		FEAT	109	127	II	CULT	0	not reported	DISC	16 Apr 96	ASM feature
29	16		FEAT	102.5	127	II	CULT	0	11.44	DISC	16 Apr 96	ASM feature
30	17		FEAT	110.5	120–121.5	II	CULT	0	not reported	DISC	16 Apr 96	ASM feature
31	18		FEAT	131	100.5–140.5	II	CULT	0	not reported	DISC	16 Apr 96	ASM feature

PD No.	Feature No.	Subfeature	Excavation Unit	Northing	Easting	Stratum	Stratum Type	Level	Depth [a]	Recovery Mode	Date	Comments
32	19		FEAT	131	111	II	CULT	0	not reported	DISC	16 Apr 96	ASM feature
33	20		FEAT	131	123	II	CULT	0	not reported	DISC	16 Apr 96	ASM feature
34	21		FEAT	100	95–99	II	CULT	0	not reported	DISC	16 Apr 96	ASM feature
35	22		FEAT	100	94	II	CULT	0	not reported	DISC	16 Apr 96	ASM feature
36	23		FEAT	100	86.5	II	CULT	0	not reported	DISC	16 Apr 96	ASM feature
37	24		FEAT	90	103	II	CULT	0	not reported	DISC	16 Apr 96	ASM feature
38	25		FEAT	90	95	II	CULT	0	not reported	DISC	16 Apr 96	ASM feature
39	26		FEAT	131	111	II	CULT	0	not reported	DISC	16 Apr 96	ASM feature
40	27		FEAT	110.5	99–100	II	CULT	0	not reported	DISC	16 Apr 96	ASM feature
41	28		FEAT	100	82–85.5	II	CULT	0	not reported	DISC	16 Apr 96	ASM feature
42	29		FEAT	110.5	92.5–97	II	CULT	0	not reported	DISC	16 Apr 96	ASM feature
43	30		FEAT	131	121	II	CULT	0	not reported	DISC	16 Apr 96	ASM feature
44	31		FEAT	101	107	II	CULT	0	not reported	DISC	16 Apr 96	ASM feature
45	32		FEAT	138.5	95	II	CULT	0	not reported	DISC	16 Apr 96	CES feature
46	33		FEAT	138.5	88–91	II	CULT	0	not reported	DISC	16 Apr 96	CES feature
47	34		FEAT	118.5	95–97	II	CULT	0	not reported	DISC	16 Apr 96	CES feature
48	35		FEAT	118.5	84–87	II	CULT	0	not reported	DISC	16 Apr 96	CES feature
49	36		FEAT	84	80	II	CULT	0	not reported	DISC	16 Apr 96	CES feature
50	37		FEAT	73	82	II	CULT	0	not reported	DISC	16 Apr 96	CES feature
51	38		FEAT	73	79.5	II	CULT	0	not reported	DISC	16 Apr 96	CES feature
52	31		TR 2	100–100.7	105–110	II	TB	1	not reported	S4	16 Apr 96	screened trench backdirt
53	39		FEAT	112.25	125.75	II	CULT	0	11–11.35	DISC	16 Apr 96	burial
54	40		FEAT	113.02	128.39	II	CULT	0	11.02–11.1	DISC	16 Apr 96	burial
55	39		FEAT	112.25	125.75	IIb	BRL	1	11–11.35	S4	16 Apr 96	
56			SU 56	110–120	117–129.5	II	CULT	1	10.41–10.94	GS	17 Apr 96	above F 15
57			SU 57	100–110	117–129.5	II	CULT	1	10.67–11.37	GS	17 Apr 96	above F 16
58			TP 58	111.64	128.71	II	CULT	0	10.65–11.18	INIT	17 Apr 96	1 × 1
59			TP 58	111.64	128.71	I	DIST	1	10.65–10.78	S4	17 Apr 96	
60			TP 60	107.96	127.47	I	DIST	0	10.76–11.31	INIT	17 Apr 96	
61			TP 60	107.96	127.47	II	CULT	1	10.76–10.86	S4	17 Apr 96	1 × 1
62			TP 58	111.64	128.71	II	CULT	2	10.78–10.98	S4	17 Apr 96	1 × 1 m
63	41		FEAT	111.64	128.71	II	CULT	0	10.78–11.11	DISC	17 Apr 96	

PD No.	Feature No.	Subfeature	Excavation Unit	Northing	Easting	Stratum	Stratum Type	Level	Depth [a]	Recovery Mode	Date	Comments
64	41		FEAT	111.64	128.71	II	CULT	1	10.78–11.11	S4	17 Apr 96	
65	42		FEAT	105.8	125.91	II	CULT	0	11.44	DISC	17 Apr 96	sherds from fill exposed when filling
66	42		FEAT	105.8	125.91	IIa	fill	1	11.44	GS	17 Apr 96	
67			TP 58	111.64	128.71	II	CULT	3	10.98–11.18	S4	17 Apr 96	
68			TP 60	107.96	127.47	II	CULT	2	10.86–11.06	S4	19 Apr 96	
69			TP 60	107.96	127.47	II	CULT	3	11.06–11.26	S4	19 Apr 96	
70			TP 60	107.96	127.47	II	CULT	4	11.26–11.31	S4	19 Apr 96	
71			TP 71	107.99	118.09	II	CULT	0	10.28–10.98	INIT	19 Apr 96	2 × 2 m
72			TP 71	107.99	118.09	I	DIST	1	10.28–10.38	S4	19 Apr 96	
73			TP 71	107.99	118.09	II	CULT	2	10.38–10.58	S4	19 Apr 96	
74			TP 71	107.99	118.09	II	CULT	3	10.58–10.78	S4	19 Apr 96	
75	214		FEAT	117	126	IIa	BRL	1	40 cmbs	GS	19 Apr 96	partial jar and human bone in SU 57, app. location
76	43		FEAT	106.42	120.48	II	CULT	0	11.16–11.3	DISC	19 Apr 96	
77	43		FEAT	106.42	120.48	IIa	fill	1	11.23	GS	19 Apr 96	
78			TP 71	107.99	118.09	II	CULT	4	10.78–10.98	S4	19 Apr 96	
79	44		ART	118.55	119.4	IIb	FLR	2	10.78	PP	19 Apr 96	
80			SU 80	112–120	106–117	II	CULT	1	9.91–10.33	GS	19 Apr 96	above F 5
81	44		FEAT	116	119.5	II	CULT	0	10.33–10.78	DISC	23 Apr 96	pit house
82	45		FEAT	117.75	112.81	II	CULT	0	10.33	DISC	23 Apr 96	pit with rocks; poss. hearth
83	46		FEAT	117.69	109.68	II	CULT	0	10.27	DISC	23 Apr 96	pit with metate slab
84	47		FEAT	116.84	109.79	II	CULT	0	10.26	DISC	23 Apr 96	small pit
85	48		FEAT	117.34	110.34	II	CULT	0	10.28	DISC	23 Apr 96	pit
86	49		FEAT	113.93	112.05	II	CULT	0	10.55	DISC	23 Apr 96	pit with rocks
87	50		FEAT	116.32	111.78	II	CULT	0	10.43	DISC	23 Apr 96	pit
88	51		FEAT	114.99	113.71	II	CULT	0	10.69	DISC	23 Apr 96	pit
89	52		FEAT	115.2	115.6	II	CULT	0	10.62	DISC	23 Apr 96	hearth cut into by pit
90	53		FEAT	113.34	116.45	II	CULT	0	10.82	DISC	23 Apr 96	pit cutting into hearth
91	54		FEAT	115.28	112.58	II	CULT	0	10.3	DISC	23 Apr 96	pit
92	55		FEAT	113.5	114.69	II	CULT	0	10.81	DISC	23 Apr 96	pit
93	56		FEAT	115.5	114.87	II	CULT	0	10.7	DISC	23 Apr 96	posthole

PD No.	Feature No.	Subfeature	Excavation Unit	Northing	Easting	Stratum	Stratum Type	Level	Depth [a]	Recovery Mode	Date	Comments
94	57		FEAT	116.76	107.61	II	CULT	0	10.33	DISC	23 Apr 96	pit
95	58		FEAT	118.12	107.42	II	CULT	0	10.29	DISC	23 Apr 96	pit
96	59		FEAT	118.85	106.32	II	CULT	0	10.14	DISC	23 Apr 96	pit
97	60		FEAT	119.69	106.46	II	CULT	0	10.06	DISC	23 Apr 96	pit
98	61		FEAT	119.04	107.46	II	CULT	0	10.18	DISC	23 Apr 96	pit
99	62		FEAT	112.67	112.43	II	CULT	0	10.6	DISC	23 Apr 96	pit with rocks; ground stone
100	63		FEAT	116.81	110.81	II	CULT	0	10.31	DISC	23 Apr 96	pit
101	64		FEAT	118.93	112.78	II	CULT	0	10.36	DISC	23 Apr 96	pit
102	65		FEAT	119.14	113.27	II	CULT	0	10.21	DISC	23 Apr 96	plaster-lined pit
103			TP 103	115.1	118.73	II	CULT	0	10.38–10.78	INIT	24 Apr 96	1 × 1 over F 44
104			TP 103	115.1	118.73	I	DIST	1	10.38–10.48	S4	24 Apr 96	
105			TP 103	115.1	118.73	II	CULT	2	10.48–10.58	S4	24 Apr 96	
106			TP 103	115.1	118.73	II	CULT	3	10.58–10.68	S4	24 Apr 96	
107			TP 103	115.1	118.73	IIa	RFL	4	10.68–10.78	S4	24 Apr 96	
108			TP 108	121.27	110.18	II	CULT	0	9.73–10.25	INIT	24 Apr 96	1 × 1
109			TP 108	121.27	110.18	I	DIST	1	9.73–9.85	S4	24 Apr 96	
110			TP 108	121.27	110.18	II	CULT	2	9.85–10.05	S4	24 Apr 96	
111			TP 108	121.27	110.18	IIa	fill/RFL	3	10.05–10.26	S4	24 Apr 96	
112	44		FEAT	116	119.5	IIa	RFL	1	10.68–10.78	GS	25 Apr 96	
113	44		ART	114.1	119.3	IIb	FLR	2	10.78	PP	25 Apr 96	metate
114	44		ART	114.7	118.2	IIb	FLR	2	10.78	PP	25 Apr 96	ground stone
115	44		ART	115.85	118.65	IIb	FLR	2	10.78	PP	25 Apr 96	metate
116	44		ART	116.6	118.95	IIb	FLR	2	10.78	PP	25 Apr 96	metate
117	44		FEAT	116	119.5	IIb	FLR	2	10.78	S4	25 Apr 96	pit house floor artifacts
118			SU 118	120–125	108.5–120	II	CULT	1	9.69–10.21	GS	25 Apr 96	around F 5
119	66		FEAT	116.53	122.23	II	CULT	0	10.77	DISC	25 Apr 96	pit
120			SU 57	107–110	126.5–129.5	II	CULT	1	10.76–11.31	GS	25 Apr 96	overburden
121	67		FEAT	115.58	121.27	II	CULT	0	10.77	DISC	25 Apr 96	pit
122			SU 122	96–106.5	92.5–100.5	II	CULT	1	9.91–10.3	GS	25 Apr 96	around F 21
123	68		FEAT	96.26	93.89	II	CULT	0	10.43	DISC	25 Apr 96	pit with rocks
124	69		FEAT	96.4	95.13	II	CULT	0	10.48	DISC	25 Apr 96	pit
125	70		FEAT	99.36	94.01	II	CULT	0	10.3	DISC	25 Apr 96	pit

PD No.	Feature No.	Subfeature	Excavation Unit	Northing	Easting	Stratum	Stratum Type	Level	Depth [a]	Recovery Mode	Date	Comments
126	71		FEAT	101.23	93.55	II	CULT	0	10.33	DISC	25 Apr 96	pit
127	72		FEAT	0	0	II	CULT	0	0	DISC	26 Apr 96	pit same as F 206
128	73		FEAT	114.1	116.82	II	CULT	0	10.99	DISC	26 Apr 96	pit
129	74		FEAT	117.68	116.88	II	CULT	0	10.76	DISC	26 Apr 96	pit
130	75		FEAT	119.26	118.42	II	CULT	0	10.64	DISC	26 Apr 96	pit with a rock on top
131	76		FEAT	117.27	121.23	II	CULT	0	10.77	DISC	26 Apr 96	pit
132	77		FEAT	117.66	121.54	II	CULT	0	10.77	DISC	26 Apr 96	pit
133	78		FEAT	118.08	120.91	II	CULT	0	10.77	DISC	26 Apr 96	pit
134	5		N2	120.2	111	IIa	fill/RFL	1	10.16–10.25	S4	30 Apr 96	
135	5		S2	120.2	111	IIa	fill/RFL	1	10.19–10.23	S4	30 Apr 96	
136	79		FEAT	117.76	111.45	II	CULT	0	10.27	DISC	30 Apr 96	pit with spindle whorl and biface
137	80		FEAT	114.82	112.47	II	CULT	0	10.44–10.64	DISC	30 Apr 96	pit
138	81		FEAT	103.99	92.76	II	CULT	0	10.29	DISC	30 Apr 96	pit house
139	82		FEAT	114.8	112.47	II	CULT	0	10.24	DISC	30 Apr 96	pit house?
140	83		FEAT	105.4	94.6	II	CULT	0	10.3	DISC	30 Apr 96	pit
141	84		FEAT	103.79	95.18	II	CULT	0	10.46	DISC	30 Apr 96	pit
142	85		FEAT	105.28	97	II	CULT	0	10.23	DISC	30 Apr 96	large pit
143	86		FEAT	104.6	97.61	II	CULT	0	10.3	DISC	30 Apr 96	pit with rocks
144	87		FEAT	104.3	97.48	II	CULT	0	10.29	DISC	30 Apr 96	pit with rocks
145	88		FEAT	104.57	98.2	II	CULT	0	10.31	DISC	30 Apr 96	pit with rocks
146	89		FEAT	104.84	98.76	II	CULT	0	10.34	DISC	30 Apr 96	pit
147	90		FEAT	104.86	99.43	II	CULT	0	10.36	DISC	30 Apr 96	pit
148	91		FEAT	104.31	99.45	II	CULT	0	10.4	DISC	30 Apr 96	pit with one rock
149	92		FEAT	103.5	98.89	II	CULT	0	10.41	DISC	30 Apr 96	pit
150	93		FEAT	104.58	99.95	II	CULT	0	10.4	DISC	30 Apr 96	pit with large rock
151	94		FEAT	105.8–103.3	98.45–100.5	II	CULT	0	10.41	DISC	30 Apr 96	pit structure? intrudes F 92 and F 93
152	95		FEAT	101.28	98.01	II	CULT	0	10.3	DISC	30 Apr 96	rock cluster intrudes F 21
153	96		FEAT	101.41	99.71	II	CULT	0	10.43	DISC	30 Apr 96	pit with rocks
154	97		FEAT	101.37	100.22	II	CULT	0	10.45	DISC	30 Apr 96	pit with rocks— hearth (ash)
155	98		FEAT	100.36	99.53	II	CULT	0	10.44	DISC	30 Apr 96	pit with rocks

PD No.	Feature No.	Subfeature	Excavation Unit	Northing	Easting	Stratum	Stratum Type	Level	Depth [a]	Recovery Mode	Date	Comments
156	99		FEAT	100.48	100.19	II	CULT	0	10.48	DISC	30 Apr 96	pit/posthole
157	100		FEAT	98.98	100.15	II	CULT	0	10.53	DISC	30 Apr 96	pit
158	101		FEAT	97.86	98.24	II	CULT	0	10.47	DISC	30 Apr 96	pit structure
159	102		FEAT	97.29	100.24	II	CULT	0	10.66	DISC	30 Apr 96	pit-hearth (ashy fill), intrudes F 101
160	103		FEAT	97.09	99.09	II	CULT	0	10.59	DISC	30 Apr 96	hearth—white ash and charcoal
161	104		FEAT	96.77	99.6	II	CULT	0	10.65	DISC	30 Apr 96	pit filled with gravels
162	105		FEAT	123.05	110.35	II	CULT	0	10.09	DISC	30 Apr 96	pit intrusive to F 5
163	105		FEAT	123.05	110.35	IIa	fill	1	10.09–10.31	S4	30 Apr 96	
164	106		FEAT	95.88	99.22	II	CULT	0	10.72	DISC	30 Apr 96	pit
165	107		FEAT	96.06	98.7	II	CULT	0	10.36	DISC	30 Apr 96	pit
166	108		FEAT	96.22	98.16	II	CULT	0	10.54	DISC	30 Apr 96	pit with rocks
167	109		FEAT	96.87	98.14	II	CULT	0	10.6	DISC	30 Apr 96	pit with gravels
168	110		FEAT	96.02	97.23	II	CULT	0	10.54	DISC	30 Apr 96	pit
169	16		FEAT	102.5	127	II	fill	1	11.44–11.46	S4	01 May 96	
170	111		FEAT	117.2	124	II	CULT	0	10.76	DISC	01 May 96	
171	42		FEAT	105.8	125.91	IIc	PH fill	3	11.44–11.6	S4	01 May 96	
172	16		FEAT	102.5	127	IIb	FLR	2	11.46	S4	01 May 96	
173	16		ART	102.1	125.8	IIb	FLR	2	11.46	PP	01 May 96	spindle
174	16		ART	102.08	125.47	IIb	FLR	2	11.46	PP	01 May 96	ceramic scoop
175	16		FEAT	102.5	127	IIc	PH fill	3	11.46	S4	01 May 96	postholes
176	112		FEAT	122.8	109.6	II	CULT	0	10.13	DISC	02 May 96	pit
177	112		FEAT	122.8	109.6	IIa	fill	1	10.13–10.41	S4	02 May 96	
178	113		FEAT	115.8	113.34	II	CULT	0	10.52	DISC	02 May 96	pit
179	114		FEAT	118.75	113.32	II	CULT	0	10.38	DISC	02 May 96	pit
180	112		FEAT	122.8	109.6	IIb	fill	2	10.41–10.64	S4	02 May 96	
181	115		FEAT	117.36	122.92	II	CULT	0	8.76	DISC	02 May 96	pit
182	116		FEAT	122.58	114.15	II	CULT	0	10.18	DISC	02 May 96	pit
183	117		FEAT	124.2	114.41	II	CULT	0	10.16	DISC	02 May 96	pit
184	118		FEAT	124.48	112.29	II	CULT	0	10	DISC	02 May 96	pit
185	119		FEAT	123.69	110.78	II	CULT	0	10.02	DISC	02 May 96	pit
186	120		FEAT	124.27	110.65	II	CULT	0	10.05	DISC	02 May 96	pit

PD No.	Feature No.	Subfeature	Excavation Unit	Northing	Easting	Stratum	Stratum Type	Level	Depth [a]	Recovery Mode	Date	Comments
187	121		FEAT	124.45	109.3	II	CULT	0	10.07	DISC	02 May 96	pit
188	15		FEAT	109	127	IIb	FLR	2	11.31	GS	02 May 96	
189	15		FEAT	109	127	IIc	PH fill	3	11.31–11.56	S4	03 May 96	
190	39		FEAT	112.25	125.75	IIa	BRL fill	1	11–11.35	S4	06 Apr 96	
192	213		FEAT	101.25	106.44	II	CULT	0	10.54–10.86	DISC	03 May 96	
193	15	01	FEAT	108.16	128.3	IIb	HRTH fill	1	11.31–11.37	C	06 May 96	
194	5		N2	120.2	111	IIc	PH fill	3	10.25–10.6	S4	06 May 96	
195	125		FEAT	121.1	113.23	II	CULT	0	10.28	DISC	06 May 96	pit
196	126		FEAT	115.45	123.23	II	CULT	0	10.76	DISC	06 May 96	pit with rocks
197	127		FEAT	116.03	123.91	II	CULT	0	10.92	DISC	06 May 96	pit with rocks
198	128		FEAT	115.87	126.83	II	CULT	0	11.01	DISC	06 May 96	pit
199	129		FEAT	117.33	128.66	II	CULT	0	11.17	DISC	06 May 96	pit
200	130		FEAT	116.68	127.9	II	CULT	0	11.07	DISC	06 May 96	roasting pit
201	131		FEAT	116.45	128.84	II	CULT	0	11.14	DISC	06 May 96	pit
202	132		FEAT	114.68	128.91	II	CULT	0	11.04–11.14	DISC	06 May 96	burial
203	133		FEAT	115.9	129.05	II	CULT	0	11.18	DISC	06 May 96	pit?
204	134		FEAT	113.06	127.51	II	CULT	0	11.17	DISC	06 May 96	pit
205	135		FEAT	114.06	127.13	II	CULT	0	11.2	DISC	06 May 96	pit
206	136		FEAT	114.71	125.38	II	CULT	0	8.76	DISC	06 May 96	pit house
207	137		FEAT	117.5	124.13	II	CULT	0	11.01	DISC	06 May 96	pit house?
208	138		FEAT	113.11	126.08	II	CULT	0	11	DISC	06 May 96	small pit with rocks
209	5	01	FEAT	120.92	111.4	IIb	HRTH fill	2	10.16	NS	06 May 96	hearth fragment N2
210	5	02	FEAT	120.04	111.3	IIb	HRTH fill	2	10.18	NS	06 May 96	hearth fragment S2
211	5	03	FEAT	122	111.14	IIc	PT fill	3	10.22–10.54	S4	06 May 96	pit in wall trench
212	5	04	FEAT	121.25	111.05	IIc	PT fill	3	10.19–10.51	S4	06 May 96	pit
213	139		FEAT	114	121.5	II	CULT	0	10.9	DISC	07 May 96	pit house below F 44
214	140		FEAT	111.8	122	II	CULT	0	11.88	DISC	07 May 96	pit with rocks; poss. burial
215	5		S2	120.2	111	IIc	PH fill	3	10.23	S4	07 May 96	
216	15		FEAT	109	107	IIc	SFLR	3	11.65	S4	07 May 96	pit below floor
217	15		FEAT	109	107	IIc	SFLR	3	11.65	S4	07 May 96	pit below floor
218	44	01	FEAT	115.3	120.66	IIc	HRTH fill	2	10.78–10.87	C	07 May 96	hearth
219	44		FEAT	116	119.5	IIa	RFL	1	10.68–10.78	S4	07 May 96	

PD No.	Feature No.	Subfeature	Excavation Unit	Northing	Easting	Stratum	Stratum Type	Level	Depth [a]	Recovery Mode	Date	Comments
220	44	02	FEAT	115.3	120.34	IId	PT fill	2	10.78–10.88	C	07 May 96	ash deposit behind hearth
221	141		FEAT	111.25	121.99	II	CULT	0	10.99	DISC	07 May 96	pit
222	142		FEAT	111.21	124.74	II	CULT	0	11.03	DISC	07 May 96	burial: elliptical pit with rocks
223	143		FEAT	111.09	123.3	II	CULT	0	11.02	DISC	07 May 96	pit with rocks
224	144		FEAT	112.39	123.18	II	CULT	0	10.93	DISC	07 May 96	burial with rocks and bowl
225	145		FEAT	113.1	124.61	II	CULT	0	10.93	DISC	07 May 96	burial: elliptical pit with rocks
226	146		FEAT	113.46	123.04	II	CULT	0	10.94	DISC	07 May 96	pit: poss. burial
227	147		FEAT	115.06	123.03	II	CULT	0	10.75	DISC	07 May 96	burial: femur exposed
228	148		FEAT	113.52	124.53	II	CULT	0	10.95	DISC	07 May 96	pit: poss. burial
229	149		FEAT	116.59	124.33	II	CULT	0	11.14	DISC	07 May 96	pit
230	150		FEAT	117	119	II	CULT	0	10.65	DISC	08 May 96	pit house
231	52	01	FEAT	114.1	115.35	IIb	HRTH fill	2	10.78–10.83	C	08 May 96	
232	43	01	FEAT	106.59	119.86	IIb	HRTH fill	2	11.29–11.47	C	08 May 96	
233	139		TP 233	114	121.5	II	CULT	0	10.9	INIT	08 May 96	
234	151		FEAT	102.26	95.41	II	CULT	0	10.52	DISC	08 May 96	burial
235	139		TP 233	114	121.5	IIa	fill	1	10.9–11.1	S4	08 May 96	
236	152		FEAT	103.36	94.75	II	CULT	0	10.52	DISC	08 May 96	pit
237	150		TP 237	116.8–118.8	117.2–118.2	II	CULT	0	10.78–10.91	INIT	08 May 96	
238	150		TP 237	116.8–118.8	117.2–118.2	IIa	fill	1	10.78–10.91	S4	08 May 96	
239	147		FEAT	115.6	123.03	IIb	BRL	1	10.75	S4	09 May 96	
240	147		FEAT	115.6	123.03	IIa	BRL fill	1	10.75	S4	09 May 96	
241	151		FEAT	102.26	95.41	IIa	BRL	2	10.52–10.65	S4	09 May 96	upper adobe cap
242	151		FEAT	102.26	95.41	IIb	BRL fill	1	10.52–10.65	S4	09 May 96	fill of rodent den
243	151	and F 156	FEAT	101.66	95.31	Id	RDNT	2	10.52–10.65	S	09 May 96	
244	151		ART	102.23	95.5	IIa	BRL	1	10.52	PP	09 May 96	partial bowl
245	151		ART	102.37	95.6	IIa	BRL	1	10.52	PP	09 May 96	partial bowl
246	151		ART	102.49	95.46	IIa	BRL	1	10.52	PP	09 May 96	whole bowl
247	151		FEAT	102.26	95.41	IIb	BRL fill	2	10.65–10.93	S	09 May 96	burial pit fill mixed with F 202
248	153		FEAT	109.02	122.07	II	CULT	0	11.05	DISC	09 May 96	

PD No.	Feature No.	Subfeature	Excavation Unit	Northing	Easting	Stratum	Stratum Type	Level	Depth [a]	Recovery Mode	Date	Comments
249	154		FEAT	109.13	121.23	II	CULT	0	11.06	DISC	09 May 96	
250	155		FEAT	107.93	121.7	II	CULT	0	11.11	DISC	09 May 96	
251	156		FEAT	102	95.31	II	CULT	0	10.65–10.83	DISC	10 May 96	burial
252	156		FEAT	102	95.31	IIb	BRL	1	10.65–10.83	S4	10 May 96	
253	156		FEAT	102	95.31	IIa	BRL fill	1	10.65–10.83	S4	10 May 96	
254	40		FEAT	113.02	128.39	IIb	BRL	1	11.02–11.1	S4	13 May 96	
255	40		FEAT	113.02	128.39	IIa	BRL fill	1	11.02–11.1	S4	13 May 96	
256	132		FEAT	114.68	128.91	IIb	BRL	1	11.04–11.14	S4	13 May 96	
257	132		FEAT	114.68	128.91	IIa	BRL fill	1	11.04–11.14	S4	13 May 96	
258	51		FEAT	114.99	113.71	IIa	fill	1	10.69–11.2	S4	13 May 96	
259	50		FEAT	116.32	111.78	IIa	fill	1	10.43–10.91	S4	13 May 96	
260	216		FEAT	115.2	115.6	IIa	fill	1	10.62–10.76	S4	13 May 96	
261	139		ART	113.42	122.21	IIb	FLR	2	11.08	PP	13 May 96	palette
262	157		FEAT	107.57	121.39	II	CULT	0	11.13	DISC	14 May 96	pit
263	158		FEAT	107.3	120.91	II	CULT	0	11.23	DISC	14 May 96	pit
264	159		FEAT	106.63	121.23	II	CULT	0	11.31	DISC	14 May 96	pit
265	160		FEAT	105.38	121.57	II	CULT	0	11.32	DISC	14 May 96	pit
266	161		FEAT	105.31	119.91	II	CULT	0	11.34	DISC	14 May 96	pit
267	162		FEAT	105.96	119.86	II	CULT	0	11.32	DISC	14 May 96	pit
268	163		FEAT	106.32	119.11	II	CULT	0	11.26	DISC	14 May 96	pit filled with rock and gravel
269	164		FEAT	107.12	119.36	II	CULT	0	11.24	DISC	14 May 96	pit with rock
270	165		FEAT	107.91	118.96	II	CULT	0	11.22	DISC	14 May 96	pit with bone tool
271	166		FEAT	107.79	118.35	II	CULT	0	11.13	DISC	14 May 96	pit with rocks and gravel
272	167		FEAT	108.52	118.11	II	CULT	0	11.09	DISC	14 May 96	pit
273	168		FEAT	108.07	116.91	II	CULT	0	11.05	DISC	14 May 96	pit
274	169		FEAT	106.02	118.09	II	CULT	0	11.18	DISC	14 May 96	pit
275	170		FEAT	104.66	117.1	II	CULT	0	11.15	DISC	14 May 96	pit
276	171		FEAT	103.85	118.43	II	CULT	0	11.28	DISC	14 May 96	pit
277	172		FEAT	103.36	117.36	II	CULT	0	11.03	DISC	14 May 96	roasting pit with rock
278	173		FEAT	104.73	117.85	II	CULT	0	11.22	DISC	14 May 96	rock-filled pit
279	174		FEAT	104.7	118.43	II	CULT	0	11.27	DISC	14 May 96	rock-filled pit

PD No.	Feature No.	Subfeature	Excavation Unit	Northing	Easting	Stratum	Stratum Type	Level	Depth [a]	Recovery Mode	Date	Comments
280	175		FEAT	104.59	119.07	II	CULT	0	11.29	DISC	14 May 96	pit
281	176		FEAT	102.8	119.92	II	CULT	0	11.24	DISC	14 May 96	pit with rock
282	177		FEAT	105.97	118.85	II	CULT	0	11.26	DISC	14 May 96	pit
283	178		FEAT	113.25	119	II	CULT	0	10.87–11.25	DISC	14 May 96	pit
284	178		FEAT	113.25	119	IIa	fill	1	10.87–11.05	S4	14 May 96	
285	178		FEAT	113.25	119	IIb	fill	2	11.05–11.25	S4	14 May 96	
286	53		FEAT	113.34	116.45	IId	fill	1	10.82–11.11	S4	14 May 96	pit
287	179		FEAT	115.2	117.2	II	CULT	0	11.07	DISC	16 May 96	2 superimposed pits
288	179		FEAT	115.2	117.2	IIa	fill	1	11.07–11.39	S4	16 May 96	pit intrusive to F 215
289	179	01	FEAT	115.36	117.29	IIa	fill	1	11.07–11.29	S4	16 May 96	
290	179	02	FEAT	115.05	117.03	IIa	fill	2	11.27–11.39	S4	16 May 96	
291	291		TP 291	111.86	106.99	II	CULT	0	10.16–10.7	INIT	16 May 96	TP above F 213
292			TP 291	111.86	106.99	I/II	DIST/CULT	1	10.16–10.36	S4	16 May 96	TP above F 213
293			TP 291	111.86	106.99	II	CULT	2	10.36–10.7	S4	16 May 96	
294	144		FEAT	112.39	123.18	IIa	fill	1	10.91–11.24	S4	16 May 96	
295	144	01	FEAT	112.46	123.92	IIa	BRL	1	11.1	S4	16 May 96	bird skeleton
296	144	02	FEAT	112.37	123.69	IIb	fill	1	11.1–11.21	C	16 May 96	ash pit
297	144	03	ART	112.03	123.1	IIa	fill	1	10.98	PP	16 May 96	hammer stone
298	144	03	ART	112.13	123.08	IIa	fill	1	10.97	PP	16 May 96	ground stone frag.
299	144	03	ART	112.04	123	IIa	fill	1	10.95	PP	16 May 96	flaked stone
300	144	03	ART	112.07	123.14	IIa	fill	1	11	PP	16 May 96	recon. bowl
301	5	05	FEAT	120	109.24	IIc	PT fill	3	10.19–10.49	S4	16 May 96	
302	5	06	FEAT	118.94	111.1	IIc	PT fill	3	10.14–10.64	S4	16 May 96	
303			TP 303	101	107	II	CULT	0	10.16–10.7	INIT	16 May 96	above F 213
304			TP 303	101	107	II	CULT	1	10.16–10.7	NS	16 May 96	above F 213
305	213		FEAT	101.25	106.44	IIc	BRL	2	10.54–10.86	S4	17 May 96	
306	213		FEAT	101.25	106.44	IIa	BRL	2	10.54–10.67	S4	17 May 96	cairn
307	213		FEAT	101.25	106.44	IIb	BRL fill	2	10.54–10.86	S4	17 May 96	
308	44		SAMP	114.15	118.5	IIb	FLR	2	10.78	PP	17 May 96	pollen under rock
309	44		ART	114.7	118.3	IIb	FLR	2	10.78	PP	17 May 96	ground stone frag.
310	44		SAMP	114.7	118.3	IIb	FLR	2	10.78	PP	17 May 96	under 309
311	44		ART	114.6	118.15	IIb	FLR	2	10.78	PP	17 May 96	ground stone

PD No.	Feature No.	Subfeature	Excavation Unit	Northing	Easting	Stratum	Stratum Type	Level	Depth [a]	Recovery Mode	Date	Comments
312	44		ART	114.76	118.06	IIb	FLR	2	10.78	PP	17 May 96	hammer stone
313	44		ART	114.93	118.11	IIb	FLR	2	10.78	PP	17 May 96	hammer stone
314	44		ART	114.99	118.63	IIb	FLR	2	10.78	PP	17 May 96	hammer stone
315	44		ART	115.2	118.32	IIb	FLR	2	10.78	PP	17 May 96	ground stone
316	44		ART	115.06	118.28	IIb	FLR	2	10.78	PP	17 May 96	ground stone
317	44		ART	115.66	118.7	IIb	FLR	2	10.78	PP	17 May 96	ground stone
318	44		SAMP	115.85	118.65	IIb	FLR	2	10.78	PP	17 May 96	pollen under 115
319	44		ART	116.52	119.42	IIb	FLR	2	10.78	PP	17 May 96	partial RV
320	44		SAMP	116.52	119.42	IIb	FLR	2	10.78	PP	17 May 96	pollen under 319
321	44		SAMP	116.9	119.2	IIb	FLR	2	10.78	PP	17 May 96	beam
322	44		ART	117.2	119.35	IIb	FLR	2	10.78	PP	17 May 96	metate
323	44		SAMP	117.2	119.35	IIb	FLR	2	10.78	PP	17 May 96	pollen under 322
324	44		ART	117.48	119.56	IIb	FLR	2	10.78	PP	17 May 96	hammer stone under 322
325	44		ART	117.5	119.31	IIb	FLR	2	10.78	PP	17 May 96	ground stone under 322
326	44		ART	116.14	119.33	IIb	FLR	2	10.78	PP	17 May 96	mano
327	44		FEAT	116	119.5	IIb	FLR	2	10.78	S4	17 May 96	floor artifacts
328	44		SAMP	116.6	118.95	IIb	FLR	2	10.78	PP	17 May 96	pollen under 116
329	44		SAMP	115.17	118.01	IIb	FLR	2	10.78	PP	17 May 96	post
330	44		ART	117.6	118.6	IIb	FLR	2	10.78	PP	17 May 96	metate
331	180		FEAT	103.05	95.74	II	CULT	0	10.55	DISC	17 May 96	pit
332	181		FEAT	102.43	94.46	II	CULT	0	10.49	DISC	17 May 96	pit
333	182		FEAT	101.01	95.19	II	CULT	0	10.62	DISC	17 May 96	pit
334	183		FEAT	105.1	125.5	II	CULT	0	11.54	DISC	17 May 96	pit
335	184		FEAT	106.6	126	II	CULT	0	11.46	DISC	17 May 96	pit
336	185		FEAT	105.4	127.3	II	CULT	0	11.49	DISC	17 May 96	pit with rocks
337	186		FEAT	106.2	127.6	II	CULT	0	11.47	DISC	17 May 96	pit with intrusive pot? burial
338	187		FEAT	104.66	123.6	II	CULT	0	11.37	DISC	17 May 96	large pit with rocks
339	188		FEAT	111.2	126.36	II	CULT	0	11.13	DISC	17 May 96	pit
340	189		FEAT	119.6	116.35	II	CULT	0	10.42	DISC	17 May 96	
341	190		FEAT	119.56	114.6	II	CULT	0	10.31	DISC	22 May 96	
342			TR 342	113.14–121.33	75.78–82.67	II/III	TB	1	0–20 cmbs	INT	22 May 96	

205

PD No.	Feature No.	Subfeature	Excavation Unit	Northing	Easting	Stratum	Stratum Type	Level	Depth [a]	Recovery Mode	Date	Comments
343			TR 343	140	110–130	II/III	TB	1	0–60 cmbs	INIT	22 May 96	
344	191		FEAT	140.5	114.08	II	CULT	0	9.37	DISC	22 May 96	TR 343 N face
345	191		PROF	140.5	114.08	II	CULT	1	9.37–9.57	PROF	22 May 96	
346	192		FEAT	140.5	115	II	CULT	0	9.37	DISC	22 May 96	TR 343 N face
347	192		PROF	140.5	115	II	CULT	1	9.37–9.6	PROF	22 May 96	
348	193		FEAT	140.62	116.79	II	CULT	0	9.4	DISC	22 May 96	
349	193		PROF	140.62	116.79	II	CULT	1	9.4–9.71	PROF	22 May 96	
350	194		FEAT	140.57	118.34	II	CULT	0	9.65	DISC	22 May 96	
351	194		PROF	140.57	118.34	II	CULT	1	9.65–9.89	PROF	22 May 96	
352	195		FEAT	140.46	129.24	II	CULT	0	10.05	DISC	22 May 96	
353	195		PROF	140.46	129.24	II	CULT	1	10.05–10.33	PROF	22 May 96	
354	196		FEAT	139.84	128.82	II	CULT	0	10.07	DISC	22 May 96	
355	196		PROF	139.84	128.82	II	CULT	1	10.07–10.32	PROF	22 May 96	
356	197		FEAT	140	126.6	II	CULT	0	10.17	DISC	22 May 96	
357	197		PROF	140	126.6	II	CULT	1	10.17–10.32	PROF	22 May 96	
358	198		FEAT	140.05	125.11	II	CULT	0	9.87	DISC	22 May 96	
359	198		PROF	140.05	125.11	II	CULT	1	9.87–10.05	PROF	22 May 96	
360	199		FEAT	140	118.22	II	CULT	0	9.76	DISC	22 May 96	
361	199		PROF	140	118.22	II	CULT	1	9.76–10.2	PROF	21 May 96	
362	200		FEAT	140	116.44	II	CULT	0	9.37	DISC	21 May 96	
363	200		PROF	140	116.44	II	CULT	1	9.5	PROF	21 May 96	
364	201		FEAT	140.46	129.86	II	CULT	0	10.05	DISC	21 May 96	
365	201		PROF	140.46	129.86	II	fill	1	10.05	PROF	21 May 96	
366	202		FEAT	101.81	95.39	II	CULT	0	10.43	DISC	04 Jun 96	pit into FS 151; 156 intrusive
367	202		FEAT	101.81	95.39	IIa	fill	1	10.43	NS	04 Jun 96	
368	203		FEAT	114	121.9	II	CULT	0	11.03	DISC	04 Jun 96	pit beneath F 139 floor
369	204		FEAT	112.9	120.6	II	CULT	0	10.84	DISC	04 Jun 96	pit
370	205		FEAT	112.6	120.1	II	CULT	0	10.84	DISC	04 Jun 96	pit adjacent to F 204
371	206		FEAT	113.52	118.06	II	CULT	0	11	DISC	04 Jun 96	pit
372	207		FEAT	113.4	117.4	II	CULT	0	10.63	DISC	04 Jun 96	pit
373	208		FEAT	118.6	117.85	II	CULT	0	10.78	DISC	04 Jun 96	pit in F 150
374	208		FEAT	118.6	117.85	IIa	fill	1	10.78–11.17	S4	04 Jun 96	

PD No.	Feature No.	Subfeature	Excavation Unit	Northing	Easting	Stratum	Stratum Type	Level	Depth [a]	Recovery Mode	Date	Comments
375	209		FEAT	114.65	120.64	II	CULT	0	10.98	DISC	04 Jun 96	pit in F 139
376	210		FEAT	117	118	II	CULT	0	10.91	DISC	04 Jun 96	pit SBAVS by floor F 150 intrusive by PHs
377	211		FEAT	117	115.5	II	CULT	0	10.33	DISC	04 Jun 96	structure predating F 52
378	212		FEAT	116	118	II	CULT	0	10.33	DISC	04 Jun 96	set of superimposed houses that includes F 44, 139, 52, 150, 211
379	212		FEAT	116	118	IIa	fill	1	10.33–11.1	NS	04 Jun 96	
380	212	01	FEAT	114.78	112.38	IIa	PH fill	3	10.47–10.77	S4	04 Jun 96	PH 4
381	212	02	FEAT	114.74	113.1	IIa	PH fill	3	10.59	S4	05 Jun 96	PH 6
382	212	03	FEAT	114.33	112.8	IIa	PH fill	3	10.58	S4	05 Jun 96	
383	212	04	FEAT	115.3	113.18	IIa	PH fill	3	10.61	S4	05 Jun 96	PH 7
384	212	05	FEAT	116.67	113.37	IIa	PH fill	3	10.43	S4	05 Jun 96	PH 11
385	212	06	FEAT	117.07	113.65	IIa	PH fill	3	10.42	S4	05 Jun 96	
386	212	07	FEAT	117.55	113.85	IIa	PH fill	3	10.32	S4	05 Jun 96	PH 12
387	212	08	FEAT	117.3	114.3	IIa	PH fill	3	10.54	S4	05 Jun 96	
388	212	09	FEAT	117.77	114.25	IIa	PH fill	3	10.42	S4	05 Jun 96	PH 15
389	212	10	FEAT	117.7	114.67	IIa	PH fill	3	10.42	S4	05 Jun 96	PH 16
390	212	11	FEAT	118.04	114.81	IIa	PH fill	3	10.49	S4	05 Jun 96	
391	212	12	FEAT	118.43	114.49	IIa	PH fill	3	10.4	S4	05 Jun 96	
392	212	13	FEAT	118.73	114.46	IIa	PH fill	3	10.35	S4	05 Jun 96	PH 17
393	212	14	FEAT	119.38	115.14	IIa	PH fill	3	10.33	S4	05 Jun 96	PH 18
394	212	15	FEAT	119.38	115.61	IIa	PH fill	3	10.38	S4	05 Jun 96	PH 19
395	212	16	FEAT	119.17	115.96	IIa	PH fill	3	10.42	S4	05 Jun 96	PH 20
396	212	17	FEAT	118.53	115.66	IIa	PH fill	3	10.54	S4	05 Jun 96	
397	212	18	FEAT	118.96	116.35	IIa	PH fill	3	10.41	S4	05 Jun 96	PH 21
398	212	19	FEAT	118.8	116.98	IIa	PH fill	3	10.44	S4	05 Jun 96	PH 65
399	212	20	FEAT	118.55	116.26	IIa	PH fill	3	10.51	S4	05 Jun 96	PH 23
400	212	21	FEAT	117.94	115.32	IIa	PH fill	3	10.58	S4	05 Jun 96	PH 22
401	212	22	FEAT	117.68	115.32	IIa	PH fill	3	10.59	S4	05 Jun 96	PH 24
402	212	23	FEAT	117.36	114.9	IIa	PH fill	3	10.58	S4	05 Jun 96	PH 14
403	212	24	FEAT	116.88	114.9	IIa	PH fill	3	10.58	S4	05 Jun 96	
404	212	25	FEAT	116.62	114.72	IIa	PH fill	3	10.58	S4	05 Jun 96	

PD No.	Feature No.	Subfeature	Excavation Unit	Northing	Easting	Stratum	Stratum Type	Level	Depth[a]	Recovery Mode	Date	Comments
405	212	26	FEAT	116.33	114.24	IIa	PH fill	3	10.62	S4	05 Jun 96	
406	212	27	FEAT	114.2	113.84	IIa	PH fill	3	10.77	S4	05 Jun 96	
407	212	28	FEAT	113.75	113.85	IIa	PH fill	3	10.85	S4	05 Jun 96	
408	212	29	FEAT	113.9	114.39	IIa	PH fill	3	10.88	S4	05 Jun 96	
409	212	30	FEAT	114.7	115	IIa	PH fill	3	10.8	S4	05 Jun 96	PH 29
410	212	31	FEAT	114.82	115.11	IIa	PH fill	3	10.8	S4	05 Jun 96	
411	212	32	FEAT	114.55	114.95	IIa	PH fill	3	10.8	S4	05 Jun 96	
412	212	33	FEAT	114.92	115.34	IIa	PH fill	3	10.8	S4	05 Jun 96	PH 8
413	212	34	FEAT	116.33	115.74	IIa	PH fill	3	10.73	S4	05 Jun 96	
414	212	35	FEAT	117.15	115.46	IIa	PH fill	3	10.69	S4	05 Jun 96	
415	212	36	FEAT	117.36	115.8	IIa	PH fill	3	10.66	S4	05 Jun 96	PH 25
416	212	37	FEAT	117.9	116.44	IIa	PH fill	3	10.5	S4	05 Jun 96	
417	212	38	FEAT	118.09	116.77	IIa	PH fill	3	10.68	S4	05 Jun 96	
418	212	39	FEAT	118.14	117.1	IIa	PH fill	3	10.77	S4	05 Jun 96	
419	212	40	FEAT	118.96	117.56	IIa	PH fill	3	10.68	S4	05 Jun 96	
420	212	41	FEAT	118.15	117.48	IIa	PH fill	3	10.88	S4	05 Jun 96	PH 66
421	212	42	FEAT	117.65	117.28	IIa	PH fill	3	10.88	S4	05 Jun 96	PH 63
422	212	43	FEAT	117.58	117.06	IIa	PH fill	3	10.88	S4	05 Jun 96	
423	212	44	FEAT	117.48	116.83	IIa	PH fill	3	10.8	S4	05 Jun 96	
424	212	45	FEAT	117.62	116.75	IIa	PH fill	3	10.86	S4	05 Jun 96	PH 28
425	212	46	FEAT	117.3	116.53	IIa	PH fill	3	10.8	S4	05 Jun 96	
426	212	47	FEAT	117.14	116.96	IIa	PH fill	3	10.85	S4	05 Jun 96	
427	212	48	FEAT	117.09	117.3	IIa	PH fill	3	10.89	S4	05 Jun 96	
428	212	49	FEAT	117.44	117.34	IIa	PH fill	3	10.89	S4	05 Jun 96	
429	212	50	FEAT	117.6	117.53	IIa	PH fill	3	10.89	S4	05 Jun 96	
430	212	51	FEAT	117.67	117.58	IIa	PH fill	3	10.89	S4	05 Jun 96	PH 62
431	212	52	FEAT	118	117.54	IIa	PH fill	3	10.9	S4	05 Jun 96	PH 61
432	212	53	FEAT	118.2	117.68	IIa	PH fill	3	10.9	S4	05 Jun 96	
433	212	54	FEAT	118.31	117.71	IIa	PH fill	3	10.91	S4	05 Jun 96	
434	212	55	FEAT	118.72	118.18	IIa	PH fill	3	10.95	S4	05 Jun 96	
435	212	56	FEAT	118.49	118.14	IIa	PH fill	3	10.94	S4	05 Jun 96	
436	212	57	FEAT	118.26	118.08	IIa	PH fill	3	10.93	S4	05 Jun 96	

PD No.	Feature No.	Subfeature	Excavation Unit	Northing	Easting	Stratum	Stratum Type	Level	Depth [a]	Recovery Mode	Date	Comments
437	212	58	FEAT	117.66	117.93	IIa	PH fill	3	10.9	S4	05 Jun 96	
438	212	59	FEAT	117.64	117.83	IIa	PH fill	3	10.9	S4	05 Jun 96	
439	212	60	FEAT	117.38	118.15	IIa	PH fill	3	10.91	S4	05 Jun 96	
440	212	61	FEAT	117.09	117.87	IIa	PH fill	3	10.91	S4	05 Jun 96	
441	212	62	FEAT	116.92	117.4	IIa	PH fill	3	10.91	S4	05 Jun 96	
442	212	63	FEAT	116.78	117.72	IIa	PH fill	3	10.91	S4	05 Jun 96	
443	212	64	FEAT	116.48	118.05	IIa	PH fill	3	10.93	S4	05 Jun 96	
444	212	65	FEAT	116.56	117.4	IIa	PH fill	3	10.93	S4	05 Jun 96	
445	212	66	FEAT	116.22	117.92	IIa	PH fill	3	10.93	S4	05 Jun 96	
446	212	67	FEAT	116.28	117.75	IIa	PH fill	3	10.94	S4	05 Jun 96	PH 59
447	212	68	FEAT	116.56	117.24	IIa	PH fill	3	10.93	S4	05 Jun 96	
448	212	69	FEAT	116.43	117.05	IIa	PH fill	3	10.98	S4	05 Jun 96	
449	212	70	FEAT	116.26	117.03	IIa	PH fill	3	10.97	S4	05 Jun 96	
450	212	71	FEAT	116.1	116.94	IIa	PH fill	3	10.97	S4	05 Jun 96	PH 37
451	212	72	FEAT	116.18	116.76	IIa	PH fill	3	10.97	S4	05 Jun 96	
452	212	73	FEAT	116.07	116.61	IIa	PH fill	3	10.97	S4	05 Jun 96	
453	212	74	FEAT	115.9	116.55	IIa	PH fill	3	10.97	S4	05 Jun 96	
454	212	75	FEAT	115.75	116.7	IIa	PH fill	3	11.02	S4	05 Jun 96	PH 36
455	212	76	FEAT	115.66	116.84	IIa	PH fill	3	11.02	S4	05 Jun 96	
456	212	77	FEAT	115.79	117.51	IIa	PH fill	3	10.99	S4	05 Jun 96	
457	212	78	FEAT	115.79	117.88	IIa	PH fill	3	10.98	S4	05 Jun 96	PH 57
458	212	79	FEAT	115.62	117.62	IIa	PH fill	3	10.99	S4	05 Jun 96	
459	212	80	FEAT	115.52	117.42	IIa	PH fill	3	10.99	S4	05 Jun 96	
460	212	81	FEAT	115.31	117.56	IIa	PH fill	3	11.03	S4	05 Jun 96	
461	212	82	FEAT	115.34	117.94	IIa	PH fill	3	11.05	S4	05 Jun 96	
462	212	83	FEAT	115.1	117.92	IIa	PH fill	3	11.05	S4	05 Jun 96	PH 56
463	212	84	FEAT	114.75	117.64	IIa	PH fill	3	10.96	S4	05 Jun 96	PH 55
464	212	85	FEAT	114.7	117.36	IIa	PH fill	3	10.96	S4	05 Jun 96	PH 54
465	212	86	FEAT	115.13	116.59	IIa	PH fill	3	11.01	S4	05 Jun 96	PH 43
466	212	87	FEAT	115.35	116.48	IIa	PH fill	3	10.98	S4	05 Jun 96	PH 35
467	212	88	FEAT	114.65	116.12	IIa	PH fill	3	10.96	S4	05 Jun 96	PH 34
468	212	89	FEAT	114.5	116.32	IIa	PH fill	3	10.96	S4	05 Jun 96	

PD No.	Feature No.	Subfeature	Excavation Unit	Northing	Easting	Stratum	Stratum Type	Level	Depth [a]	Recovery Mode	Date	Comments
469	212	90	FEAT	114.4	116.41	IIa	PH fill	3	11.01	S4	05 Jun 96	
470	212	91	FEAT	114.3	117.02	IIa	PH fill	3	11.01	S4	05 Jun 96	PH 52
471	212	92	FEAT	114.37	117.29	IIa	PH fill	3	11	S4	05 Jun 96	
472	212	93	FEAT	114.35	117.43	IIa	PH fill	3	11	S4	05 Jun 96	
473	212	94	FEAT	114.5	117.54	IIa	PH fill	3	10.99	S4	05 Jun 96	PH 53
474	212	95	FEAT	114.26	117.24	IIa	PH fill	3	11	S4	05 Jun 96	PH 41
475	212	96	FEAT	114.04	117.13	IIa	PH fill	3	11.01	S4	05 Jun 96	PH 40
476	212	97	FEAT	114.05	117.56	IIa	PH fill	3	11	S4	05 Jun 96	
477	212	98	FEAT	114.03	117.84	IIa	PH fill	3	11	S4	05 Jun 96	PH 45
478	212	99	FEAT	113.36	117.72	IIa	PH fill	3	10.99	S4	05 Jun 96	PH 44
479	212	100	FEAT	113.1	117.15	IIa	PH fill	3	10.85	S4	05 Jun 96	PH 42
480	212	101	FEAT	112.85	116.66	IIa	PH fill	3	10.85	S4	05 Jun 96	
481	212	102	FEAT	113.07	116.65	IIa	PH fill	3	11.13	S4	06 Jun 96	intrudes F 53
482	212	103	FEAT	113.23	116.18	IIa	PH fill	3	11.13	S4	06 Jun 96	intrudes F 53
483	212	104	FEAT	112.78	115.8	IIa	PH fill	3	10.79	S4	06 Jun 96	
484	212	105	FEAT	112.9	115.5	IIa	PH fill	3	10.78	S4	06 Jun 96	
485	212	106	FEAT	112.94	115.33	IIa	PH fill	3	10.76	S4	06 Jun 96	
486	212	107	FEAT	113.01	115.17	IIa	PH fill	3	10.75	S4	06 Jun 96	
487	212	108	FEAT	113.6	115.06	IIa	PH fill	3	10.77	S4	06 Jun 96	
488	212	109	FEAT	116.04	116	IIa	PH fill	3	10.97	S4	06 Jun 96	
489	212	110	FEAT	113.62	116.12	IIa	PH fill	3	10.99	S4	06 Jun 96	
490	212	111	FEAT	113.88	115.86	IIa	PH fill	3	10.98	S4	06 Jun 96	PH 9
491	212	112	FEAT	114.1	115.72	IIa	PH fill	3	10.98	S4	06 Jun 96	PH 10
492	212	113	FEAT	114.25	115.81	IIa	PH fill	3	10.98	S4	06 Jun 96	PH 10
493	212	114	FEAT	114.54	115.79	IIa	PH fill	3	10.92	S4	06 Jun 96	
494	212	115	FEAT	114.7	115.86	IIa	PH fill	3	10.88	S4	06 Jun 96	PH 33
495	212	116	FEAT	114.95	115.98	IIa	PH fill	3	10.96	S4	06 Jun 96	PH 39
496	212	117	FEAT	115.3	115.98	IIa	PH fill	3	10.99	S4	06 Jun 96	
497	212	118	FEAT	115.53	116	IIa	PH fill	3	10.99	S4	06 Jun 96	
498	212	119	FEAT	115.73	116.04	IIa	PH fill	3	10.98	S4	06 Jun 96	
499	212	120	FEAT	115.99	116.18	IIa	PH fill	3	10.97	S4	06 Jun 96	
500	212	121	FEAT	116.12	116.1	IIa	PH fill	3	10.97	S4	06 Jun 96	

PD No.	Feature No.	Subfeature	Excavation Unit	Northing	Easting	Stratum	Stratum Type	Level	Depth [a]	Recovery Mode	Date	Comments
501	212	122	FEAT	116.37	116.14	IIa	PH fill	3	10.97	S4	07 Jun 96	PH 31
502	212	123	FEAT	116.47	116.04	IIa	PH fill	3	10.97	S4	07 Jun 96	
503	212	124	FEAT	116.46	116.31	IIa	PH fill	3	10.97	S4	07 Jun 96	
504	212	125	FEAT	116.54	116.6	IIa	PH fill	3	10.98	S4	07 Jun 96	
505	212	126	FEAT	116.66	116.58	IIa	PH fill	3	10.98	S4	07 Jun 96	
506	212	127	FEAT	116.8	116.67	IIa	PH fill	3	10.98	S4	07 Jun 96	
507	212	128	FEAT	116.7	116.83	IIa	PH fill	3	10.99	S4	07 Jun 96	
508	212	129	FEAT	116.68	116.9	IIa	PH fill	3	10.99	S4	07 Jun 96	
509	212	130	FEAT	116.8	117.15	IIa	PH fill	3	10.98	S4	07 Jun 96	PH 30
510	212	131	FEAT	116.88	116.95	IIa	PH fill	3	10.94	S4	07 Jun 96	
511	212	132	FEAT	117	116.66	IIa	PH fill	3	10.91	S4	07 Jun 96	
512	212	133	FEAT	116.85	116.1	IIa	PH fill	3	10.84	S4	07 Jun 96	
513	212	134	FEAT	118.6	118.76	IIa	PH fill	3	10.97	S4	07 Jun 96	
514	212	135	FEAT	118.6	119.1	IIa	PH fill	3	10.96	S4	07 Jun 96	
515	212	136	FEAT	118.75	119.4	IIa	PH fill	3	10.67	S4	07 Jun 96	PH 42
516	212	137	FEAT	118.77	119.61	IIa	PH fill	3	10.72	S4	07 Jun 96	
517	212	138	FEAT	118.88	120.09	IIa	PH fill	3	10.77	S4	07 Jun 96	
518	212	139	FEAT	118.94	120.53	IIa	PH fill	3	10.76	S4	07 Jun 96	
519	212	140	FEAT	118.84	120.97	IIa	PH fill	3	10.78	S4	07 Jun 96	
520	212	141	FEAT	118.55	120.99	IIa	PH fill	3	10.78	S4	07 Jun 96	
521	212	142	FEAT	118.62	121.16	IIa	PH fill	3	10.83	S4	07 Jun 96	
522	212	143	FEAT	177.77	121.21	IIa	PH fill	3	10.83	S4	07 Jun 96	PH 71
523	212	144	FEAT	177.25	121.35	IIa	PH fill	3	10.73	S4	07 Jun 96	PH 76
524	212	145	FEAT	116.71	121.48	IIa	PH fill	3	10.75	S4	07 Jun 96	PH 77
525	212	146	FEAT	116.45	121.32	IIa	PH fill	3	10.76	S4	07 Jun 96	PH 75
526	212	147	FEAT	115.87	121.36	IIa	PH fill	3	10.76	S4	07 Jun 96	PH 74
527	212	148	FEAT	115.6	121.29	IIa	PH fill	3	10.76	S4	07 Jun 96	
528	212	149	FEAT	115.5	121.09	IIa	PH fill	3	11	S4	07 Jun 96	
529	212	150	FEAT	115.42	121.28	IIa	PH fill	3	11	S4	07 Jun 96	
530	212	151	FEAT	115.28	121.6	IIa	PH fill	3	11.01	S4	07 Jun 96	
531	212	152	FEAT	115.09	122.05	IIa	PH fill	3	11.05	S4	07 Jun 96	
532	212	153	FEAT	115.39	122.51	IIa	PH fill	3	10.85	S4	07 Jun 96	

PD No.	Feature No.	Subfeature	Excavation Unit	Northing	Easting	Stratum	Stratum Type	Level	Depth [a]	Recovery Mode	Date	Comments
533	212	154	FEAT	115.22	122.74	IIa	PH fill	3	10.85	S4	07 Jun 96	
534	212	155	FEAT	115.02	122.92	IIa	PH fill	3	10.85	S4	07 Jun 96	
535	212	156	FEAT	114.85	121.2	IIa	PH fill	3	11	S4	07 Jun 96	
536	212	157	FEAT	114.72	121.22	IIa	PH fill	3	11	S4	07 Jun 96	
537	212	158	FEAT	113.75	121.12	IIa	PH fill	3	10.98	S4	07 Jun 96	
538	212	159	FEAT	114.07	120.76	IIa	PH fill	3	10.97	S4	07 Jun 96	
539	212	160	FEAT	113.91	120.5	IIa	PH fill	3	10.97	S4	07 Jun 96	
540	212	161	FEAT	113.54	120.09	IIa	PH fill	3	10.96	S4	07 Jun 96	
541	212	162	FEAT	113.22	120.02	IIa	PH fill	3	10.9	S4	07 Jun 96	
542	212	163	FEAT	113.62	119.78	IIa	PH fill	3	10.96	S4	07 Jun 96	
543	212	164	FEAT	113.25	119.6	IIa	PH fill	3	10.9	S4	07 Jun 96	
544	212	165	FEAT	113.7	119.45	IIa	PH fill	3	10.93	S4	07 Jun 96	
545	212	166	FEAT	113.94	118.7	IIa	PH fill	3	10.96	S4	07 Jun 96	PH 51
546	212	167	FEAT	113.82	118.5	IIa	PH fill	3	10.96	S4	07 Jun 96	PH 50
547	212	168	FEAT	113.4	118.43	IIa	PH fill	3	10.98	S4	07 Jun 96	PH 49
548	212	169	FEAT	113.12	118.14	IIa	PH fill	3	11.04	S4	07 Jun 96	
549	212	170	FEAT	112.91	118.4	IIa	PH fill	3	11	S4	07 Jun 96	PH 48
550	212	171	FEAT	112.75	118.04	IIa	PH fill	3	10.99	S4	07 Jun 96	PH 47
551	212	172	FEAT	112.84	117.85	IIa	PH fill	3	10.99	S4	07 Jun 96	PH 46
552	212	173	FEAT	113.14	117.83	IIa	PH fill	3	10.99	S4	07 Jun 96	
553	212	174	FEAT	117.15	116.2	IIa	PH fill	3	10.7	S4	07 Jun 96	PH 27
554	212	97, 98	FEAT	114.04	117.7	IIa	PH fill	3	11	S4	07 Jun 96	
555	73		FEAT	114.1	116.82	IIa	fill	1	10.96–11.06	S4	07 Jun 96	
556	212	70, 71, 72	FEAT	116.2	116.9	IIa	PH fill	3	10.97	S4	07 Jun 96	
557	212	75, 76	FEAT	115.7	116.77	IIa	PH fill	3	11.02	S4	07 Jun 96	
558	212	109, 120, 121	FEAT	116.05	116.09	IIa	PH fill	3	10.97	S4	07 Jun 96	488, 499, 500
559	74		FEAT	117.68	116.88	IIa	fill	1	10.76–10.89	S4	07 Jun 96	
560	212	112, 113	FEAT	114.18	115.77	IIa	PH fill	3	10.98	S4	07 Jun 96	491–492
561	80		FEAT	114.9	112.5	IIa	fill	1	10.47–10.64	S4	07 Jun 96	
562	55		FEAT	113.54	114.65	IIa	fill	1	10.81–11.06	S4	07 Jun 96	
563	186		FEAT	106.2	127.6	IIa	fill	1	11.47	S4	07 Jun 96	
564	208		FEAT	118.6	117.85	IIa	fill	1	10.91–11.17	S4	07 Jun 96	

PD No.	Feature No.	Subfeature	Excavation Unit	Northing	Easting	Stratum	Stratum Type	Level	Depth [a]	Recovery Mode	Date	Comments
565	210		W2	117	118	IIa	fill	1	10.91–11.29	S4	07 Jun 96	
566	203		FEAT	114	121.9	IIa	fill	1	11.03	GS	07 Jun 96	
567	78		FEAT	118.08	120.91	IIa	fill	1	10.83–11.08	S4	07 Jun 96	
568	212		FEAT	116	118	IIc	PH fill	3	10.33–11.07	S4	07 Jun 96	misc. postholes; unprovenienced
569	156		ART	102.03	95.41	IIb	BRL	1	10.65–10.83	PP	10 Jun 96	shell bracelet on right upper arm
570	156		ART	102	95.31	IIb	BRL	1	10.65–10.83	PP	10 Jun 96	shell bracelet on left upper arm
571	15		FEAT	109	127	IIc	SFLR	3	11.59	S4	11 Jun 96	
572	44		ART	114.85	120.6	IIb	FLR	2	10.78	PP	11 Jun 96	ground stone
573	144	03	FEAT	112.07	123.14	IIa	fill	1	10.94–11.09	S4	11 Jun 96	
574	213		FEAT	101.25	106.44	II	CULT	0	10.54–10.86	DISC	13 Aug 96	duplicate of 192, 192 supersedes
575	214		FEAT	117	126	II	CULT	0	40.00 cmbs	DISC	14 Aug 96	
576	5		N2	120.2	111	IIb	FLR	2	10.25	NS	28 May 97	
577	5		S2	120.2	111	IIb	FLR	2	10.23	NS	28 May 97	
578	215		FEAT	115.5	117	II	CULT	0	10.78	DISC	28 May 97	
579	216		FEAT	115.2	115.6	II	CULT	0	10.8	DISC	28 May 97	

[a] All depths are in meters below datum (mbd), except those noted as centimeters below surface (cmbs).

Codes on Provenience Forms and in Table A.1

Excavation units
General
    Site: entire site area
    Locus: designated locus (naturally bounded area of site)
    Area: designated area (arbitrarily defined unit of the site, e.g. excavation area)
Features (nonhouse)
    FEAT: entire feature treated as single unit
    N2: north one-half
    E2: east one-half
    S2: south one-half
    W2: west one-half
Houses
    FEAT: entire house excavated as single unit
    Q1: first quarter
    Q2: second quarter
    Q3: third quarter
    Q4: fourth quarter
    E: entryway (if present and definable)
    Q1–Q4: composite recovered from all quarters (used when house is otherwise subdivided for recovery of artifacts and samples; distinct from FEAT when entire house treated as single recovery unit)
    H1: first half
    H2: second half
    HRTH: intramural hearth (because it is a subordinate feature)
    PH: intramural posthole (same note as hearth)
    PIT: intramural pit (same note as hearth)
Artifacts and samples:
    ART: point-provenienced artifacts
    SAMP: point-specific sample (when location of sample is more restricted than excavation unit)
Nonfeature excavation units (and arbitrary sample units in features):
    TR: trench
    TP: test pit
    SU: stripping unit
    PROF: profile (vertical two-dimensional surface, such as the sidewall of a trench)

Stratum type
SURF: surface
NATS: natural soil or sediments
DIST: disturbed deposits
CULT: culture bearing horizon
DIST/CULT: mixed disturbed and cultural deposits
RDNT: rodent disturbance
TB: trench backdirt (also includes backdirt from stripping units and hand trenches)
Fill: feature fill
RFL: roof fall
Fill/RFL: mixed fill and roof fall deposits
FLR: floor (contact only)
SFLR: subfloor
BRL: burial associations (only items associated with burial; not fill items)
BRL Fill: burial fill (bulk objects from fill around an above interment; not part of funerary deposit)
MDN: midden
PH Fill: intramural posthole fill, within houses
HRTH Fill: intramural hearth fill
PT Fill: intramural pit fill

Recovery mode

DISC: discovery (for features only)

INIT: initiation (beginning of an arbitrary unit, this pd number will be the unit name

PROF: profile

S4: screened, ¼-inch mesh

S8: screened, ⅛-inch mesh

S: screened, other mesh, specify on provenience record form in excavation methods

NS: null set, not screened, no collections made

GS: not screened, grab sample of artifacts recovered

PP: point provenienced artifact or sample

C: composite sample taken from multiple proveniences

SAMP: pollen, flotation, or other nonartifactual sample taken from unscreened context (such as recovery of flotation samples for macrobotanical extraction from extramural hearths)

Example of the Feature and Subfeature List

Table B.1. Type and Location of Features and Subfeatures at El Macayo

Feature Number & Feature Type	Subfeature	Subfeature Type	PD No.	North	East	Depth (mbd)
Feature 1						
Burials: cremation			14	100	109	
Feature 2						
Burials: cremation			15	101	107.25	
Feature 3						
Pit			16	120	103	
Feature 4						
Pit			17	111	102	
Feature 5						
Pit house			18	120.2	111	10.11
Pit house	01	hearth	209	120.92	111.4	10.16
Pit house	02	hearth	210	120.04	111.3	10.18
Pit house	03	pit	211	122	111.14	10.22
Pit house	04	pit	212	121.25	111.05	10.19
Pit house	05	pit	301	120	109.24	10.19
Pit house	06	pit	302	118.94	111.1	10.14
Pit house	07	posthole fill	580	119.81	112.06	10.16
Pit house	08	posthole fill	581	119.67	112.24	10.18
Pit house	09	posthole fill	582	119.54	112.02	10.24
Pit house	10	posthole fill	583	119.32	112.23	10.18
Pit house	11	posthole fill	584	119.69	111.07	10.19
Pit house	12	posthole fill	585	119.78	111.35	10.19
. . .						
Feature 213						
Burials: human			192	101.25	106.44	10.54
Feature 214						
Burials: human			575	117	126	40

Feature Number & Feature Type	Subfeature	Subfeature Type	PD No.	North	East	Depth (mbd)
Feature 215						
Pit house			578	115.5	117	10.78
Feature 216						
Pit			579	115.2	115.6	10.62
Feature 217						
Pit			191	107.7	127.25	11.4
Feature 218						
Pit			693	108	126.6	11.41
Feature 219						
Pit/posthole			694	108.88	127.4	11.41

Note: A complete list of the features and subfeatures is archived at the Arizona State Museum.
Key: mbd = meters below datum

APPENDIX C

Ceramic Data

Robert A. Heckman

Table C.1. Ceramic Attribute Key for El Macayo Ceramic Analysis

Code	Ware and Type
1000	**El Macayo**
1010	Local red-on-brown
1015	Local black-on-red
1020	Local black-on-brown
1025	Local purple-on-brown
1030	Local black-on-white (slip)
10000	**Hohokam Buff Ware**
10100	Estrella Red-on-gray
10110	Estrella Red-on-gray (incised)
10120	Estrella (incised)
10200	Sweetwater Red-on-gray
10210	Sweetwater Red-on-gray (incised)
10215	Sweetwater Red-on-gray (pattern incised)
10220	Sweetwater (incised)
10225	Sweetwater (pattern incised)
10250	Sweetwater or Snaketown Red-on-gray
10260	Sweetwater or Snaketown Red-on-gray (incised)
10270	Sweetwater or Snaketown (incised)
10300	Snaketown red-on-dense paste
10310	Snaketown red-on-dense paste (incised)
10400	Snaketown Red-on-buff
10410	Snaketown Red-on-buff (incised)
10420	Snaketown (incised only)
10449	Indeterminate Pioneer
10450	Snaketown or Gila Butte Red-on-buff
10500	Gila Butte Red-on-buff
10510	Gila Butte Red-on-buff (incised)
10520	Gila Butte (incised only)
10550	Gila Butte or Santa Cruz Red-on-buff
10600	Santa Cruz Red-on-buff
10650	Santa Cruz or Sacaton Red-on-buff
10700	Sacaton Red-on-buff
10800	Casa Grande Red-on-buff
10995	Indeterminate red-on-buff
10999	Indeterminate buff (no paint)

Code	Ware and Type
12000	**Tucson Basin Brown Ware**
12100	Estrella style
12200	Sweetwater style
12250	Sweetwater or Snaketown style
12400	Snaketown style
12500	Cañada del Oro Red-on-brown
12501	Cañada del Oro Red-on-brown, white slip
12550	Cañada del Oro or Rillito Red-on-brown
12600	Rillito Red-on-brown
12620	Rillito or Rincon Red-on-brown, style A
12712	Rincon Red-on-brown, style A
12713	Rincon Red-on-brown, style A, white slip
12715	Rincon Red-on-brown, style B
12716	Rincon Red-on-brown, style B, white slip
12717	Rincon Red-on-brown, style B, white slip, black paint
12730	Rincon Polychrome
12731	Rincon Polychrome, black paint, white slip ext., red slip int.
12740	Rincon Red-on-brown, style B or C
12745	Indeterminate Rincon Red-on-brown
12748	Rincon Red-on-brown, style C
12754	Rincon Red-on-brown, indeterminate style
12762	Rincon Red-on-brown, style C or Tanque Verde Red-on- brown
12800	Tanque Verde Red-on-brown
12801	Tanque Verde Red-on-brown, white slip
12802	Tanque Verde Red-on-brown, white slip, black paint
12803	Tanque Verde Red-on-brown, black paint
12830	Tanque Verde Polychrome
12999	Indeterminate Tucson Basin red-on-brown
14000	**San Simon Brown Ware**
14100	Dos Cabezas Red-on-brown
14150	Dos Cabezas or Pinaleno Red-on-brown
14200	Pinaleno Red-on-brown
14250	Pinaleno or Galiuro Red-on-brown
14300	Galiuro Red-on-brown
14400	Cerros Red-on-white
14410	Cerros Red-on-white (Galiuro style)
14420	Cerros Red-on-white (Encinas style)
14500	Encinas Red-on-brown
14999	Indeterminate San Simon red-on-brown
16000	**Papagueria area**
16100	Vamari Red-on-brown
16200	Topawa Red-on-brown
16999	Indeterminate red-on-brown (Papagueria)
18000	**Trincheras ware**
18101	Trincheras Purple-on-red (specular)
18102	Trincheras Purple-on-red (nonspecular)
18200	Trincheras (Altar) Polychrome
18300	Nogales Polychrome
18301	Nogales Polychrome (purple only)

Code	Ware and Type
18302	Nogales Polychrome (black only)
18303	Nogales Polychrome (red only)
20000	**Upper/Middle Santa Cruz area**
20100	Rio Rico Polychrome
20200	Ramanote Red-on-brown
20300	Canelo Brown-on-yellow
20400	Santa Cruz Polychrome
20401	Santa Cruz Polychrome (red only)
20402	Santa Cruz Polychrome (black only)
99000	**Other painted wares**
99010	San Carlos Red-on-brown
99011	San Carlos Red-on-brown (white slip)
99500	Salado White-on-red
99999	Indeterminate painted
	Unpainted types
100	Plain ware
110	Vahki Plain
120	Gila Plain
170	Mogollon Brown Ware (southern variant)
180	Type I (santac)
181	Type II (santac)
182	Type III (santac)
183	Type IV (santac)
198	Indeterminate plain ware
200	Red ware
210	Vahki Red
215	San Francisco Red
220	Sacaton Red
225	Rincon Red
230	Trincheras Red
235	Gila Red
240	Salt Red
245	San Carlos Red
270	Sells Red
275	Peck Red
280	Papago Red
	Textured ware
298	Indeterminate red ware
299	Indeterminate plain or red ware
1998	Indeterminate intrusive unpainted
1999	Indeterminate unpainted

Interior Code	Exterior Code	Surface Finish
11	211	Blackened
12	212	Smudged
20	220	Hand smoothed
21	221	Hand smoothed, blackened
22	222	Hand smoothed, fire cloud
30	230	Uniformly polished

Interior Code	Exterior Code	Surface Finish
31	231	Uniformly polished, blackened
32	232	Uniformly polished, fire cloud
40	240	Striated polished
41	241	Striated polished, blackened
42	242	Striated polished, fire cloud
50	250	Striated polished, zonal
51	251	Striated polished, zonal, blackened
52	252	Striated polished, zonal, fire cloud
60	260	Washed
61	261	Washed, blackened
62	262	Washed, fire cloud
70	270	Slipped, hand smoothed
71	271	Slipped, hand smoothed, blackened
72	272	Slipped, hand smoothed, fire cloud
80	280	Slipped, uniformly polished
81	281	Slipped, uniformly polished, blackened
82	282	Slipped, uniformly polished, fire cloud
90	290	Slipped, striated polished
91	291	Slipped, striated polished, blackened
92	292	Slipped, striated polished, fire cloud
100	300	Scraped or wiped
110	310	Scored
120	320	Incised
150	350	Unfinished
199	399	Indeterminate

Code	Temper
100	Sand
110	Sand and mica (< 50% biotite)
111	Sand and mica (> 50% biotite)
115	Sand and mica (< 50% biotite and muscovite)
116	Sand and mica (> 50% biotite and muscovite)
120	Sand and mica (< 50% muscovite)
121	Sand and mica (> 50% muscovite)
125	Sand and mica (< 50% muscovite and phlogopite)
126	Sand and mica (> 50% muscovite and phlogopite)
130	Sand and mica (< 50% phlogopite)
131	Sand and mica (> 50% phlogopite)
140	Rhyolitic sand
145	Granitic sand
150	Gneissic sand
180	Sand (quartz)
181	Quartz
182	Fine quartz
190	Fine sand
210	Phyllitic sand
410	Diabase
499	Indeterminate igneous
500	Granitic gneiss

Code	Temper
600	Phyllite
610	Sand and phyllite
650	Phyllite and schist
700	Schist
710	Sand and schist
799	Indeterminate metamorphic
899	Indeterminate crushed rock
900	Sherd
910	Sand and sherd
950	Other
999	Indeterminate

Code	Vessel Form
10	Hemispherical bowl
11	Subhemispherical bowl
12	Incurved bowl
14	Outcurved bowl
16	Flare-rimmed bowl
17	Shouldered bowl
29	Indeterminate bowl
30	Globular jar
32	Shouldered jar
35	Neckless jar
37	Flare-rimmed jar
49	Indeterminate jar
50	Plate
60	Pitcher
65	Beaker
70	Cauldron
75	Pinch pot
80	Scoop
85	Effigy vessel
95	Other
110	Miniature hemispherical bowl
111	Miniature subhemispherical bowl
112	Miniature incurved bowl
114	Miniature outcurved bowl
116	Miniature flare-rimmed bowl
130	Miniature globular jar
132	Miniature shouldered jar
135	Miniature neckless jar
137	Miniature flare-rimmed jar
199	Indeterminate

Code	Vessel Part
10	Rim
11	Rim/neck
21	Neck
22	Neck/shoulder
23	Shoulder

Code	Vessel Part
24	Shoulder/base
25	Base
26	Base/body
30	Indeterminate body

Code	Rims
	Interior rim diameter (cm)
	Interior throat diameter (cm)
	Form
10	Direct
20	Straight
30	Slight flare (70–89 degrees)
31	Moderate flare (45–69 degrees)
32	Pronounced flare (< 45 degrees)
40	Slightly everted (60–80 degrees)
41	Moderately everted (45–59 degrees)
42	Sharply everted (< 45 degrees)
50	Slightly recurved (80–90 degrees)
51	Moderately recurved (70–79 degrees)
52	Sharply recurved (< 70 degrees)
99	Indeterminate/not applicable
	Finish
10	Flat
15	Tapered
20	Rounded
30	Interior bevel
31	Exterior bevel
32	Beveled, both sides
40	Interior bulge or overhang
41	Exterior bulge or overhang
42	Bulged or overhung, both sides
50	Variable
99	Indeterminate/not applicable

Code	Modifications
10	Burned
20	Repair hole
30	Stained (pigment)
40	Use wear
50	Sooted
60	Kill hole
70	Multiple (specify)
80	Other (specify)
90	None

	Other Attributes
	Count (number of sherds)
	Thickness (mm)

Table C.2. Example of the Painted Ceramic Database

Rec. No.	Prov. No.	Ceramic Type	Interior Finish	Exterior Finish	Temper	Vessel Form	Vessel Part	Rim Form	Rim Finish	Shoulder Type	n	Thickness (mm)	Modification
1	301	Trincheras P/red (nonspec)	SP	scraped or wiped	sand	indet. jar	indet. body	indet./na	indet./na	indet./na	1	5	none
2	301	Cañada del Oro or Rillito R/br			sand	fl-rim bowl	rim	mod. flare	int. bevel	indet./na	1	5	none
3	189	Rincon R/br, style C	UP	UP	sand	indet. bowl	indet. body	indet./na	indet./na	indet./na	1	6	none
4	189	Indet. Tucson Basin r/br	nr	nr	sand	indet. jar	indet. body	indet./na	indet./na	indet./na	1	4	none
5	189	Indet. Tucson Basin r/br	nr	nr	sand	indet. jar	indet. body	indet./na	indet./na	indet./na	1	4	none
6	343	Trincheras P/red (spec)	SP	HS	sand	subhem. bowl	rim	direct	int. bulge	indet./na	1	5	none
7	343	Trincheras P/red (spec)	UP	SP	sand	subhem. bowl	rim	direct	tapered	indet./na	1	6	none
8	343	Trincheras P/red (spec)	UP	SP	sand	subhem. bowl	rim	direct	int. bulge	indet./na	1	4	none
9	343	Santa Cruz R/b	HS	HS	schist	fl-rim bowl	rim	mod. flare	int. bevel	indet./na	1	6	none
10	343	Indet. r/b	HS	HS	schist	indet. bowl	indet. body	indet./na	indet./na	indet./na	1	4	none
⋮													
588	77	local bl/red	slipped, UP	slipped, UP	sand/mica (<50% phlog.)	indet. bowl	indet. body	indet./na	indet./na	indet./na	1	5	none
589	415	Trincheras (Altar) Polychrome	scraped or wiped	UP	sand/mica (<50% phlog.)	indet. jar	indet. body	indet./na	indet./na	indet./na	1	4	none
590	61	local r/br	HS	indet.	sand	indet. bowl	indet. body	indet./na	indet./na	indet./na	1	6	none
591	61	local r/br	unfinished	HS, black	sand	indet. jar	indet. body	indet./na	indet./na	indet./na	1	7	none
592	61	local r/br	UP	UP	sand	indet. jar	indet. body	indet./na	indet./na	indet./na	1	5	none
593	105	local r/br	HS	HS	sand	indet. bowl	indet. body	indet./na	indet./na	indet./na	1	5	none
594	259	local r/br	unfinished	HS	sand/mica (<50% phlog.)	indet. jar	indet. body	indet./na	indet./na	indet./na	1	6	none
595	235	local r/br	UP, black	UP	sand/mica (<50% phlog.)	subhem. bowl	rim	direct	rounded	indet./na	1	5	none

Key: bl/red = black-on-red; black = blackened; fl-rim = flare-rimmed; HS = hand smoothed; indet. = indeterminate; int. = interior; mod. = moderate; na = not applicable; nonspec = nonspecular; nr = not recorded; Prov. = Provenience; P/red = Purple-on-red; phlog. = phlogopite; R/b = Red-on-buff; R/br = Red-on-brown; Rec. = record; SP = striated polished; spec = specular; subhem. = subhemispherical; UP = uniformly polished

Table C.3. Unpainted, Red-Slipped Database

Record No.	Prov. No.	Ceramic Type	Interior Finish	Exterior Finish	Temper
1	78	red ware	slip, uniformly polished	slip, uniformly polished, fire clouded	sand/mica (< 50% phlog.)
2	78	red ware	slip, striated polished	slip, striated polished	sand
3	238	red ware	striated polished	slip, uniformly polished	sand/mica (< 50% phlog.)
4	111	San Francisco Red	slip, uniformly polished, fire clouded	slip, uniformly polished, fire clouded	sand
5	56	red ware	slip, striated polished	slip, striated polished, fire clouded	sand

Key: phlog. = phlogopite

Table C.4. Unpainted (Plain Ware) Rim Sherd Database

Rec. No.	Prov. No.	Ceramic Type	Interior Finish	Exterior Finish	Temper	Vessel Form	Rim Form	Rim Finish	Thickness (mm)	Interior Rim Diam. (cm)	Interior Throat Diam. (cm)	n	Modif.
1	219	Type II	HS	SP	sand/mica (<50% phlog.)	indet. jar	indet./na	rounded	6	indet./na	indet./na	1	none
2	219	Type II	HS	HS	sand	indet. jar	indet./na	rounded	7	indet./na	indet./na	1	none
3	219	Type II	HS, black	HS, black	sand	indet. jar	indet./na	rounded	7	indet./na	indet./na	1	none
4	219	Type II	UP, black	UP, black	sand	subhem. bowl	direct	rounded	7	18	18	1	none
5	219	Type II	UP	SP	sand	subhem. bowl	direct	flat	7	10	10	1	none
6	219	Type II	HS	SP	sand	neckless jar	direct	flat	7	8	8	1	none
7	219	Type II	HS, black	HS, fire cl	sand	indet. bowl	indet./na	rounded	7	indet./na	indet./na	1	none
8	219	Type II	UP	UP	sand	hem. bowl	slight evert	flat	5	indet./na	indet./na	1	burn
9	219	Type I	HS	scraped or wiped	sand	indet. bowl	indet./na	rounded	9	21	21	1	none
10	219	Type I	HS	HS	sand	neckless jar	direct	flat	7	13	13	1	none
...													
310	302	Type II	UP	UP	sand	indet. jar	indet./na	rounded	6	indet./na	indet./na	1	none
311	395	Type I	unfinished	unfinished	sand	indet.	indet./na	indet./na	7	indet./na	indet./na	1	none
312	171	Type II	HS, black	HS	sand	neckless jar	direct	rounded	5	10	10	1	none
313	567	red ware	slipped, SP	slipped, SP, fire cl	sand/mica (<50% phlog.)	subhem. bowl	direct	rounded	6	25	25	1	none
314	567	Type II	HS	HS	sand	indet.	indet./na	flat	9	indet./na	indet./na	1	none
315	238	Type III	scraped or wiped	SP	sand	flare-rimmed jar	mod. flare	int. bulge	5	20	17	1	none
316	238	Type II	SP	SP	sand	indet. bowl	indet./na	rounded	6	indet./na	indet./na	1	none
317	238	Type II	SP	SP, fire cl	sand	indet.	indet./na	rounded	6	indet./na	indet./na	1	none
318	238	Type II	scraped or wiped	HS	sand	indet. jar	indet./na	flat	6	indet./na	indet./na	1	none
319	238	Type II	HS	SP, fire cl	sand/mica (<50% phlog.)	indet. jar	indet./na	rounded	6	14	indet./na	1	burn
320	175	Type II	unfinished	scraped or wiped	sand	indet.	indet./na	rounded	6	indet./na	indet./na	1	none
321	175	Type IV	HS, black	SP	schist	indet.	indet./na	rounded	6	indet./na	indet./na	1	none
322	122	Type III	scraped or wiped	HS	sand	indet. jar	straight	rounded	6	18	18	1	none

Key: black = blackened; Diam. = diameter; fire cl = fire clouded; gran. = granitic; hem. = hemispherical; HS = hand smoothed; indet. = indeterminate; int. = interior; mod. = moderate; Modif. = modification; na = not applicable; phlog. = phlogopite; pro. = pronounced; Prov. = provenience; Rec. = record; Sp = striated polished; subhem. = subhemispherical; UP = uniformly polished

Table C.5. Unpainted (Plain Ware) Body Sherd Database

Record No.	Prov. No.	Ceramic Type	Interior Finish	Exterior Finish	Temper	Vessel Form	Vessel Part	n	Thickness (mm)
1	78	Type III	scraped or wiped	indet.	sand	indet.	indet. body	1	9
2	78	Type III	scraped or wiped	hand smoothed	sand	indet.	indet. body	1	5
3	78	Type III	unfinished	hand smoothed	sand	indet.	indet. body	1	6
4	78	Type III	scraped or wiped	hand smoothed	sand	indet.	indet. body	1	5
5	78	Type III	scraped or wiped	hand smoothed	sand	indet.	indet. body	1	5
6	78	Type III	hand smoothed	hand smoothed	sand	indet.	indet. body	1	7
7	78	Type IV	hand smoothed	striated polished	schist	indet.	indet. body	1	6
8	78	Type IV	hand smoothed	striated polished	schist	indet.	indet. body	1	4
9	78	Type II	striated polished	uniformly polished	sand	indet.	indet. body	1	5
10	78	Type II	striated polished, fire clouded	uniformly polished, fire clouded	sand/mica (<50% phlog.)	indet.	indet. body	1	1.1
...									
550	74	Type II	hand smoothed, blackened	hand smoothed	sand/mica (<50% phlog.)	indet.	indet. body	1	9
551	74	Type II	hand smoothed	uniformly polished	sand	indet.	indet. body	1	6
552	74	Type II	hand smoothed, fire clouded	uniformly polished, fire clouded	sand	indet.	indet. body	1	4
553	74	Type II	hand smoothed	uniformly polished	sand	indet.	indet. body	1	5
554	74	Type II	hand smoothed	uniformly polished	sand	indet.	indet. body	1	6
555	74	Type II	hand smoothed	uniformly polished	sand	indet.	indet. body	1	6
556	74	Type II	hand smoothed	uniformly polished	sand	indet.	indet. body	1	6
557	74	Type II	hand smoothed	hand smoothed	sand	indet.	indet. body	1	6
558	74	Type II	hand smoothed, blackened	hand smoothed	sand	indet.	indet. body	1	6
559	74	plain ware[a]	indet.	indet.	indet.	indet.	indet. body	66	indet.
560	72	Type III	scraped or wiped	hand smoothed, fire clouded	sand	indet.	indet. body	1	5
561	72	Type II	hand smoothed, blackened	uniformly polished, blackened	sand/mica (<50% phlog.)	indet.	indet. body	1	6

Key: indet. = indeterminate; phlog. = phlogopite
[a] Attributes were not recorded on plain ware body sherds smaller than a quarter dollar.

Descriptions of Locally Manufactured Painted Pottery

This section presents descriptions of several unusual, potentially "local," and heretofore undescribed ceramic entities from El Macayo. No attempt was made to define new types per se; instead, detailed descriptions of these ceramics are presented, including local red-on-brown, black-on-brown, purple-on-tan, and black-on-red. The identification of "local" painted ceramics at El Macayo was based largely on technological attributes. The format used to organize the descriptions follows the format pioneered by Colton (e.g., Colton and Hargrave 1937). It has been modified, however, so as not to be confused with a formal type description. As explained in Chapter 3, these sherds and one reconstructible vessel appear to have been locally produced. Further research, however, is needed prior to identifying manufacturing locale and establishing these ceramics as formal types. The following descriptions are presented in an effort to further our knowledge concerning the ceramics of the middle Santa Cruz River valley.

Local Red-on-brown and Local Black-on-brown

Designation: Local red-on-brown; local black-on-brown

Distribution: Middle Santa Cruz River valley: Nogales to Arivaca Junction, Arizona

Provenience: El Macayo, AZ EE:9:107 (ASM)

Period, Phase: Appears to be contemporaneous with the Hohokam Sedentary period

Time: ca. A.D. 1000–1150

Associated Ceramics: Rincon Red-on-brown, Trincheras Purple-on-red

Construction: Coil and hand modeled

Firing Atmosphere: Oxidizing to neutral

Paste:
Color: Light brown to an orange, reddish brown; 2.5YR 5/6, 5/8 red to a 5YR 6/6–6/8 reddish yellow (Munsell 1994). A carbon streak is often present.

Temper: Sand (well sorted)
   Texture: Medium-coarse to fine, subangular to subrounded particles
   Inclusions: 0.03–1 mm; opaque and translucent quartz dominate; pink and reddish granitic grains, and varying amounts of phlogopite mica

Fracture: Soft and rounded to medium hard and subangular

Walls: Uneven. Thickness: 0.6–1 cm

Finish: Variable; often unfinished prior to tool polishing, leaving coil marks in the low, unpolished areas; other sherds exhibit a greater degree of finishing, or obliteration of the coil joints, prior to tool polishing; in either case, the surface is uneven, which is most notable on bowl exteriors
   Color: Dark brown to tan; 7.5YR 5/6, 5/8 strong brown to 7.5YR 6/3, 6/4 light brown (Munsell 1994)
   Fire Clouds: Common

Forms: Bowls and jars

Decoration:
Local red-on-brown:
   Paint: Weak, watery red hematite pigment. Color: Red; 10R 5/8, 4/8 red (Munsell 1994)

Local black-on-brown:
   Paint: Weak, watery mineral pigment. Color: Black; 7.5YR 3/1 (Munsell 1994)

Design: All of the rim sherds have a painted lip. The design motifs are consistent with the design elements, motifs, and arrangements exhibited on Rincon Red-on-brown: paneled and plaited, straight line designs employing curvilinear and rectilinear scrolls, fringe, and solid triangular elements (see Figure 3.7). The execution of the design is sloppy and poorly done in comparison with Rincon Red-on-brown. Most of the sherds identified as local red-on-brown have the strongest stylistic similarities with the later stylistic expressions of Rincon Red-on-brown: Greenleaf's (1975:60) late variant of Rincon Red-on-brown at Punta De Agua, Deaver's (1984:262) Rincon Style C, and Wallace's (1985:121, 1986:53) Late Rincon Red-on-brown. The designs also share stylistic affinities with Withers's (1973:27) Topawa Red-on-brown and Greenleaf's (1975:54) Topawa Red-on-brown, Tucson variety (see McGuire 1982:182–184, for a discussion on the typological validity of Topawa Red-on-brown).

Comparisons: Rincon Red-on-brown and Rincon Black-on-brown have a denser paste; paddle-and-anvil construction; thick, even, red or black paint; and better execution of the design. Vamori Red-on-brown and Topawa Red-on-brown are similar stylistically but are paddle-and-anvil construction, with an even surface finish.

Remarks: No chronometric dates can be associated directly with these sherds; therefore, the above dates are based on design-style similarities shared with defined examples of Rincon Red-on-brown. Most of the sherds from El Macayo that were typed as local red-on-brown show an "openness" of the design field characteristic of the late Sedentary style in the Tucson Basin. All of the bowl sherds of this type in the collection have an interior design.

The characteristics that distinguish local red-on-brown from Rincon Red-on-brown sherds are strikingly similar to the characteristics that Di Peso (1956:321–323) used to distinguish Ramanote Red-on-brown from Tanque Verde Red-on-brown during his analysis of the pottery from the Paloparado site. He observed that the designs on Ramanote Red-on-brown were sloppily executed when compared with Tanque Verde Red-on-brown and that the paint was watery and less vivid. The local red-on-brown sherds from El Macayo may represent the antecedent to Ramanote Red-on-brown; together these types may express a local red-on-brown series spanning the Sedentary and Classic periods in the middle Santa Cruz River valley.

An inspection of the sherds from the Potrero Creek site (AZ EE:9:53 [ASM]) research collection, housed at the ASM, revealed that some of the sherds labeled as Rincon Red-on-brown conform with the description of the local red-on-brown sherds from El Macayo.

Local Purple-on-tan

Designation: Local purple-on-tan

Distribution: Middle Santa Cruz River valley: Nogales to Arivaca Junction, Arizona

Provenience: El Macayo, AZ EE:9:107 (ASM)

Period, Phase: Appears to be contemporaneous with the Hohokam Sedentary period

Time: ca. A.D.1000–1150

Associated Ceramics: Trincheras Purple-on-red, Nogales Polychrome, Trincheras Polychrome, Rincon Red-on-brown

Construction: Coil and hand modeled

Firing Atmosphere: Oxidizing to neutral

Paste:
Color: Reddish brown; 2.5YR 4/4 reddish brown, to 2.5YR 4/6 red (Munsell 1994). No carbon streak.

Temper: Sand
Texture: Fine to medium coarse, angular to subangular
Inclusions: 0.05–1.5 mm; opaque, translucent, and transparent quartz dominate; booklets and individual platelets of phlogopite mica; several small, dark silicate inclusions (possibly pyroxene, hornblende, or weathered garnet)

Fracture: Friable and rounded

Walls: Uneven. Thickness: 0.7 cm

Surface: Interior: tan or cream colored wash. Exterior: no slip or wash

Finish: Variable. Interior: hand smoothed, tool polished, uniform finish slightly undulating. Exterior: hand-smoothed, tool-polished, uneven-finish coil joints visible in low, unfinished areas
Color: Wash 10YR 7/3 or 7/4 very pale brown (Munsell 1994)
Fire Clouds: Common

Forms: Subhemispherical bowl

Decoration:
Paint: Iron rich, specular hematite (igneous or metamorphic). Color: Crimson; 10R 3/2–3/4 dusky red (Munsell 1994)

Design: Interior, poorly executed, repeated, curvilinear interlocking scrolls, painted lip, possibly a quartered layout

Comparisons: Trincheras Purple-on-red differs in its coil-and-scrape construction and absence of a cream-colored slip; Vamori Red-on-brown differs based on its paddle-and-anvil construction and the use of a red, ocherous hematite paint; the apparently local red-on-brown pottery from El Macayo (see previous description) differs in its use of a red hematite pigment for paint and lack of a slip or wash. Di Peso's (1956:361) Nogales Purple-on-red, a variant of the Trincheras series, was defined based on its "tan base color and in being much better made." This latter characteristic would clearly distinguish it from the above described purple-on-tan.

Remarks: A partial bowl was recovered from Feature 144.03 (see Figure 3.8). This subhemispherical bowl was technologically identical to local red-on-brown pottery in every respect other than the application of a tan wash and the purple/red specular paint. The design style, apparently consisting of large, repeated interlocking scrolls, is consistent with designs on Trincheras Purple-on-red (see Di Peso 1956:Plate 99), although the poor draftsmanship of the design is more consistent with the local red-on-brown pottery.

Reinhard (1978:237) describes two vessels, recovered from cremations at AZ EE:9:68 in Nogales, that correspond technologically and stylistically to the purple-on-tan vessel from El Macayo.

Local Black-on-red

Designation: Local black-on-red

Distribution: Middle Santa Cruz River valley: Nogales to Arivaca Junction, Arizona

Provenience: El Macayo, AZ EE:9:107 (ASM)

Period, Phase: Appears to be contemporaneous with the Hohokam Sedentary period

Time: circa A.D. 1000–1150

Associated Ceramics: Local red-on-brown (see previous description); Nogales Polychrome; Rincon Red-on-brown; Trincheras Purple-on-red

Construction: Coiled and smoothed

Firing Atmosphere: Oxidizing to neutral

Paste:
Color: Reddish brown; 2.5YR 4/8, 5/8 red and 2.5YR 5/4, 5/3 reddish brown (Munsell 1994)

Temper: Sand (well sorted)
Texture: Medium fine sand, with subangular to rounded particles
Inclusions: 0.05–1 mm; opaque quartz is most abundant (translucent quartz is present); reddish granitic grains, dark-subangular to rounded-silicate particles (possibly pyroxene hornblende or weathered garnet), and a few, small individual platelets of phlogopite mica

Fracture: Medium hard and angular with some rounding

Walls: Striated. Thickness: 0.5–7 cm

Surface: Red slip, interior and exterior approximately 0.02–0.03 mm thick
Finish: Zonal, striated polish, no polishing over the decoration. Color: Red; 10R 4/6, 4/8 red (Munsell 1994)
Fire Clouds: None

Forms: Bowls only

Decoration:
Paint: Dark blackish brown, mineral pigment. Color: 2.5Y 2.5/1 black to 7.5YR 3/1 very dark gray (Munsell 1994)

Design: Only one sherd was large enough to provide information on its design (see Figure 3.9). This partial vessel had a thin band painted midway down the interior of the vessel, with large solid diamonds centered along the band at regular intervals. This simple-banded design shows little stylistic similarities with any previously described pottery type.

Comparisons: Trincheras Purple-on-red can be distinguished from this black-on-red pottery based on the color of the slip, and the color of the mineral pigment used as paint.

Remarks: Although only five local black-on-red sherds, representing two bowls (see Figure 3.9), were found at El Macayo, these ceramics merit special recognition because of the possibility that they represent a "hybrid" of several regional ceramic traditions. The simple banded design (although the elements are unique) is similar to that of Trincheras Purple-on-red. The slip, in color and appearance, has affinities to some of the contemporary red wares (e.g., Rincon Red) as well as later Papaguería red wares (e.g., Sells Red, Valshni Red). These black-on-red sherds may be related to the appearance of red wares and polychromes (with red-slipped surfaces), which occurs during the middle to late Sedentary period in the Tucson Basin, contemporaneous with El Macayo.

APPENDIX D

Additional Stone Artifact Data

Anthony Della Croce

Table D.1. Example of a Portion of the Flaked Stone Debitage Database

PD No.	Material	Cortex (% Coverage)	Color	Size Class [a]	Debitage Type	Platform Type	Complete-ness	Edge Damage?	Heat Treated?	n
61	aphanitic igneous	0	n/a	2	tertiary	single facet	proximal	no	no	1
61	chert	0	brown	2	tertiary	single facet	complete	no	no	1
61	chert	0	brown	2	tertiary	single facet	proximal	no	no	1
61	chert	0	gray	2	tertiary	single facet	complete	no	no	1
61	chert	0	gray	2	tertiary	single facet	proximal	no	no	1
61	chert	0	gray	3	indet.	none	fragmented	no	no	1
61	chert	0	gray	3	tertiary	single facet	complete	no	no	1
61	metamorphic	0	n/a	4	tertiary	single facet	split	no	no	1
61	rhyolite	0	n/a	2	indet.	none	fragmented	no	no	1
61	rhyolite	0	n/a	2	tertiary	single facet	complete	no	no	1
61	rhyolite	0	n/a	4	indet.	none	fragmented	no	no	1
68	aphanitic igneous	0	n/a	2	tertiary	single facet	complete	no	no	1
68	aphanitic igneous	1–90	n/a	4	secondary	cortical	complete	no	no	1
68	aphanitic igneous	1–90	n/a	7	tertiary	single facet	complete	no	no	1
68	chert	0	brown	2	indet.	none	fragmented	no	no	1
. . .										
294	rhyolite	0	n/a	3	tertiary	single facet	complete	no	no	1
294	rhyolite	0	n/a	4	indet.	none	fragmented	no	no	1
294	rhyolite	0	n/a	4	indet.	none	fragmented	no	no	1
294	rhyolite	0	n/a	4	tertiary	single facet	complete	no	no	1
294	rhyolite	0	n/a	4	tertiary	single facet	complete	no	no	1
294	rhyolite	0	n/a	4	tertiary	single facet	complete	no	no	1
294	rhyolite	0	n/a	5	tertiary	none	distal	no	no	1
294	sandstone	0	n/a	3	tertiary	single facet	proximal	no	no	1
301	rhyolite	0	n/a	3	tertiary	single facet	complete	yes	no	1
302	rhyolite	0	n/a	5	tertiary	single facet	complete	yes	no	1

Key: indet. = indeterminate; n/a = not applicable; PD = provenience designation
[a] Size classes are as follows: 1 = 0–1 cm; 2 = 1–2 cm; 3 = 2–3 cm; 4 = 3–4 cm; 5 = 4–5 cm; 6 = 5–6 cm; 7 = 6–7 cm; 8 = 7–8 cm; 9 = 8–9 cm; 10 = 9–10 cm.

Table D.2. Example of a Portion of the Flaked Stone Shatter Database

PD No.	Material	Color	Size Class [a]	n
74	rhyolite	n/a	2	1
74	aphanitic igneous	n/a	1	1
74	aphanitic igneous	n/a	1	1
74	aphanitic igneous	n/a	3	1
74	chert	gray	1	1
74	chert	gray	1	1
74	chert	gray	2	1
74	chert	gray	3	1
74	chert	gray	3	1
74	chert	gray	3	1
74	chert	brown	2	1
74	chert	white	2	1
. . .				
285	aphanitic igneous	n/a	2	1
285	chert	gray	2	1
301	chalcedony	n/a	2	1
288	chert	gray	2	1
288	chert	gray	2	1
288	chert	gray	2	1
294	phaneritic igneous	n/a	2	1
294	rhyolite	n/a	2	1
294	rhyolite	n/a	2	1
177	rhyolite	n/a	2	1
177	rhyolite	n/a	2	1
177	aphanitic igneous	n/a	2	1
177	chert	gray	2	1
177	chert	gray	2	1
177	chert	gray	3	1

Key: n/a = not applicable; PD = provenience designation
[a] Size classes are as follows: 1 = 0–1 cm; 2 = 1–2 cm; 3 = 2–3 cm.

Table D.3. Example of a Portion of the Ground Stone Database

PD No.	Type	Plan View	Material	Texture	Condition	Pigment?	Heat Treated?	Manufacture	Degree Manufacture	Use Type	Multiple Use	Use Surfaces (n)	Length (cm)	Width (cm)	Thickness (cm)	n
1	grinding slab	ovoid	igneous	medium	whole	no	no	abraded	min. shaping	single	n/a	1	52.0	38.0	20.0	1
52	grinding slab	irregular	granite	coarse	whole	no	no	abraded	mod. shaping	single	n/a	1	35.0	28.0	19.0	1
52	pendant	irregular	unknown	medium	whole	no	no	abraded	mod. shaping	single	n/a	n/a	1.8	0.5	0.5	1
56	basin mano	square	igneous	medium	whole	no	no	abraded	mod. shaping	single	n/a	1	15.4	9.7	3.6	1
56	flat mano or hand stone	square	igneous	medium	whole	no	no	pecked & abraded	mod. shaping	single	n/a	2, opposite	14.0	9.9	3.4	1
57	metate	broken	granite	coarse	incomplete	no	no	abraded	indet.	single	n/a	indet.	n/a	n/a	n/a	1
67	mano	broken	igneous	coarse	incomplete	no	yes, light	indet.	indet.	indet.	n/a	indet.	n/a	n/a	n/a	1
78	3/4 groove axe	irregular	igneous	fine	whole	no	no	pecked & abraded	exten. shaping	single	n/a	2, opposite	12.7	7.5	5.2	1
78	bead	cylindrical	igneous	fine	whole	no	no	drilled	exten. shaping	single	n/a	n/a	1.0	0.6	0.6	1
78	bordered palette	square	igneous	fine	whole	yes	no		mod. shaping	indet.	n/a	n/a	5.6	4.8	0.9	1
78	mano	broken	igneous	coarse	incomplete	no	no	abraded	indet.	indet.	n/a	indet.	n/a	n/a	n/a	1
78	pendant	spherical	chert	medium	whole	no	no	drilled	exten. shaping	single	n/a	n/a	1.8	1.8	0.6	1
78	polishing stone	rectangular	igneous	fine	whole	no	no	pecked & abraded	exten. shaping	multiple	pestle	multiple	7.0	2.5	2.5	1
...																
322	metate	broken	andesite	indet.	incomplete	no	yes, light	indet.	indet.	indet.	n/a	1	n/a	n/a	n/a	29
322	metate	broken	andesite	indet.	incomplete	no	yes, light	indet.	indet.	indet.	n/a	1	n/a	n/a	n/a	1
322	metate	broken	andesite	indet.	incomplete	no	yes, light	indet.	indet.	indet.	n/a	1	n/a	n/a	n/a	6
322	metate	broken	andesite	indet.	incomplete	no	yes, light	indet.	indet.	indet.	n/a	1	n/a	n/a	n/a	1
325	metate	broken	igneous	medium	incomplete	no	no	indet.	indet.	indet.	n/a	1	n/a	n/a	n/a	1
326	basin mano	irregular	igneous	medium	whole	no	no	natural	min. shaping	single	n/a	1	16.5	9.0	4.7	1
330	basin metate	broken	granite	medium	incomplete	no	yes, light	pecked & abraded	mod. shaping	single	n/a	1	33.0	38.0	20.0	1
409	basin mano	ovoid	igneous	medium	whole	no	no	abraded	mod. shaping	single	n/a	1	14.6	10.2	4.7	1
464	bead	cylindrical	turquoise	fine	whole	no	no		exten. shaping	single	n/a	n/a	0.7	0.7	0.3	1
564	basin mano	disk	granite	medium	whole	no	no	abraded	mod. shaping	single	n/a	1	14.4	13.2	3.0	1
572	mano	irregular	igneous	medium	whole	no	yes, light	abraded	min. shaping	single	n/a	2, opposite	14.0	10.6	8.2	1

Key: exten. = extensive; indet. = indeterminate; min. = minimal; mod. = moderate; PD = provenience designation

APPENDIX E

Shell Analysis Recording Form

Sharon F. Urban

SHELL ARTIFACT—DETAILED ANALYSIS *SANTAC*

Site: __E E : 0 9 : 1 0 7__ (ASM) Locus: ___ Feature: ___ ___ ___ Subfeat.: ___ ___ ___ . ___ ___

North: ___ 1 0 7 . 9 9 - ___ ___ ___ . ___ ___

E : ___ 1 1 8 . 0 9 - ___ ___ ___ . ___ ___   Feature Type: ___ ___ ___

Stratum: ___ II / Cult ___ Level: 0 4   Unit #: I P 7 1

Prov.Bag: ___ 7 8 . ___ ___   Coll. Type: S 4   Age: ___ ___ ___ . ___

Comments: Cat # 90   Recovery S4   Depth 10.78   Depth II 10.98

Genus/Species: *Spondylus / chama* ___ Code: ___

Description: A slightly beveled circular shaped bead/pendant from the dorsal margin of the shell. The bead/pendant was formed by grinding both the exterior + interior and biconically drilling a perforation in the middle of the shell. The interior side has some of vesicula-pumice like appearance that the other side has. One side of the interior has a natural deep pit, the other side of the interior has the mussel scar. With in these two natural features the shell has the characteristic markings of Spondylus/Chama pinkish-purple coloration (and perhaps a tinge of yellow orange — But not the bright orange that would make it very Spondylus).

Artifact Code: ___ ___

Whole Valve Bead- ___
Disk Bead- ___
Cylindrical Bead- ___
Other Bead- ___
Whole Valve Pendant- ___
Geometric Pendant- ___
Zoomorphic Pendant- ___
Anthro. Pendant- ___
Other Pendant- *Bead*
Plain Bracelet- ___
Decorated Bracelet- ___
Bracelet In Process- ___
Plain Ring- ___
Decorated Ring- ___
Ring In Process- ___
Geometric- ___
Carved Shell- ___
Perforated Shell- ___
Utilitarian- ___
Other: ___ - ___
Manufacturing Residue - ___
Wk. Frag. - Unknown Form- ___
Unworked Fragment- ___
Whole Shell- ___

Measurements: 18.33 x 17.92 x 6.76   Diameter: 3.00
Weight: 2.4 grams   Percent: 100 %

Condition: Good   Photo #:

Drawing:

Portion of band remaining

Portion of valve employed (if known)

Shurban

Site No.:	AZ EE:9:107(ASM)	Object:	Bracelet/Pendant
Provenience:	Feat 15; Quad 1	Species:	Glycymeris
Field No.:	PD 571	Origin:	Gulf of California
Date Found:	Not given.	Length:	6.55cms
Recorder:	Not given.	Diameter: Width:	6.25cms
Date Analyzed:	July 1, 1996	Height: Thickness:	0.55cms

Description: Specimen is complete. It is ring shaped in plan view while being

biplanar in cross-section. Both the upper and lower surfaces as well as the inner edge

have been ground to shape. Upper surface grinding has been such that the inflated umbo

has been reduced to a mere projection at the back of the shell. There is a conical

hole in the beak from the interior edge. Specimen is much reduced from the original

valve and is quite flat. Exterior surface has two sections of the band that have been

carved with two sets of parallel notches (both "u" and "v" shaped grooves) that are

diagonally across the surface of the band, but are not parallel. Color is an off

white.

Bracelet – portion of
band remaining

Portion of valve employed
(if known)

Drawings: Plan view done to scale with use
surface(s) indicated in red.

Scale 1:1

x

Table F.1. Example of a Portion of the Unworked Bone Database

Case	Feature No.	PD No.	Cat. No.	Class	Taxon	Size	Body Part	Portion	Side	Fusion	Breakage	% Present[a]	Burning	Gnawing	Working	Weathering	n
1	186	563	562	mammal	Canis sp.	medium	tibia (distal)	distal	left	fused	new breaks	75	unburned	absent	none	unkn.	1
2	186	563	562	mammal	Canis sp.	medium	radius (proximal)	proximal	right	fused	new breaks	75	unburned	absent	none	unkn.	1
3	186	563	562	mammal	Canis sp.	medium	ulna (proximal)	shaft	right	unkn. or n/a	old & new breaks	50	unburned	absent	none	unkn.	1
4	186	563	562	mammal	Canis sp.	medium	ulna (proximal)	proximal	right	fused	new breaks	15	unburned	absent	none	unkn.	1
5	186	563	562	mammal	Canis sp.	medium	radius (distal)	distal	left	fused	new breaks	25	unburned	absent	none	unkn.	1
6	186	563	562	mammal	Canis sp.	medium	radius (proximal)	proximal	left	fused	new breaks	25	unburned	present	none	unkn.	1
7	186	563	562	mammal	Canis sp.	medium	tibia-tibiotarsus (shaft or complete)	distal	right	unkn. or n/a	old breaks	30	unburned	present	none	unkn.	1
8	186	563	562	mammal	Canis sp.	medium	ilium	fragment	right	unkn. or n/a	indet. breaks	15	unburned	absent	none	unkn.	1
9	186	563	562	mammal	Canis sp.	medium	ulna (distal)	distal	right	fused	new breaks	30	unburned	absent	none	unkn.	1
10	186	563	562	mammal	Canis sp.	medium	metatarsal-tarsometatarsus (shaft or complete)	complete	left	fused	none	100	unburned	absent	none	unkn.	6
⋮																	
186	213	307	299	mammal	unidentified	very small–small	indet.	fragment	unkn.	unkn. or n/a	old breaks		unburned	absent	none	good condition	1
187	0	122	149	mammal	Lepus californicus	small	metatarsal-tarsometatarsus (shaft or complete)	complete	unkn.	fused	none	100	unburned	absent	none	good condition	1
188	0	122	149	mammal	Artiodactyla	large	tibia-tibiotarsus (shaft or complete)	shaft	unkn.	unkn. or n/a	old & new breaks	10	unburned	absent	none	good condition	1
189	151	242	505	mammal	Artiodactyla	large	longbone (indet.)	fragment	unkn.	unkn. or n/a	old & new breaks		unburned	absent	none	good condition	1
190	40	255	306	mammal	Rodentia	very small	femur (shaft or complete)	shaft	unkn.	unfused or immature	none	90	unburned	absent	none	good condition	1

243

Case	Feature No.	PD No.	Cat. No.	Class	Taxon	Size	Body Part	Portion	Side	Fusion	Breakage	% Present [a]	Burning	Gnawing	Working	Weathering	n
191	40	255	306	mammal	Rodentia	very small	tibia-tibiotarsus (shaft or complete)	shaft	unkn.	unfused or immature	none	90	unburned	absent	none	good condition	1
192	40	255	306	mammal	Rodentia	very small	longbone (indet.)	shaft	unkn.	unfused or immature	none	60	unburned	absent	none	good condition	1
193	40	255	306	mammal	Rodentia	very small	ribs-carapace	shaft	unkn.	unkn. or n/a	old breaks		unburned	absent	none	good condition	9
194	212.96	475	722	mammal	Artiodactyla	large	antler/horn core	fragment	unkn.	unkn. or n/a	old breaks		possible heat alteration	present	none	slightly weathered	1
195	16	175	280	mammal	Artiodactyla	large	vertebra, thoracic	fragment	axial	unkn. or n/a	old & new breaks	10	unburned	absent	none	good condition	1
196	16	175	280	mammal	Artiodactyla	large	vertebra (indet.)	fragment	axial	unkn. or n/a	old & new breaks	10	unburned	absent	none	good condition	1
197	212.70	556	263	mammal	unidentified	large	longbone (indet.)	fragment	unkn.	unkn. or n/a	old breaks		unburned	absent	none	slightly weathered	1
198	0	105	104	mammal	unidentified	large	ribs-carapace	anterior	unkn.	unkn. or n/a	old & new breaks		unburned	present	none	slightly weathered	1
199	0	105	104	mammal	unidentified	medium–large	longbone (indet.)	fragment	unkn.	unkn. or n/a	old breaks		possible heat alteration	absent	none	good condition	1
200	212.16	395	645	unknown	unidentified	small	longbone (indet.)	fragment	unkn.	unkn. or n/a	old & new breaks		unburned	absent	none	good condition	1
201	51	258	401	mammal	unidentified	small	longbone (indet.)	shaft	unkn.	unkn. or n/a	old breaks		unburned	absent	none	good condition	1
202	151	242	241	unknown	unidentified	unkn.	indet.	fragment	unkn.	unkn. or n/a	indet. breaks		unrecorded	unrec.	unrec.	unrecorded	1
203	151	242	241	mammal	unidentified	very small	ribs-carapace	fragment	unkn.	unkn. or n/a	old breaks		unburned	absent	none	good condition	1
204	0	68	39	reptile	*Gopherus agassizi*	medium	plastron	posterior	unkn.	unkn. or n/a	old & new breaks	5	unburned	absent	none	good condition	1
205	144	294	477	unknown	unidentified	very small–small	longbone (indet.)	fragment	unkn.	unkn. or n/a	new breaks		unburned	absent	none	good condition	1
206	0	106	113	mammal	unidentified	unkn.	longbone (indet.)	fragment	unkn.	unkn. or n/a	old breaks	—	unburned	absent	none	good condition	1

Key: indet. = indeterminate; unkn. = unknown; unrec. = unrecorded
[a] Percentages recorded in increments of 5 percent

Archaeomagnetic Sampling, Analysis, and Dating at El Macayo

William L. Deaver & Barbara A. Murphy

Introduction

Archaeomagnetic dating samples were collected from three hearths at El Macayo (AZ EE:9:107 ASM; Site Latitude: 31.37° N; Site Longitude: 249.07° E; Magnetic Declination: 12.5° E). Each hearth represents a pit structure. The available archaeological information (Table G.1) indicates that these features may range in age from the Early Formative to the Middle Formative period (ca. A.D. 650–1150). The only firm chronological information available is that Feature 44 was constructed after Feature 52. Two of the three samples yielded archaeomagnetic results that we consider reliable; the sample from Feature 43 did not exhibit a coherent magnetic signal. Archaeomagnetic dates are consistent with the expected ages (Table G.2). These dates indicate that Feature 44 probably dated to the later part of the Middle Formative period and that Feature 52 was slightly older but still within the Middle Formative period. Statistical comparison of the archaeomagnetic signals corresponding to Features 44 and 52 indicates that these two abandonment events occurred at detectably different points in time. The statistical comparison and the values of the archaeomag-

netic dates are consistent with the archaeological evidence that Feature 52 was abandoned some time before Feature 44 was constructed.

Principles of Archaeomagnetic Dating

Two fundamental principles underlie archaeomagnetic dating. The first principle is that many desert sediments contain ferromagnetic minerals that, under certain conditions, will acquire a magnetic remanence parallel to the prevailing magnetic field. The most common situation is when sediments and soils at archaeological sites were heated to relatively high temperatures, such as occurred with the use of hearths and cooking pits, or such as occurred during the destruction of a structure by fire (for more information on this and other processes see Aitken 1974; Butler 1992; Eighmy and Howard 1991; Eighmy and Sternberg 1990; Irving 1964; McElhinny 1973; Sternberg 1982, 1990; Tarling 1983). The magnetic remanence is acquired upon

Table G.1. Archaeological Contexts for Archaeomagnetic Samples from El Macayo

Sample Number	Sample Context	Archaeological Phase or Period	Estimated Calendrical Age
-1ua	Feature 44.01: pit house hearth	Middle Formative	A.D. 725–1150
-2ua	Feature 52.01: pit house hearth	Middle Formative	A.D. 725–1150
-3ua	Feature 43.01: pit house hearth	Early or Middle Formative	A.D. 650–1150

Note: All sample numbers prefixed with the site number AZ EE:9:107 (ASM).

Table G.2. Calendrical Archaeomagnetic Dates

Sample Number	Sample Context	Archaeomagnetic Dates at 95% Confidence
-1ua	Feature 44.01	A.D. 1005 (1150) 1245
-2ua	Feature 52.01	A.D. 930 (950, 975) 1020
-3ua	Feature 43.01	no date

Note: All sample numbers prefixed with the site number AZ EE:9:107 (ASM).

cooling, and once established, this magnetization is stable and enduring.

The second principle is that the direction and strength of the prevailing magnetic field is constantly changing, a phenomenon referred to as *secular variation*. Although both the direction and strength of the magnetic field change, archaeomagnetic studies in the southwestern United States have concentrated on documenting directional secular variation. Changes in the direction of the magnetic field are typically monitored by shifts in the apparent location of the magnetic north pole. Change in the apparent location of the magnetic north pole is commonly referred to as *polar drift* or *polar wander*. Because of polar wander, each archaeomagnetic remanence is an observation of the apparent location of the magnetic north pole at a specific point in time.

We refer to the moment that the remanence is acquired as the *archaeomagnetic event*. To have meaning in archaeological analyses, we must associate the archaeomagnetic event with a specific archaeological event.[1] In the case of hearths and cooking pits that were probably reused, we assume that each heating and cooling cycle successfully erased any previously acquired magnetization and a new remanence was acquired. Following this logic, the recorded remanence represents the last heating and cooling cycle associated with that feature. When these firepits are associated with structures, we assume that the last use and abandonment of the hearth corresponds to the abandonment of the structure. In the case of samples collected from walls and floors heated during the burning of structures, the archaeomagnetic event is clearly equivalent to the destruction event. In most situations the archaeomagnetic event probably corresponds to an archaeological abandonment event, but at the most unresolved level, the archaeomagnetic event represents some archaeological event that occurred sometime within the use life of the archaeological feature.

Experimental Methods

An archaeomagnetic sample consists of a set of individually oriented and measured specimens obtained from the baked archaeological sediments. We follow standard sampling procedures as described by Eighmy (1990) and apply laboratory procedures well established at the Paleomagnetic Laboratory, Department of Geosciences, University of Arizona.

We have adopted a sample designation protocol similar to that used by the Archaeometric Laboratory at Colorado State University. Most archaeological sites from which we have obtained archaeomagnetic samples have been assigned unique designations in inventories maintained by private, local, state, or federal agencies. The archaeomagnetic sample number is prefaced with this site inventory designation. Within each archaeological site, samples are numbered sequentially. In Arizona, sites often have been assigned designations in several inventory systems. When this occurs, we use the site designation that will be used in the archaeological report in which the archaeomagnetic data will appear. On occasion, we obtain samples from a site that was previously studied by Colorado State University. In these situations, we attempt to assign a series of numbers that do not duplicate the previous sample numbers. To avoid potential duplication, we suffix our sample number with the initials "ua" to indicate that the sample was measured at the Archaeomagnetic Program, University of Arizona.

Typically, 12 specimens were collected from baked sediments or soil representing the same archaeomagnetic event. Each specimen was carefully isolated from the remaining matrix and was surrounded by an aluminum mold. The mold was leveled and filled with plaster encasing each specimen. This procedure preserved the integrity of the specimens and allowed us to control for the orientations of the molds. The azimuth of the mold surrounding each specimen was always measured relative to magnetic north using a Brunton compass. The axis along which the azimuth was measured, the sample number, and the specimen designation were etched into the plaster on top of the specimen. Weather permitting, the azimuth was also measured using a sun compass. When corrected for the geographic location, time of year, and time of day, the sun azimuth provides the orientation of the specimen relative to true north. The difference between the magnetic and sun azimuths is the *local magnetic declination* at the time of sampling. We averaged the individual differences between the sun and magnetic azimuths to obtain an *average magnetic declination* for the sampling sites. We have opted for this procedure because we do not always obtain a sun azimuth for each specimen. The local magnetic declination is determined by taking the average difference between the sun and magnetic azimuths for all samples from the archaeological site.

After collection, the samples were returned to the laboratory and stored in a magnetically shielded room with an average field intensity < 200 nT. During analysis, all specimens were stored in a Mu metal shield for additional protection. All measurements were made with a cryogenic magnetometer. Initially, we measured the natural remanent magnetization (NRM) of each specimen and then computed preliminary sample averages to evaluate the cohesiveness of the NRM. Our experience has been that samples characterized by large variance rarely improve during further analysis and probably represent materials that have a weak and unreliable remanence (Sternberg 1982). Even if we recover a measurable archaeomagnetic remanence, the poor precision makes archaeomagnetic dating useless. Sample means with very large confidence intervals (for example $\alpha 95 \geq 9°$) at NRM are not analyzed beyond the NRM stage.

The magnetic profiles of archaeomagnetic samples from the Southwest are fairly consistent. Experimental evidence indicates that magnetite or titanomagnetite is the primary carrier of the remanence (Sternberg 1982:34–37). The archaeomagnetic signal that we are interested in is often overlain by a weaker secondary component acquired during the several hundred years of burial. Alternating field (AF) demagnetization is a useful and appropriate means of removing the secondary magnetization (Sternberg 1990:20). All specimens are demagnetized at peak AF strengths of 2.5, 5.0, 7.5, 10, 15, 20, 30, 40, 50, 60, 70, and 80 mT. This series of measurements provides a broad spectrum of data for evaluating the magnetic profile of each specimen. The results of AF demagnetization are analyzed by principal component analysis (Kirschvink 1980) to obtain the declination and inclination of the remanence for each specimen. No fewer than four demagnetization steps are used, and only specimens with minimum angular deviations of less than 5.0° are considered reliable and are used for computing the sample means.

Sample means were obtained by averaging the individual specimen directions using statistical methods based on the Fisherian distribution of points on a sphere. Use of these methods is long established in paleomagnetic studies (Fisher 1953; Irving 1964; McElhinny 1973). Specimens that exhibited irregular demagnetization behavior or that deviated excessively from the other specimens were considered as potential outliers. Each was evaluated individually for physical or experimental evidence to explain the deviation. If there was corroborating evidence that one specimen was different from the others, it was deleted from computation of the final mean. If there was no physical or experimental

evidence, the specimen was evaluated as a potential statistical outlier. Specimens that deviated from the mean by more than 3 standard deviations were considered as outliers and were deleted from computation of the mean. By convention, a virtual geomagnetic pole (VGP) is computed for each sample mean direction (Shuey et al. 1970). The resulting VGP is a standardized measure that facilitates comparison of data from across a relatively large region.

Archaeomagnetic Dating

Because of polar wander, each archaeomagnetically determined VGP has a temporal moment that we refer to as T. It is the value of T that we try to ascertain through archaeomagnetic dating. We make a distinction between two types of archaeomagnetic dating: *calendrical dating* and *relative dating*. The primary difference between calendrical and relative dating is not in the analytical methods, but in the referents. The objective in calendrical dating is to determine when events occurred according to the modern Christian calendar by reference to a master polar wander curve that has been independently calibrated. The objective in relative dating is to determine when archaeological events occurred relative to other archaeomagnetically documented archaeological events. These two forms of dating are similar, but each addresses different kinds of chronological questions, and each is capable of achieving different levels of chronological resolution. Relative dating is the most straightforward and is the more refined temporal method. If a researcher's goal is to associate the age of an archaeomagnetic event to a cultural chronology, or to differentiate between contemporaneous and noncontemporaneous events, or to order archaeological events, relative dating is the most appropriate choice. If a researcher's goal is to determine when an archaeological event occurred in years A.D./B.C., then the calendrical approach is more appropriate.

Calendrical Dating

Calendrical dating is a pattern-matching technique similar to dendrochronological dating and is not a radiometric technique such as radiocarbon dating (Sternberg 1990). Therefore, determining the age of an archaeomagnetic event of unknown age requires first having a master reconstruction of the pattern of ancient polar wander that is calibrated in years A.D./B.C. The polar wander path, or "master dating curve" as it is often called, is constructed from archaeological contexts where the age of the archaeomagnetic events can be estimated by independently derived dates. In the Southwest, these independent dates are produced by dendrochronology, radiocarbon assays, or cross-dated ceramic associations.[2]

We used the SWCV590 dating curve developed by the Archaeometric Laboratory at Colorado State University (Eighmy 1991) to date these samples. This curve is constructed using Sternberg's (1982:59–64; see also Sternberg and McGuire 1990) moving-window method with 40-year windows advanced by 25-year intervals. Although this is not the only dating curve that has been developed, it is the curve most widely used. Consequently, we maintain its use to foster comparability with the archaeomagnetic dates presented by Colorado State University.

We have adopted a format for the presentation of the calendrical dates that is similar to that for modern radiocarbon calibrations: A.D. 950 (1000) 1050. This date consists of a 95 percent confidence interval surrounding a *best-fit* date.[3] We apply the mathematical dating procedure established by Sternberg (1982:104–105; see also Sternberg and McGuire 1990) to obtain the 95 percent confidence interval. This procedure applies the statistical methods of McFadden and Lowes (1981) for the comparison of paleomagnetic directions.[4] The statistics are all interpreted at the 0.05 significance level, and the dates associated with the master VGPs are applied to the VGP of unknown age following the guidelines suggested by Sternberg.

The best-fit date is intended as a measure of the central tendency of the 95 percent confidence date. Because the ancient pattern of polar wander appears as a squiggly line on the surface of the earth, sample VGPs rarely intercept the polar wander curve, but rather tend to cluster around this curve. Although the best-fit date is not the interception of the measured value with the polar wander curve, it does represent the point along the polar wander curve to which the sample VGP is most similar. Our objective in presenting the best-fit date is to present information about the inherent structure of the 95 percent confidence date range.

We obtain the best-fit date by calculating the angular distance between the sample VGP and the master VGPs comprising the dating curve; we refer to this statistic as *angle*. The best-fit date is that segment of the master dating curve for which angle takes on the minimum value. Typically in evaluating the values for angle, we encounter one of two situations. The first type is what we refer to as the "unimodal situation." Within each 95 percent confidence date, there is one minimum value with all other values becoming progressively larger on either side of this minimum. These are straightforward to interpret; the value of the best-fit date is the midpoint of the age window associated with the master VGP at this minimum value. The second type is what we refer to as the "bimodal situation." The plot of the angles exhibits two major troughs of differing magnitudes. These troughs result because the curve loops back on itself. When archaeomagnetic dates span these loops, we often encounter the bimodal situation. One minimum value

represents the best fit on the early side of the loop, and the other represents the best fit on the late side of the loop. As an example, given a 95 percent date range of A.D. 930–1350, the best-fit dates may be A.D. 1025 and 1300. These are the smallest values obtained on either side of A.D. 1150, which represents the apex of the A.D. 1000–1200 loop (see Eighmy 1991). Occasionally there are other minor troughs as well, but we are only interested in the minimum values on either side of the loops. The best-fit date represents the central tendency of the 95 percent confidence date, and we include it to illustrate that the 95 percent confidence dates are not necessarily symmetrical.[5]

Calendrical dating, as it is currently implemented, has three limitations for resolving the age of archaeomagnetic events. The first and most common limitation is that multiple, mutually exclusive, date options may be assigned to a single archaeomagnetic VGP. We cannot distinguish archaeomagnetically which date option is most correct. It is the responsibility of the archaeologists to evaluate these date options against other lines of evidence to determine the most probable date. The second limitation is that the resolution of archaeomagnetic dates is not directly proportional to the uncertainty of the sample VGP. Rather the resolution is dependent upon the period of time to which the unknown sample dates, the precision of the dating curve, and the distance of the sample VGP from the curve (Sternberg et al. 1990). Increasing the number of specimens to provide for a more accurate and precise estimation of the VGP for a critical context will not result in a more precise archaeomagnetic date using this mathematical dating method. A third limitation is that often seemingly strong and reliable archaeomagnetic determinations do not date. In recent years we have observed that this phenomenon tends to occur with samples expected to date to the periods ca. A.D. 800 and ca. A.D. 1100. Although the moving-window method used to generate the polar wander curve has the desirable effect of reducing errors associated with independently dating archaeomagnetic events, it also has the undesirable effect of smoothing some of the real variation in the polar wander path. In the case of the A.D. 800 and A.D. 1100 loops, the effect is to reduce the magnitude of these loops. Precisely measured samples that fall along these loops may not date because the polar wander curve underestimates the course of polar wander.

Relative Dating

In relative dating we apply many of the same methods and procedures used in calendrical dating, but the referents are different. The location of each VGP_i is taken as a proxy for the age, T_i, of the associated archaeological event. For a set of VGPs (VGP_1, VGP_2, ... VGP_n) there is an equivalent set of temporal moments (T_1, T_2, ... T_n). Thus, the spatial relationships among the VGPs are equivalent to the temporal relationships among the associated archaeological events. We can then evaluate a hypothesis such as $T_1 = T_2$ by evaluating the equivalent hypothesis that $VGP_1 = VGP_2$. Similarly, based on the assumption that polar wander will tend to be linear over short periods of time, we can identify the linear trajectory inherent in a distribution of VGPs and arrange them into an objective relative sequence based on the position of the VGPs relative to the linear trajectory.

Assessing Contemporaneity of Archaeomagnetic Events

The goal of this analysis is to evaluate the hypothesis if $T_i = T_j$, and thus identify contemporaneous events. An apparently simple solution would be to evaluate the calendrical dates obtained above to determine if the date ranges for any set of samples overlap. If the estimated calendrical dates overlapped, then there would seem to be some probability that the archaeomagnetic events were contemporary. However, many archaeomagnetic events with overlapping calendrical dates can be shown empirically to be temporally discrete (see Deaver 1988b:114).[6] This seemingly contradictory situation arises because we can measure the location of the ancient VGP more precisely than we can estimate when the VGP was in a particular location. The most direct way of assessing whether or not any two archaeomagnetic events could have occurred at the same time is to statistically compare the calculated VGPs.

To do this, we apply the statistical methods of McFadden and Lowes (1981). These are the same methods used to compare a VGP of unknown age with the archaeomagnetic dating curve. In this situation, however, we use these methods to evaluate the similarity or dissimilarity between any two archaeomagnetically determined VGPs. We perform a series of pairwise comparisons between VGPs in preselected data sets. The null hypothesis is that the two archaeomagnetic VGPs being compared are the same ($VGP_1 = VGP_2$). If the computed probability for the F statistic is greater than 0.95, we reject the null hypothesis and conclude that $VGP_1 \neq VGP_2$. It follows then that $T_1 \neq T_2$. Alternatively, if the computed probability for the F statistic is equal to or less than 0.95, we must accept the null hypothesis and conclude that the difference between the VGPs is due to chance alone, and thusly $T_1 \approx T_2$. The ages of the two events are not necessarily equal, but they cannot be differentiated at the desired level of significance.

Whenever, the temporal span represented by $VGP_1 \ldots VGP_n$ is large enough that the pattern of polar wander loops back on itself, we will derive spurious comparisons because archaeomagnetic events of dissimilar age will have similar VGPs. Consequently, it is helpful to create separate datasets for this analysis. Subsets should be selected on the basis of

the expected or measured age of the archaeological event and the general character of polar wander as depicted in the SWCV590 curve. Generally, these comparisons can be performed for three periods: A.D. 600–800, A.D. 800–1100, and A.D. 1100–1800. Within these periods, the overall direction of polar wander appears to be unidirectional.

Determining a Relative Sequence of Events

The goal of this analysis is to provide an independent temporal ordering of archaeological contexts based on the relative position of the archaeomagnetic VGPs so that diachronic trends in the archaeological record may be perceived. This analysis uses the same data subsets defined for the contemporaneity evaluations for similar reasons. We must have some degree of confidence that, over the period of time represented by the subset of $T_1 \ldots T_n$, the polar wander was unidirectional. This assumption appears to be generally true when the data subsets are restricted to the three calendrical periods delimited above. Even if we cannot exactly segregate the archaeological contexts to these three periods, such as would occur with archaeological contexts expected to date near the boundaries, we can still derive important sequential information with the loss of some resolution near the beginning or end of these periods.

The VGPs were analyzed by adapting Engebretson and Beck's (1978) procedures for measuring the shape of directional data to the archaeological situation at hand. As in the other archaeomagnetic dating procedures, the spatial locations of the VGPs are taken as proxies for the ages of the archaeomagnetic events relative to one another. This analysis is accomplished in two steps. First, it is necessary to ascertain whether time is a major determinant of the VGP locations. Second, in those cases where time is found to be a determinant, a series of mathematical transformations are performed to assign values to the VGPs reflecting the relative ages of the archaeomagnetic events.

Whether or not time is a major determinate of this distribution is ascertained by evaluating the shape of the VGP distribution. We assume that the distribution of VGPs will be elliptical when time is a significant determinant to the VGP locations. Conversely, when the distribution of VGPs is circular, we assume that time is not a major factor, and that the dispersion of VGPs is determined primarily by random sampling errors. It is not time per se that creates the ellipticity of the VGP distribution. Rather, it is the effects of polar wander that occur over time that create the ellipticity. The ellipticity of the data set is measured by an eccentricity statistic, e. The value of e varies from 0 for a circular distribution to 1 for a linear distribution. Data sets with values of e near 1 are judged to be elliptical.[7]

For elliptical distributions we estimate the major semi-axis, l_f, for the distribution. This is the axis along which the VGPs are elongated. Accepting that the elongation is due to polar wander, l_f is then the general course of polar wander through these VGPs. It is not the polar wander path, but a general approximation of the overall trend of the polar wander path. Consequently, l_f also represents the general timeline through the events represented by the VGPs. The ages of the VGPs are determined according to their position relative to l_f. Variation perpendicular to l_f is caused by random sampling error and the nonlinearity of the true polar wander path. Although this method orders the VGPs, it cannot independently determine the direction in which time is progressing. Information on the direction of time is obtained from the cumulative knowledge we have amassed first on how past secular variation correlates with the archaeological periods and phases, and second, how this correlates with known archaeological cultural sequences (Deaver 1989c; Eighmy and McGuire 1988).

Determining the relative sequence for a data set involves six sequential steps. (1) A composite VGP is calculated for each data subset. (2) The VGPs are rotated so that the composite VGP is coincident with the Earth's rotation axis. (3) The three directional cosines, XYZ[8], are calculated for each VGP. (4) After these coordinates are calculated, the data points are projected orthogonally onto the XY plane by setting $z = 0$. The composite mean of the distribution is now the origin on the XY plane. Because the data points are all located relatively near the Earth's rotation axis, any distortion resulting from "flattening" the distribution of VGPs from the surface of the sphere onto the XY plane is inconsequential. (5) The e statistic and the slope of l_f are calculated. (6) The data set is once again rotated around the composite mean so that l_f is coincident with the X axis. The relative age of each data point can now be determined by the value X_r, which is the X coordinate of each VGP after this last rotation. The value of X_r can vary between -1 and 1, but because the VGPs are located near the Earth's rotation axis,

the actual values for sample VGPs typically vary over a range much smaller than this.

For the periods before A.D. 800 and after A.D. 1150, the direction of polar wander was easterly; thus, the values for X_r will have a positive correlation with the progression of time. For these periods, the value of X_r for each VGP is taken as the measure of the relative date.[9] For the period A.D. 800–1150, the direction of polar wander was westerly; thus, there will be a negative correlation between the value of X_r and the progression of time. It is important to note that the rate of polar wander was not constant; therefore a given distance does not correspond to an exact number of calendar years. Furthermore because of the looping character of polar wander, the relative archaeomagnetic dates assigned are specific to a given data set; the values cannot be compared from one data set to another.

Results

The values of the archaeomagnetic signals from these three samples are presented in Table G.3. As noted earlier, the sample AZ EE:9:107(ASM)-3ua showed large dispersion of the individual specimen measurements as indicated by the large value of $\alpha95$ and the correspondingly small value of k. The other two samples exhibited strongly coherent directions that we consider reliable. Archaeomagnetic dates were obtained only for the two samples showing acceptable levels of precision. These dates are presented in Table G.2 and are consistent with the expected archaeological ages. Statistical comparison of these two VGPs indicates that they are significantly different ($p = 1.00$) and thus represent two distinct archaeological events. Furthermore, the date for sample AZ EE:9:107(ASM)-2ua is older than the date for sample AZ EE:9:107(ASM)-1ua; this is consistent with the stratigraphic information that shows that Feature 44 was

Table G.3. Final Archaeomagnetic Data

Sample Number	N_2/N_1 [a]	Paleodirection					Virtual Geomagnetic Pole			
		Inc.[b]	Dec.[c]	J_r [d]	$\alpha95$	k [e]	Latitude	Longitude	dm [f]	dp [f]
-1ua	12/12	56.78	346.24	1.19E-03	2.8	234.05	77.18	190.66	4.12	2.99
-2ua	8/12	48.32	356.13	9.30E-05	3.0	342.98	86.08	128.40	3.93	2.57
-3ua	9/9	62.93	311.06	5.32E-04	15.2	12.39	49.90	192.27	23.92	15.80

Note: All sample numbers prefixed with the site number AZ EE:9:107 (ASM).

[a] N_2 = number of specimens used in computation of mean; N_1 = number of specimens collected
[b] inclination
[c] declination
[d] intensity of magnetic moment in Gauss
[e] k = precision parameter
[f] dm and dp are the errors associated with the virtual geomagnetic pole location

constructed sometime after Feature 52 was abandoned and partially destroyed.

Endnotes

1. In his seminal discussion of archaeological dating theory, Dean (1978) defines four events that are of importance in archaeological dating. These are: the target event (E_t), the dated event (E_d), the reference event (E_r), and the bridging event (E_b). E_t is the archaeological event that we wish to date, E_d is the event we are dating, E_r is the potentially datable event most closely related to E_t, and E_b is the event or events that link E_d with E_t. In archaeomagnetic analysis, E_d is the archaeomagnetic event, and in most situations E_r is an archaeological abandonment event.

2. The ages are not perfectly known and are a source of potentially significant error. While at the University of Arizona, Robert S. Sternberg developed a moving-window method for smoothing archaeomagnetic data that explicitly accounts for the age uncertainties in the independent dating of the archaeomagnetic events. This method is now commonly used by us and the Archaeometric Laboratory of Colorado State University to generate master dating curves from a collection of archaeomagnetic events of known age.

3. The 95 percent confidence date range is equivalent with the *Residual Date Range* presented by the Archaeometric Laboratory at Colorado State University. The Archaeometric Laboratory does not provide a date comparable to our *best-fit* date.

4. The equations of McFadden and Lowes (1981) are also applied to obtain relative dates.

5. In some analyses, researchers have combined and averaged archaeomagnetic dates from independent events to obtain a more finely resolved estimate for the dates of archaeological phases and periods (see Dean 1991; Eighmy and McGuire 1988). These analyses have turned to the statistical analysis of radiocarbon dates as a model. The researchers assumed that the 95 percent confidence date range was quasi-normal and took the midpoint as the estimate of the mean. However, this is not always the case. The tendency for the best-fit date to be near one end or the other of the 95 percent confidence range, is not random, but is rather patterned. The midpoint of the 95 percent confidence range consistently overestimates the best-fit date in some cases, consistently underestimates the best-fit date in other cases, or indicates a single mean date when in fact there are two competing best-fit dates.

6. In the example cited, two samples from the site of Las Colinas were obtained from hearths in two pit structures that were dated to the Sacaton phase on the basis of associated ceramics. The interpreted archaeomagnetic dates for one sample was A.D. 900–1070 and for the other sample was A.D. 860–1030. Based on the archaeological age and the overlap of the archaeomagnetic dates, it seemed that these two structures were possibly contemporary. However, the results of the pairwise comparison of the mean VGPs indicated that the VGPs were different ($p > 0.999$); thus, the archaeomagnetic events were not contemporaneous. This example illustrates the typical situation in archaeological and archaeomagnetic dating where at each level of inference the resolution of the dating information becomes more refined.

7. Although the procedures of Engebretson and Beck (1978) provide for calculating a value of e for a set of directional data, they do not provide a method of assigning a probability to a calculated value of e. We cannot determine for a data set what value of e would be significant at a desired level of significance, and the decision on whether or not a data set is sufficiently elongated for this analysis is based on our judgement that values of e greater than 0.5 indicate strongly elliptical data sets. In most of our applications the value of e is usually much greater.

8. x = cosine (longitude) × cosine (latitude); y = sine (longitude) × cosine (latitude); z = sine (latitude)

9. The location of the sample VGPs are not perfectly known, and there is error associated with assigning relative dates to the VGPs. Furthermore, the errors in locating the sample VGPs are not constant from one sample to the next. Because of these issues, the sequence of the VGPs should not be taken as an exact ordering, but rather emphasis should be placed on the trend in the data set. We suggest that before the relative order of two sample VGPs is accepted as presented, the researcher should evaluate the results of the contemporaneity evaluation of these two VGPs. If the VGPs are not contemporary, then the relative order of the two VGPs is probably valid. We also offer the following bootstrap method for estimating the error in the relative placement of each sample. The estimated 95 percent confidence interval for the calculated relative age is approximately sine(dm × dp)$^{-1/2}$, where dm and dp are the errors given for the VGP location.

Inventory of Human Burials and Repatriated Artifacts

Table H.1. Summary of Human Burials Identified at AZ EE:9:107

Feature No.	Burial Type	Institution	Treatment and Disposition
1	cremation	ASM (1987)	Exposed in test trench; profiled; unexcavated.
2	cremation	ASM (1987)	Exposed in test trench by ASM; profiled; unexcavated. Location excavated by SRI in exhuming Feature 213; determined not to be a cremation. Miscellaneous remains recovered in Test Pit 291.
19	inhumation	ASM (1987)	Exposed in test trench; profiled; unexcavated.
31	inhumation	ASM (1987) SRI (1996)	Remains disturbed by ASM trenching; collected and archived at ASM. Additional remain recovered by SRI; repatriated.
32	inhumation	CES (1991)	Excavated; remains collected; archived at ASM.
39	inhumation	SRI (1996)	Remains exposed during mechanical stripping; excavated; remains collected; repatriated.
40	inhumation	SRI (1996)	Remains exposed during mechanical stripping; excavated; remains collected; repatriated.
132	inhumation	SRI (1996)	Remains exposed during mechanical stripping; excavated; remains collected; repatriated.
146	inhumation?	SRI (1996)	Elliptically shaped pit discovered during mechanical stripping; no human remains exposed; unexcavated.
147	inhumation	SRI (1996)	Remains exposed during mechanical stripping; excavated; remains collected; repatriated.
148	inhumation?	SRI (1996)	Elliptically shaped pit discovered during mechanical stripping; no human remains exposed; unexcavated.
151	inhumation	SRI (1996)	Remains exposed during mechanical stripping; excavated; remains collected; repatriated.
156	inhumation	SRI (1996)	Remains exposed during mechanical stripping; excavated; remains collected; repatriated.
213	inhumation	SRI (1996)	Remains exposed during reexcavation of ASM trench; excavated; remains collected; repatriated.
214	inhumation	SRI (1996)	Remains disturbed during mechanical stripping; collected; repatriated.

Table H.2. Repatriated Items from Excavations at AZ EE:9:107

Catalog No.	PD No.	Feature No.	Feature Type	Unit	Stratum Type	Artifact Category	Bags
152	122			SU 122	CULT	human bone	1
169	293			TP 291	CULT	human bone	1
182	134	5	pit house	N2	RFL	human bone	1
292	52	31	inhumation	TR 2	TB	human bone	2
304	55	39	inhumation	feature	BRL	human bone	1
307	254	40	inhumation	feature	BRL	human bone	5
309	255	40	inhumation	feature	BRL FILL	human bone, fragments in soil	1
459	256	132	inhumation	feature	BRL	human bone	1
490	239	147	inhumation	feature	BRL	human bone	1
498	241	151	inhumation	feature	BRL	ground stone, nonutilitarian, beads	1
499	241	151	inhumation	feature	BRL	human bone	4
502	241	151	inhumation	feature	BRL	worked shell, beads	1
508	244	151	inhumation	ART	BRL	ceramics reconstructible vessel, plain ware bowl	1
511	245	151	inhumation	ART	BRL	ceramics reconstructible vessel, plain ware bowl	1
514	246	151	inhumation	ART	BRL	ceramics reconstructible vessel, plain ware bowl	1
522	243	151 & 156	inhumation	feature	RDNT	human bone	1
525	191	156	inhumation	ART	BRL	ground stone, nonutilitarian, turquoise pendant	1
526	252	156	inhumation	feature	BRL	human bone	3
530	569	156	inhumation	ART	BRL	worked shell, bracelet	1
531	570	156	inhumation	ART	BRL	worked shell, bracelet	1
295	305	213	inhumation	feature	BRL	human bone	2
293	307	213	inhumation	feature	BRL FILL	human bone	1
76	75	214	inhumation	feature	BRL	human bone	1
724	75	214	inhumation	feature	BRL	ceramic reconstructible vessel, plain ware jar	1

Note: These burial items were repatriated on October 24, 1996, as per the Agreement on Burial Discoveries (Case No. 95-24).
Key: ART = point-provenienced artifact; BRL = burial associations; BRL FILL = burial fill; CULT = culture-bearing horizon; N2 = north one-half; RNDT = rodent disturbance; RFL = roof fall; SU = stripping unit; TB = trench backdirt; TP = test pit; TR = trench

REFERENCES CITED

Adams, David K., and Andrew C. Comrie
1997   The North American Monsoon. *Bulletin of American Meteorological Society* 78:2,197–2,213.

Adams, Kim
1994   Archaeological Assessment of a Parcel along the El Paso Natural Gas Company California Line (Number 2143) near Nogales, Santa Cruz County, Arizona. Archaeological Consulting Services. Manuscript on file, Arizona State Museum Library, University of Arizona, Tucson.

Adams, Kim, and Teresa L. Hoffman
1995   Archaeological Assessment of a Proposed Fiber Optic Cable Right-of-Way between Tucson, Pima County and Nogales, Santa Cruz County, Arizona. Archaeological Consulting Services. Manuscript on file, Arizona State Museum Library, University of Arizona, Tucson.

Adler, Michael A.
1996   *The Prehistoric Pueblo World, A.D. 1150–1300.* University of Arizona Press, Tucson.

Agenbroad, Larry D.
1967   Cenozoic Stratigraphy and Paleo-Hydrology of the Redington–San Manuel Area: San Pedro Valley, Arizona. Unpublished Ph.D. dissertation, Department of Geosciences, University of Arizona, Tucson.

Ahler, S. A.
1989   Mass Analysis of Flaking Debris: Studying the Forest Rather Than the Trees. In *Alternative Approaches to Lithic Analysis*, edited by D. Henry and G. Odell, pp. 85–118. Archaeological Papers of the American Anthropological Association No. 1.

Aitken, M. J.
1974   *Physics and Archaeology.* 2nd ed. Clarendon Press, Oxford.

Altschul, Jeffrey H., Rein Vanderpot, Robert A. Heckman, and César A. Quijada
1997   The Periods Between: Archaic and Formative Cultures of the Upper and Middle San Pedro Valley. Paper prepared for the 1997 Amerind Foundation Seminar "The Archaeology of a Land Between: Regional Dynamics in the Prehistory and History of Southeastern Arizona," October. Manuscript on file, Statistical Research, Tucson.

American Ornithologists' Union
1975   *Check-List of North American Birds.* 5th ed. Prepared by a Committee of the American Ornithologists' Union, Port City Press, Baltimore.

Anyon, Roger, Patricia A. Gilman, and Steven A. LeBlanc
1981   A Reevaluation of the Mogollon-Mimbres Archaeological Sequence. *The Kiva* 46:209–226.

Ayres, James E.
1970   Two Clovis Fluted Points from Southern Arizona. *The Kiva* 35:121–124.

Ball, S. H.
1941   *The Mining of Gems and Ornamental Stone by American Indians.* Bureau of American Ethnology Bulletin No. 128. Anthropological Papers No. 13. Smithsonian Institution, Washington, D.C.

Barkley, F. A.
1934   The Statistical Theory of Pollen Analysis. *Ecology* 15:283–289.

Bartlett, Katherine
1935   Prehistoric Mining in the Southwest. *Museum Notes* 7(10):41–44. Museum of Northern Arizona, Flagstaff.

1966   Prehistoric Mining in the Southwest. *Lapidary Journal* 20:316–319.

Barton, C. Michael, Kay Simpson, and Lee Fratt
1981   *Tumacacori Excavations 1979–1980: Historical Archeology at Tumacacori National Monument.* Publications in Archeology No. 17. Western Archeological and Conservation Center, National Park Service, Tucson.

Barz, David D.
1995   A Cultural Resources Survey of a 4.2 Mile Long Segment of Interstate-19 Right-of-Way between Tubac and Chavez Siding Road Interchanges in Northwestern Santa Cruz County, Arizona. Archaeological Research Services. Manuscript on file, Arizona State Museum Library, University of Arizona, Tucson.

Bayman, James
1987   The Southern Segment of the Tubac Presidio, an Archaeological Reconnaissance, Pima County, Arizona. Manuscript on file, Arizona State Museum Library, University of Arizona, Tucson.

Beaubien, Paul
1937   *Excavations at Tumacacori, 1934.* Southwestern Monuments Special Report No. 15. Manuscript on file, Western Archaeological and Conservation Center, National Park Service, Tucson.

Bequaert, Joseph C., and Walter B. Miller
1973   *The Mollusks of the Arid Southwest with an Arizona Check List.* University of Arizona Press, Tucson.

Blake, W. P.
1899   Aboriginal Turquoise Mining in Arizona and New Mexico. *The American Antiquarian* 21(183):278–284.

Bohrer, Vorsila L.
1981   Methods of Recognizing Cultural Activity from Pollen in Archaeological Sites. *The Kiva* 46:135–142.

1984   Domesticated and Wild Crops in the CAEP's Study Area. In *Prehistoric Cultural Development in Central Arizona: Archaeology of the Upper New River Region,* edited by P. M. Spoerl and G. J. Gumerman, pp. 183–259. Occasional Paper No. 5. Center for Archaeological Investigations, Southern Illinois University, Carbondale.

Bowen, Thomas
1972   A Survey and Re-evaluation of the Trincheras Culture, Sonora, Mexico. Manuscript on file, Arizona State Museum Library Archives, AT-94-85, University of Arizona, Tucson.

1976   Esquema de la Historia de la Cultura Trincheras. In *Sonora: Antropología del Desierto,* edited by B. Braniff C. and R. S. Felger, pp. 267–279. Colección Cientifica 27, Instituto Nacional de Antropología e Historia, Mexico City.

Braniff Cornejo, Beatriz
1992   *La Frontera Protohistorica Pima-Opata en Sonora, Mexico.* 3 vols. Instituto Nacional del Antropología e Historia, Culhuacan, Mexico.

Brown, David E. (editor)
1994   *Biotic Communities: Southwestern United States and Northwestern Mexico.* University of Utah Press, Salt Lake City.

Brown, David E., and Charles H. Lowe
1980   Biotic Communities of the Southwest Map. One sheet, scale: 1:1,000,000. University of Utah Press, Salt Lake City.

Brown, Jeffrey L.
1967   An Experiment in Problem-Oriented Highway Salvage Archaeology. *The Kiva* 33:60–66.

Brown, Jeffrey L., and Paul F. Grebinger
1969   A Lower Terrace Compound at San Cayetano del Tumacacori. *The Kiva* 34:185–198.

Bruder, J. Simon
1992   Cultural Resources Class III Inventory for the Mariposa Road (State Route 189) Upgrading Project, Santa Cruz County, Arizona. Letter report to Sverdrup Corporation. Manuscript on file, Arizona State Museum Library, University of Arizona, Tucson.

Bryan, Kirk
1925   *The Papago Country, Arizona.* U.S. Geological Survey Water-Supply Paper No. 499. Government Printing Office, Washington, D.C.

Bryant, Vaughn M., Jr.
1969   Pollen Analysis of Late-Glacial and Post-glacial Texas Sediments. Unpublished Ph.D. dissertation, Department of Botany, University of Texas, Austin.

Buikstra, J. E., and D. H. Ubelaker (editors)
1994   *Standards for Data Collection from Human Skeletal Remains.* Research Series No. 44. Arkansas Archaeological Survey, Fayetteville.

Bullock, Peter Y., and Alan Cooper
1999   Ancient DNA and Macaw Identification in the American Southwest: A Progress Report. Manuscript on file, Office of Archaeological Studies, Museum of New Mexico, Santa Fe.

Burton, Jeffery F.
1992a   *San Miguel de Guevavi: The Archeology of an Eighteenth Century Jesuit Mission on the Rim of Christendom.* Publications in Archeology No. 57. Western Archeological and Conservation Center, National Park Service, Tucson.

1992b   *Remnants of Adobe and Stone: The Surface Archeology of the Guevavi and Calabazas Units, Tumacacori Historical Park, Arizona.* Publications in Archeology No. 59. Western Archeological and Conservation Center, National Park Service, Tucson.

Butler, Robert F.
1992   *Paleomagnetism: Magnetic Domains to Geologic Terranes.* Blackwell Scientific Publications, Boston.

Carpenter, John, and Guadalupe Sanchez
1997   *Prehistory of the Borderlands: Recent Research in the Archaeology of Northern Mexico and the Southern Southwest.* Archaeological Series No. 186. Arizona State Museum, University of Arizona, Tucson.

Carpenter, John L., and Charles Tompkins
1995   *An Archaeological Assessment for the Mariposa Canyon Borrow Pit in Nogales, Arizona.* Technical Report No. 95-8. Tierra Right-of-Way Services, Ltd., Tucson.

1998   An Archaeological Resource Survey for the Proposed Expansion of the Rio Rico Sanitary Landfill, Santa Cruz County, Arizona. SWCA, Inc. Manuscript on file, Arizona State Museum Library, University of Arizona, Tucson.

Caywood, Louis R.
1965   Field notes. Manuscript on file, Western Archeological and Conservation Center, National Park Service, Tucson.

Ciolek-Torrello, Richard S.
1995   The Houghton Road Site, the Agua Caliente Phase, and the Early Formative Period in the Tucson Basin. *Kiva* 60:531–574.

Cockrum, E. Lendell
1960   *The Recent Mammals of Arizona: Their Taxonomy and Distribution.* University of Arizona Press, Tucson.

Colton, Harold S.
1939   *Prehistoric Cultural Units and Their Relationships in Northern Arizona.* Bulletin No. 17. Museum of Northern Arizona, Flagstaff.

1946   *The Sinagua: A Summary of the Archaeology of the Region of Flagstaff, Arizona.* Bulletin No. 22. Museum of Northern Arizona, Flagstaff.

1955   *Checklist of Southwestern Pottery Types.* Ceramic Series No. 2. Museum of Northern Arizona, Flagstaff.

Colton, Harold S., and Lyndon L. Hargrave
1937   *Handbook of Northern Arizona Pottery Wares.* Bulletin No. 11. Museum of Northern Arizona, Flagstaff.

Cooke, R. U., and R. W. Reeves
1976   *Arroyos and Environmental Change in the American Southwest.* Oxford University Press, Oxford.

Crown, Patricia L., and W. James Judge (editors)
1991   *Chaco & Hohokam: Prehistoric Regional Systems in the American Southwest.* School of American Research Press, Santa Fe.

Cunningham, Robert D., Jr.
1972   An Archaeological Survey in Central Southern Arizona or Site Seeking at Rio Rico, July 20, 1972. Manuscript on file, Arizona State Museum Library, University of Arizona, Tucson.

Danson, Edward B.
1946   An Archaeological Survey of the Santa Cruz River Valley from the Headwaters of the Town of Tubac, Arizona. Manuscript on file, Arizona State Museum Library, University of Arizona, Tucson.

1957   Pottery Type Descriptions. In *Excavations, 1940, at University Indian Ruin*, by Julian D. Hayden, pp. 219–231. Technical Series No. 5. Southwest Parks and Monuments Association, Globe, Arizona.

Dart, Alan
1994   *Archaeological Testing Results and Data Recovery Plan for the Tubac-Tumacacori Volunteer Fire Department at the Peck Canyon Fire Station Site, AZ DD:8:145 (ASM)*. Archaeological Report No. 94-1. Old Pueblo Archaeology Center, Tucson.

Dean, Jeffrey S.
1988   Dendrochronology and Paleoenvironmental Reconstruction on the Colorado Plateaus. In *The Anasazi in a Changing Environment*, edited by G. J. Gumerman, pp. 119–167. Cambridge University Press, Cambridge.

1991   Thoughts on Hohokam Chronology. In *Exploring the Hohokam: Prehistoric Desert Peoples of the American Southwest*, edited by G. J. Gumerman, pp. 61–149. Amerind Foundation, Dragoon, Arizona.

Dean, Jeffrey S., William H. Doelle, and Janet D. Orcutt
1994   Adaptive Stress, Environment, and Demography. In *Themes in Southwest Prehistory*, edited by G. J. Gumerman, pp. 53–86. School of American Research Press, Santa Fe.

Deaver, William L.
1984   Pottery. In *Hohokam Habitation Sites in the Northern Santa Rita Mountains*, vol. 2, by Alan Ferg, Kenneth C. Rozen, William L. Deaver, Martyn D. Tagg, David A. Phillips, Jr., and David A. Gregory, pp. 237–419. Archaeological Series No. 147. Arizona State Museum, University of Arizona, Tucson.

1988a   Ceramics. In *Excavations at Fastimes (AZ AA:12:384), a Rillito Phase Site in the Avra Valley*, edited by Jon S. Czaplicki and John C. Ravesloot, pp. 139–174. Hohokam Archaeology along Phase B of the Tucson Aqueduct Central Arizona Project, vol. 2. Archaeological Series No. 178(2). Arizona State Museum, University of Arizona, Tucson.

1988b   Identifying Contemporary Archaeological Events through Comparison of Archaeomagnetic Directions. In *The 1982–1984 Excavations at Las Colinas: The Site and Its Features*, by D. A. Gregory, W. L. Deaver, S. K. Fish, R. Gardiner, R. W. Layhe, F. L. Nials, and L. S. Teague, pp. 73–120. Archaeological Series No. 162, Vol. 2. Arizona State Museum, University of Arizona, Tucson.

1989a   Ceramics. In *Excavations at Water World (AZ AA:16:94), a Rillito Phase Ballcourt Village in the Avra Valley*, edited by Jon S. Czaplicki and John C. Ravesloot, pp. 153–192. Hohokam Archaeology along Phase B of the Tucson Aqueduct Central Arizona Project, vol. 3. Archaeological Series No. 178(3). Arizona State Museum, University of Arizona, Tucson.

1989b   Pottery and Other Ceramic Artifacts. In *The 1979–1983 Testing at Los Morteros (AZ AA:12:57 ASM), a Large Hohokam Village Site in the Tucson Basin*, by Richard C. Lange and William L. Deaver, pp. 27–82. Archaeological Series No. 177. Arizona State Museum, University of Arizona, Tucson.

1989c   Southwestern Archaeomagnetic Secular Variation: The Hohokam Data. In *The 1982–1984 Excavations at Las Colinas: Syntheses and Conclusions*, by L. S. Teague and W. L. Deaver, pp. 7–42. Archaeological Series 162, Vol. 6. Arizona State Museum, University of Arizona, Tucson.

1998   Scorpion Point Village. In *Descriptions of Habitation and Nonagricultural Sites*, edited by Richard Ciolek-Torrello, pp. 3–87. Vanishing River: Landscapes and Lives of the Lower Verde Valley: The Lower Verde Archaeological Project, vol. 1. CD-ROM. SRI Press, Tucson.

Deaver, William L., and Richard Ciolek-Torrello
1995   Early Formative Period Chronology for the Tucson Basin. *Kiva* 60:481–529.

Di Peso, Charles C.
1956   *The Upper Pima Indians of San Cayetano del Tumacacori*. Publication No. 7. Amerind Foundation, Dragoon, Arizona.

1974   *Casas Grandes, a Fallen Trading Center of the Gran Chichimeca*, vols. 1–3, edited by Gloria J. Fenner. Amerind Foundation Series No. 9. Amerind Foundation, Dragoon, Arizona and Northland Press, Flagstaff.

1979   Prehistory: Southern Periphery. In *Southwest*, edited by Alfonso Ortiz, pp. 152–161. Handbook of North American Indians, vol. 10, William C. Sturtevant, general editor. Smithsonian Institution Press, Washington, D.C.

Doelle, William H.
1985 *Excavations at the Valencia Site: A Preclassic Hohokam Village in the Southern Tucson Basin.* Anthropological Papers No. 3. Institute for American Research, Tucson.

1988 Preclassic Community Patterns in the Tucson Basin. In *Recent Research on Tucson Basin Prehistory: Proceedings of the Second Tucson Basin Conference*, edited by William H. Doelle and Paul R. Fish, pp. 277–312. Anthropological Papers No. 10. Institute for American Research, Tucson.

Doelle, William H., Frederick W. Huntington, and Henry D. Wallace
1987 Rincon Phase Reorganization in the Tucson Basin. In *The Hohokam Village: Site Structure and Organization,* edited by D. E. Doyel, pp. 71–95. AAAS Publication No. 87-15. Southwestern and Rocky Mountain Division of the American Association for the Advancement of Science, Glenwood Springs, Colorado.

Doelle, William H., and Henry D. Wallace
1986 *Hohokam Settlement Patterns in the San Xavier Project Areas, Southern Tucson Basin.* Technical Report No. 84-6. Institute for American Research, Tucson.

Dongoske, Kurt E.
1993 Burial Population and Mortuary Practices. In *Archaic Occupation on the Santa Cruz Flats: The Tator Hills Archaeological Project*, edited by Carl D. Halbirt and T. Kathleen Henderson, pp. 173–182. Northland Research, Flagstaff.

Douglas, Michael W., Robert A. Maddox, Kenneth Howard, and Sergio Reyes
1993 The Mexican Monsoon. *Journal of Climate* 6:1,665–1,677.

Downum, Christian E.
1993 *Between Desert and River: Hohokam Settlement and Land Use in the Los Robles Community.* Anthropological Papers No. 57. University of Arizona Press, Tucson.

Downum, Christian E., Paul R. Fish, and Suzanne K. Fish
1994 Refining the Role of Cerros de Trincheras in Southern Arizona Settlement. *Kiva* 59:271–296.

Doyel, David E.
1977a *Excavations in the Middle Santa Cruz River Valley, Southeastern Arizona.* Contributions to

Highway Salvage Archaeology in Arizona No. 44. Arizona State Museum, University of Arizona, Tucson.

1977b Rillito and Rincon Period Settlement Systems in the Middle Santa Cruz River Valley: Alternative Models. *The Kiva* 43:93–110.

1984 From Foraging to Farming: An Overview of the Preclassic in the Tucson Basin. *The Kiva* 49:147–166.

1987 *The Hohokam Village: Site Structure and Organization.* AAAS Publication No. 87-15. Southwestern and Rocky Mountain Division of the American Association for the Advancement of Science, Glenwood Springs, Colorado.

Drewes, Harald
1972 *Structural Geology of the Santa Rita Mountains, Southeast of Tucson, Arizona.* U.S. Geological Survey Professional Paper No. 746. Government Printing Office, Washington D.C.

DuBois, Susan M., and Ann W. Smith
1980 *The 1887 Earthquake in San Bernardino Valley, Sonora: Historic Accounts and Intensity Patterns in Arizona.* Special Paper No. 3. State of Arizona Bureau of Geology and Mineral Technology, University of Arizona, Tucson.

Eckholm, Gordon F.
1939 Results of an Archaeological Survey of Sonora and Northern Sinoloa. *Revista Mexicana de Estudios Antropologicos* 3(1):7–11. Sociedad Mexicana de Antropologia, Mexico City.

1940 The Archaeology of Northern and Western Mexico. In *The Maya and Their Neighbors*, edited by C. L. Haya, pp. 307–320. D. Appleton-Century Co., New York.

Eighmey, James E.
1994 Cultural Resources Survey of a ca. One-Half Mile Long Segment of Frank Reed Road Right-of-Way for Interstate 19 to State Route 89 in Nogales, Santa Cruz County, Arizona. Archaeological Research Services. Manuscript on file, Arizona State Museum Library, University of Arizona, Tucson.

Eighmy, Jeffrey L.
1990 Archaeomagnetic Dating: Practical Problems for the Archaeologist. In *Archaeomagnetic Dating*, edited by J. L. Eighmy and R. S. Sternberg, pp. 33–64. University of Arizona Press, Tucson.

1991   Archaeomagnetism: New Data on the Southwest USA Master Virtual Geomagnetic Pole Curve. *Archaeometry* 33(2):201–214.

Eighmy, Jeffrey L., and Jerry B. Howard
1991   Direct Dating of Prehistoric Canal Sediments Using Archaeomagnetism. *American Antiquity* 56(1):88–102.

Eighmy, Jeffrey L., and Randall H. McGuire
1988   *Archaeomagnetic Dates and the Hohokam Phase Sequence.* Archaeometric Lab Technical Series No. 3. Colorado State University, Fort Collins.

Eighmy, Jeffrey L., and Robert S. Sternberg
1990   *Archaeomagnetic Dating.* University of Arizona Press, Tucson.

El Najjar, Mahmoud T., Dennis J. Ryan, Christy G. Turner II, and Betsy Lozoff
1976   The Etiology of Porotic Hyperostosis among the Prehistoric and Historic Anasazi Indians of the Southwestern United States. *American Journal of Physical Anthropology* 44:447–488.

Elson, Mark D., and James Gundersen
1992   The Mineralogy and Sourcing of Argillite Artifacts: A Preliminary Examination of Procurement, Production, and Distribution Systems. In *Artifact and Specific Analyses,* edited by M. D. Elson and D. B. Craig, pp. 429–462. The Rye Creek Project: Archaeology in the Upper Tonto Basin, vol. 2. Anthropological Papers No. 11. Center for Desert Archaeology, Tucson.

Engebretson, David C., and Myrl E. Beck, Jr.
1978   On the Shape of Directional Data Sets. *Journal of Geophysical Research* 83(B12):5,979–5,982.

Erdtman, G.
1960   The Acetolysis Method: A Revised Description. *Svensk Botanisk Tidskrift* Bd. 54:561–564.

Ezzo, Joseph, A., and William L. Deaver
1998   *Watering the Desert: Late Archaic Farming at the Costello-King Site.* Technical Series 68. Statistical Research, Tucson.

Fazekas, I. G., and F. Kosa
1978   *Forensic Fetal Osteology.* Akademiai Kiado, Budapest.

Fish, Paul R., and Suzanne K. Fish
1994   Southwest and Northwest: Recent Research at the Juncture of the United States and Mexico. *Journal of Archaeological Research* 2(1):3–44.

Fish, Suzanne K.
1998   *The Cerro de Trincheras Settlement and Land Use Survey.* Preliminary report submitted to the National Geographic Society for Grant 5856–97. Manuscript on file, Arizona State Museum, University of Arizona, Tucson.

Fish, Suzanne K., and Paul R. Fish
2000   In the Trincheras Heartland. Paper presented at the 65th Annual Meeting of the Society for American Archaeology, Philadelphia.

Fish, Suzanne K., Paul R. Fish, and John H. Madsen
1992   Evolution and Structure of the Classic Period Marana Community. In *The Marana Community in the Hohokam World,* edited by S. K. Fish, P. R. Fish, and J. H. Madsen, pp. 20–40. Anthropological Papers of the University of Arizona No. 36. University of Arizona Press, Tucson.

Fisher, R. A.
1953   Dispersion on a Sphere. *Proceedings of the Royal Society of London* A217:295–305.

Fontana, Bernard L.
1971   Calabasa of the Rio Rico. *The Smoke Signal* 24:66–88.

Fox, Sherry C.
1991   The Human Skeletal Remains from AZ EE:9:107 (ASM). In *Archaeological Investigations in Nogales, Arizona: A Limited Testing Program at AZ EE:9:107 (ASM),* by Laurie V. Slawson, pp. 18–20. Cultural and Environmental Systems, Tucson.

Fratt, Lee
1981a   *Tumacacori Plaza Excavation 1979: Historical Archeology at Tumacacori National Monument, Arizona.* Publications in Anthropology No. 16. Western Archeological and Conservation Center, National Park Service, Tucson.

1981b   *Tumacacori Excavations 1979–1980: Historical Archeology at Tumacacori National Monument, Arizona.* Publications in Anthropology No. 17. Western Archeological and Conservation Center, National Park Service, Tucson.

Frick, Paul S.
1954   An Archaeological Survey in the Central Santa Cruz Valley, Southern Arizona. Unpublished Master's thesis, Department of Anthropology, University of Arizona, Tucson.

Fulton, William S.
1934a   *Archaeological Notes on Texas Canyon, Arizona.* Museum of the American Indian Contribution, vol. 12, No. 1. Heye Foundation, New York.

1934b   *Archaeological Notes on Texas Canyon, Arizona.* Museum of the American Indian Contribution, vol. 12, No. 2. Heye Foundation, New York.

1938   *Archaeological Notes on Texas Canyon, Arizona.* Museum of the American Indian Contribution, vol. 12, No. 3. Heye Foundation, New York.

Fulton, William S., and Carr Tuthill
1940   *An Archaeological Site near Gleeson, Arizona.* Amerind Foundation Papers No. 1. Dragoon, Arizona.

Gardiner, Ronald
1987   *The History of AZ EE:9:109: A Military Camp in Nogales, Arizona, 1916 through 1918.* Cultural Resource Management Division, Arizona State Museum, University of Arizona, Tucson. Prepared for Santa Cruz County Planning and Zoning, Department of Public Works.

Gardiner, Ronald, and Bruce B. Huckell
1987   Report on the Mapping and Testing of AZ EE:9:107, AZ EE:9:108, and AZ EE:9:109 at Nogales, Arizona, Bureau of Land Management Land Proposed as the Site for the New Santa Cruz County Administration Complex. Manuscript on file, Arizona State Museum, University of Arizona, Tucson.

Gasser, Robert, E., and Scott M. Kwiatkowski
1991a   Food for Thought: Recognizing Patterns in Hohokam Subsistence. In *Exploring the Hohokam: Prehistoric Desert Peoples of the American Southwest,* edited by George J. Gumerman, pp. 417–460. Amerind Foundation, Dragoon, Arizona, and University of New Mexico Press, Albuquerque.

1991b   Regional Signatures of Hohokam Plant Use. *Kiva* 56:207–226.

Gilbert, B. Miles, Larry D. Martin, and Howard G. Savage
1981   *Avian Osteology.* Missouri Archaeological Society, Columbia.

Gladwin, Harold S., Emil W. Haury, Edwin B. Sayles, and Nora Gladwin
1937   *Excavations at Snaketown: Material Culture.* Medallion Papers No. 25. Gila Pueblo, Globe, Arizona. Reprinted 1965 by the University of Arizona Press, Tucson.

Gladwin, Winifred, and Harold S. Gladwin
1929a   *The Red-on-buff Culture of the Gila Basin.* Medallion Papers No. 3. Gila Pueblo, Globe, Arizona.

1929b   *The Red-on-buff Culture of the Papagueria.* Medallion Papers No. 4. Gila Pueblo, Globe, Arizona.

Goree, Patricia
1972   December 15, 1972, Visit to AZ EE:9:85 (ASM). Notes to the files, dated January 4, 1973. Additional Site Information, Arizona State Museum, University of Arizona, Tucson.

Grebinger, Paul F.
1971a   Hohokam Cultural Development in the Middle Santa Cruz Valley, Arizona. Unpublished Ph.D. dissertation, Department of Anthropology, University of Arizona, Tucson.

1971b   The Potrero Creek Site: Activity Structure. *The Kiva* 37:30–52.

Greeley, M. N.
1987   The Early Influence of Mining in Arizona. In *History of Mining in Arizona,* vol. 1, edited by J. M. Canty and M. N. Greeley, pp. 13–50. Mining Club of the Southwest Foundation, American Institute of Mining Engineers, Tucson Section, and Southwestern Minerals Exploration Association, Tucson.

Greenleaf, J. Cameron
1975   *Excavations at Punta de Agua in the Santa Cruz River Basin, Southeastern Arizona.* Anthropological Papers of the University of Arizona No. 26. University of Arizona Press, Tucson.

Gregory, Teresa L., Edgar K. Huber, and Matthew A. Sterner
1999   *An Archaeological Survey of Portions of Country Club Road and Other Adjacent Areas in Santa Cruz County, Nogales, Arizona.* Technical Report 98-39. Statistical Research, Tucson.

Gumerman, George J. (editor)
1991   *Exploring the Hohokam: Prehistoric Peoples of the American Southwest.* Amerind Foundation, Dragoon, and University of New Mexico Press, Albuquerque.

Halbirt, Carl D., and T. Kathleen Henderson (editors)
1993   *Archaic Occupation on the Santa Cruz Flats: The Tator Hills Archaeological Project.* Northland Research, Flagstaff.

Hall, E. Raymond, and Keith R. Kelson
1959   *The Mammals of North America.* Ronald Press, New York.

Hall, Stephen A.
1981   Deteriorated Pollen Grains and the Interpretation of Quaternary Pollen Diagrams. *Review of Paleobotany and Palynology* 32:193–206.

Hargrave, Lyndon L.
1970   *Mexican Macaws: Comparative Osteology and Survey of Remains from the Southwest.* Anthropological Papers of the University of Arizona No. 20. University of Arizona Press, Tucson.

Harrington, E. R.
1939   Digging for Turquoise in America's First Mines. *New Mexico Magazine* 17(7):12.

1940   Chalchihuitl—A Story of Early Turquoise Mining in the Southwest. *Engineering and Mining Journal* 141:57–58.

Harvey, J. R., and J. R. Harvey
1938   Turquoise among the Indians and a Colorado Turquoise Mine. *Colorado Magazine* 25:186–192.

Hastings, James R., and Raymond M. Turner
1965   *The Changing Mile: An Ecological Study of Vegetation Change with Time in the Lower Mile of an Arid and Semiarid Region.* University of Arizona Press, Tucson.

Hathaway, Jeffrey B.
1996   Cultural Resources Survey of Two Highway Segments along State Route 82 between Nogales and the Junction of State Route 90 (from Mileposts 1.2 to 28.0 and Mileposts 45.3 to 51.2) in Santa Cruz and Southwestern Cochise Counties, Arizona. Archaeological Research Services. Manuscript on file, Arizona State Museum Library, University of Arizona, Tucson.

Haury, Emil W.
1932   *Roosevelt 9:6, a Hohokam Site of the Colonial Period.* Medallion Papers No. 11. Gila Pueblo, Globe, Arizona.

1934   *The Canyon Creek Ruin and Cliff Dwellings of the Sierra Ancha.* Medallion Papers No. 14. Gila Pueblo, Globe, Arizona.

1936   *Some Southwestern Pottery Types, Series IV.* Medallion Papers No. 19. Gila Pueblo, Globe, Arizona.

1937   Pottery Types at Snaketown. In *Excavations at Snaketown: Material Culture*, by Harold S. Gladwin, Emil W. Haury, E. B. Sayles, and Nora Gladwin, pp. 169–229. Medallion Papers No. 25. Gila Pueblo, Globe, Arizona.

1950   *The Stratigraphy and Archaeology of Ventana Cave.* University of Arizona Press, Tucson, and University of New Mexico Press, Albuquerque.

1957   An Alluvial Site on the San Carlos Indian Reservation, Arizona. *American Antiquity* 23:2–27. Reprinted in *Emil W. Haury's Prehistory of the American Southwest*, edited by J. J. Reid and D. E. Doyel, pp. 146–189. University of Arizona Press, Tucson, 1986.

1976   *The Hohokam: Desert Farmers and Craftsmen: Excavations at Snaketown, 1964–1965.* University of Arizona Press, Tucson.

1986   An Alluvial Site on the San Carlos Reservation. In *Emil Haury's Prehistory of the American Southwest*, edited by J. J. Reid and D. E. Doyel, pp. 146–189. University of Arizona Press, Tucson.

Haynes, C. Vance, Jr., and Bruce B. Huckell
1986   *Sedimentary Successions of the Prehistoric Santa Cruz River, Tucson, Arizona.* Arizona Bureau of Mines Open File Report, Tucson.

Heckman, Robert A., Barbara K. Montgomery, and Stephanie M. Whittlesey
2000   *Prehistoric Painted Pottery of Southeastern Arizona.* Technical Series 77. Statistical Research, Tucson.

Heckman, Robert A., and Stephanie M. Whittlesey
1999   Ceramics. In *Investigations at Sunset Mesa Ruin*, edited by R. Ciolek-Torrello, E. K. Huber, and R. B. Neily, pp. 87–133. Technical Series 66. Statistical Research, Tucson.

Heidke, James M.

1986 Plainware Ceramics. In *Archaeological Investigations at the Tanque Verde Wash Site: A Middle Rincon Settlement in the Eastern Tucson Basin*, by Mark D. Elson, pp. 181–231. Anthropological Papers No. 7. Institute for American Research, Tucson.

1988 Ceramic Production and Exchange: Evidence from Rincon Phase Contexts. In *Recent Research on Tucson Basin Prehistory: Proceedings of the Second Tucson Basin Conference*, edited by W. H. Doelle and P. R. Fish, pp. 387–410. Anthropological Papers No. 10. Institute for American Research, Tucson.

Hemmings, Ernest Thomas

1970 Early Man in the San Pedro Valley, Arizona. Unpublished Ph.D. dissertation, Department of Anthropology, University of Arizona, Tucson.

Hinton, Thomas B.

1955 A Survey of Archaeological Sites in the Altar Valley, Sonora. *The Kiva* 21(3–4):1–12.

Hirschboeck, K. K.

1987 Catastrophic Flooding and Atmospheric Circulation Anomalies. In *Catastrophic Flooding*, edited by L. Mayer and D. Nash, pp. 23–56. Allen and Unwin, Boston.

Holloway, Richard G.

1981 Preservation and Experimental Diagenesis of the Pollen Exine. Unpublished Ph.D. dissertation, Department of Biology, Texas A&M University, College Station, Texas.

1984 Analysis of Surface Pollen from Alberta, Canada by Polar Ordination. *Northwest Science* 58:18–28.

1989 Experimental Mechanical Pollen Degradation and Its Application to Quaternary Age Deposits. *Texas Journal of Science* 41:131–145.

1996 Synthetic Overview of Palynological Data from the El Paso Natural Gas Project, McKinley and San Juan Counties, New Mexico. Quaternary Services Technical Report Series, Report No. 96-004. Manuscript on file, WCRM, Inc., Bloomfield, New Mexico.

Huber, Edgar K.

1996 *Inventory, National Register Recommendations, and Treatment Plan for Prehistoric Archaeological Resources*. Draft. Cultural Resource Management Plan for the Fairfield Canoa Ranch Property, vol. 2. Technical Series. Statistical Research, Tucson.

Huckell, Bruce B.

1982 *The Distribution of Fluted Points in Arizona: A Review and an Update*. Archaeological Series No. 145. Arizona State Museum, University of Arizona, Tucson.

1984a *The Archaic Occupation of the Rosemont Area, Northern Santa Rita Mountains, Southeastern Arizona*. Archaeological Series No. 147(1). Arizona State Museum, University of Arizona, Tucson.

1984b The Paleo-Indian and Archaic Occupation of the Tucson Basin: An Overview. *The Kiva* 49:133–145.

1988 Late Archaic Archaeology of the Tucson Basin: A Status Report. In *Recent Research on Tucson Basin Prehistory: Proceedings of the Second Tucson Basin Conference*, edited by William H. Doelle and Paul R. Fish, pp. 57–80. Anthropological Papers No. 10. Institute for American Research, Tucson.

1990 Late Preceramic Farmer-foragers in Southwestern Arizona: A Cultural and Ecological Consideration of the Spread of Agriculture into the Arid Southwestern United States. Unpublished Ph.D. dissertation, Department of Arid Lands Resources Sciences, University of Arizona, Tucson.

1995 *Of Marshes and Maize: Preceramic Agricultural Settlements in the Cienega Valley, Southeastern Arizona*. Anthropological Papers of the University of Arizona No. 59. University of Arizona Press, Tucson.

Huckell, Bruce B., Martyn D. Tagg, and Lisa W. Huckell

1987 *The Corona de Tucson Project: Prehistoric Use of a Bajada Environment*. Archaeological Series No. 174. Arizona State Museum, University of Arizona, Tucson.

Huckell, Lisa W.

1987 Archaeobotanical Remains. In *The Corona de Tucson Project: Prehistoric Use of a Bajada Environment*. Archaeological Series No. 174. Arizona State Museum, University of Arizona, Tucson.

1992 Plant Remains. In *On the Frontier: A Trincheras–Hohokam Farmstead, Arivaca, Arizona*. Technical Series 30. Statistical Research, Tucson.

Huett, Mary Lou

1995   The Cultural Resources Inventory of a 6.15-Acre Parcel for the Nogales Housing Authority in Santa Cruz County, Arizona. Cultural and Environmental Systems. Manuscript on file, Arizona State Museum Library, University of Arizona, Tucson.

Huntington, Ellsworth

1912   The Fluctuating Climate of North America—The Ruins of the Hohokam. In *Annual Report of the Board of Regents of the Smithsonian Institution*, pp. 383–397. Smithsonian Institution, Washington, D.C.

1914   *The Climate Factor as Illustrated in Arid America*. Publication No. 192. Carnegie Institution of Washington, Washington, D.C.

Irving, E.

1964   *Palaeomagnetism and Its Application of Geological and Geophysical Problems*. John Wiley, New York.

Jácome, Felipe Carlos

1986   *The Nogales Wash Site: Preliminary Report of the Nogales City Dump Archaeological Project*. Pimeria Alta Historical Society, Nogales, Arizona.

Jobson, R. W.

1986   Stone Tool Morphology and Rabbit Butchering. *Lithic Technology* 15(1):9–20.

Johnson, Alfred E.

1960   The Place of the Trincheras Culture of Northern Sonora in Southwest Archaeology. Unpublished Master's thesis, Department of Anthropology, University of Arizona, Tucson.

1963   The Trincheras Culture of Northern Sonora. *American Antiquity* 29:174–186.

Johnston, B.

1964   A Newly Discovered Turquoise Mine of Prehistory, Mohave County, Arizona. *The Kiva* 29:76–83.

1966   Ancient Turquoise Mine and Tunnel with Tools Re-discovered near Kingman, Arizona. *Lapidary Journal* 20:309–313.

Jones, F. A.

1904   History and Mining of Turquoise in the Southwest. *The Mining World* 31:1,251–1,252.

1909   Notes on Turquoise in the Southwest: Concerning Its Original Workings, Its Geology and Its Modern Method of Mining. *South-Western Mines* 1(12):1–2.

Karlstrom, Thor V. N.

1988   Alluvial Chronology and Hydrological Change of Black Mesa and nearby Regions. In *The Anasazi in a Changing Environment*, edited by G. J. Gumerman, pp. 45–91. Cambridge University Press, Cambridge.

Kelly, Isabel T., James Officer, and Emil W. Haury

1978   *The Hodges Ruin: A Hohokam Community in the Tucson Basin*. Anthropological Papers of the University of Arizona No. 30. University of Arizona Press, Tucson.

Kessell, John L.

1970   *Mission of Sorrows: Jesuit Guevavi and the Pimas, 1691–1767*. University of Arizona Press, Tucson.

Kirschvink, J. L.

1980   The Least-Squares Line and Plane and the Analysis of Paleomagnetic Data. *Journal of the Royal Physics Society* 62:699–718.

Krogman, W. M.

1978   *The Human Skeleton in Forensic Medicine*. Charles C. Thomas, Springfield, Illinois.

Lascaux, Annick

1998   A Class III Archaeological Inventory of Fifty-eight 30-meter Diameter Light and Power Pole Locations along the International Border, Nogales, Santa Cruz County, Arizona. SWCA, Inc. Manuscript on file, Arizona State Museum Library, University of Arizona, Tucson.

Lekson, Stephen H.

1990   Sedentism and Aggregation in Anasazi Archaeology. In *Perspectives on Southwestern Prehistory*, edited by P. E. Minnis and C. L. Redman, pp. 333–340. Westview Press, Boulder, Colorado.

Leney, L., and R. W. Casteel

1975   Simplified Procedure for Examining Charcoal Specimens for Identification. *Journal of Archaeological Science* 2:153–159.

Lindsay, Lee W., Jr.

1993   Archaeological Survey of the Proposed Development Site, Bonito Villa Partners. Statistical

Research. Manuscript on file, Arizona State Museum Library, University of Arizona, Tucson.

Lite, Jeremy A.
1992 A Cultural Resources Survey of Existing and Proposed Arizona Department of Transportation Right-of-Way at the Intersection of Business-19 and State Route 189 in Nogales, Santa Cruz, County, Arizona. Archaeological Research Services. Manuscript on file, Arizona State Museum Library, University of Arizona, Tucson.

1996a A Cultural Resources Survey of 5.2 Miles of Business-19 Right-of-Way (Milepost 0.0 to 5.2) in Nogales, Arizona, Santa Cruz County, Arizona. Project Report No. 96:84. Archaeological Research Services. Manuscript on file, Arizona State Museum Library, University of Arizona, Tucson.

1996b A Cultural Resources Survey of 1.1 Miles of State Route 189 (Mariposa Road) Right-of-Way from Milepost 0.0 to 0.3 and Milepost 3.0 to 3.8, Santa Cruz County, Arizona. Project Report No. 96:85. Archaeological Research Services. Manuscript on file, Arizona State Museum Library, University of Arizona, Tucson.

Lite, Jeremy A., and Matthew M. Palus
1997 A Cultural Resources Survey of Existing and Proposed Arizona Department of Transportation Right-of-Way at the Intersection of Business 19 and State Route 189 in Nogales, Santa Cruz County, Arizona. Project Report 97:39. Archaeological Research Services. Manuscript on file, Arizona State Museum Library, University of Arizona, Tucson.

Lite, Jeremy A., Jennifer K. Tweedy, and Teresa L. Cadiente
1996 A Cultural Resources Survey of 30 Miles of Interstate-19 Right-of-Way along the Santa Cruz River Valley between Nogales and Amado (Kilometers 0.0 to 48.3, Mileposts 0.0 to 30), Santa Cruz County, Arizona. Project Report 96:83. Archaeological Research Services. Manuscript on file, Arizona State Museum Library, University of Arizona, Tucson.

Lovejoy, C. O., R. S. Meindl, T. R. Pryzbeck, and R. P. Mensforth
1985 Chronological Metamorphosis of the Auricular Surface of the Ilium: A New Method for the Determination of Age at Death. *American Journal of Physical Anthropology* 68:15–28.

Lumholtz, Karl S.
1912 *New Trails in Mexico.* Scribner, New York.

Lyman, R. Lee
1994 *Vertebrate Taphonomy.* Cambridge University Press, Cambridge.

Mabry, Jonathan B.
1997 Rewriting Prehistory: Recent Discoveries at Cienega Phase Sites in the Santa Cruz Floodplain. *Archaeology in Tucson Newsletter* 11(3):1, 6–7. Center for Desert Archaeology, Tucson.

Mabry, Jonathan B. (editor)
1998a *Archaeological Investigations of Early Village Sites in the Middle Santa Cruz Valley.* Anthropological Papers No. 19. Center for Desert Archaeology, Tucson.

1998b *Paleoindian and Archaic Sites in Arizona.* Technical Report No. 97-7. Center for Desert Archaeology, Tucson.

Mabry, Jonathan B., and Jeffery J. Clark
1994 Early Village Life on the Santa Cruz River. *Archaeology in Tucson Newsletter* 8(1):1–5. Center for Desert Archaeology, Tucson.

Mabry, Jonathan B., and James P. Holmlund
1998 Canals. In *Archaeological Investigations of Early Village Sites in the Middle Santa Cruz Valley: Analyses and Syntheses,* edited by J. B. Mabry, pp. 283–298. Anthropological Papers No. 19, Part 1. Center for Desert Archaeology, Tucson.

Mabry, Jonathan B., Deborah L. Swartz, Helga Wocherl, Jeffery J. Clark, Gavin H. Archer, and Michael W. Lindeman
1997 *Archaeological Investigations of Early Village Sites in the Middle Santa Cruz Valley: Descriptions of the Santa Cruz Bend, Square Hearth, Stone Pipe, and Canal Sites.* Anthropological Papers No. 18. Center for Desert Archaeology, Tucson.

Maldonaldo, Ronald P.
1987 An Archaeological Survey of a Proposed 20-Acre Subdivision in Nogales, Arizona. Cultural and Environmental Systems. Manuscript on file, Arizona State Museum Library, University of Arizona, Tucson.

Maresh, M. M.
1955   Linear Growth of Long Bones of Extremities from Infancy through Adolescence. *American Journal of Diseases of Children* 89:725–742.

Martin, A. C., and W. D. Barkley
1961   *Seed Identification Manual.* University of California Press, Berkeley.

Martin, Paul S.
1963   *The Last 10,000 Years.* University of Arizona Press, Tucson.

Martynec, Richard, Sandra Martynec, and Duane E. Peter
1994   *Cultural Resources Survey and Monitoring of the Nogales, Arizona, Sector of the U.S.–Mexican Border.* Miscellaneous Reports of Investigation No. 34. Geo-Marine, Plano, Texas.

Matson, R. G.
1991   *The Origins of Southwestern Agriculture.* University of Arizona Press, Tucson.

McElhinny, M. W.
1973   *Paleomagnetism and Plate Tectonics.* Cambridge University Press, London.

McFadden, P. L., and F. J. Lowes
1981   The Discrimination of Mean Directions Drawn from Fisher Distributions. *Geophysical Journal of the Royal Astronomical Society* 34:163–189.

McGee, W. J.
1895   The Beginning of Agriculture. *American Anthropologist* 8:350–375.

McGuire, Randall H.
1982   Problems in Culture History. In *Hohokam and Patayan: Prehistory of Southwestern Arizona,* edited by R. H. McGuire and M. B. Schiffer, pp. 150–222. Academic Press, San Diego.

McGuire, Randall H., and Ann V. Howard
1987   The Structure and Organization of Hohokam Shell Exchange. *The Kiva* 52:113–146.

McGuire, Randall H., and Michael B. Schiffer
1982   *Hohokam and Patayan: Prehistory of Southwestern Arizona.* Academic Press, New York.

McGuire, Randall H., and Maria Elisa Villalpando C.
1993   *An Archaeological Survey of the Altar Valley, Sonora, Mexico.* Archaeological Series No. 184.

Arizona State Museum, University of Arizona, Tucson.

McGuire, Randall H., Maria Elisa Villalpando C., Victoria D. Vargas, Emiliano Gallaga M.
1999   Cerro de Trincheras and the Casas Grandes World. In *The Casas Grandes World,* edited by C. F. Schaafsma and C. L. Riley, pp. 134–146. University of Utah Press, Salt Lake City.

McKusick, Charmion R.
1974   Bird Remains. In *Casas Grandes: A Fallen Center of the Gran Chichimeca,* vol. 9, by Charles C. Di Peso, John B. Rinaldo, and Gloria J. Fenner, pp. 267–308. Amerind Foundation, Dragoon, Arizona, and Northland Press, Flagstaff.

Montero, Laurene G.
1993   Archaeological Clearance Survey for Proposed Boundary Fencing at Sonoita Creek State Natural Area Park, Santa Cruz County, Arizona. Arizona State Parks. Manuscript on file, Arizona State Museum Library, University of Arizona, Tucson.

Montgomery, F. H.
1977   *Seeds and Fruits of Plants of Eastern Canada and Northeastern United States.* University of Toronto Press, Toronto.

Moore-Jansen, P., S. D. Ousley, and R. L. Jantz
1994   *Data Collection Procedures for Forensic Skeletal Material.* Report of Investigations No. 48. University of Tennessee, Knoxville.

Munsell Color
1994   *Munsell Soil Color Charts.* Rev. ed. New Windsor, New York.

Nations, Dale, and Edmund Stump
1981   *The Geology of Arizona.* Kendall-Hunt, Dubuque, Iowa.

Neily, Robert B.
1991   Archaeological Survey of the El Paso Natural Gas Company Twin Buttes Pipeline, Pima and Santa Cruz Counties, Arizona. Archaeological Consulting Services. Manuscript on file, Arizona State Museum Library, University of Arizona, Tucson.

1994   *Archaeological Investigations near Nogales, Arizona and Site Testing at the Buena Vista Ranch Site, AZ EE:9:151 (ASM).* Technical Report 93-21. Statistical Research, Tucson.

Neily, Robert B., and Thomas R. Euler
1987   A Cultural Resource Inventory of Bureau of Land Management Land Proposed for the New Santa Cruz County Administrative Complex. Manuscript on file, Cultural Resource Management Division, Arizona State Museum, University of Arizona, Tucson.

Nelson, Richard S.
1991   *Hohokam Marine Shell Exchange and Artifacts.* Archaeological Series No. 179. Arizona State Museum, University of Arizona, Tucson.

O'Brien, P. M., E. Bassett, and A. E. Rogge
1989   Archaeological Investigation along the Santa Cruz 115kV Transmission Line Corridor: Amado to Tubac Segment. Dames and Moore. Manuscript on file, Arizona State Museum Library, University of Arizona, Tucson.

Olson, Matthew
1998   An Archaeological Resource Survey of 12.6 Acres near Tubac, Santa Cruz County, Arizona. SWCA, Inc. Manuscript on file, Arizona State Museum Library, University of Arizona, Tucson.

Palus, Matthew M.
1997   A Cultural Resources Survey of 10.8 Miles of State Route 289 Right-of-Way (between Milepost 0.0 and 10.8), the Pena Blanca Road in Coronado National Forest, Santa Cruz County, Arizona. Archaeological Research Services. Manuscript on file, Arizona State Museum Library, University of Arizona, Tucson.

Panshin, A. J., and C. de Zeeuw
1980   *Textbook of Wood Technology.* 4th ed. McGraw-Hill, New York.

Parry, W. J., and R. L. Kelly
1987   Expedient Core Technology and Sedentism. In *The Organization of Core Technology*, edited by J. K. Johnson and C. A. Morrow, pp. 285–304. Westview Press, Boulder.

Phillips, David A., Jr.
1989   Prehistory of Chihuahua and Sonora, Mexico. *Journal of World Prehistory* 3:373–401.

1995   Archaeological Survey of a Proposed Fire Station near Nogales, Santa Cruz County, Arizona. SWCA, Inc. Manuscript on file, Arizona State Museum Library, University of Arizona, Tucson.

Plog, Fred, George J. Gumerman, Robert C. Euler, Jeffrey S. Dean, Richard H. Hevly, and Thor N. V. Karlstrom
1988   Anasazi Adaptive Strategies: The Model, Predictions, and Results. In *The Anasazi in a Changing Environment*, edited by G. J. Gumerman, pp. 230–276. Cambridge University Press, Cambridge.

Reinhard, Karl J.
1978   Prehistoric Cremations from Nogales, Arizona. *The Kiva* 43:231–252.

Reinhard, Karl J., and T. Michael Fink
1982   The Multi-individual Cremation Phenomenon of the Santa Cruz Drainage. *The Kiva* 47:151–161.

Richardson, M. L., S. D. Clemmons, and J. C. Walker
1979   *Soil Survey of Santa Cruz and Parks of Cochise and Pima Counties, Arizona.* U.S. Department of Agriculture, Soil Conservation Service and Forest Service in cooperation with the Arizona Agricultural Experiment Station. Government Printing Office, Washington, D.C.

Roberts, Heidi
1993   An Archaeological Survey of 1.2 Acres of the Tubac-Tumacacori Volunteer Fire Department, Santa Cruz County, Arizona. SWCA, Inc. Manuscript on file, Arizona State Museum Library, University of Arizona, Tucson.

Robinson, William J.
1976   Mission Guevavi: Excavations in the Convento. *The Kiva* 42:135–175.

Roth, Barbara J.
1989   Late Archaic Settlement and Subsistence in the Tucson Basin. Unpublished Ph.D. dissertation, Department of Anthropology, University of Arizona, Tucson.

1992   An Archaeological Survey of a U.S. West Right-of-Way along State Route 189 in Nogales, Santa Cruz County, Arizona. Tierra Right-of-Way Services, Ltd. Manuscript on file, Arizona State Museum Library, University of Arizona, Tucson.

1995   Regional Land Use in the Late Archaic of the Tucson Basin: A View from the Upper Bajada. In *Early Formative Adaptation in the Southern Southwest*, edited by B. J. Roth, pp. 37–48. Monographs in World Archaeology No. 5. Prehistory Press, Madison, Wisconsin.

Rothweiler, Thomas S., and Mary Jane Gregory
1980 National Register of Historic Places Nomination Form for the Old Nogales City Hall and Station. Arizona State Historic Preservation Office, Phoenix.

Rouse, Irving
1972 *Introduction to Prehistory: A Systematic Approach.* McGraw-Hill, New York.

Rozen, Kenneth C.
1984 Flaked Stone. In *Hohokam Habitation Sites in the Northern Santa Rita Mountains*, edited by A. Ferg, K. C. Rozen, W. L. Deaver, M. D. Tagg, D. A. Phillips Jr., and D. A. Gregory, pp. 421–604. Archaeological Series No. 147(2), pt. I. Arizona State Museum, University of Arizona, Tucson.

Sauer, Carl O., and Donald Brand
1931 Prehistoric Settlements of Sonora with Special Reference to Cerros de Trincheras. *University of California Publications in Geography* 5(3):67–148. University of California, Berkeley.

Sayles, E. B.
1937 Stone Implements and Bowls. In *Excavations at Snaketown, Material Culture,* by Harold S. Gladwin, Emil W. Haury, E. B. Sayles, and Nora Gladwin, pp. 101–120. Medallion Papers No. 25. Gila Pueblo, Globe, Arizona.

1945 Material Culture. In *The San Simon Branch: Excavations at Cave Creek and in the San Simon Valley*, vol. I. Medallion Papers No. 29. Gila Pueblo, Globe, Arizona.

1983 *The Cochise Cultural Sequence in Southeastern Arizona.* Anthropological Papers of the University of Arizona No. 42. University of Arizona Press, Tucson.

Sayles, E. B., and Ernst Antevs
1941 *The Cochise Culture.* Medallion Papers No. 29. Gila Pueblo, Globe, Arizona.

Scantling, Frederick H.
1940 Excavations at the Jackrabbit Ruin, Papago Indian Reservation, Arizona. Unpublished Master's thesis, Department of Anthropology, University of Arizona, Tucson.

Schiffer, Michael B.
1987 *Formation Processes of the Archaeological Record.* University of New Mexico Press, Albuquerque.

Schopmeyer, C. S.
1974 *Seeds of Woody Plants in the United States.* USDA Agriculture Handbook No. 450. U.S. Department of the Interior, Forest Service, Washington, D.C.

Schott, Michael
1986 Technological Organization and Settlement Mobility: An Ethnographic Examination. *Journal of Anthropological Research* 42:175–188.

Schour, J., and M. Massler
1944 Development of the Human Dentition. Chart distributed by the American Dental Association.

Schwalen, H. C., and R. J. Shaw
1957 *Ground Water Supplies of Santa Cruz Valley of Southern Arizona between Rillito Station and the International Boundary.* Technical Bulletin No. 288. Agricultural Experiment Station, University of Arizona, Tucson.

Scott, Barry G.
1995 U.S. West Communication Highway 82 Cable Replacement Archaeological Survey. Iguana Archaeological Research. Manuscript on file, Arizona State Museum Library, University of Arizona, Tucson.

Scott, E. C.
1979 Dental Wear Scoring Technique. *American Journal of Physical Anthropology* 51:213–218.

Sellers, William D., and Richard H. Hill
1974 *Arizona Climate, 1931–1972.* University of Arizona Press, Tucson.

Seymour, Deni
1990 *A Methodological Perspective on the Use and Organization of Space: A Case Study of Hohokam Structures from Snaketown, Arizona.* Ph.D. dissertation, Department of Anthropology, University of Arizona, Tucson. University Microfilms, Ann Arbor.

1991a A Cultural Resources Inventory of the Proposed Guevavi Ranch Preserve, Santa Cruz County, Arizona. SWCA, Inc. Manuscript on file, Arizona State Museum Library, University of Arizona, Tucson.

1991b Results of the Supplemental Survey for the Guevavi Ranch Preserve, Santa Cruz County, Arizona. SWCA, Inc. Manuscript on file, Arizona State Museum Library, University of Arizona, Tucson.

1992   Site Card for AZ EE:9:153 (ASM). Site Files, Arizona State Museum, University of Arizona, Tucson.

Seymour, Gregory
1991   A Cultural Resource Survey for a Proposed Buried Fiber Optic Line along the I-19 Frontage Road. SWCA, Inc. Manuscript on file, Arizona State Museum Library, University of Arizona, Tucson.

Shelley, Steven D., and Jeffrey H. Altschul
1987   *Cultural Resources Literature Search and Survey of Portions of Nogales Wash and Potrero Creek, Southern Arizona.* Technical Series 6. Statistical Research, Tucson.

Shenk, Lynette O.
1976   *San Jose de Tumacacori: An Archeological Synthesis and Research Design.* Prepared for the Western Archeological and Conservation Center, National Park Service. Manuscript on file, Arizona State Museum Library, University of Arizona, Tucson.

Shenk, Lynette O., and George A. Teague
1975   *Excavations at the Tubac Presidio.* Archaeological Series No. 85. Arizona State Museum, University of Arizona, Tucson.

Shuey, R. T., E. R. Cole, and M. J. Mikulich
1970   Geographic Correction of Archaeomagnetic Data. *Journal of Geomagnetism and Geoelectricity* 22:485–489.

Simonis, Don
1983   AZ EE:9:1 (BLM), Cultural Resources-Field Inventory Site Form. Manuscript on file, Bureau of Land Management, Denver.

Slawson, Laurie V.
1991   *Archaeological Investigations in Nogales, Arizona: A Limited Testing Program at AZ EE:9:107 (ASM).* Technical Series No 27. Cultural and Environmental Systems, Tucson.

1995   A Cultural Resources Inventory of the Hacienda del las Flores Subdivision Right-of-Way North of Nogales, Arizona. Cultural and Environmental Systems. Manuscript on file, Arizona State Museum Library, University of Arizona, Tucson.

Smith, B. H.
1984   Patterns of Molar Wear in Hunter-Gatherers and Agriculturalists. *American Journal of Physical Anthropology* 63:39–56.

Snow, David H.
1990   Tener Comal y Metate: Protohistoric Rio Grande Maize Use and Diet. In *Perspectives on Southwestern Prehistory,* edited by P. E. Minnis and C. L. Redman, pp. 289–300. Westview Press, Boulder.

Stacy, Pheriba V. K.
1974   Cerros de Trincheras in the Arizona Papagueria. Unpublished Ph.D. dissertation, Department of Anthropology, University of Arizona, Tucson.

Stebbins, Robert C.
1954   *Amphibians and Reptiles of Western North America.* McGraw-Hill, New York.

Sternberg, Robert S.
1982   *Archaeomagnetic Secular Variation of Direction and Paleointensity in the American Southwest.* Ph.D. Dissertation, Department of Geosciences, University of Arizona, Tucson.

1990   The Geophysical Basis of Archaeomagnetic Dating. In *Archaeomagnetic Dating,* edited by J. L. Eighmy and R. S. Sternberg, pp. 5–28. University of Arizona Press, Tucson.

Sternberg, Robert S., Richard C. Lange, Barbara A. Murphy, William A. Deaver, and Lynn S. Teague
1990   Archaeomagnetic Dating at Las Colinas, Arizona, USA. In *Archaeometry '90: Proceedings of the 27th International Symposium on Archaeometry,* edited by E. Pernicka and G. A. Wagner, pp. 597–606. Birkhauser, Basel, Switzerland.

Sternberg, Robert S., and Randall H. McGuire
1990   Techniques for Constructing Secular Variation Curves and for Interpreting Archaeomagnetic Dates. In *Archaeomagnetic Dating,* edited by J. L. Eighmy and R. S. Sternberg, pp. 109–136. University of Arizona Press, Tucson.

Stone, Bradford W.
1994   Cultural Resources Survey of a 2.3 Mile Long Segment of the Old Tucson Road North of Nogales, South-Central Santa Cruz County, Arizona. Archaeological Research Services, Inc. Manuscript on file, Arizona State Museum Library, University of Arizona, Tucson.

1995 Cultural Resources Survey of an Aggregate Materials Source and Alternative Sources within the Interstate-19 Traffic Median North of the Mariposa Road/Interstate-19 Traffic Interchange. Archaeological Research Services. Manuscript on file, Arizona State Museum Library, University of Arizona, Tucson.

Stuart-Macadam, P.
1985 Porotic Hyperostosis: Representative of a Childhood Condition. *American Journal of Physical Anthropology* 66:391–398.

Sullivan, Mark E.
1993 A Cultural Resource Inventory of a 7.06-Acre Parcel in the City of Nogales. Cultural and Environmental Systems. Manuscript on file, Arizona State Museum Library, University of Arizona, Tucson.

1996 A Cultural Resource Inventory of Approximately 7.6 Miles of Trails on State Land surrounding Patagonia Lake, Santa Cruz County, Arizona. Technical Report No. 96-26. Aztlan Archaeology, Tucson.

Swartz, Deborah L.
1995 *An Archaeological Survey for Mining Activity South of Patagonia, Arizona.* Letter Report No. 95:106. Center for Desert Archaeology, Tucson.

1999a *Archaeological Survey of a Proposed Water Pipeline and Forebay along South River Road in Santa Cruz County, North of Nogales, Arizona.* Letter Report No. 98:208. Center for Desert Archaeology, Tucson.

1999b *Archaeological Survey of 3.1 Miles along Interstate 10 between Ruby Road and Rio Rico Drive in Santa Cruz County, North of Nogales, Arizona.* Letter Report 99:123. Center for Desert Archaeology, Tucson.

1999c *Data Recovery at AZ EE:9:117 (ASM), a Small Site along the Santa Cruz River North of Nogales, Arizona.* Technical Report No. 99-1. Center for Desert Archaeology, Tucson.

Szuter, Christine R.
1991 *Hunting by Prehistoric Horticulturalists in the American Southwest.* Garland Publishing, New York.

Szuter, Christine R., and Frank Bayham
1984 Techniques of Salt-Gila Aqueduct Project Faunal Analysis. In *Environment and Subsistence,* edited by L. S. Teague and P. L. Crown, pp. 21–31. Hohokam Archaeology along the Salt Gila Aqueduct Central Arizona Project, vol. VII. Archaeological Series No. 150. Arizona State Museum, University of Arizona, Tucson.

Tarling, D. H.
1983 *Paleomagnetism: Principles and Applications in Geology, Geophysics, and Archaeology.* Chapman and Hall, London.

Teris, Lee, and David Doak
1995 A Cultural Resource Survey of Two Proposed Roads through Pena Blanca Highlands, Santa Cruz County, Arizona. SWCA, Inc. Manuscript on file, Arizona State Museum Library, University of Arizona, Tucson.

Thiel, Homer J.
1995 *A Survey of 4.1 Miles of South River Road, Santa Cruz County, Arizona.* Letter Report No. 95-121. Center for Desert Archaeology, Tucson.

Ubelaker, Donald H.
1984 *Human Skeletal Remains.* Taraxacum Press, Washington, D.C.

Van Buren, Mary, James M. Skibo, and Alan P. Sullivan III
1992 The Archaeology of an Agave Roasting Location. In *The Marana Community in the Hohokam World,* edited by S. K. Fish, P. R. Fish, and J. H. Madsen, pp. 88–96. Anthropological Papers of the University of Arizona No. 56. University of Arizona Press, Tucson.

Van West, Carla R.
1994 Proposal to Conduct Archaeological Data Recovery, AZ EE:9:107 (ASM). Statistical Research, Tucson. Submitted to Public Works Department, Santa Cruz County.

Van West, Carla R., and Jeffrey H. Altschul
1998 Environmental Variability and Agricultural Economics along the Lower Verde River, A.D. 750–1450. In *Overview, Synthesis, and Conclusions,* edited by S. M. Whittlesey, R. Ciolek-Torrello, and J. H. Altschul, pp. 337–392. Vanishing River: Landscapes and Lives of the Lower Verde Valley: The Lower Verde Archaeological Project. SRI Press, Tucson.

Van West, Carla R., Richard S. Ciolek-Torrello, John R. Welch, Jeffrey H. Altschul, Karen R. Adams, Steven D. Shelley, and Jeffrey A. Homburg
2000 Subsistence and Environmental Interactions. In *Salado*, edited by J. S. Dean, pp. 27–56. Amerind Foundation Publication No. 4. University of New Mexico Press, Albuquerque.

Villalpando, Maria Elisa
1997 La Tradicion Trincheras y Los Grupos Consteros del Desierto Sonorense. In *Prehistory of the Borderlands: Recent Research in the Archaeology of Northern Mexico and Southern Southwest,* edited by J. Carpenter and G. Sanchez, pp. 95–111. Archaeological Series No. 186. Arizona State Museum, University of Arizona, Tucson.

Vivian, Gordon
1955 Stabilization Requirements for Southwestern National Monuments, pt. 2. Manuscript on file, Western Archeological and Conservation Center, National Park Service, Tucson.

Walker, Philip L.
1985 Anemia among Prehistoric Indians of the American Southwest. In *Health and Disease in the Prehistoric Southwest*, edited by C. Merbs and R. Miller, pp. 139–164. Anthropological Research Papers No. 34. Department of Anthropology, Arizona State University, Tempe.

Wallace, Henry D.
1985 Decorated Ceramics. In *Excavations at the Valencia Site: A Preclassic Hohokam Village in the Southern Tucson Basin*, by William H. Doelle, pp. 81–135. Anthropological Papers No. 3. Institute for American Research, Tucson.

1986 *Rincon Phase Decorated Ceramics in the Tucson Basin.* Anthropological Papers No. 1. Institute for American Research, Tucson.

1997 Presence or Parlance? The Meaning of "Hohokam" and Concepts of Culture, A.D. 800 to 1050, in Southeastern Arizona. Paper presented at the seminar "The Archaeology of a Land Between: Regional Dynamics in the Prehistory and History of Southeastern Arizona." Amerind Foundation, Dragoon, Arizona.

Wallace, Henry D., James M. Heidke, and William H. Doelle
1995 Hohokam Origins. *Kiva* 60(4):575–618.

Warren, A. Helene, and F. Joan Mathien
1985 Prehistoric and Historic Mining in the Cerrillos District: Time and Place. In *Southwestern Culture History: Collected Papers in Honor of Albert H. Schroeder*, edited by C. H. Lange, pp. 93–127. Papers of the Archaeological Society of New Mexico No. 10. Ancient City Press, Santa Fe.

Warren, A. Helene, and R. H. Weber
1979 Indian and Spanish Mining in the Galisteo and Hagan Basins. In *Archaeology and History of Santa Fe Country*, edited by R. V. Ingersoll and J. R. Callender, pp. 7–11. Special Publication No. 8. New Mexico Geological Society, Socorro.

Wasley, William W.
1968 Archaeological Survey in Sonora, Mexico. Paper presented at the Annual Meeting of the Society for American Archaeology, Santa Fe. Manuscript on file, Arizona State Museum, University of Arizona, Tucson.

Waters, Michael R.
1987 Holocene Alluvial Geology and Geoarchaeology of AZ BB:13:14 and the San Xavier Reach of the Santa Cruz River, Arizona. In *The Archaeology of the San Xavier Bridge Site (AZ BB:13:14), Tucson Basin, Southern Arizona*, edited by John C. Ravesloot, pp. 39–60. Archaeological Series No. 171. Arizona State Museum, University of Arizona, Tucson.

1988 The Impact of Fluvial Processes and Landscape Evolution on Archaeological Sites and Settlement Patterns along the San Xavier Reach of the Santa Cruz River. *Geoarchaeology* 3:205–219.

Weaver, David S.
1977 New Methods for the Determination of Sex, Age, and Rates of Growth of Infant and Child Skeletal Remains in Prehistoric American Indian Populations. Unpublished Ph.D. dissertation, Department of Anthropology, University of New Mexico, Albuquerque.

Webb, Robert H., and Julio L. Betancourt
1992 *Climatic Variability and Flood Frequency of the Santa Cruz River, Pima County, Arizona.* U.S. Geological Survey Water-Supply Paper No. 2379. U.S. Government Printing Office, Washington, D.C.

Weigand, Philip C.

1982a Mining and Mineral Trade in Prehistoric Zacatecas. *Anthropology* 6(1–2):87–134.

1982b Sherds Associated with Turquoise Mines in Southwestern U.S.A. *Pottery Southwest* 9(2):4–6.

1994 Observations on Ancient Mining within the Northwestern Regions of the Mesoamerican Civilization, with Emphasis on Turquoise. In *Quest of Mineral Wealth: Aboriginal and Colonial Mining and Metallurgy in Spanish America,* edited by A. K. Craig and R. C. West, pp. 21–35. Geosciences and Man 33, K. Mathewson and G. Stone, general editors. Department of Geography and Anthropology, Louisiana State University, Baton Rouge.

Welch, John R., and Daniela Triadan

1991 The Canyon Creek Turquoise Mine, Arizona. *Kiva* 56:145–164.

Western Regional Climate Center (WRCC)

2000 Western U.S. Climate Historical Summaries; Climatological Data Summaries (Temperature and Precipitation); Arizona Climate Summaries; Nogales, Nogales Old Nogales, and Nogales 6N. <http://wrcc.sage.dri.edu/summary/climsaz.html>

Whalen, Norman M.

1971 Cochise Culture Sites in the Central San Pedro Drainage, Arizona. Unpublished Ph.D. dissertation, Department of Anthropology, University of Arizona, Tucson.

Wheat, Joe Ben

1955 *Mogollon Culture Prior to A.D. 1000.* Memoirs of the American Anthropological Association No. 82, and Memoirs of the Society for American Archaeology No. 10. American Anthropological Association and Society for American Archaeology, Menasha and Salt Lake City.

Whittaker, J. C.

1994 *Flintknapping: Making and Understanding Stone Tools.* University of Texas Press, Austin.

Whittlesey, Stephanie M.

1987 Plain and Red Ware Ceramics. In *The Archaeology of the San Xavier Bridge Site (AZ BB:13:14), Tucson Basin, Southern Arizona,* edited by J. C. Ravesloot, pp. 181–204. Archaeological Series No. 171. Arizona State Museum, University of Arizona, Tucson.

1992 Ceramics. In *On the Frontier: A Trincheras-Hohokam Farmstead, Arivaca, Arizona,* edited by S. M. Whittlesey and R. S. Ciolek-Torrello, pp. 39–51. Technical Series 30. Statistical Research, Tucson.

1995 Ceramics. In *Early Farmers of the Sonoran Desert: Archaeological Investigations at the Houghton Road Site, Tucson, Arizona,* edited by R. Ciolek-Torrello, pp. 127–167. Technical Series 72. Statistical Research, Tucson.

1996 Culture History: Prehistoric Narratives for Southern Arizona. In *Background and Research Design for Prehistoric Archaeological Resources,* by Carla R. Van West and Stephanie M. Whittlesey, pp. 45–80. Draft. Cultural Resource Management Plan for the Fairfield Canoa Ranch Property, vol. 1. Technical Series. Statistical Research, Tucson.

1998 Rethinking the Core-Periphery Model of the Pre-Classic Period Hohokam. In *Overview, Synthesis, and Conclusions,* edited by S. M. Whittlesey, R. S. Ciolek-Torrello, and J. H. Altschul, pp. 597–628. Vanishing River: Landscapes and Lives of the Lower Verde Valley: The Lower Verde Archaeological Project. SRI Press, Tucson.

1999 Engendering the Mogollon Past: Theory and Mortuary Data from Grasshopper Pueblo. In *Sixty Years of Mogollon Archaeology: Papers from the Ninth Mogollon Conference, Silver City, New Mexico, 1996,* edited by S. M. Whittlesey, pp. 39–48. SRI Press, Tucson.

Whittlesey, Stephanie M., and Richard S. Ciolek-Torrello

1992 *On the Frontier: A Trincheras-Hohokam Farmstead, Arivaca, Arizona.* Technical Series 30. Statistical Research, Tucson.

1996 The Archaic-Formative Transition in the Tucson Basin. In *Early Formative Adaptations in the Southern Southwest,* edited by B. J. Roth, pp. 49–64. Prehistory Press, Madison.

Whittlesey, Stephanie M., Richard S. Ciolek-Torrello, and Matthew A. Sterner

1994 *Southern Arizona: The Last 12,000 Years: A Cultural-Historic Overview for the Western Army National Guard Aviation Training Site.* Technical Series 48. Statistical Research, Tucson.

Wilcox, David R.

1987 New Models of Social Structure at the Palo Parado Site. In *Exploring the Hohokam: Prehistoric Desert Peoples of the American Southwest,* edited by G. J. Gumerman, pp. 281–319. Amerind Foundation, Dragoon, Arizona, and University of New Mexico Press, Albuquerque.

Wilson, Marjorie
1974 National Register of Historic Places Nomination Form for Pete Kitchen's El Potrero Ranch. Arizona State Historic Preservation Office, Phoenix.

1977 National Register of Historic Places Nomination Form for the Santa Cruz County Courthouse. Arizona State Historic Preservation Office, Phoenix.

Withers, Arnold M.
1941 Excavations at Valshni Village, Papago Indian Reservation, Arizona. Unpublished Master's thesis, Department of Anthropology, University of Arizona, Tucson.

1973 *Excavations at Valshni Village, Arizona.* The Arizona Archaeologist No. 7. Arizona Archaeological Society, Phoenix.

Woodson, M. Kyle, Thomas E. Jones, and Joseph S. Crary
1999 Exploring Late-Prehistoric Mortuary Patterns of Southeastern Arizona and Southwestern New Mexico. In *Sixty Years of Mogollon Archaeology: Papers from the Ninth Mogollon Conference, Silver City, New Mexico, 1996*, edited by S. M. Whittlesey, pp. 67–79. SRI Press, Tucson.

Woodward, Arthur
1936 A Shell Bracelet Manufactory. *American Antiquity* 2:117–125.

Zedeño, M. Nieves
1994 *Sourcing Prehistoric Ceramics at Chodistaas Pueblo, Arizona: The Circulation of People and Pots in the Grasshopper Region.* Anthropological Papers No. 58. University of Arizona Press, Tucson.

Statistical Research, Inc., is committed to distributing the results of cultural resource management studies to a wide audience. Toward this goal, we maintain three publication series, designed to achieve different objectives and reach different readers.

SRI Press produces broad-interest volumes in archaeology, anthropology, history, and ethnography. These studies will appeal to professional archaeologists, avocational archaeologists, and general readers. Titles include:

- *Islanders and Mainlanders: Prehistoric Context for the Southern California Coast and Channel Islands,* edited by Jeffrey H. Altschul and Donn R. Grenda. 2001.

- *Sixty Years of Mogollon Archaeology: Proceedings of the Ninth Mogollon Conference, Silver City, New Mexico,* edited by Stephanie M. Whittlesey. 1999.

- *Vanishing River: Landscapes and Lives of the Lower Verde Valley.* CD (3 volumes) and book. 1998.

The SRI Technical Series presents the results of our most significant cultural resource management projects and is aimed toward a professional audience. A limited number of these reports are printed and perfect bound. Out-of-print volumes can be photocopied as requested. Titles include:

- *Prehistoric Painted Pottery of Southeastern Arizona,* by Robert A. Heckman, Barbara K. Montgomery, and Stephanie M. Whittlesey (Technical Series 77, 2000; includes 10 color plates). An easy-to-understand, well-illustrated guide to the painted ceramics of culturally diverse southeastern Arizona.

- *Of Stones and Spirits: Pursuing the Past of Antelope Hill,* edited by Joan S. Schneider and Jeffrey H. Altschul (Technical Series 76, 2000, book and CD). The culmination of nearly a decade of research on the archaeology, ethnography, and history of Antelope Hill, known for its abundant prehistoric and historical-period rock art and its prehistoric use as a quarry and production locus for milling implements.

- *The Desert Training Center/California-Arizona Maneuver Area, 1942–1944: Historical and Archaeological Contexts,* by Matt C. Bischoff (Technical Series 75, 2000). An in-depth look at this massive World War II–era military training facility in the California and Arizona desert.

- From the Desert to the Mountains: Archaeology of the Transition Zone: The State Route 87–Sycamore Creek Project. Vol. 1: *Prehistoric Sites,* edited by Rein Vanderpot, Eric Eugene Klucas, and Richard Ciolek-Torrello (Technical Series 73, 1999). The results of archaeological investigations at 29 prehistoric sites in the Sycamore Creek valley and Mazatzal Mountains of central Arizona.

- *Early Farmers of the Sonoran Desert: Archaeological Investigations at the Houghton Road Site, Tucson, Arizona,* edited by Richard Ciolek-Torrello (Technical Series 72, 1998). An investigation of early farmers of the Sonoran Desert through archaeological evidence recovered from the eastern Tucson Basin of southern Arizona.

- *Watering the Desert: Late Archaic Farming at the Costello-King Site,* by Joseph A. Ezzo and William L. Deaver (Technical Series 68, 1998). Archaeological investigations of a 2,500–3,000-year-old farming camp, with evidence of ditch irrigation, on the Santa Cruz River near Tucson, Arizona.

- *Investigations at Sunset Mesa Ruin,* edited by Richard Ciolek-Torrello, Edgar K. Huber, and Robert B. Neily (Technical Series 66, 1999). A comprehensive study of a Rincon phase settlement and a Mexican homestead near the confluence of the Rillito and Santa Cruz Rivers in the northern Tucson Basin.

SRI's Technical Report series provides an outlet for all cultural resource management reports conducted under contract. These compliance reports can be photocopied as needed.

The titles listed above, along with selected others, can be obtained from the University of Arizona Press at 1230 North Park Avenue, Suite 102, Tucson, AZ 85719, or (800) 426-3797 (outside Arizona) or (520) 626-4218. For a complete list of the three series, write to SRI at P.O. Box 31865, Tucson, AZ 85751-1865.